Democratic passions

Manchester University Press

Democratic passions

The politics of feeling in British popular radicalism, 1809–48

Matthew Roberts

MANCHESTER UNIVERSITY PRESS

Copyright © Matthew Roberts 2022

The right of Matthew Roberts to be identified as the author
of this work has been asserted by them in accordance with
the Copyright, Designs and Patents Act 1988.

Published by Manchester University Press
Oxford Road, Manchester M13 9PL

www.manchesteruniversitypress.co.uk

British Library Cataloguing-in-Publication Data
A catalogue record for this book is available from the British
Library

ISBN 978 1 5261 3704 3 hardback
ISBN 978 1 5261 7886 2 paperback

First published 2022

The publisher has no responsibility for the persistence or
accuracy of URLs for any external or third-party internet
websites referred to in this book, and does not guarantee
that any content on such websites is, or will remain, accurate
or appropriate.

Typeset by Newgen Publishing UK

Contents

List of figures

Acknowledgements

For someone who took the better part of a decade to publish their first monograph (in 2020), the appearance of a second in less than two years might be construed as rushed. But one of the main reasons why my last monograph took so long to appear was because I was also working on this book alongside. In some respects, *Democratic passions* emerged out of the research I undertook for my previous book, which, among other things, explored the 'emotional' engagement of Chartists with key antecedent radical heroes. In other respects, the genesis of the present book predated this, and traces its origins to my exposure as a student and then as a lecturer to cultural history at the University of York in the early 2000s. It was my good fortune to take on the teaching of an undergraduate module 'Mind, Ritual and Anthropology'. It was while exploring the first word in that module title and, it must be confessed, in the frantic casting around for material to make what was largely a medieval-based module into a more familiar and comfortably modern one that I stumbled across a newly published book: William Reddy's *Navigation of Feeling* (2003), as well as the beginnings of the emergence of a new field, the history of emotions. At that time (and clearly in defiance of my training as a cultural historian) I remember thinking, surely an emotion was the same thing in the present as it was at any time in the past (or indeed anywhere on the globe)? The discovery of just how mistaken that assumption was has proved endlessly liberating and has allowed me to approach afresh the well-traversed field of popular politics in nineteenth-century Britain, though with what success I leave for the reader to judge. In hindsight, what was even more fortuitous was that I co-taught that module with Rob Boddice, now one of the leading authorities on the history of emotions. As the references in this book will attest, Rob's work has been a major influence and source of inspiration.

To those unfamiliar with popular radicalism in nineteenth-century Britain, the scope of this book may seem rather limited. After all, it is not even a study of radicalism, but something more specific called popular radicalism (defined in the introduction). As those who do know this field will vouch, each of the selected radical leaders and the movements which grew up around them – the rebirth of radicalism in the first decade of the nineteenth century, the post-war mass platform culminating in Peterloo, radical freethought, the Reform Bill agitation, Owenism, the factory and anti-Poor Law movements, Chartism, and Irish Repeal – have generated voluminous historiographies in their own right. The present work would not have been possible but for the sturdy shoulders of several generations of historians, and more recently, literary scholars, who have done much to shape my understanding of these topics. This is by way of prefacing the fact that, to make the project manageable, the decision was taken to focus on individual radical leaders, though not in isolation from their working-class supporters. To concede that there is much more to be said about the politics of feeling in radicalism and protest, let alone modern British politics and social movements, is an understatement.

I have tried to address two very different constituencies in this book: first, historians of popular politics, social movements and political culture (diverse in themselves); and, second, historians of emotion. To the first group, what follows should be read as a contribution to writing the cultural history of politics, a project which has stalled somewhat in the wake of the linguistic turn. I am conscious that the second constituency may find my eclectic approach to the field – of a magpie-like scavenging of concepts and methods, and the resulting bricoleur patchwork – rather frustrating. Though in my defence, I cite Jan Plamper (admittedly from as long ago as 2012 – and as others have pointed out, the field of history of emotions has come a long way since then): 'the entire conceptual vocabulary of the history of emotions is still too new to make such hard-and-fast distinctions, rather than creatively combining such theoretical building blocks'.[1] I hope that the close attention to the affective language used by politicians and their plebeian supporters may contribute something to debates about the shift from passions to emotions in the nineteenth century, as well as to related discussions about the location of feelings in the human body, and their political significance.

A number of individuals and institutions have contributed to the production of this book, and it is a pleasure to record my thanks. At Sheffield Hallam, Doug Hamilton, Chris Hopkins and Clare Midgley kindly and constructively read various iterations of funding applications for study leave, which helped me with the scoping of the project as well as giving me time to complete it. Beyond Hallam, fellow scholars of nineteenth-century Britain and British politics have answered queries, passed on useful information and responded enthusiastically to various airings of chapters, as well as providing opportunities for those airings at seminar series and conferences: Joan Allen, Richard Allen, Fabrice Bensimon, Michael Brown, the late Malcolm Chase,

Jennifer Davey, Peter Gurney, Ian Haywood, Geoff Hicks, Anthony Howe, Lucy Matthew-Jones, Matthew McCormack, Rohan McWilliam, Simon Morgan, Katrina Navickas, Stephanie Olsen, Colin Reid, Kathyrn Rix, Edward Royle, Mike Sanders, Tom Scriven, Martin Spychal, and Tony Taylor. I would also like to thank Rob Boddice, Robert Poole and Mike Sanders for acting as referees for various grant applications. I owe a particular debt of gratitude to, once again, Rob Boddice and Miles Taylor for help at the initial stages in shaping the material into a coherent project, though any remaining deficiencies are mine entirely. Thomas Dixon also deserves thanks for allowing me to share some of my initial thoughts on the Queen Caroline agitation on his *History of Emotions Blog*. I also record my thanks to the Trustees of the Scouloudi Foundation, administered by the Institute of Historical Research, the Huntington Library, San Marino, California, and the Library Company of Philadelphia in conjunction with the Historical Society of Pennsylvania. Fellowships from these three bodies gave me the opportunity to work, respectively, on the neglected Richard Oastler papers at Columbia and Yale universities, the Richard Carlile papers held by the Huntington Library, and the William Cobbett papers in Philadelphia. The penultimate set of individuals that I would like to single out are the team at Manchester University Press, especially Emma Brennan, and the production team at Newgen Publishing UK for shepherding the project through to publication. Finally, I thank my family – Roz, Fran and Bron – for their love and support. Having them all around much more than would ordinarily have been the case due to the pandemic has made working at home much more enjoyable.

Note

1 Jan Plamper, *The History of Emotions* (Oxford: Oxford University Press, 2012), p. 70.

Abbreviations

Archival repositories and collections

BL   British Library, London
BM   British Museum, London
HSP   Historical Society of Pennsylvania, Philadelphia
HO   Home Office files, TNA
TNA   The National Archives, Kew
TS   Treasury Solicitor's papers, TNA

Journals

EHR   *English Historical Review*
EHCS   *Emotions: History, Culture, Society*
HJ   *Historical Journal*
LHR   *Labour History Review*

Newspapers and periodicals

CWPR   *Cobbett's Weekly Political Register*
FP   *Fleet Papers*
NS   *Northern Star*

Organisations

LWMA   London Working Men's Association

Introduction: The Queen Caroline agitation of 1820

In August 1820 one of the most sensational trials in modern British history began in the House of Lords. Under the terms of the aptly named Bill of Pains and Penalties, Queen Caroline – the estranged wife of the new King, George IV – was put on trial for adultery.[1] This was demanded by the King who wanted to prevent Caroline from becoming queen with the hope that a guilty verdict would be grounds for divorce, his latest attempt to rid himself of the woman he had never wanted to marry. Negotiations were opened with the Queen by Lord Liverpool's government in the hope that she would accept an increase in her allowance in return for staying out of the country and renouncing her claims. This offer Caroline refused, and she returned to Britain on 5 June to take up her rightful claim to be crowned. When she returned to Britain a constitutional crisis ensued which pitted the King and his ministers against much of parliament and the people.

The Queen Caroline agitation was followed closely by virtually the whole country, with public opinion firmly behind the Queen. The King was widely reviled as a symbol of a corrupt and reactionary regime. Feelings ran high both inside and outside of parliament. The self-serving Whig Henry Brougham, who acted as Caroline's legal advocate, remarked: 'It is impossible to describe the universal, and strong, even violent, feelings of the people, not only in London but all over the country, upon the subject of the Queen.'[2] The role of heightened feeling in the affair has certainly not gone unnoticed by historians. But this has been interpreted either as little more than a relatively safe and diversionary opportunity for radicals to vent their feelings in the aftermath of the government clampdown on radicalism in 1819–20, or as a function of the melodramatic register in which the affair was discussed.[3] There was more than frustration and melodrama at stake in 1820. While the Caroline agitation hardly marked the moment when the passions entered politics (a greater claim could be made for the French Revolution),[4] never before had feelings been so politicised. The Romantic essayist William Hazlitt for one recognised this: the cause of the Queen was 'the only question I have ever known that excited a thorough popular feeling. It struck its roots into the heart of the nation'.[5] The popular radical journalist William Cobbett concurred, judging the agitation a 'new and unparalleled subject, which excites the feelings of every creature, and sets in motion a greater mass of passion than ever before existed in the breasts of the people'.[6]

Dror Wahrman has argued that the Caroline agitation signalled the unprecedented political relevance of public opinion, and that invoking it had become part of 'the rhetorical game rules' of politics.[7] This book is concerned with a different aspect of those game rules – the nature of feeling and its place in politics, and more specifically popular politics. It should be read as a contribution to the cultural history of politics, but one which seeks to recapture the experiential dimension of popular politics, a dimension which has been lost in the wake of the 'linguistic turn' with its tendency to reduce politics to language.[8] To paraphrase Jan Plamper on the Russian Revolution, radicalism became known to the working classes not (just) through reading newspaper articles or listening to speeches at rallies, but also through the sights, sounds and smells of the mass platform, the tavern and the coffee shop along with the attendant feelings associated with these spaces and places.[9] Even abstract ideas and concepts often assumed sensorial form. Public opinion, political identities and loyalties were based just as much on sentiment as they were abstract ideas or ideology.[10] Late Georgian and early Victorian politicians were just as likely to talk of 'public feeling', the 'sentiments of the people' or the 'temper' of the popular mind.[11] The very language of politics, particularly that surrounding the relationship between politics, protest and the people, often centred around feeling and bodily sensation: agitation, outrage, excitement, suffering, inflammation, distress, terror.

Leading the campaign outdoors in favour of the Queen were the popular radicals. The Tory MP Edward Bootle-Wilbraham complained to a friend that 'Radicalism has taken the shape of affection for the Queen'.[12] Bootle-Wilbraham meant this disparagingly with the implication that what previously had been a movement of principle – of measures not men – had been reduced to the popular adulation of Caroline. For all his barb, the Tory MP had hit inadvertently on the centrality of feeling. The popular radical leaders who are at the heart of this study presided over an extra-parliamentary movement for democratic and social rights. During the two peaks of mass mobilisation in the 1810s and 1840s (two peaks which mark the chronological boundaries of this study), radical leaders spoke for hundreds of thousands and eventually millions of working-class men and women. This book explores the affective politics of key radical leaders in the first half of the nineteenth century, when the movement for democracy took off. It is organised around seven of the most influential and popular radical leaders, with a chapter on each and the movements that grew up around them, roughly in chronological order: William Cobbett, Richard Carlile, Robert Owen, Richard Oastler, Joseph Rayner Stephens, William Lovett and Daniel O'Connell.[13]

As with the response to Queen Caroline so with popular radicalism more generally: the role of feeling, though much remarked upon, has not been explored in a systematic way.[14] There are two reasons why historians of popular radicalism have neglected feeling. First, the history of emotions is still a relatively new field, and only recently has some suggestive work by historians and literary scholars begun to explore the role played by feelings, though none of them have engaged in a sustained, critical way with the burgeoning literature on the history of emotions.[15] Second, there is a tendency for modern historians to exaggerate the rationality of popular politics. According to these accounts, popular radicalism was politically focused and largely peaceful in contrast to the violence and spontaneity of pre-industrial protest.[16] This over-rationalisation of popular radicalism is a reaction to an older historiography that viewed popular radicalism as hunger protest, a rebellion of the belly not the head. Underpinning the hunger-protest model was the assumption that the rational political content of radicalism was, at best, incidental to the irrational masses who were whipped up into frenzies by unprincipled demagogues, such as the post-war hero of the mass platform Henry Hunt or the Chartist leader Feargus O'Connor a generation later.[17] As this book will suggest, it is possible – as well as necessary – to restore the centrality of feeling in popular radicalism without the condescending imputation of irrationality. Let us return to Queen Caroline to explore the place, nature and significance of feeling in the political culture of the period.

Feelings on trial

From the very beginning it was clear that feelings were on trial in 1820. Ministers, magistrates and spies declaimed the way in which the trial had been sensationalised out of doors through appeals to the passions of the multitude.[18] Earlier in the case, the Queen was accused of having succumbed to evil, sordid passions unbecoming of a woman of her station. As this accusation implies, there was a hierarchy of feelings which mapped on to a social hierarchy – noble sentiment at the top and base passion at the bottom, and the two were intimately linked. Indulging these lusty passions made the Queen little better than a common prostitute, or so the unfortunate inference drawn by the Queen's defence implied.[19] We will encounter this set of affective assumptions many times in the following pages: distinct sets of feeling rules existed for separate social classes, as well as between men and women, the inference being that different classes felt differently.[20]

When those like Caroline, who, if was felt in elite circles, ought to have known better – an accusation also levelled at gentleman radical leaders – they were assumed to be suffering from disordered passions, and/or deadened senses. The latter underscores the importance of 'braiding ... the senses and emotions'; after all, as we have already seen with public opinion, one's capacity for feeling is intimately related to the senses.[21] Cobbett for one was fully alive to this braiding. As he commented at the height of the agitation: 'When the passions are deeply engaged, when strong feeling exists, when men are looking about them for the cause of what give them offence, their eyes and ears are open.'[22] The parallel drawn between the Queen and the common prostitute, and the deadened senses of both, hinted at the widely held assumption in elite circles that the working classes either had a diminished capacity for feeling, or – somewhat paradoxically – that they were sub-human creatures of base passion. In either case, the masses were seen as brutish.[23] The Queen's partisans contested this, juxtaposing Her Majesty's and their own refined feelings against the cold-hearted and cruel King and his ministers: George was literally the embodiment of a bloated, unfeeling and insensate ruling class.[24] Cobbett, berating Brougham's limp and unfeeling defence of the Queen, similarly asserted that 'The public have feeling as well as the members of parliament'.[25] Cobbett was making the point that would become the affective cornerstone of popular radicalism: ordinary people not only had the capacity for refined feelings – in this case, chivalric masculinity, but unlike the abandoned aristocracy and profligate royalty, they were neither unfeeling nor lacking in restraint.[26] Radicals also invoked the senses to underscore their disgust at the King and his ministers: 'the vile breath of faction' whose 'pestilent breath would consume the fruits of the country', ran one satirical pro-Queen pamphlet.[27] This subversive yoking of feeling and senses had significant radical potential as the case study of William Cobbett in chapter 1 shows.

These affective blasts and counter-blasts had important consequences for political citizenship as it furnished political elites with a further justification for excluding working people from the political nation. In the late eighteenth and early nineteenth century, the political citizen was defined as 'autonomous, rational, reasonable, calm, self-controlled and sane', and, we might also add, white. The antithesis of the political citizen – the mob, protesters, radicals, blacks and women, including depraved queens – were denigrated as 'irrational ..., excitable, disorderly and passionate'.[28] This gendered understanding was made legible on the body by equating a slavish submission to the appetites of the body as feminine weakness.[29] While the focus of this book is on the male radical leaders who championed the demo-cratic cause of the people, not least because of the existence of rich source material from which to reconstruct their affective politics, this is contextual-ised in relation to the broader gendered politics of citizenship. The manifold ways in which this gender politics was anchored in affective assumptions is explored in several chapters: in the discussion of the radical infidel Richard Carlile's feminism and his hostility towards homosexuality (chapter 2); on the ways in which Owenite socialism was undercut by gendered notions of feeling (chapter 3); in the sentimental vision of the working-class family sketched by Tory-radicals in the 1830s (chapters 4 and 5); and in the place of domestic affection in moral-force Chartism (chapter 6). In addition to class and gender, some attention is also paid – in chapters 1 and 4 – to race. Some radicals advanced the claims of the white working class to citizenship by erecting distinctions between the rational white working class and an irrational black 'other' who, at best, did not deserve sympathetic priority, and, at worst, deserved no sympathy at all.

Popular radicals had to walk a fine line: asserting that working-class men were men of feeling without giving affective hostages to fortune that they were creatures of passion. Fear of the mob, protest and radicalism was noth-ing new by the early nineteenth century. Within the political elite, negative feelings, especially anger, came to be associated with revolution, terror and war – what might be termed the affective legacy of the French Revolution. In the shadow of 1790s, the view gained ground that the political sphere ought to be an arena of cool, rational debate – a Habermasian public sphere which accented restraint and reason.[30] In practice, this was neither achiev-able nor often desirable as the scurrilous print culture of the Queen Caroline agitation attests.[31] Feeling was far too powerful as a mobiliser of popular support to be jettisoned.

Nonetheless, those who transgressed the set of feeling rules prescribed by the elite were viewed as dangerous, subversive and deviant. As far as the government and the loyalists were concerned in 1820, behind the apparent radical displays of 'royal disloyalty', which attached itself to the coattails of the Queen, lurked the Jacobin threat.[32] This serves as a reminder of the need to study radicalism in its loyalist mirror image. This book sheds new light on the relationship between protest movements and the state by showing how one of the central issues at stake in the conflict between radicals and their oppressors was the feelings of the propertied classes: with questions of law – and life and death in the cases of those convicted of treason – resting on little more than the subjective states of propertied feeling. The right of public meeting and petitioning parliament also turned on feeling.[33] While it was the constitutional right of the people to petition parliament and hold meetings to facilitate that, the draconian Six Acts of 1819 underlined that this was only legal until loyal and peaceable subjects felt great terror.[34] In language which was characteristic during this period, the radicals in 1819–20 stood accused of exciting feelings of contempt towards government.[35]

Among those radical supporters of the Queen was the unlikely figure of Richard Carlile (whose affective politics are the focus of chapter 2). As an austere republican he had, initially, dismissed the queen's case as humbug, but he soon changed his tune to the extent that he, too, found it impossible to resist being sentimental. 'An involuntary tear has oft trickled down my cheeks on reading of your cause', he told the Queen from his prison cell in Dorchester gaol where he was serving a long prison sentence for blasphemy.[36] Carlile was not alone: when the Queen died of a bowel obstruction in August 1821, the nation wept – at least according to the *Times*, and entered a period of national mourning.[37] Cobbett's response was even more sentimental. On learning of the queen's death, he wrote: 'I have twice parted from wife and daughters in a way that placed the seas between us. ... But never, until yesterday, did I know what it was to feel my heart sink in me.'[38]

Radical feeling rules

In the aftermath of the agitation, there is no doubt that Carlile and other radicals set about trying to create and practice a rational politics of 'pure reason' unsullied by the kind of sentimentalism that he and other radicals had poured out in defence of the Queen. This shift has traditionally been interpreted as part of a 'march of mind' and the rise of respectability in the 1820s, but historians have not fully appreciated that an important cause and consequence of this shift was affective.[39] Some of this undoubtedly stemmed from a reaction to the Caroline agitation, which, once the dust began to settle, left some radicals feeling sullied and embarrassed by the episode, with both King and Queen now viewed as scornful objects of contempt.[40] The melodramatic register of the radical response to Caroline failed not because it trivialised politics, but because of emotional over-heating. Thus, the failure of radicalism in 1820 was not so much aesthetic as affective, and Carlile appreciated this more than most as we will see in chapter 2. Far from the affair 'leading nowhere', indicative of the backward-looking nature of radicalism, or merely serving as an opportunity to vent,[41] it represented a crescendo of sentimental radicalism and its displacement by the rise and consolidation of a different set of feeling rules. The aftermath of the agitation, once tempers had cooled, marked a key moment when the assumption that the public sphere ought to be an arena characterised by restraint and decency was consolidated.[42] Carlile personified – by turns – two relatively discrete and rival forms of affective politics, a shorthand term used here to denote the set of feeling rules which shaped popular radical expression in the first half of the nineteenth century. On the one hand was ascetic radicalism; on the other, sentimental radicalism. Both had deep roots, but essentially traced their origins to the late eighteenth century, the former to the radical wing of the Enlightenment, the latter to the Romantic reaction against the age of reason.

Ascetic radicalism was a set of feeling rules which emphasised restraint, rationality and aversion to unbridled passion, and which advanced claims to citizenship on the basis that it was both possible and necessary for the working classes to curb their base passions. Rational Dissent was one source of this affective politics, as was a commonwealthman and country party critique of luxury. An enduring puritan distrust of the sensual was another. Christian asceticism, neo-stoicism and Spartan austerity were also ante-cedents, each of which linked 'emotional and corporeal "looseness" and "softness" '.[43] Not for nothing did radicals speak of 'tax-eaters' and bloated establishments. While Christianity was one wellspring, somewhat paradox-ically, freethought was another. The idea that man was a slave to his pas-sions played into the grasping hands of clerics who preached that Christ's passion – suffering by proxy – enslaved mankind by inculcating feelings of guilt and depravity. As we will see in chapter 2, Carlile tried to assuage these feelings. Initially, asceticism (and freethought for that matter) had been practised mainly by middle-class radical Dissenters who wished to distance themselves from the riotous mob and the sensual aristocracy, and it formed part of William Godwin and Mary Wollstonecraft's reaction to the senti-mentalism of the Burkean and loyalist response to the French Revolution.[44] Yet as with radicalism more broadly in response to the French Revolution, this ascetic current was democratised and by the early nineteenth century when radicalism re-emerged it was being appropriated as a riposte to the charge that popular radicals appealed to base passions which frequently accompanied the state's assault on dangerous enthusiasm.[45] Ascetic radi-cals also asserted that everyone had the same capacity for feeling, and thus were entitled to political rights. But some ascetic radicals – Carlile, for example – qualified this universalism, for reasons that will be explored in chapters 2 and 6.

Asceticism has connotations of austerity, self-denial, stoicism; in short, a mental state free of feeling in the face of suffering. Ascetic radicals were averse to sentimental effusions; hence, for example, their hostility to poetry (except that which 'was founded in truth', to add Cobbett's own cryptic caveat).[46] This is not to imply that ascetic radicals disclaimed all appeals to feeling, or were themselves some kind of unfeeling automata; only that their stated aversion to appeals to the passions was an important part of their affective politics.[47] In short, the purpose was not to purge passion but master it and integrate it into one's private and public life – indeed, the two spheres of public and private were intimately linked.[48]

As the first chapter on William Cobbett argues, ascetic radicalism was also about expressing the right feelings in the right place at the right time. Drawing attention to episodes when this failed to happen was part of the armoury of radicalism in its many battles with the state and its propertied supporters. Further, ascetic radicalism could also be used to mark out distinct positions and rivalries within the radical movement. The politics of feeling was central to the rivalry among British radical leaders and their followers as the final chapter on the tempestuous relationship between the Chartists and the Irish radical Daniel O'Connell shows only too clearly. We need to be wary when historical actors, whether elites or radical leaders, claim to be acting only in accordance with reason – the latter was no less an affective construct than more open and explicit appeals to feeling. Thomas Dixon usefully reminds us that 'The so-called "Age of Reason" was also an age of ostentatious weeping, violent passions, religious revivals'.[49] As the chapters on Carlile, the socialist Robert Owen and the Chartist William Lovett each demonstrate, the path to 'pure reason' was paved with affective tensions. This was because its adherents often struggled to practise what they preached, to say nothing of the fact that the destination of 'pure reason' was meant to be a state of happiness – a recently politicised term. For ascetic radicals it was both the responsibility of individuals and the state to guarantee a level of happiness; sentimental radicals, by contrast, laid that responsibility almost entirely at the feet of the state.[50]

As with the Romantic movement, of which it formed a part, the immediate roots of sentimental radicalism can be traced to tensions within the Enlightenment and its prioritising of reason over feeling. An associated eighteenth-century precursor was the emergence of the culture of sensibility in which men and women, especially of the rising middle classes, demonstrated their refinement through elevating their softer feelings such as sympathy and love.[51] Armed with this heightened feeling, sentimental radicalism emerged in reaction to the perceived coolness and unfeeling associated with the age of reason (however much the latter was also an affective construct). Romantic literature, it has been argued, was 'the most powerful register of the period's gravitational pull toward feeling'.[52] Lest we assume that these changes in feeling rules were confined to the world of culture and the arts, it is worth recalling Isaiah Berlin's definition of the age of Romanticism as one of the few periods in human history when the arts exercised a tyranny over all other aspects of life, with politics no exception.[53] This study builds on the work of literary scholars and historians who have, in the words of Miles Taylor, registered the 'long reach of romanticism'.[54] Romanticism in its radical mode did much to shape the form of popular politics from the 1790s. The democratic implications of works such as *Lyrical Ballads*, which suggested that the outward trappings of refinement – fine clothes – were not a precondition for deep feeling. This romantic current was appropriated and further democratised in the cultural stylistics of popular radical leaders.[55]

Several key aspects of sentimental radicalism registered this impact: the intense outpouring of feeling for radical leaders, who like romantic leaders were invariably flawed heroes; a militant and heartfelt assertion of the right of working-class people to express their feelings; the deliberate crafting of an affective politics that not only appealed to intense feelings, but often sought to exacerbate those feelings, and channel them towards radical goals. In licensing the expression of intense feelings, sentimental radicalism came close at times to the 'emotional over-heating' that the historian William Reddy diagnosed in the affective politics of the Jacobins in the French Revolution. Chapter 5 explores via a case study of the fiery renegade Methodist preacher Joseph Rayner Stephens what happens when individuals get caught between different feeling rules (or emotional regimes to use Reddy's concept). Chapter 6 probes the tensions between emotional regimes and what Reddy terms emotional refuges to cast new light on the first Chartist Convention of 1839.[56] In both cases, Reddy's concepts are tested and refined as a way of spotlighting some of the tensions and contradictions within sentimental radicalism, and between the latter and ascetic radicalism. Sentimental radicalism drew much of its strength and appeal from a cluster of negative feelings, or base/bad passions in the language of the period – anger, hatred, fear, vengeance, outrage, rage – but it could also appeal to nobler feelings – love, fraternity and, above all, sympathy. But sentimental radicalism, like ascetic radicalism, was not just based on particular clusters of feeling; it also explored what place feelings had, and ought to have, in politics. In drawing – sometimes explicitly and self-consciously; other times subconsciously – on melodrama and the Gothic aesthetic, the hallmark of sentimental radicalism was an excess of feeling. Hence the use of these lenses – especially the Gothic – to explore the affective politics of the Tory-radical factory reformer and anti-Poor Law campaigner Richard Oastler in chapter 4, and Feargus O'Connor in chapter 7. When wielded by those like Oastler and Stephens, sentimental radicalism was akin to nemesis in the classical Greek sense of the term (though in both cases it was refracted through their Christianity): the enactment of retributive justice based on feelings of righteous indignation against those who display hubris before the divine order of things.

As far as the enemies of radicalism were concerned, and indeed those radicals who adhered to the rival affective politics of ascetic radicalism, sentimental radicalism was dark, dangerous, and raw. Far from being the expression of authentic feeling that it claimed, sentimental radicalism was attacked for unduly inflaming the passions of the people. It was little more than a theatrical form of popular politics that subversively blurred the boundaries between the stage and the platform. As the pair of chapters on Joseph Rayner Stephens and his friend Richard Oastler show, as theatrical as their politics might appear, it was anything but playful. Far from unnecessarily inflaming the passions of the people, Stephens and Oastler laid that charge at the door of the enemies of the people, the advocates of cold, unfeeling liberal political economy. To illuminate this Tory-radical critique of liberal political economy, *Democratic passions* draws on Thomas Haskell's concept of an 'ethical shelter', which he developed to explain why humanitarianism developed in response to chattel slavery but not wage slavery after 1750. Haskell defines an ethical shelter as a mental space which 'enables us all … to maintain a good conscience, in spite of doing nothing concretely about most of the world's suffering'. Rob Boddice has refined Haskell's concept by highlighting the affective basis of an ethical shelter which is central to its success and failure. This enables Boddice to build an explanatory model of an ethical shelter that foregrounds the conditions under which failure to elicit sympathy can occur, and this model is used to explain why Tory-radicalism ultimately failed to elicit sympathy for the plight of the vulnerable.[57] Both Stephens and Oastler were deeply religious men, and their affective politics of sympathy was powered not just by Romanticism but also evangelical religion – another wellspring of sentimental radicalism.[58] The cultural stylistics of sentimental radicalism politicised the democratic language invented by the radical Romantic poets as a way of conveying feeling in a much more direct way, as compared, for example, to ornate classical poetry or elite forms of classical oratory.

Popular radicalism in the first half of the nineteenth century was beset by affective tensions and contradictions between these two rival and relatively discrete sets of feeling rules, a tension that it never satisfactorily resolved and which played a part in the failure of the movement to secure many of its goals. True, the two forms of affective politics sometimes blurred at the edges – for example, ascetic and sentimental radicals alike berated the enemies of the people for their callousness – and as we have seen with Carlile sometimes individual radicals moved between the two. Further, there were also subtle differences within as well as between ascetic and sentimental radicals. Certainly, as this book will show, there was no linear shift from excess of feeling to restraint akin to Norbert Elias's civilising process, a teleology which has been convincingly demolished by historians of emotion.[59] The shifting affective terrain of popular radicalism went in cycles with either ascetic or sentimental radicalism in the ascendancy, contingent on a whole range of factors explored in this book. Sometimes the two co-existed uneasily within the same movement – Chartism being a case in point as shown in chapters 6 and 7. But these caveats aside, presenting popular radicalism as riven by two rival forms of affective politics not only does justice to the subtleties of the diverse ways in which radicals politicised feeling, it also sheds new light on the popular political culture of the period by drawing on the new and burgeoning field of the history of emotions.

The history of emotions

Democratic passions has two broader purposes. The first is to show, by way of a case study of popular radicalism in the first half of the nineteenth century, how the history of emotions can be used to shed new light on British political history and popular/social movements. Second, this book seeks to contribute to recent debates among historians of emotion, not through further discussions about what the history of emotions might entail (several very good introductions now exist).[60] Rather, it seeks to recover what popular radicals themselves thought about feelings as part of a broader exploration of the place of feelings in the political culture of the period. This is not to suggest that we jettison the seminal work of those historians such as William Reddy and Barbara Rosenwein; on the contrary, but we now need historical research that puts these perspectives into practice and that tests them in ways that pay careful attention to the affective language used by historical actors in a particular time and place. This is especially needed in relation to non-elite voices as most of the focus in the British context has been on what theologians, philosophers, scientists and psychologists thought and felt about emotion.

Some of the most recent work on the history of working-class feeling has focused on individuals in the private sphere of the home and family as revealed in highly personal narratives such as autobiographies and diaries. While this body of emerging work has certainly not studied the individual in isolation from society, the emphasis is nonetheless on the individual worker in the private sphere: of the home as an important site of emotional attachment in radical politics, or the emotional ties of family that working-class men and women drew on to support them in the arduous life of being a radical. A parallel development within the field of history of emotion has been the rise of embodied emotions which has shifted the focus towards the question of what do emotions do to our bodies: 'the daily effects of feeling, doing, and communicating emotions'.[61] This book is more concerned with feeling in the public sphere rather than an exploration of what emotions do to individuals, though it shares the approach to ideas as embodied thoughts. *Democratic passions* explores how political leaders crafted appeals and identities that politicised feelings, and how political elites constructed feeling rules that sought to discipline and disable popular politics.[62]

There is an emerging consensus 'that emotions have both biological and cultural components and that societies influence the expression, repression and meaning of feelings by giving them names and assigning values to some and not others'.[63] If anything, the consensus is shifting even further towards culture as demonstrated by Rob Boddice's recent work on biocultural approaches to the brain.[64] A trans-historical concept of emotion actually obfuscates rather than clarifies the affective life of those in the past.[65] As the history of emotions has begun to expand, scholars have come to adopt a much more critical awareness of the concepts that they use, as well as of the affective vocabulary of those they study. The modern concept of the emotions – 'conceived as a set of morally disengaged, bodily, non-cognitive and involuntary feelings', which began to emerge in the eighteenth century was only cemented in the second half of the nineteenth century.[66] Before that, people spoke of sentiments, affections, appetites, feelings and, above all, passions – the latter being the most commonly used generic term to describe the affective realm in the eighteenth and early nineteenth centuries. Only occasionally was the word emotion used, and as this book will show, when it was it meant something quite different and much more specific than what is understood by that term today.[67] As the case studies of radical leaders show, where historical actors locate the source of feeling in the body and the language they use to describe those feelings has political implications.

This is more than mere semantics: the modern concept of emotion – as a psychological category – was invented precisely to detach the affective realm from the moral and theological discourses in which feeling, especially sentiments and affections, had hitherto been conceptualised and discussed.[68] In addition, 'Emotion words are now acknowledged themselves to effect what emotions are like; that is, how they are experienced and perceived'.[69] Far from being 'hardwired', research into neuroplasticity has shown how the brain is continually shaped by its environment (a view that would have been taken as axiomatic by Robert Owen). It is precisely because of this latest scientific and psychological research, along with a longer-standing assumption that the 'nature/culture dyad' is self-defeating when researching the history of emotions (can we ever really know whether people in the past felt as we do?), that some historians are now suggesting that we do away completely with this binary. Thus, it is imperative for historians to determine how the historical actors being studied understood the affective realm. It is not enough to explore the role of, say, anger in Chartism. We must go further and ask not just what did Chartists mean by anger but also how they understood the relationship between affect and politics, how they conceptualised feelings more generally, and, further still, how representative that conceptualisation was in comparison to other contemporary theories of feeling.

One possible solution to these difficulties might be to assemble an affective repertory that is sensitive to the contemporary ways in which feelings were named and described during the period under review. But this approach lends itself too easily to keyword searching for feelings – rage, fury, indignation – the problem being that historical actors do not always name the feelings that they are expressing (or that we, as historians, deem them to be expressing) to say nothing of the thorny issue that meanings shift.[70] For example, we might – in line with a long literary and historical pedigree – associate sentimental radicalism with a nostalgic longing for 'the world we have lost'.[71] While there is no doubt that many radicals did indeed wish to restore a lost golden age, to label this feeling as nostalgia is anachronistic because the word was not used in that sense until the turn of the twentieth century (before then it was roughly synonymous with feelings of homesickness).[72] On one level we might retort, does this matter? Once we realise that the very labelling of feelings shapes what is felt, it does matter. Further, by using anachronistic definitions of nostalgia we run the risk of importing presentist assumptions into the past – that nostalgia is either a politically disabling feeling because it is focused on the past rather than the present, or – somewhat paradoxically – it licenses a right-wing populism. Neither of these meanings would have occurred to those like Richard Oastler and Joseph Rayner Stephens.

The problem is not just that language and meaning evolve, bodies do as well. In any case, we are not privy to the faces or bodies of historical actors (only, occasionally, representations), and even if we were, these are unreliable indicators of feeling. Not only is the expression of feeling culturally and spatially specific but the ways in which feelings are expressed is inseparable from the way they are felt. Those in the past and present who maintain that there *are* biological universals when it comes to feelings are engaged in a political act which seeks to efface cultural difference, and the very necessity for a history of emotions.[73] Hence the decision to focus here on the broader place of feelings in popular radicalism, and the attempt to pay close attention to affective language and bodily practice. What follows, then, is a study of how radical leaders theorised and politicised the passions, and of the role played by feelings in the relationship between leaders and the led. Following the lead of scholars such as Joanna Bourke and Rob Boddice, this study also asks: what are feelings *doing* in the political sphere?[74] As we have seen with the Queen Caroline agitation, feelings do certain things: they disqualify certain people from participating in politics, such as women and some men, while pathologising radicals.

Definitions, space and scope

I have opted for the more neutral term 'feeling' as a descriptive, portmanteau term for bodily sensations and their associated affective dimensions.
A range of alternative terms are now available – emotion, moral economy,
experience – but the problem with some of these concepts for those not
particularly versed in the history of emotions is that terms such as 'moral
economy' are already heavily freighted and often problematic. The focus
here is on affective politics (or feeling rules, which is used interchangeably).
This is conceived primarily as a loose heuristic device to explore the use
made of feelings in any form of political activity and the response they elicited, along with the ways in which feelings were managed and the rules
which controlled their expression. The term 'affective', though not unprob-
lematic, is more apposite, partly because it has none of the contemporary,
and thus ahistorical, connotations that terms such as 'emotional' possess (or
the negative connotations that the word passion possessed during the first
half of the nineteenth century). In addition, by the early nineteenth century,
'affect' and 'affective' were not used as they are today – as the domain of
the irrational and automatic bodily response. Rather, they were viewed as
part of the faculties in a way that did not often posit a fundamental separation between thought and feeling. As Lynn Hunt and Margaret Jacob
have argued, the term 'affective' 'conveys better than any other [term] the
combination of internal (emotional) state and bodily (external) expression
or disposition'.[75]

   In short, affective politics speaks to the notion of embodied thought, and
reason as something felt.[76] While it is perfectly possible for different political
movements to have their own distinctive affective politics, the advantage of
the concept over others on offer, notably Rosenwein's emotional communities or Reddy's emotional regimes, is that it foregrounds *utility*. By utility
I mean the specific role played by feelings in a particular kind of politics in
a specific time and place rather than making the grander and reified claim
that these expressions of feeling were coterminous with a discrete community or regime. A more important dynamic that can be isolated in affective
politics is space. It matters where things were said: what was 'public' and
'private' space, for example, could profoundly shape what was said, how
it was said and received.[77] The affective politics of radical leadership could
look quite different from the perspective of the radical underworld, or from
that of the mass platform. These differences stemmed in part from the different performative conventions associated with specific places. As Katie
Barclay has argued in relation to the performance of masculinity, 'power
… is produced through negotiations between men, who draw on a broad
range of cultural resources in a performance that is embodied and located

in place'.[78] Chapter 6 on Lovett explores the contrasting embodied feeling rules of coffee shops and pubs. Differing conventions and audiences associated with particular spaces could also shape affective politics.

Democratic passions casts new light on the relationship between political leaders and their largely working-class constituencies of support by showing how each of the leaders claimed to give voice to the feelings of the masses, while at the same time shaping how those feelings were expressed. It deliberately excludes 'middle-class radicalism' – the Anti-Corn Law League, anti-slavery, moral and Manchester radicalism. Benthamite utilitarianism is also excluded, though the legacy of Bentham's utilitarian conception of happiness on Robert Owen is explored in chapter 3, where the case for including Owen as a radical is also made.[79] This is partly for reasons of manageability; but also because much less attention has been paid in the modern history of emotions to the working class and their icons/leaders. While these middle-class radical movements certainly had their populist elements, their leaders tended to be much more politically, if not quite socially, accepted as part of the elite at least in the eyes of many working-class radicals. At the same time, this will also necessitate some analysis of the relationship between popular radicalism and its enemies – which could include middle-class radicals (as chapter 7 illustrates) who, in other contexts might serve as allies. As chapter 6 shows, there was scope for common affective ground between middle-class radical Unitarians and ascetic radicals, both of whom invested heavily in feelings of domestic kindness and affection.

One final note of delimitation. Much of what follows is a study of English political culture, with the notable exception of the final chapter. Chapter 7 uses the affective politics of the Irish Catholic leader Daniel O'Connell to explore the place of feelings in Irish popular politics as well as the role they played in the relationship between British and Irish radicals. In the absence of more detailed research on the politics of feelings in the separate four nations it is unclear to what extent distinct affective politics existed in Ireland, Scotland and Wales. On the other hand, given the manifold ways in which English, Irish, Scottish and Welsh popular politics were interwoven during this period – as recent work has underlined – we should be cautious in assuming that distinct affective politics can be neatly mapped onto geography.[80] Such reductionism runs the risk of perpetuating stereotypes – sometimes resorted to by the enemies of radicalism during this period – of the temperamental and excitable Celt.[81] As the case studies of O'Connell and Feargus O'Connor suggest, neither of these Irishmen were – despite the accusations of one to the other, and their enemies – creatures of their passions. Although they were far removed from the ascetic radicalism of a Cobbett or a Carlile, their sentimental radicalism was no less carefully constructed.

Notes

1 Lady Cowper noted that 'A Bill of Pains and Penalties is an awkward name; it sounds to the ignorant as if she was going to be fried or tortured in some way'. Flora Fraser, *The Unruly Queen: The Life of Queen Caroline* (London: Papermac, 1996), p. 399.

2 Henry Brougham, *The Life and Times of Henry, Lord Brougham*, vol. 2 (New York, 1871), p. 279.

3 Iorwerth Prothero, *Artisans and Politics in Early Nineteenth-Century London: John Gast and his Times* (Folkestone: Dawson, 1979), p. 136; Iain McCalman, *Radical Underworld: Prophets, Revolutionaries, and Pornographers in London, 1795–1840* (Oxford: Oxford University Press, 1993), pp. 176–7; Thomas W. Laqueur, 'The Queen Caroline affair: politics as art in the reign of George IV', *Journal of Modern History*, 54 (1982), 417–66.

4 Lynn Hunt and Margaret Jacob, 'The affective revolution in 1790s Britain', *Eighteenth-Century Studies*, 34 (2001), 497.

5 P.P. Howe (ed.), *The Complete Works of William Hazlitt*, vol. 10 (London: J.M. Dent, 1930–34), p. 136.

6 *CWPR*, 17 June 1820.

7 Dror Wahrman, 'Public opinion, violence, and the limits of constitutional politics', in James Vernon (ed.), *Re-Reading the Constitution: New Narratives in the Political History of England's Long Nineteenth Century* (Cambridge: Cambridge University Press, 1996), p. 111.

8 For a critique of this aspect of linguistic turn, see Katrina Navickas, *Protest and the Politics of Space and Place, 1789–1848* (Manchester: Manchester University Press, 2016), pp. 4–5. Several historians of emotion have cited similar dissatisfactions arising out of the linguistic turn as a factor in the rise of the history of emotion. 'AHR conversation: the historical study of emotions', *American Historical Review*, 117 (2012), 1494.

9 Jan Plamper, 'Sounds of February, smells of October: the Russian Revolution as sensory experience', *American Historical Review*, 126 (2021), 1–26. The sensory dimension of radicalism has begun to be explored in recent work on music: Kate Bowan and Paul A. Pickering, *Sounds of Liberty: Music, Radicalism and Reform in the Anglophone World, 1790–1914* (Manchester: Manchester University Press 2017); David Kennerley, 'Strikes and singing classes: Chartist culture, "rational recreation" and the politics of music after 1842', *EHR*, 135 (2020), 1165–94.

10 Dror Wahrman, ' "Middle-class" domesticity goes public: gender, class, and politics from Queen Caroline to Queen Victoria', *Journal of British Studies*, 32 (1993), 396.

11 TNA, HO 40/14, J.D. Whitaker to Home Office, 7 July 1820, fol. 13v. Cobbett, to take another example, wrote to Queen Caroline to inform her of the true 'sentiments of the people'. HSP, William Cobbett Papers, 2129, Folder 15, Cobbett to the Queen, 10 June 1820.

12 Edward Wilbraham to Lord Colchester, 12 September 1820, in Lord Colchester (ed.), *Diary and Correspondence of Charles Abbot, Lord Colchester*, vol. 3

(London, 1861), p. 164. Sir Robert Peel defined public opinion at this time as a 'great compound of folly, weakness, prejudice, wrong feeling, right feeling, obstinacy, and newspaper paragraphs'. Peel to J.W. Croker, 23 March 1820, in Louis J. Jennings (ed.), *The Croker Papers*, vol. 1 (London, 1884), p. 170.

13 Two absences from this cast of radical leaders demand explanation. The first is Sir Francis Burdett, who was central to the revival of radicalism in the first decade of the nineteenth century. While Burdett's popularity did not reach its meridian until 1810, and although his political career was far from over, his influence and popularity significantly waned thereafter – as did his radicalism. The second is Henry Hunt, the hero of the post-war mass platform. Although Hunt is not the focus of a separate chapter, some attention is paid to his affective politics through a comparison with the radical infidel Richard Carlile, with whom he locked swords in the 1820s. The other reason for demoting Hunt to a cameo appearance is that, in contrast to Cobbett and Carlile, he left no voluminous set of papers. The existence of the latter has proved invaluable for shedding light on the private musings of Carlile and Cobbett on their own affective politics.

14 E.g., E.P. Thompson: 'Strike a spade into the working-class culture of the north at any time in the Thirties, and passion seems to spring from the ground.' *The Making of the English Working Class* (New York: Vintage, 1966), p. 802. Or George Kitson Clark: the 1830s and 1840s were 'more heavily charged with emotion than anything we know'. G.S.R. Kitson Clark, 'The romantic element – 1830 to 1850', in J.H. Plumb (ed.), *Studies in Social History: A Tribute to G.M. Trevelyan* (London: Longman, 1955), p. 236.

15 E.g., Miles Taylor has shown how the poetry of the Chartist leader Ernest Jones addressed feeling: *Ernest Jones, Chartism, and the Romance of Politics, 1819–1869* (Oxford: Oxford University Press, 2003), a theme also developed in Simon Rennie, *The Poetry of Ernest Jones: Myth, Song, and the 'Mighty Mind'* (Cambridge: Legenda, 2016). Tom Scriven pays some attention to the role of emotions in the moral politics of Chartism: *Popular Virtue: Continuity and Change in Radical Moral Politics, 1820–70* (Manchester: Manchester University Press 2017), pp. 52–8. Ian Haywood explores what he terms 'virtuous public excitement' in popular radical print culture in the 1830s: Ian Haywood, *The Revolution in Popular Literature: Print, Politics and the People, 1790–1860* (Cambridge: Cambridge University Press, 2004). And Michael Sanders discusses the affective dimensions of the Chartist imaginary: 'The platform and the stage: the primary aesthetics of Chartism', in Peter Yeandle, Katherine Newey and Jeffrey Richard (eds), *Politics, Performance and Popular Culture: Theatre and Society in Nineteenth-Century Britain* (Manchester: Manchester University Press 2016), pp. 44–58.

16 John Belchem, *'Orator' Hunt: Henry Hunt and English Working Class Radicalism* (London: Breviary, 2012); Dorothy Thompson, *The Chartists: Popular Politics in the Industrial Revolution* (New York: Pantheon, 1984); Gareth Stedman Jones, *The Language of Class: Studies in Working-Class History, 1832–1982* (Cambridge: Cambridge University Press, 1983), pp. 90–178. For an early critique of the over-rationalisation of popular protest, see John Bohstedt, *Riots*

and Community Politics in England and Wales, 1790–1810 (Cambridge, MA: Harvard University Press, 1983), pp. 10–11.

17 For examples of this older historiography, see J.L. Hammond and Barbara Hammond, *The Town Labourer: The New Civilization* (London: Longmans, 1917); G.D.H. Cole, *Chartist Portraits* (London: Macmillan, 1941); Malcolm I. Thomis, *The Luddites: Machine-Breaking in Regency England* (Newton Abbot: David and Charles, 1970).

18 E.g., TNA, HO 40/15, 'J.S. [John Shegoe/g] to Robert Baker, 10 July 1820, f. 33.

19 *Hansard*, House of Lords, 18 August, vol. 2, cols 675, 694, 7 September 1820, vol. 2, col. 1388, 26 October 1820, vol. 3, col. 1223.

20 E.g., Janet Oppenheim, *'Shattered Nerves': Doctors, Patients, and Depression in Victorian England* (New York: Oxford University Press, 1991) pp. 104, 106.

21 Rob Boddice and Mark Smith, *Emotion, Sense, Experience* (Cambridge: Cambridge University Press, 2020), p. 3. See also Plamper, 'Sounds of February, smells of October'.

22 *CWPR*, 25 November 1820.

23 Rob Boddice, *The History of Emotions* (Manchester: Manchester University Press, 2018), p. 99. See also G.J. Barker-Benfield, *The Culture of Sensibility: Sex and Society in the Eighteenth Century* (Chicago: University of Chicago Press, 1992), p. 132; Nicola Eustace, *Passion is the Gale: Emotion, Power, and the Coming of the American Revolution* (Chapel Hill: University of North Carolina Press, 2008), pp. 70–2; Joanna Bourke, *What it Means to be Human: Reflections from 1791 to the Present* (London: Virago, 2011), chapter 6.

24 E.A. Smith (ed.), *A Queen on Trial: The Affair of Queen Caroline* (Stroud: Alan Sutton, 1993), pp. 103–4, 147; Corinna Wagner, *Pathological Bodies: Medicine and Political Culture* (Berkeley: University of California Press, 2013), chapter 5.

25 *CWPR*, 8 June 1820.

26 Louise Carter, 'British masculinities on trial in the Queen Caroline affair of 1820', *Gender & History*, 20 (2008), 261.

27 *The Queen and Magna Charta, or the Thing that John Signed* (London, 1820), pp. 20, 22.

28 Michael T. Davis, 'The mob club? The London Corresponding Society and the politics of civility in the 1790s', in Michael T. Davis and Paul A. Pickering (eds), *Unrespectable Radicals? Popular Politics in the Age of Reform* (Aldershot: Ashgate, 2008), p. 25.

29 Christopher E. Forth, *Fat: A Cultural History of the Stuff of Life* (London: Reaktion, 2019), pp. 49, 98, 103.

30 Wagner, *Pathological Bodies*, pp. 106, 190; Leonore Davidoff and Catherine Hall, *Family Fortunes: Men and Women of the English Middle Class, 1780–1850* (London: Hutchinson, 1987), p. 437; Andrew M. Stauffer, *Anger, Revolution, and Romanticism* (Cambridge: Cambridge University Press, 2005), pp. 1, 174; Stefan Collini, 'The idea of "character" in Victorian political thought', *Transactions of the Royal Historical Society*, 35 (1985), 29–50; Martin Wiener, *Men of Blood: Violence, Manliness and Criminal Justice in Victorian England* (Cambridge: Cambridge University Press, 2004); Joanne Begiato, *Manliness in Britain: 1760–1900* (Manchester: Manchester University Press 2020),

chapter 2. For a critique of the 'rational' public sphere (mainly in relation to early American history), see John L. Brooke, 'Reason and passion in the public sphere: Habermas and the cultural historians', *Journal of Interdisciplinary History*, 29 (1998), 43–67; Nicole Eustace, 'Emotion and political change', in Susan J. Matt and Peter N. Stearns (eds), *Doing Emotions History* (Urbana, Chicago and Springfield: University of Illinois Press, 2014), pp. 163–83.

31 For the print culture of the Caroline agitation, see Marcus Wood, *Radical Satire and Print Culture, 1790–1822* (Oxford: Oxford University Press, 1994); McCalman, *Radical Underworld*, pp. 162–77.

32 BM Satires 13895, 'The Radical Ladder', by George Cruikshank (1820).

33 On petitioning, see 'The transformation of petitioning', special issue of *Social Science History*, 43 (2019); Richard Huzzey and Henry Miller, 'Petitions, parliament and political culture: petitioning the House of Commons, 1780–1918', *Past and Present*, 248 (2020), 123–64. For recent work on the relationship between radicalism and the state, see Malcolm Chase, *1820: Disorder and Stability in the United Kingdom* (Manchester: Manchester University Press 2013); Navickas, *Protest and the Politics of Space and Place*; Robert Poole, *Peterloo: The English Uprising* (Oxford: Oxford University Press, 2019); Jason McElligott and Martin Conboy (eds), *The Cato Street Conspiracy: Plotting, Counter-Intelligence and the Revolutionary Tradition in Britain and Ireland* (Manchester: Manchester University Press 2020).

34 Seditious Meetings Prevention Bill, 60 Geo. III, chapter 6, copy in *Parliamentary Debates, Vol. XLI* (London, 1820), pp. 1655–6.

35 TNA, HO 40/14, 'R.H.' (of Hull) to Home Office, 28 September 1820, fol. 297v.

36 *Black Dwarf*, 15 November 1820; *Republican*, 8 December 1820; McCalman, *Radical Underworld*, p. 162.

37 *The Times*, 8 August 1821.

38 *CWPR*, 18 August 1821. This sentimentalism was not just show for public consumption. As he wrote privately to a friend, 'I have never before known what depression of spirits was; but I really feel it now'. HSP, William Cobbett Papers, 2129, Folder 16, Cobbett to S. Clarke, 17 August 1821.

39 Vic Gatrell, *City of Laughter: Sex and Satire in Eighteenth-Century London* (London: Atlantic, 2006), chapters 17–18; McCalman, *Radical Underworld*, chapter 9.

40 See, for example, the satirical image, *The Stool of Repentance; The Scorn of the World*, 1821, published by the London radical William Benbow. National Portrait Gallery, London, NPG D48677.

41 For these interpretations of the Caroline agitation, see, respectively: J. Anne Hone, *For the Cause of Truth: Radicalism in London, 1796–1821* (Oxford: Oxford University Press, 1982), p. 317; Craig Calhoun, *The Question of Class Struggle: Social Foundations of Popular Radicalism during the Industrial Revolution* (Chicago: University of Chicago Press, 1982), pp. 105–15; Prothero, *Artisans and Politics*, p. 141; Anna Clark, 'Queen Caroline and the sexual politics of popular culture in London, 1820', *Representations*, 31 (1990), 50.

42 Calhoun, *Question of Class Struggle*, p. 109; Gatrell, *City of Laughter*, p. 530; Iain McCalman, 'Unrespectable radicalism: infidels and pornography in early nineteenth-century London', *Past and Present*, 104 (1984), 84–6.

43 Forth, *Fat*, p. 158.

44 Rob Boddice, *A History of Feelings* (London: Reaktion, 2019), p. 118. For the influence of Godwin and Wollstonecraft's affective politics on popular radicals, see Matthew Roberts, 'Romantic memory? Forgetting, remembering and feeling in the Chartist pantheon of heroes, 1790–1840', in Matthew Roberts (ed.), *Memory and Modern British Politics: Commemoration, Tradition, Legacy, 1789 to the Present* (London: Bloomsbury, forthcoming).

45 E.g., *Trial of Thomas Hardy for High Treason* (London, 1794), p. 67; *Trial of Edward Marcus Despard for High Treason* (London, 1803), p. 48; *Trial of Robert Emmet for High Treason* (London, 1803), p. 22.

46 HSP, Cobbett Papers, 2129, Folder 10, Cobbett to Miss Mitford, 18 March 1810.

47 My reading of asceticism has been influenced by: Geoffrey Galt Harpham, *The Ascetic Imperative in Culture and Criticism* (Chicago: Chicago University Press, 1987); Rob Boddice, *Pain: A Very Short Introduction* (Oxford: Oxford University Press, 2017), p. 17 and chapter 6. As Boddice observes, 'restraint is a form of expression, but also inescapably a form of action to change how a feeling feels'. Boddice, *History of Emotions*, p. 62.

48 In this respect it was congruent with what John Tosh has termed 'manly simplicity'. Although closely identified with the middle classes, this was a gendered code which transcended class and, in contrast to elite notions of gentlemanly politeness, it was socially inclusive, open to all men and offered a route for self-betterment rather than waiting for structural reform to improve the condition of the people. Bound up with notions of character, this form of manliness emphasised, *inter alia*, self-discipline, thrift, courage, 'toughness of heart'. John Tosh, 'Gentlemanly politeness and manly simplicity in Victorian England', *Transactions of the Royal Historical Society*, 12 (2001), 455–72. See also Matthew McCormack and Matthew Roberts, 'Chronologies in the history of British political masculinities, c.1700–2000', in Matthew McCormack (ed.), *Public Men: Masculinity and Politics in Modern Britain* (Basingstoke: Palgrave, 2007), pp. 187–202.

49 Thomas Dixon, *Weeping Britannia: Portrait of a Nation in Tears* (Oxford: Oxford University Press, 2015), p. 72. See also Eustace, *Passion is the Gale*, pp. 439–48; Boddice, *History of Feelings*, chapter 4.

50 The American Revolution marked a new departure in asserting the natural right to happiness, when Jefferson substituted property in the phrase 'life, liberty and property' for happiness in the Declaration of Independence. But as Nicole Eustace has recently argued, this effectively equated happiness with property ownership. Radicals soon came to realise that the happiness of the rich 'was socially created and materially grounded in processes of exploitation'. Nicole Eustace, 'Emotional pursuits and the American Revolution', *Emotion Review*, 12 (2020), 148, 150. The idea that it was the state's responsibility to guarantee happiness was novel, and from the point of view of most of the elite, dangerous

and unattainable. See Joanna Innes, 'Happiness contested: happiness and politics in the eighteenth and early nineteenth centuries', in Michael J. Braddick and Joanna Innes (eds), *Suffering and Happiness in England, 1550–1850: Narratives and Representations* (Oxford: Oxford University Press, 2017), p. 106.

51 Barker-Benfield, *Culture of Sensibility*.

52 See Joel Faflak and Richard C. Sha, 'Feeling Romanticism', in Joel Faflak and Richard C. Sha (eds), *Romanticism and the Emotions* (Cambridge: Cambridge University Press, 2016), p. 2. The relationship between Romanticism and emotion was, of course, much more complex than this. As well as the above collection, see the special issue 'Romanticism and affect studies', *Romantic Circles Praxis Volume* (2018).

53 Isaiah Berlin, *The Roots of Romanticism*, ed. Henry Hardy (London: Pimlico, 1999), p. xi.

54 Taylor, *Ernest Jones*, p. 10. I am well aware of the complexities and contested nature of Romanticism, and of the similarly contested and evolving nature of Romantic Studies – the shift away from canonical figures and tropes to the popular and discordant, along with the tensions between Romanticism and Enlightenment. I discuss these issues at greater length in Roberts, 'Romantic memory?'.

55 Kevin Gilmartin, *Print Politics: The Press and Radical Opposition in Early Nineteenth-Century England* (Cambridge: Cambridge University Press, 1996); Philip Harling, 'William Hazlitt and radical journalism', *Romanticism*, 3 (1997), 53–65; David Worrall, *Theatric Revolution: Drama, Censorship and Romantic Period Sub-Cultures, 1773–1832* (Oxford: Oxford University Press, 2006); Jon Mee, *Print, Publicity and Popular Radicalism in the 1790s: The Laurel of Liberty* (Cambridge: Cambridge University Press, 2016).

56 Reddy defines an emotional regime as: 'a normative order for emotions ... which require individuals to express normative emotions and to avoid deviant emotions'. Emotional refuge as: 'A relationship, ritual, or organization ... that provides safe release from prevailing emotional norms and allows relaxation of emotional effort ... which may shore up or threaten the existing emotional regime'. William M. Reddy, *The Navigation of Feeling: A Framework for the History of Emotions* (Cambridge: Cambridge University Press, 2001), p. 129. Throughout this book, I have generally opted for the looser definition of feeling rules rather than Reddy's more specific concept of emotional regimes, except where the latter seemed particularly apt for elucidating the power dynamics of affective politics (chapters 5 and 6).

57 Thomas L. Haskell, 'Capitalism and the origins of the humanitarian sensibility, part 1', *American Historical Review*, 90 (1985), 339–61 (quote at 352); Boddice, *Science of Sympathy*, pp. 8–10.

58 Dixon, *Weeping Britannia*, chapter 5. For the role played by evangelicalism in Oastler and Stephens's affective politics, and the concept of an ethical shelter, see Matthew Roberts, 'Tory-radical feeling in Brontë's *Shirley* and early Victorian England', *Victorian Studies*, 68 (2020), 39–42.

59 Norbert Elias, *The Civilizing Process* (Oxford, 1994 [1939]). A similar teleology can be detected in Peter Gay's argument that modern politics was premised on the

sublimation of aggression. Peter Gay, *The Cultivation of Hatred: The Bourgeois Experience Victoria to Freud* (New York, 1993), chapter 3. For a powerful critique of this teleology, see Barbara H. Rosenwein, *Emotional Communities in the Early Middle Ages* (Ithaca: Cornell University Press, 2006), pp. 7–10.

60 For critical introductions to the field, see Jan Plamper, *The History of Emotions: An Introduction* (Oxford: Oxford University Press, 2012); Barbara Rosenwein and Riccardo Cristiani, *What is the History of Emotions?* (Cambridge: Polity, 2018); Boddice, *History of Emotions*.

61 Dolores Martín-Moruno and Beatriz Pichel, 'Introduction', in Dolores Martín-Moruno and Beatriz Pichel (eds), *Emotional Bodies: The Historical Performativity of Emotions* (Urbana, Chicago and Springfield: University of Illinois Press, 2019), pp. 5–6.

62 Thomas Dixon, *From Passions to Emotions: The Creation of a Secular Psychological Character* (Cambridge: Cambridge University Press, 2003); Barbara Rosenwein, *Generations of Feeling: A History of Emotions, 600–1700* (Cambridge: Cambridge University Press, 2015); Michael Brown, 'Surgery, identity and embodied emotion: John Bell, James Gregory and the Edinburgh "medical war"', *History*, 104 (2019), 19–41; Rob Boddice, *Humane Professions: The Defence of Experimental Medicine, 1876–1914* (Cambridge: Cambridge University Press, 2021). See also Carolyn Steedman, *An Everyday Life of the English Working Class: Work, Self and Sociability in the Early Nineteenth Century* (Cambridge: Cambridge University Press, 2013); Ruth Mather, 'The home-making of the English working-class: radical politics and domestic life in late Georgian England, c.1790–1820' (PhD dissertation, Queen Mary, University of London, 2016), p. 174; Julie-Marie Strange, *Fatherhood and the British Working-Class, 1865–1914* (Cambridge: Cambridge University Press, 2015); Emma Griffin, *Breadwinner: An Intimate History of the Victorian Economy* (New Haven: Yale University Press, 2020), chapter 8.

63 Susan J. Matt and Peter N. Stearns, 'Introduction', in Matt and Stearns, *Doing Emotions History*, p. 2.

64 Boddice, *History of Emotions*, pp. 142–67.

65 Dixon, *Passions to Emotions*; pp. 2, 25; Rosenwein, *Generations of Feeling*; Boddice, *History of Emotions*, pp. 35, 45–6.

66 Dixon, *Passions to Emotions*, pp. 3, 17–18.

67 While the term 'passions' did operate as something of an umbrella term for feelings, strictly speaking, by the late eighteenth century, the term meant intense, often violent, inward stirrings of the soul, and was distinguished from the affections which denoted milder appetites and sentiments. Thomas Dixon, '"Emotion": the history of a keyword in crisis', *Emotion Review*, 4 (2012), 340.

68 As Rob Boddice and Mark Smith have recently underlined, in the eighteenth and early nineteenth centuries, morality, feeling and the senses were conflated. Boddice and Smith, *Emotion, Sense, Experience*, pp. 12, 15. For a recent critical overview of changing affective vocabulary, see Susan J. Matt, 'What were emotions? Definitions and understandings, 1780–1920', in Susan J. Matt (ed.), *A Cultural History of the Emotions in the Age of Romanticism, Revolution and Empire* (London: Bloomsbury, 2019), pp. 1–16.

69 Boddice, *History of Emotions*, p. 46.

70 *Ibid.*, p. 57. This is not to suggest that we abandon all attempts to label feelings in the past, a nihilistic desideratum that is neither desirable nor achievable. At the same time, it is important to recognise the provisional and contingent nature of our portraits of the affective lives of those we study, especially when we use, if only for heuristic purposes, words from contemporary emotional vocabulary. On this thorny issue, see Thomas Dixon, 'What is the history of anger a history of?', *EHCS*, 4 (2020), 1–34.

71 The literature on this is vast, but key works include: Peter Laslett, *The World We Have Lost* (London: Methuen, 1965); Mark Keay, *William Wordsworth's Golden Age Theories during the Industrial Revolution* (Basingstoke: Palgrave, 2001); Alistair Bonnett, *Radicalism and the Politics of Nostalgia* (London: Bloomsbury, 2010).

72 'Nostalgia, 2', OED Online (Oxford: Oxford University Press University Press, 2020), www-oed-com.hallam.idm.oclc.org/view/Entry/128472 [accessed 23 March 2021].

73 For a trenchant critique of the dangers of this kind of essentialism, see Boddice, *History of Emotions*, chapters 2, 5. See also '*AHR* conversation', 1491.

74 Joanna Bourke, 'Fear and anxiety: writing about emotion in modern history', *History Workshop Journal*, 55 (2003), 121, 125; Rob Boddice, 'The affective turn: historicizing the emotions', in Cristian Tileagă and Jovan Byford (eds), *Psychology and History: Interdisciplinary Explorations* (Cambridge: Cambridge University Press, 2014), pp. 147–65.

75 Hunt and Jacob, 'The affective revolution in 1790s Britain', p. 496.

76 See the *OED Online*, for examples of the way in which 'affective' was used in the early nineteenth century: 'Affective, adj.' *OED Online* (Oxford: Oxford University Press University Press, 2020), www.oed.com/view/Entry/3357 [accessed 1 March 2021]. Rachel Hewitt, *A Revolution of Feeling: The Decade that Forged the Modern Mind* (London: Granta, 2017), p. 7; cf. Rosenwein and Cristiani, *What is the History of Emotions?*, pp. 11, 17–19, 83.

77 Christina Parolin, *Radical Spaces: Venues of Popular Politics in London, 1790-c.1845* (Canberra: ANU Press, 2010); Navickas, *Protest and the Politics of Space and Place*.

78 Katie Barclay, *Men on Trial: Performing Emotion, Embodiment and Identity in Ireland, 1800–45* (Manchester: Manchester University Press 2018), p. 26.

79 For a recent discussion of Owen's ambiguous political stance, and one that locates him in the context of rational Dissent, see Gareth Stedman Jones, 'Millennium and enlightenment: Robert Owen and the second coming of truth', *History of European Ideas*, 47 (2021), 1–20.

80 On the links between British and Irish radicalism, see Chase, *1820*; Jonathan Jeffrey Wright, 'An Anglo-Irish radical in the late Georgian metropolis: Peter Finnerty and the politics of contempt', *Journal of British Studies*, 53 (2014), 660–84; Matthew Roberts, 'Daniel O'Connell, repeal, and Chartism in the age of Atlantic revolutions', *Journal of Modern History*, 90 (2018), 1–39; Tim Murtagh, 'The shadow of the pikeman: Irish craftsmen and British radicalism', in McElligott and Conboy, *Cato Street*, pp. 135–52. On the close links between

English and Welsh radicals, see Malcolm Chase, *The Chartists: Perspectives and Legacies* (London: Merlin, 2015), chapter 6; and on Scotland, Gordon Pentland, *Radicalism, Reform and National Identity in Scotland, 1820–1833* (Woodbridge: Royal Historical Society, 2008); Gordon Pentland, *The Spirit of the Union: Popular Politics in Scotland, 1815–1820* (London: Pickering & Chatto, 2011).

81 E.g., 'The intellectual organisation of the Irish people ... confers imagination and passion in a far higher degree than reasoning and judgement', *Blackwood's Magazine*, quoted in the *Sligo Journal*, 27 November 1829. 'Thank God! we are Saxons! ... flanked by the savage Celt [who] is a slave to the passions', *Economist*, quoted in *Hampshire Telegraph*, 6 May 1848.

1

William Cobbett's anti-'feelosofee'

William Cobbett (1763–1835) began his working life as a ploughboy in Surrey, born into relatively humble circumstances as the son of a yeoman farmer and innkeeper. A restless youth who craved adventure and the expanse of wider horizons, he eventually enlisted in the West Norfolk 54th Foot and was stationed in New Brunswick in the years immediately following the American war of independence, rising to the rank of sergeant major. Cobbett served in the army for nearly eight years, during which time he became aware of the corruption of the officer class who were defrauding his fellow subalterns. Determined to whistle-blow, he secured his discharge and began proceedings against his superiors in 1792, until he was forced to abandon the suit when he realised that the army and government were closing ranks against him. And so he fled with his wife, Nancy, to France, before emigrating to the United States, where he would remain until 1800. Shortly after his arrival at Philadelphia, Cobbett set up in a trade in which he would spend the rest of his life: a journalist with side interests in printing, publishing and bookselling, including a growing and ultimately voluminous catalogue of works from his own pen. By the time he died in 1835, having spent his twilight years combining his journalism with a career that had eluded him until 1832 – as an MP – Cobbett had authored some twenty million words. The bulk of this oeuvre was published in his long-running and hugely popular periodical the *Political Register*.

Cobbett was the most widely read journalist of his day – 'a kind of fourth estate in the politics of the country', in William Hazlitt's famous description. An anti-Jacobin turned radical, Cobbett was infamous for his invective and brutal sparring with a growing cast of villains who were held responsible for impoverishing the people, about whom he cared deeply. Unsurprisingly, he was seen by friend and foe alike as an instinctive and sometimes brutish creature of his passions.[1] Unsuspecting historians have also followed this assessment.[2] The caricatured image of Cobbett as an unthinking writer wielding uncontrolled invective has been punctured by Leonora Nattrass's literary analysis of his writing: 'the highly-wrought self-consciousness of his writings are always striving for a calculated effect', with the purpose being to 'mobilize its reader's emotions and ideas in certain directions'.[3] Cobbett's skill was in making his writing look instinctive. As Hazlitt astutely observed, Cobbett was strong in 'bodily perception', which he juxtaposed against those like Joseph Priestley whose bodies were merely the envelopes of their minds. It was precisely because he thought with his body that Cobbett's writing appeared so instinctive and immediate: while reason plods, sense perception leaps, a view that Hazlitt derived from Francis Hutcheson.[4] Cobbett's widely attested brutality – even the appreciative Hazlitt wrote of Cobbett's 'great mutton-fist' and his 'unwieldly bulk' – has obscured the fact that he could be an intensely sensitive man of feeling, shaped just as much by the age of sensibility and Romanticism as any other writer who came of age in the late eighteenth century.[5] James Grande has read Cobbett's private correspondence as a form of 'sentimental radicalism', anchored in his cultural and stylistic indebtedness to Edmund Burke.[6] While hugely insightful, Nattrass and Grande have little to say about the nature, purpose and significance of feelings in Cobbett's published writing, or how exactly he politicised feeling and with what effect – the focus of this chapter. There was much more to Cobbett's affective politics than sentimentalism and indebtedness to Burke's insistence that feeling, not reason, should guide human action, though that certainly played a part. This chapter shifts the interpretative emphasis towards asceticism in Cobbett's radicalism.[7]

Cobbett's biographers have understandably struggled to explain the twists and turns in a political career that lasted from the 1790s to the 1830s. Paying attention to the way he deploys the language of feeling underscores the fundamental continuities in his political career. While principles might be exchanged – from loyalism to radicalism – fidelity to one's feelings was, for him, sacrosanct. Cobbett's double volte-face – from radical to Tory, Tory to radical – is less dramatic than historians have sometimes argued. He rediscovered his radicalism in response to his many encounters with Old Corruption – the name given to the deleterious effects of the concentration of political power in the hands of a parasitic elite – as part of the general radical revival in the 1800s. In short, Cobbett became radical to further his patriotic feelings.[8] Focusing on his affective politics restores some coherence of purpose to his political career. This is about more than simply noting his unique position among radical leaders of being able to give voice to the feelings of rural workers (the focus of Dyck's study).[9] Rather, it is also about recognising that Cobbett was one of the loudest radical voices in the early nineteenth century who denounced the unfeeling callousness of the elite and the emerging ideology of liberal political economy – what he derisively dubbed 'Scotch *feelosofee*', a quip widely quoted by historians but one whose affective significance has gone unnoticed.

This chapter focuses mainly on the first decade of Cobbett's radicalism, c.1809–20, and for two reasons. First, this was a formative period in which he articulated the affective politics which would endure for the rest of his public life. Second, because key episodes during this period – his trial for seditious libel in 1810, and his election campaign at Coventry in 1820 – have not received the attention they merit. The chapter explores the origins of one of the central goals of Cobbett's radicalism: positioning himself and subsequently soldiers and labourers as men of feeling as part of his campaign to further their enfranchisement. It takes as its point of departure Hazlitt's notion that Cobbett was a bodily thinker by showing how he politicised the senses in ways that celebrated, like Paine, 'the socially levelling implications of the bonds of feeling'.[10] But he went further than Paine in asserting that it was the hard-hearted, senseless elite who were unfeeling, not the people. Focusing on the ways in which Cobbett was vilified by his enemies – which, as the first section shows, frequently turned on accusations that he was brutish and suffered from disordered passions and hardened senses – helps to explain the centrality of this goal. By rereading Cobbett's autobiography, 'the progress of a ploughboy', and through a close reading of his seditious libel of 1809 and the resulting trial, the next section explores the ways in which Cobbett challenged the widely held assumption that working-class men lacked refined sensibility. Attention is also paid to the ways in which he developed a radical version of patriotic feeling to challenge political corruption and the desiccated, unfeeling patriotism espoused by the elite in the final stages of the Napoleonic Wars.[11] Cobbett had to walk an affective tightrope on behalf of the poor – a man of feeling, but not a creature of his passions. For all his invective and apparent instinctive outrage, Cobbett also preached a version of ascetic radicalism, as the third section argues. His ascetic radicalism was, however, a Georgian incarnation, which had its violent and crude manifestations (at least as far as the subsequent Victorian variant was concerned). Ascetic radicalism for Cobbett was about displaying appropriate feeling in the right contexts. A charge he frequently made against his enemies was that they failed in this, and in failing rendered themselves unfit to govern.

The progress of an unfeeling brute

As E.P. Thompson remarked, 'in tone will be found at least one half of Cobbett's political meaning'.[12] While this tone was central to Cobbett's affective politics and was the cornerstone of his popularity with the masses, unsurprisingly his invective soon made for a growing list of enemies, some of whom would stop at nothing to put him behind bars and ruin him financially. Cobbett's enemies tried to turn his tone against him – he was a creature of passion, suffered from disordered passions or, worse still, was an unfeeling brute. Writing in the *New Times* in 1817, a hostile correspondent cautioned Cobbett that 'Strong passions are like strong drink! the repeated indulgence of the one is as weakening to the mind, as that of the other is to the body'. But worse than the disordered state of his own passions was the effect that he had on others: 'no state can be safe or tranquil, where the passions of men are kept in such a perpetual state of fury and agitation, as that which is produced by Cobbett's seditious publications'.[13] Imputations of brutishness were frequently visited on him, both in text and image. In some of the earliest caricatures in which he features, Cobbett is depicted as a bullish, stocky yokel, holding rolled-up copies of his writing which are transformed into club-like weapons, or alternatively with a menacing pitchfork.[14] His bodily excess – Cobbett was some six feet tall and widely depicted as portly (no doubt exaggerated in visual satire) – along with the violence he threatened offended the class and gendered norms of polite society.[15]

Gillray's satirical *Life of William Cobbett*, a set of eight prints published in 1809, no doubt with government prodding, was one of the most stinging loyalist attacks on the recent Tory-turned-radical.[16] Its effectiveness stemmed not merely from Gillray's portrait of Cobbett as a traitorous Jacobin, but also from the way in which it equated Jacobinism with disordered passion and brutishness. In the first plate, Cobbett is depicted as a young boy not just tormenting the farmyard animals but appearing almost as one of them, billed as 'goode entertainment for man and beaste'. In a print from the previous year, Gillray virtually reduced Cobbett to the level of a pig as the leader of the 'Hampshire Hogs'. Cobbett had recently purchased a house and estate at Botley in Hampshire, which provided satirists with a ready-made lampoon for years to come.[17] In Gillray's latest spoof, we learn that at the tender age of seven Cobbett was already displaying 'a taste for plunder and oppression' and that he 'beat all the little girls of the town'. The imputation of cruelty is further underlined here by the inference that Cobbett has transgressed the gendered norms of chivalric masculinity by beating girls rather than boys.[18] The third plate alleges that Cobbett was a cruel sergeant during his time in the army who resorted to 'caning and kicking'.[19] The penultimate print brings Cobbett's career up to date and shows him revelling in Jacobin excess and delighting in the cruelty he was able to inflict on the poor and infirm as lord of the manor of Botley.[20] Most, if not all, of these allegations were unfounded – Cobbett always spoke out against cruelty to animals and counselled kindness towards them, for example – but the veracity of these charges is not the key to their significance, at least not as far as his enemies were concerned.[21] It was the imputation of unfeeling brutishness that rendered him an unfit employer and a dangerous radical. He would face similar charges for the rest of his political career.[22] At best Cobbett was portrayed as a defective character, with, for example, 'a vile temper'; at worst, he was sub-human – 'a knavish brute'.[23]

In the eyes of his detractors, no single episode confirmed Cobbett's brutishness more than his macabre disinterring of Thomas Paine's bones from the latter's grave on his New York farm.[24] Cobbett had crossed the Atlantic once again in 1817, fleeing from what would almost certainly have been another period of imprisonment for sedition (or debt). His intention on returning to Britain in November 1819 was laudable enough: to give Paine the burial he had been denied in the United States by consecrating a memorial which, Cobbett hoped, would serve as a rallying point for the radical movement then in desperate need of succour. He arrived back in Britain with Paine's bones three months after the Peterloo Massacre when a peaceful crowd of radical reformers on St Peter's Fields in Manchester had been mown down by the yeomanry and army, killing some twenty and injuring hundreds more. Unusually for Cobbett, the lack of popular enthusiasm for his *deus ex machina* suggests that he had misread the popular mood. The lack of enthusiasm for Paine's bones may have stemmed less from any feelings of embarrassment and revulsion at Cobbett's macabre actions – the view taken by his loyalist enemies – and more from fears of how the authorities would react given the clampdown on radicalism in the shape of the draconian Six Acts. Either way, popular feeling was paramount, and this was not lost on Cobbett who noted the disjunction between his own cheerful feelings on returning to Britain, eager to resume his radicalism, and that of his friends who were gloomy.[25]

With the failure of Cobbett's scheme, it was left to the loyalists to make capital out of the 'bones fiasco'. The very sacrilegious act of disinterring Paine's bones was proof positive of Cobbett's infidelity and disordered passions: 'he hugs the excommunicated relics with impious affection', a reference to Paine's own infidelity as the author of the 'atheist' *Age of Reason* and, by proxy, Cobbett's.[26] The whole episode overshadowed Cobbett's first attempt to stand for parliament at Coventry in 1820, where the ghost of Paine was present in more ways than one.[27] The Evangelical *Christian Observer* could barely conceal its satisfaction that Cobbett's 'ridiculous partiality for the bones of Tom Paine ... seems to have disgusted even the Radicals of Coventry'.[28] Ironically – because the feeling was one that Cobbett frequently expressed towards his enemies – disgust was uppermost in the loyalist response. This was because the episode took place against the background of rising concern with grave-robbing: one print labelled Cobbett a 'Political champion turned resurrection man'.[29] The grave-robber was a hardened criminal insensitive to feelings of common decency.

The disgusting nature of the episode was further underlined by scurrilous accounts which dwelt on the apparently gruesome details of how Cobbett had planned and executed the disinterring, relying for the most part on a former black servant of Paine's, 'one Quacho, a free Negro man'. The latter was reluctant to dig up the bones fearing that they would be too rotten, partly on account of the lapse of time (Paine had died a decade earlier) but also because of Paine's widely attested alcoholism and poor hygiene. Quacho recalled 'oh God, how he [s]tink!'.[30] This further served to subordinate Paine and Cobbett beneath the morality of a 'Poor innocent Negro' who, offended by noxious odours, is a man possessed of apparent greater sensibility than Cobbett who, by implication, is impervious to smell. As Rob Boddice and Mark Smith have recently suggested, the elitist charge that those who were less refined were creatures of their passions was intimately linked to the assumption that there was no 'uniformity among all classes of sensory experience'.[31] The poor, for example, were thought to be hardened against filth, stench and pain.

This theme of Cobbett's hardened senses was picked up by other hostile satirists. As 'A Letter to William Cobbett' by 'A Briton' remarked: 'I will not call upon you to blush, because (I use the language adopted by yourself when formerly addressing your *now sainted hero*, Paine) "the result of villainy has eaten your cheek to the bone, and dried up the source of suffision" [sic.] Wretched apostate!'[32] Other diatribes used smell to accentuate their feelings of disgust: in one satirical image from 1817 by George Cruikshank, Cobbett belches forth poisonous fumes, personifying radicalism as 'noxious gas'.[33] Sight was also used to underline obnoxiousness: 'First comes "a monster of such frightful mein." "That to be hated needs but to be seen." ... Mark [h]is designing look, and cunning air, And see if aught but knavery is there.'[34] Like other radicals and threatening members of the lower orders, Cobbett sounded, looked and even smelled like a frightful monster whose disordered passions were linked to equally defective senses, a product of his closeness to the smells and sounds of the farmyard and barrack. These were pointed barbs, for as the next section shows, Cobbett was incredibly attuned to the sensory. He frequently invoked senses for veracity and to underline his sensitivity, which in turn, undergirded his claims to be a right-feeling person. When departing London on the first of his famous rural rides (October 1821) to find out for himself what ordinary men were thinking and feeling, and leaving the smells and sights of London behind him, Cobbett declared, 'the *smell* has a great deal to do with health'. Unlike sight and sound, tactile senses like smell and touch literally permeate the body.[35] Cobbett supported this claim with the less than plausible evidence that 'There can be no doubt that Butchers and their wives fatten upon the smell of meat'.[36]

Ploughboys and soldiers as men of feeling

The problem with berating Cobbett for his lack of refinement was that it inadvertently served to increase his affinity with those he represented. As one anti-Cobbett tract ventriloquised, 'I am your equal, bred up in a humble state of life, I can enter into your feelings'.[37] Cobbett never ceased to identify himself with the poor, especially the rural poor: 'the ploughboy that continues to warm my veins', as he put it towards the end of his life.[38] Similarly, as a former soldier he also confessed in July 1810 that 'To the army, to every soldier in it, I have a bond of attachment quite independent of any political reasoning ... I like soldiers as a class in life, better than any other description of men'. Among his reasons for this partiality, he concluded with 'having felt hardships themselves, they know how to feel for others', a characteristic contrary statement that challenged the stereotype of the soldier as callous.[39]

These references to feeling were neither unusual nor without significance. Cobbett knew only too well that one of ways in which men like him and the poor for whom he spoke were excluded from citizenship was on the basis that they were deemed to be unfeeling brutes. An anti-radical tract (possibly a radical spoof) from 1816 objected to Cobbett's claim that working men, being the same as other men, were worthy of political rights: 'You have no rights but the rights of horses and beasts of burden.'[40] Soldiers were viewed as 'mere animals, endowed only with brute instincts'. But as one soldier of the 71st Light Infantry complained at this time, the 'unnoticed soldiers [were] equally susceptible of every feeling of pain' as their social superiors.[41] Soldiers, Cobbett countered in 1817, were more than 'worthy of the vote ... I know them to be quick sighted, and to be particularly gifted at prying into any sinister caresses'.[42] Note, again, the emphasis on the senses here – in this case sight – and the allusion to corruption as sordid pleasure. Countering these accusations was part of the reason why Cobbett in his autobiographical writings presented himself as a man of sentiment. He began publishing autobiographical material as early as the 1790s, and he would continue to write instalments down to his death in 1835. Some of this autobiographical writing, as well as much else of Cobbett's published output, was directed, not towards soldiers, ploughboys or the working classes more generally, but to the propertied classes. It was this audience which needed disabusing of their prejudices that ploughboys and soldiers were brutes. Cobbett's *Advice to Young Men*, for example, was addressed to those 'in the middle and higher ranks of life'.[43]

Cobbett's first moment of intellectual awakening is told in terms of feeling curiosity and delight; his filial devotion as one of pride, his childhood one of happiness. He recalled the exhilaration he felt as a child when listening to the political debates in his father's inn, while his recollections of first love equals the sentimentalism of any similar account written during the last two decades of the eighteenth century. His running away from home as a teenager is attributed to a burning curiosity to see Kew Gardens having heard of their beauty from a local gardener. Recalling of his ramblings in the Canadian outback when stationed there in the 1780s, Cobbett remarked that 'Here was everything to delight the eye, and especially of one like me, who seems to have been born to love rural life, and trees and plants of all sorts'.[44] Notions of beauty were central to Cobbett's language, especially evident in *Rural Rides* as well as its corresponding opposite (urban) ugliness. His most palpable memory as an adolescent was the sadness he felt when he lost Swift's *Tale of a Tub*, the reading of which was central to his intellectual awakening: 'the loss gave me greater pain than I have ever felt at losing thousands of pounds'. His feeling of awesome wonder – 'between astonishment and admiration' – when he saw a fleet of ships at Portsmouth, which along with the allure of the sea, induced him to enlist in the navy (rejected). 'My heart was inflated with national pride.' This event awakened in Cobbett a desire for travel: 'I sighed for a sight of the world.' 'The things in which I had taken the most delight were neglected; the singing of the birds grew insipid, and the heart-cheering cry of the hounds ... were heard with the most torpid indifference.' Cobbett also had experience of privation (some of it, admittedly self-enforced to pay for books), remembering how in the army he had on one occasion lost his last half-penny with which to buy food: 'I buried me head under the miserable sheet and rug, and cried like a child!' (he was then about twenty years old). He also presented himself as an affectionate father, who never resorted to the cruelties of corporal punishment, recollecting that there was only one occasion on which he spoke to one of his children in an angry tone, and when he had done so 'it appeared as if my heart was gone out of my body'. This was a characteristic charge of heartlessness that he often levelled at the enemies of the working classes.[45]

The ways in which Cobbett romanticised the virtues of rural life in the imagined 'Old England' of his youth followed on naturally from these sentimental episodes in his own life. He contrasted his memories of happy labourers with the misery and wretchedness he now encountered in the rural cottage. Despite the crushing poverty of the rural poor, during his *Rural Rides* in the 1820s Cobbett never lost an opportunity to present labourers as men of refined feelings: 'Thus he proceeded to illustrate the labourers' character by pointing to evidence of their sensitivity, including their "*neatly kept and productive little gardens*", and their tenderness and leniency in child-rearing.' Adopting an almost physiocratic assumption that land was the basis of all national wealth, he democratised this notion by placing the agricultural labourer at the root of all wealth, concluding: 'With this correct idea of your own worth in your minds, with what indignation must you hear yourself called the Populace, the Rabble, the Mob, the Swinish Multitude.' In short, Cobbett's affective politics were about restoring feelings of dignity (after all, the counterpoint to indignity, and by extension indignation) and self-confidence to the poor. He challenged the perception that labourers were 'a *distinct and degraded class of persons*', a view he rejected 'with scorn'. Cobbett was fully alive to the sleight of hand involved here: 'Instead of looking into the [labourers'] misery, those who inveigh against them seem to regard them as a separate cast of beings; as a distinct and different breed of animals.' 'Have they not a right to happiness,' he retorted, 'and shall I be accused of *sedition*, because I endeavour ... to point out to them how to obtain and secure the happiness?'[46] One of the maxims he laid down in his popular self-help *Cottage Economy* was that happiness was a natural right to which all were entitled and it was blasphemy to claim that God intended man to be miserable. 'Happy poverty' was a contradiction in terms invented by parasites such as absentee clergymen.[47] Happiness was not to be the exclusive preserve of the town labourer; indeed, Cobbett believed that genuine happiness could only be found in the countryside where man was at one with nature.

It was not just in the countryside that Cobbett encountered unhappiness, as important as that discovery was in propelling him towards radicalism. By the time he witnessed the ill-effects of corruption in the countryside he was already familiar with it in the army. One of the more intense feelings that Cobbett expressed when recalling his days in the army was the indignation he felt on discovering the corruption of his officers in defrauding the men their full allowances: 'I feel an indignation at this I cannot describe', he had written in *The Soldier's Friend* (1792), exposing the corruption, and framed as giving voice to the feelings of the subaltern ranks.[48] What made this corruption even more outrageous was that he had seen subalterns – 'lads from the plough-tail' like himself – 'lay in their berths, many and many a time, actually crying on account of hunger'.[49] To add insult to injury, most of the officer class he served with were incompetent, in some cases illiterate and had to rely on men like Cobbett. Further revelations of corruption, incompetence and cruelty of army officers and their political allies during the final stages of the Napoleonic Wars was a major factor in Cobbett's conversion to radicalism, as well as the more familiar poverty of rural England that he encountered. Soldiers were hardly an insignificant minority when he began to voice their grievances: by 1809 some one in nine men were serving in the regular armed forces, navy or militia, and if volunteers and local militia units are included, the figure is closer to one in six.[50]

Cobbett's preoccupation with malfeasance in the interlocking worlds of the military and political establishment would culminate in 1809 when the

Mary Anne Clarke scandal broke. The scandal centred on a former mistress of the Duke of York who had used her influence over the Duke, then commander-in-chief of the army, for trafficking commissions. Cobbett's journey towards radicalism had begun in 1804, but it was not until 1809 in response to this scandal that the full force of that radicalism was expressed. By giving voice to these outraged feelings and speaking on behalf of soldiers, and more broadly those at home suffering from the dire consequences of corruption and a mismanaged war, Cobbett's affective politics played a central part in breaking the patriotic consensus, fragile at best, that appeared to unite Britons against Napoleon.[51] One specific issue which had outraged him during the Clarke scandal was flogging. Cobbett highlighted the cruel class-based approach to indiscipline and incompetency in the army: while common soldiers were flogged for the smallest of infractions, the 'silly boobies' who led them were rarely held to account for their gross failings and ill-treatment of men.[52] This 'partiality of punishments', which was 'so mischievous and hateful … is what no man can bear without feeling a desire to see overturned … the whole system and fabric of that government where such partiality has proceeded'.[53] The Clarke scandal crystallised the relationship between corruption, incompetence and the wave of indignation which powered Cobbett's radicalism.

Cobbett's indignation over the Clarke scandal would prove to be the first of two acts in 1809. The second act represented one of his most impassioned tirades to date in the *Political Register* in which he spoke out against the flogging of a group of militiamen at Ely in Cambridgeshire by the King's German Legion. The year had seen widespread strikes by militiamen over wages and allowances, the specific grievance of the men at Ely being a stoppage for their knapsacks. The reason why the 'mutiny' at Ely attracted national attention was because the authorities called in a guard of Hanoverian cavalry to discipline the ringleaders and administer the punishment of five hundred lashes. Cobbett was not alone among radicals in campaigning against flogging in the army, the prevalence of which had increased during the French Wars, and in the first instance he may have been following rather than leading.[54] But Cobbett not only spoke with the authority of a former soldier, he also brought to the issue his newly formed affective politics. The rising tide of indignation which had been growing within him, finally burst forth clothed in heavy sarcasm (and is worth quoting at length as the first, full and characteristic example of Cobbett's tone):

> *Five hundred lashes* each! Aye, that is right! Flog them; flog them; flog them! They deserve it, and a great deal more. They deserve flogging at every mealtime. 'Lash them daily, lash them duly.' What, shall the rascals dare to *mutiny*, and that, too when the German Legion is so near at hand! Lash them, lash them, lash them! They *deserve* it. O, yes; they merit a double-tailed cat. Base

dogs! What, mutiny for the sake of *the price of a knapsack!* Lash them! flog them! Base rascals! Mutiny for the price of a goat's skin; and, then, upon the appearance of the *German Soldiers*, they take a flogging as quietly as so many trunks of trees! – I do not know what sort of place Ely is; but I really should like to know how the inhabitants looked at one another in the face, while this scene was exhibiting in their town. I should like to have been able to see their faces, and to hear their observations to each other, at the time. – This occurrence at home will, one would hope, teach *the loyal*, a little caution in speaking of the means, which Napoleon employs (or, rather, which they say he employs), in order to get together and discipline his Conscripts. ... [T]here is scarcely one of the loyal, who has not cited these means as proof, a complete proof, that the people of France *hate Napoleon and his government, assist with reluctance in his wars*, and would *fain see another revolution*. I hope, I say, that the loyal will, hereafter, be more cautious in drawing such conclusions, now that they see, that our 'gallant defenders' not only require physical restraint in certain cases, but even a little blood drawn from their backs, and that too, with the aid and assistance of *German* troops.[55]

It was this outburst which led to Cobbett's trial for seditious libel on 15 June 1810, the delay occasioned by the government's vain hope that he would either abandon or tone down his radical journalism.[56] The extreme sarcasm and invective that Cobbett expressed was clearly a response to what he perceived as the cruelty – the unfeeling – of the authorities for the soldiers. The affective language on display in the trial was equally revealing. The Attorney-General, who led the prosecution, outlined the charge:

I ... here impute to the Defendant, that he charges the government with cruelty – that he charges the military authorities with cruelty – that he suggests to mutineers the injustice of their sentence – and that he ridicules the patience with which they endured their punishment, and the compunction with which they regretted their offence. He, the Defendant, tells you that it is said as an extreme of cruelty in the French Governor, that he drags the youth of France to join the armies, chained and handcuffed, and then compares this act of tyranny to the just punishment of the Local Militia. There is something peculiarly revolting in all this to the feelings which still distinguish the hearts and actions of generous and British men.[57]

In the initial article deemed seditious, Cobbett had dwelt on the sensory aspects of the episode to highlight the charge of cruelty – he wanted to see the faces of those in Ely who had witnessed the punishment. Reading the initial charge and subsequent remarks made by Cobbett in his defence, it was not so much the act of flogging that he attacked, but the fact that it had been inflicted by foreign troops and against men who had, in his view, been legitimately protesting at the worsening of their conditions. Thus, Cobbett's outrage was inflected by patriotic and class-based feelings. He admitted that his comparison with Napoleon was meant to 'sting' the government and to point out their hypocrisy in attacking the emperor's cruelty. Cobbett then proceeded to ask why it was not allowed to point out cruelty towards soldiers. To paraphrase Boddice and Smith, 'To introduce the concept of "cruelty" into public discourse' and to censure cruel acts in the pages of the press 'was to do more than identify cruelty; it was to literally *construct* it.'[58] As far as the Crown was concerned, Cobbett needed silencing; failure to respond would have been a tacit admission by the authorities that flogging was cruel and unwarranted – a problematic admission during a time of war when indiscipline was prevalent in the armed forces.

The basis of the charge of seditious libel against Cobbett rested entirely on the tone he had adopted. The Attorney General in his closing remarks underlined tone as the key issue: 'every individual has a right to suggest an alteration in that law [reliance on foreign troops], provided that suggestion be made in temperate and qualified terms'. Failure to do so ran the risk of 'exciting discontent in the minds of those whom it concerns', the effect of which was to bring government into 'contempt'. Cobbett responded that his words ought not be taken literally, only figuratively; if the law of seditious libel was to turn on the literal, then it would leave no room for the expression of irony or hyperbole. In emphasising tone, and by extension feeling, his trial highlights yet another way in which the state clamped down on radicalism during the French wars.[59] It was not just a matter of what was said (radical ideas), or even who was speaking (a lower-class radical), but also *how* it was expressed. There was to be no place in the public sphere for such impassioned outbursts, least of all in the armed forces or on their behalf by radical agitators. Cobbett drew attention to this very issue during the trial when he rejected the premise that the soldiers had mutinied; expressing injured feelings was not tantamount to mutiny. Thus, in effect, the state was policing which feelings could be expressed in the public sphere, an injunction which would outlast the wars and cast its shadow over radicalism for many years to come. Like politics, the law itself so often turned on feeling, something which Cobbett had been acutely aware of since the first libel action brought against him in 1803 for attacking British rule in Ireland. During the 1803 trial the choleric anti-Jacobin lord chief justice, Lord Ellenborough, had defined a libel as anything which is 'injurious to the feelings and happiness of an individual'.[60] Unfortunately for Cobbett, Ellenborough was the presiding judge at his trial in 1810, and, worse still, the jury had been packed to ensure conviction.[61]

In the 1810 trial, Cobbett tried to shift the focus of his defence to ground on which he was much more comfortable – patriotic feeling. He dwelt considerably on the constitutional and historic objections to the presence of foreign soldiers on British soil: 'This objection, then, does not proceed from any jacobinical aversion to his Majesty, but it is an objection which has been justly entertained at all times by those who had the best British feeling.' Cobbett alleged that his open expression of anger was evidence that he was not seeking to incite hatred against His Majesty; if that really had been his purpose, he retorted, then he would have done it secretly. 'When an army of foreigners is raked together in this manner,' Cobbett continued, 'when their officers command over Englishmen, and when part of them are brought to witness the flogging of our local militiamen, how can I avoid feeling the greatest indignation and feeling (as I must do) this indignation, why should I not be permitted to express it?' The inference that patriotic feeling could excuse impassioned language was a shrewd claim on Cobbett's part, and he was careful to distinguish between outraged patriotic feeling and sedition: 'And if I do express this indignation which I feel, in somewhat angry language, are you, upon that account, to presume that I am guilty of deliberately wishing and contriving to subvert the Government of the country?' He could not resist the opportunity to try and turn the trial into an indictment of the government's handling of the war, in particular its reliance on foreign troops. Again, he accented feeling: the problem with relying on foreign troops was that 'they never can participate in the feelings of Englishmen. Their attachments lie not to England but to Germany. It is impossible from the feelings of human nature, that it should be otherwise. The graves of their fathers and their properties (if they have any) lie in Germany, and there are their affections also.'[62]

The authorities were in no mood to tolerate Cobbett's attempt to construe his radicalism as patriotism. He was promptly found guilty and sentenced to imprisonment for two years in Newgate, hit with a hefty fine and, upon his release, bound over for seven years to maintain the peace. All this was evidence, as Cobbett well knew, that the government were trying to ruin him. He worried that he might die in prison, a rare indication, perhaps, of the psychological strain under which he had been labouring in the period leading up to his incarceration.[63] These fears would prove unnecessary given the relative comfort he was able to purchase for himself while in Newgate as the crayon portrait he had commissioned attests. The portrait (Figure 1.1) depicts Cobbett as a man of refinement, sensibility and seriousness, notwithstanding what looks to us as a slightly pained expression on his face. Cobbett's son, James, thought this one of the best likenesses of his father but objected to the 'air of seriousness in his face' which had 'too much of the crabbed, & not sufficient of the full & florid in [his] complexion'.[64] When copies of the portrait were published again at the time of Cobbett's death, the facial expression changed (Figure 1.2). It is unclear *what* feelings are being depicted, to say nothing of *whose* feelings are being depicted, Cobbett's or the artist's. Neither is it clear whether the artist has succeeded in depicting the desired feelings, all of which illustrates the difficulties of reading off emotions from facial expressions.[65]

Figure 1.1 William Cobbett, by John Raphael Smith (1812).

WILLIAM COBBETT, ESQ^R

Figure 1.2 William Cobbett, engraving by Henry Adlard (1835).

Naturally, Cobbett's thoughts turned to the fate of his family should he die while incarcerated. These fears were considerably allayed when he received a letter from a Mr James Paull, a Quaker farmer from Philadelphia, a friend from Cobbett's American days, offering to provide for his family should anything happen to him. Still the man of feeling many years later, Cobbett recalled the intense feelings he felt towards Paull: 'At [seventy] years of age, I feel the tears of gratitude on my cheeks as I transcribe his words.'[66] Imprisonment clearly affected Cobbett psychologically, to the extent that he found his wife's dictated letters deeply upsetting, remonstrating with her to be mindful of his feelings.[67] According to his daughter Anne, he emerged from prison a changed man – much more bitter and prone to angry outbursts. This may be attributed to the fact that he had not expected to be prosecuted given the long delay from the offence to the trial, much less be found guilty given the unpredictability of trials for seditious libel and relatively high acquittal rate. As his prison correspondence attests, he also suffered a series of personal and financial mishaps, which were rendered the more intractable and frustrating on account of his incarceration.[68] For the remainder of the 1810s, Cobbett found himself having to tread carefully: he sympathised with the plight of the Luddite machine breakers, for example, but told them to restrain their anger and channel it into support for parliamentary reform. 'Petition is the channel for your sentiments', he told them.[69] While it is true that some spies and informers, along with some of the more ardent and disaffected radicals, cited Cobbett as an inflammatory influence, in truth he discouraged violent expressions of anger and hatred – and recent attempts to suggest otherwise are wholly reliant on circumstantial evidence.[70]

Cobbett managed this tightrope walking until May 1817 when, as we have seen, another rising tide of indignation at the government's refusal to redress popular grievances led him to flee to America where he was able to continue attacking the British government with relative impunity. Little had changed by the time he returned to Britain in November 1819 when the government was framing the Six Acts. Yet again, he was forced to tread carefully and he felt keenly the atmosphere of repression, 'the "wholesome restraint" of which I continually feel' was his description of this repressive legislation.[71] Cobbett was acutely aware of the affective restraints imposed by the Six Acts, and of the way in which feeling – or the denial of the right to express it – was being politicised. The government conceded this in the very language of the legislation. The law against blasphemous and seditious libel defined these crimes as language 'tending to bring into hatred or contempt' the King or government.[72] In Cobbett's view, these acts constituted nothing less than a denial of the right of the working class to express their feelings, and symbolised the fact that aristocratic rule was now based on fear rather than affection.[73] Was it any wonder, he asked, that the 'courageous' Cato Street conspirators – who plotted to assassinate the cabinet in February 1820 – had been driven to these extremes by the 'miseries of their country'. Far from being inflamed by Cobbett's poison, the feeling of the conspirators had been 'inflamed with indignation by the proceedings at Manchester [a reference to Peterloo]'.[74]

This was the main reason why he threw himself so wholeheartedly into the cause of Queen Caroline in 1820.[75] It is hard not to interpret the radical outpouring of sentimentalism in defence of the queen as evidence of the hydraulic theory of emotions – surging feelings within demanding expression, which, if suppressed, eventually burst forth, wave-like. In this case, the repressed feelings consequent on the enactment of the Six Acts had burst forth in 'Caroline fever'. Implicitly, Cobbett appears to have subscribed to the hydraulic theory. Reflecting on the Six Acts, he warned the government 'Men resent restrains of this kind with more bitterness … than they do any other species of force'. 'Let people freely complain … let them exhaust their just anger in this way, and there is an end to the matter.'[76] But even in this moment of radical release, Cobbett's response to Caroline, though sentimental, was not unmeasured: he used sentimentalism in a calculated way as a means to ingratiate himself to the Queen and to try and manipulate her for the radical cause.[77] Far from engaging in the obscene populism which characterised much of the unrespectable radical response to the affair, Cobbett sought to 'transform … Caroline into a Burkean object of chivalry'. He juxtaposed the heartfelt response of the working classes to the plight and subsequent death of the queen with the unfeeling and cruel stance of the establishment, a calculated sentimentalism that was also designed to appeal to respectable women of all classes.[78]

Ascetic radicalism late Georgian style

There was a negative side to Cobbett's insistence that labourers and soldiers be admitted into the ranks of humanity: his virulent anti-black racism and anti-Semitism. There can be no doubt that, like many others who have advanced their own claims to citizenship, Cobbett denigrated these groups as a way of enhancing the claims of the white working class. It infuriated him that philanthropists and abolitionists were sympathetic to the plight of the enslaved blacks abroad but appeared blind to the sufferings of white labourers at home. As time passed, he clung ever closer to the argument that the white working class 'were made to endure insults and indignities such as even Negroes were never exposed to'.[79] Cobbett tried to buttress this by recourse to racist ideas of black inferiority, which included the suggestion that blacks (and Jews) lacked the capacity for refined feelings: 'the Negroes were in a state of profound ignorance; it was notorious that they had no such thing as moral sentiment'.[80] For Cobbett, as for some other British radicals, the issue was one of misplaced feeling on the part of the abolitionist; sympathy should begin at home. He went further and likened abolition to an uncontrolled passion.[81] Although a reprehensible example, Cobbett's racism brings into sharp focus the nature and significance of his brand of ascetic radicalism, the fundamental basis of which was about displaying appropriate feeling in the right context.

Attacking enemies for callousness was a favourite charge, and none deserved it more than the apologists for liberal political economy – Scotch 'feelosofee', an unfeeling ideology that Cobbett always traced to the moral philosophers of eighteenth-century Scotland. The very word 'feelosofee' is a characteristic example of his ability to encapsulate in one derogatory label the cluster of feelings of indignation and revulsion towards the 'feelosofer', the implication being that they were willing to lose all feeling for a fee. This was an accusation that he frequently levelled at the Reverend Thomas Malthus because of the latter's callous theory of surplus population. Cobbett viewed this as justification for leaving the poor to starve and preventing them from marrying and procreating. Malthus, as a minister of the Church of England, was nothing more than a state pauper who in exchange for his stipend published work which not only exonerated the authorities and the rich of any responsibility towards the care of the poor but also licensed cruelty. Cobbett reserved some of his best invective for 'unfeeling Malthus and the Scotch *feelosofers*' whose theory was predicated on the assumption that the poor were sub-human.[82] Anticipating Foucault's concept of biopower, Cobbett held Malthus responsible for the growing tendency of classifying the people as ' "the population," just as we call the animals upon a farm "the stock." ' This marked out the poor as non-citizens, while at the same time placing obligations of citizenship on them, such as paying taxes and fighting wars. It was this debasing of the poor – not just discursively but also institutionally in workhouses – which enabled the increasingly impoverished country gentlemen to 'disguise their own humiliation by their haughty and insolent deportment' towards the poor.[83]

More mischievously, Cobbett hurled the charge of inappropriate feeling at radical rivals, such as Sir Francis Burdett with whom Cobbett had fallen out by 1817, partly over money that the former had lent the latter, but also because of what Cobbett viewed as Burdett's growing patrician distaste for popular radicalism: 'a democrat in words, and an aristocrat in feeling'.[84] As we have seen with black slavery, ascetic radicalism furnished Cobbett with the means to accuse the enemies of the working class of misplaced feelings, or the failure to display what, in his view, were the right kinds of feeling demanded by the context. During the latter stages of the Napoleonic War when he began to articulate his critique of public finance, paper money and the mounting national debt, Cobbett was acutely sensitive to the changing meanings of patriotism. His worry was that as the government was forced to borrow more, it created a new class of fundholders. The proliferation of fundholders had the effect of subordinating natural love of country to personal greed and the anxieties that went with being a creditor.[85] Here Cobbett inverted Burke's argument that the unfeeling Jacobin was a threat to the affective ties of kin and locality, and shifts the blame to the fundholders and the government. By contrast, it is the working classes in the armed forces who espoused natural patriotic feeling grounded in the affective ties of home, family and chivalric masculinity.[86] Cobbett's concern was that this desiccated patriotism was infecting the countryside as well as the city, as rich landowners and farmers became enmeshed in government finance as creditors: 'The funding system was eating the heart out of the nobility; stifling every high and honourable feeling.'[87] To take another example, Cobbett wrote of how he had found his family and especially children a comfort during his imprisonment, and he contrasted this right feeling with its absence in his enemies:

> What a blessing it is to have such healthy and clever and sober and sensible and industrious and dutiful and affectionate children! The miserable, malignant, poisonous wretches, who hate me, have no such children. Their race is rotten in carcase and limbs as well as in heart. They are eaten up with infection from the top of their senseless heads to the bottom of their lazy feet.[88]

Ascetic radicalism furnished Cobbett with the means to walk the tightrope previously identified – to present himself (and those like him) as a man of refined feeling, but not a creature of his passions. It also enabled those who espoused it to denigrate the enemies of the working class as unfeeling while simultaneously monopolising nobler feelings. In the eighteenth century, nobler feelings such as indignation were 'reserved for those whose anger was dignified, honourable, and righteous', and that was men of property.[89] Cobbett challenged this elitist view by speaking of indignation rather anger, and of despising rather than of hating, for example.[90] These distinctions also enabled him to refute the charge, often made, that he deliberately excited the passions of the people. On his return from America in November 1819, Cobbett addressed the people of Lancashire (he landed at Liverpool). After assurances that he had no desire to inflame the passions of the people, he then juxtaposed his refined sensibility against that of the people's enemies who were blind to their suffering: 'The heart, which under the contemplation of the present state of the noble county of Lancashire, can retain its wonted [sic.] beat, must be formed of materials very different from those of mine.'[91]

True, on occasion, the language of hate bursts through when Cobbett addressed his enemies, or in his jealousy of rival radicals. Yet on the whole he was more measured and disciplined, a perception that was aided by the fact that he authored popular instructional works on grammar and regularly emphasised the need to express one's self clearly, carefully and correctly. This had the effect of turning vulgar language – identified with the passions – into refined language.[92] Take his famous polemic against Malthus, often cited as evidence of his impassioned invective.[93] On closer inspection, it is a carefully crafted and affectively restrained intervention: 'I have during my life detested many men; but never any one so much as you. Your book on Population contains matter more offensive to my feelings even than that of the Dungeon Bill [Cobbett's name for the suspension of Habeas Corpus].' The second sentence reinforces the measured declaration of detestation (not hate) through comparison with Cobbett's more refined sensibility – 'offensive to my feelings'. He then shifts the ground of his attack to anti-clericalism by claiming that the clergy were not just callous but cruel: 'Priests have, in all ages, been remarkable for cool and deliberate and unrelenting cruelty; but it seems to have been reserved for the Church of England to produce one who has a just claim to the atrocious pre-eminence.'[94]

At first glance, there are aspects of Cobbett's affective politics which appear to belie ascetic radicalism, such as his defence of pugilism and rural sports, pastimes increasingly threatened by the reformation of manners and new standards of respectability and decency.[95] But far from being evidence which contradicts this label, Cobbett's ascetic radicalism was anchored in the cultural mores of Georgian England, rather than anticipating the subsequent Victorian incarnation of ascetic radicalism discussed in later chapters. He spoke out against the never-ending recourse to parliamentary legislation to curb the traditional and violent pleasures of the people, viewing this as nothing less than trying to change how people felt: 'There were a set of "well-meaning" men in the country, who would have passed laws for the regulating and restraining of every feeling of the human breast, and every motion of the human frame.' Rural and athletic sports such as single stick and boxing 'string the nerves and strengthen the frame ... excite an emulation in deeds of hardihood and valour, and ... imperceptibly instil honour, generosity, and a love of glory'. Cobbett defended boxing and single stick as carefully defined and acceptable channels for the expression of the passions, which, if removed, would spill over into other areas of life and endanger peace and prosperity.[96] Rural sports were also an important means of instilling feelings of paternalism and deference as, traditionally at least, they brought lords and peasants together 'which made the poor man proud of his inferiority, and created in his breast a personal affection for his lord'.[97] Rural sports acted as the affective glue which bound together the rural community. Manly feelings were also at stake: 'The peasants of this country are brave, their forefathers were so, and notwithstanding the incessant efforts of cant and effeminacy to eradicate every manly sentiment from their minds, the sons also are brave.'[98]

In other respects, Cobbett was the archetypal ascetic radical, exemplified in his own rise from ploughboy to politician, who extolled the virtues of temperance, cleanliness, thrift, early rising and early to bed, self-improvement and education: 'Try one month what regular risings, good exercise, lean meat, little butter, little tea, and good water and wine will do; and, above all, half an hour's walking and washing before breakfast', he told his wife from his prison cell in 1811.[99] He was quick to accuse his enemies of failings, even small ones, in these departments. Cobbett was disgusted by Lord Liverpool's habit of picking his nose in public: 'I know a Prime Minister who picks his nose and regales himself with the contents. I have witnessed the worse beastly act scores of times.'[100] For Cobbett this signalled a lack of decorum, self-control and cleanliness which placed Liverpool on the sub-human level. Cobbett traced his own impeccable standards to the regimen of agricultural work and rural pursuits in which he was schooled as a young boy. He always retained a love for agriculture and rural pursuits, which he viewed as much more wholesome than the dissipations of urban life. Looking back on the menial tasks he had performed in garden and field as a young boy, he remarked that 'I never lost one particle of my passion for these healthy and rational and heart-cheering pursuits'. During his time in the army, he recalled how his 'leisure time was spent, not in the dissipations common to such a way of life, but in reading and study'.[101] Cobbett's ascetic radicalism was put forth most fully and explicitly in the conduct literature that he wrote, notably *Advice to Young Men*. Few others came close to rivalling his preaching and practising of discipline and economy: 'simplicity in dress, temperance in food and drink, the avoidance of gambling, civility without servility, and husbanding one's time'.[102] While Cobbett appears to have been a loving husband and father in the early years of his marriage, he rebuked his wife for her sentimentalism and on one occasion expressed concern that his youngest son, William, shared his mother's sentimentalism: 'I am afraid of his feeling too much.'[103] He could be prudish and censure frivolous conduct such as ladies sitting around drinking tea and gossiping. Tea was to be avoided as it weakened the nerves.[104] He also censured novel reading in ways that echoed Rousseau on the theatre: 'I deprecate *romances* of every description. It is impossible that they can do any *good*, and they may do a great deal of harm. They excite passions that ought to lie dormant; they give the mind a taste for *highly-seasoned* matter; they make matters of real life insipid.'[105] Clearly, Cobbett evidently believed that it was possible for one to exercise a degree of control over how one felt, mainly by avoiding certain activities and engaging in wholesome pursuits.

The occasion which called forth Cobbett's asceticism more than any other during his first decade as a leading radical was his campaign to stand for parliament at Coventry in 1820. Even by Georgian standards, the corruption and violence on display were remarkable, which included attempts on Cobbett's life and those of his supporters from opponents armed with knives.[106] Election corruption and bribery had disgusted him ever since he had first encountered it at Honiton in 1806, but it would reach new heights at Coventry: 'Few men, with like means, have boasted more than I have of *English humanity* and *fair-play*. But, never, since I was born, did I see any thing so disgraceful to human nature; so ferocious; so odious; so hateful.'[107] Some of this was, no doubt, sour grapes on his part in response to losing.[108] But the episode is more significant for what it reveals about Cobbett's affective politics, and in particular the way he braided the senses and emotions in articulating and practising his ascetic radicalism. As several biographers have rightly observed, the power of Cobbett's radicalism rested in part on his ability to personalise issues. In providing such a graphic and visceral account of the election in the *Political Register*, he was able to personalise his attack on electoral corruption and thus lend support to the radical campaign for parliamentary reform. He devoted considerable space to describing the crowds and especially the ruffians hired by his opponents for the purposes of intimidation:

> The scene was far more horrible than any thing of which any man, actually present, can form an idea. There were at least three score select-wretches constantly vomiting forth *imprecations* the most horrid that words can frame; intermixed with expressions peculiar to prostitutes and bullies and houses devoted to lewdness. The bottles of gin and brandy were constantly passing from mouth to mouth; and, from the mass of heads (including those of the whole crowd) which were closely jammed together, there arose, a *reek*, or *steam*, proceeding from the sweating carcasses and from the foaming and belshing [sic.] mouths of the brutes; just like the reek that rises, in a morning, from a heating dunghill. The *smell* was nauseously offensive. Every sense was disgusted.[109]

The final sentence not only adds to the graphic description of electoral corruption for Cobbett's readers, it also links unpleasant sensory overload with the excesses of electoral corruption in a way that personalises the abstractions of the latter. Disgust also functions here in the utopian way identified by Colin McGinn. According to McGinn disgust marks out the 'disjunction between how the world actually works and how we would like it to be', which, in Cobbett's case, is a democratic future purified of corruption.[110]

As Jon Lawrence has argued in relation to the culture of electioneering in the nineteenth century, it was imperative for those standing for election to display manly forbearance on the hustings as a way of demonstrating their fitness to speak for the people.[111] A central part of this was not just composure and courage, but also displaying good humour and cheerfulness. From the outset of the campaign, Cobbett cultivated 'a gentle and affable demeanour'.[112] His account of the election and of his feelings can be read as an exemplary account of 'emotion management' for candidates standing in elections, anticipating the training techniques of late twentieth century airlines for stewardesses on how to deal with difficult passengers.[113] He knew full well that, despite the many taunts, he needed to appear good-humoured: 'I defy the Rich Ruffians of Coventry to say, that the *thousand pounds a day* (for that was about the sum), which they expended on their savages, ever took that good-humour for one single moment!' Naturally, he took this a stage further and delighted in aggravating the hostile crowd: 'The way I managed the brutes was well calculated to sting them and their employers to madness.' He did this by pointing and laughing at the 'yelling beasts ... foaming with rage'.[114] But this evident delight aside, the most significant 'emotion labour' that Cobbett practised as a way of handling the ruffians was to question their humanity. 'The mere circumstance of a creature's walking upon *two legs* is no proof, that he is of the same *sort* or *kind* as I am, or as any other man of mind is', he asserted. Questioning the humanity of these brutes enabled him to substitute his anger for humour: 'I really looked at and heard these brutes, till they became a subject of amusing speculation ... I could not bring myself to feel anything like *anger* towards the poor beasts, every one of whom I sincerely regard as inferior to any of the animals abovementioned [dogs].'

Ascetic radicalism, it should be recalled, was about displaying appropriate feelings in the correct context, and here Cobbett practised what he preached: 'My *philosophy* despised the brutes', but 'I felt no *anger* against the brutes. Nor did I ever feel *anger* against a flock of crow.'[115] More broadly, his experience at Coventry also brought into sharp focus the place of feeling in the electoral culture of the period, and how the electoral system itself elicited and licensed certain feelings. Unlike many of the political elite, Cobbett did not draw the conclusion that displays of thuggery at elections made the people unfit for citizenship. It was the electoral system of corruption and bribery which turned some men into brutes. Ruffians were little more than creatures of their political masters, a bond that would be sundered by the introduction of the secret ballot, the enactment of which would guard against such displays of brute passion.[116] The corruption, intimidation and violence at Coventry had stifled the 'real feelings of the electors'. 'The people feel the force of his [Cobbett's] argument, they sympathise in his feelings', but these natural feelings had been stifled and supplanted by fear and terror. 'People are so cowed down; so timid, so afraid', Cobbett told his son. Only parliamentary reform would allow for that free expression of natural feeling. Above all, in what would become a *sine qua non* of radical parliamentary reform, there could be no such thing as a free election while feelings of fear were present.[117]

Conclusion

In contrast to other radical leaders in this study, Cobbett did not explicitly reflect on the nature of the passions. Even so, he was clearly aware of the importance of feeling in politics, both positively and negatively. He approached radicalism not primarily as an ideology, or even 'through the totality of the labourers' economic and cultural experiences', but as something deeply felt, grounded in the senses: the indignation he felt towards Old Corruption, his sympathy for the plight of the labourer and his contempt for the enemies of the people.[118] 'Cobbett's fury' is more accurately described as indignation, and it was not 'crazily intense'.[119] As we saw with his letter to Malthus, Cobbett's affective politics were carefully crafted. The ascetic radicalism that he preached and usually practised was meant to be empowering as well as disciplining. This acted as a guide for the radical leader and the people he represented; too strong an expression of feeling could be disabling. Ascetic radicalism also supplied Cobbett with the means to charge his opponents with callousness, inappropriate or misdirected displays of feeling. Above all, his affective politics constituted a fundamental challenge to those who surrendered right feeling for a price, whether in the form of access to the spoils of corruption at Westminster, the proceeds of electoral bribery, or, in the case of Malthus, a stipend and access to the ill-gotten gains of the plundering Church of England.

The charge of unfeeling was one of the most pointed, poignant and enduring of insults wielded by Cobbett. This was not just because he personalised politics, it also stemmed from the way in which he politicised the senses to sublimate anger and hatred of the establishment into disgust, enabling the radical movement to occupy the moral high ground. This would reappear in the 1820s and early 1830s culminating in his opposition to the Anatomy Act of 1832 and the New Poor Law of 1834, both of which rode roughshod over the feelings of the people.[120] In claiming that he and those he represented were men of feeling, Cobbett was doing more than just asserting the fitness of the ploughboy and soldier, or even working class more generally, for citizenship, as important as that was. It is also further recognition of just how well he knew his enemies. The ascetic radicalism he personified was a riposte to what he viewed as the nauseating hypocrisy of a puritan strand of Christian morality. These puritans sought to curb the worst excesses of the brutish masses in a reformation of manners while simultaneously hardened to the suffering of the white working class. The working classes were neither brutish nor unfeeling; rather it was the elite who were unfeeling and if some of the people displayed brutish behaviour then they had been made brutish by a malfeasant elite. Right feeling could only be restored through a combination of parliamentary reform, wholesome rural pursuits and moral conduct. Though he had little time for the irrationality of rural pursuits, Richard Carlile reached similar conclusions, albeit for different reasons, as the next chapter shows.

Notes

1 William Hazlitt, *The Character of W. Cobbett MP* (London, 1835), pp. 3, 8–9.

2 J.R. Poynter, *Society and Pauperism: English Ideas on Poor Relief, 1795–1834* (London: Routledge & Kegan Paul, 1969), p. 175.

3 Leonora Nattrass, *William Cobbett and the Politics of Style* (Cambridge: Cambridge University Press, 1995), pp. 13, 21.

4 Tom Paulin, *The Day Star of Liberty: William Hazlitt's Radical Style* (London: Faber and Faber, 1998), pp. 56, 66.

5 J.E. Morpurgo (ed.), *Cobbett's America: A Selection of the Writings of William Cobbett* (London: Folio, 1985), p. xviii.

6 James Grande, *William Cobbett, the Press and Rural England: Radicalism and the Fourth Estate, 1792–1835* (Basingstoke: Palgrave, 2014), p. 46; James Grande, John Stevenson and Richard Thomas (eds), *The Opinions of William Cobbett* (Farnham: Ashgate, 2013), p. 198. Marcus Daniel also emphasises Cobbett's indebtedness to Burke in his study of Cobbett's American journalism in the 1790s: *Scandal & Civility: Journalism and the Birth of American Democracy* (New York: Oxford University Press, 2009), pp. 218–19.

7 There are parallels here with the work of Gerd Althoff on medieval emotion as ritualised performance. Althoff argues that far from being impulsive outbursts, emotional displays in public settings such as courts followed well-understood rules of the game, and served as political announcements. For a critical summary of Althoff's work (which was published in German), see Barbara H. Rosenwein, *Emotional Communities in the Early Middle Ages* (Ithaca: Cornell University Press, 2006), pp. 12–13, 175–8.

8 Peter Spence, *The Birth of Romantic Radicalism: War, Popular Politics and English Radical Reformism, 1800–1815* (Aldershot: Scolar Press, 1996), p. 26; John Stevenson, 'William Cobbett: dimensions of patriotism', in James Grande and John Stevenson (eds), *William Cobbett, Romanticism and the Enlightenment* (London: Pickering & Chatto, 2015), p. 40.

9 Ian Dyck, *William Cobbett and Rural Popular Culture* (Cambridge: Cambridge University Press, 1992).

10 Nicole Eustace, *Passion is the Gale: Emotion, Power, and the Coming of the American Revolution* (Chapel Hill, NC: University of North Carolina Press, 2008), p. 448.

11 For all the attention devoted to the impact of the Napoleonic Wars on British society, very little has been written on the affective basis of patriotism – love of one's country. In Linda Colley's influential account of the patriotic consensus that prevailed during the French Wars, patriotism emerges largely as a rational, self-interested identity: in short, it recapitulates the desiccated patriotism that Cobbett railed against. Linda Colley, *Britons: The Forging of the Nation, 1737–1837* (New Haven: Yale University Press, 1992). Neither does patriotism feature in Rachel Hewitt's panoramic portrait of feeling in 1790s Britain, the growing ascendancy of which was surely a factor in the decline of radicalism that she traces. Rachel Hewitt, *A Revolution of Feeling: The Decade that Forged the Modern Mind* (London: Granta, 2017).

12 E.P. Thompson, *The Making of the English Working Class* (London: Victor Gollancz, 1980), p. 822; David A. Wilson, *Paine and Cobbett: The Transatlantic Connection* (Kingston and Montreal: McGill-Queen's Press, 1988), p. 125.

13 *New Times*, 15 February and 5 April 1817. For similar accusations, see *Caledonian Mercury*, 16 January 1830; *Hereford Times*, 5 December 1835; TNA, HO 42/157, 'Parliamentary Reform, by Erinus', n.d. [December 1816], fol. 650; *White Dwarf*, 10 January 1818.

14 E.g., BM Satires 10614, 'Posting to the election', by James Gillray (1806); BM Satires 11338, 'True Reform of Parliament', by James Gillray (1809), BM Satire 14194, 'Revolutionary Association', by I.R. Cruikshank (1821). For Cobbett and caricature, see Ian Haywood, 'The life of William Cobbett: caricature, hauntology and the impossibility of radical life writing in the Romantic period', in John Goodridge and Bridget Keegan (eds), *A History of British Working-Class Literature* (Cambridge: Cambridge University Press, 2017), pp. 176–94.

15 This may explain why some commentators expressed surprise when they saw Cobbett in the flesh for the first time; contrary to the repulsive way in which the caricaturists and satirists had depicted him, they found him not the least bit threatening but the embodiment of an old-fashioned country gentleman. See, for example, Samuel Bamford, *Passages in the Life of a Radical*, vol. 2 (London, 1893), pp. 20–1.

16 Richard Ingrams, *The Life and Adventures of William Cobbett* (London: HarperCollins, 2005), p. 90.

17 BM Satires 11047, 'The loyal address', by James Gillray (1808). By the time that Cobbett returned to Britain with the bones of Paine in 1819, he had been fully transmogrified into a pig: *The Loyal Man in the Moon* (1820), p. 15. Robert Cruikshank's later 'Trans-Atlantic luxury' similarly places Cobbett at the same level as farmyard animals: *Book of Wonders* (London, 1821), pp. 25–6.

18 BM Satires 11372, 'Life of William Cobbett, No. 1', by James Gillray (1809).

19 BM Satires 11384, 'Life of William Cobbett, No. 3'.

20 BM Satires 11378, 'Life of William Cobbett, No. 7'.

21 HSP, William Cobbett Papers, 2129, Folder 10, William Cobbett to Mr Adams, 27 May 1810; Folder 11, Cobbett to Anne Cobbett, 2 December 1811.

22 Anon., *Life of William Cobbett* (London, 1835), pp. 395, 194; M.L. Pearl, *William Cobbett: A Bibliographical Account of His Life and Times* (London: Oxford University Press, 1953), p. 82.

23 E.g., William Hone and George Cruikshank, *Life of Billy Cobb and the Death of Tommy Pain* (1819), pp. 11, 13.

24 For the story of Cobbett and Paine's bones, see Paul A. Pickering, 'A "grand ossification": William Cobbett and the commemoration of Tom Paine', in Paul A. Pickering and Alex Tyrrell (eds), *Contested Sites: Commemoration, Memorial and Popular Politics in Nineteenth-Century Britain* (Aldershot: Ashgate, 2004), pp. 57–80.

25 This was Cobbett's own view: bringing back Paine's bones against the background of Richard Carlile's prosecution for publishing Paine's *Age of Reason*, Cobbett judged, 'was to put public opinion ... to the severest test'. *CWPR*, 27 January 1820.

26 *Edinburgh Monthly Review*, April 1820, p. 438.

27 E.g., the broadside 'Cobbett at Coventry', American Philosophical Society, Col. Richard Gimbel Collection of Thomas Paine Papers, American Philosophical Society, William Cobbett to unknown, 25 February 1820, Box 3; *The Book of Wonders* (London, 1821), chapter 14.

28 *Christian Observer*, March 1820.

29 BM Satires 13283, 'The political champion turned resurrection man', by I.R. Cruikshank (1819).

30 'Cobbett and the Negro' (1820), broadside, Chetham's Library, Manchester, Scrapbook B.9.41.52(1). The use of approximated dialogue was a leitmotif of racist parodying of black dialect. See Hazel Waters, *Racism on the Victorian Stage: Representations of Slavery and the Black Character* (Cambridge: Cambridge University Press, 2007); Daphne A. Brooks, *Bodies in Dissent: Spectacular Performances of Race and Freedom, 1850–1910* (Durham, NC: Duke University Press, 2006).

31 Rob Boddice and Mark Smith, *Emotion, Sense, Experience* (Cambridge: Cambridge University Press, 2020), p. 5.

32 A Briton, *A Letter to William Cobbett* (Birmingham, 1819), p. 8.

33 BM Satires 12867A, 'A patriot luminary extinguishing noxious gas!!!', by George Cruikshank (1817).

34 *The Loyal Man in the Moon* (1820), reprinted in Edgell Rickword (ed.), *Radical Squibs and Loyalist Ripostes* (Bath: Adams and Dart, 1971), p. 122.

35 Martha Nussbaum, *Hidden from Humanity: Disgust, Shame and the Law* (Princeton, NJ: Princeton University Press, 2004), p. 92.

36 William Cobbett, *Rural Rides*, ed. Asa Briggs, vol. 1 (London: Dent, 1957), p. 4. To be fair to Cobbett, he was not alone in thinking along these lines: e.g., Christopher E. Forth, *Fat: A Cultural History of the Stuff of Life* (London: Reaktion, 2019), p. 221.

37 TNA, HO 40/9, 'Bill Bobbett's address to the Spa-Fields meeting', 8 December 1816, fol. 73.

38 *CWPR*, 28 September 1833.

39 *CWPR*, 21 July 1810. This stereotype came under challenge during the Napoleonic Wars, during which time the soldier came to be seen more sympathetically. See Yuval Noval Harari, *The Ultimate Experience: Battlefield Revelations and the Making of Modern War Culture, 1450–2000* (Basingstoke: Palgrave,

2008), chapter 5; Kevin Lynch and Matthew McCormack, 'Wellington's men: the British soldier of the Napoleonic wars', *History Compass*, 13 (2015), 288–96.

40 TNA, HO 40/3, 'The pernicious principles of William Cobbett addressed to the Hampden clubs in general by a gentleman', 24 December 1816, fol. 872A.

41 Nick Mansfield, *Soldiers as Citizens: Popular Politics and the Nineteenth-Century Military* (Liverpool: Liverpool University Press, 2019), pp. 4, 8.

42 *CWPR*, 13 December 1817.

43 William Cobbett, *Advice to Young Men and (Incidentally) to Young Women in the Middle and Higher Ranks of Life* (London, 1829). Similarly, Cobbett's *Paper against Gold*, which also contained some autobiographical writing, was addressed to 'tradesmen and farmers'. As Nattrass correctly observes, the unusual success of Cobbett was that he was read by all classes. Nattrass, *Cobbett*, pp. 3–4, 186–7.

44 William Cobbett, *The Autobiography of William Cobbett*, ed. William Reitzel (London: Faber & Faber, 1947), pp. 18, 38, 40–3. It should be noted that some of these autobiographical reflections were written in the 1790s, first appearing in *The Life and Adventures of Peter Porcupine* (Philadelphia, 1796).

45 *CWPR*, 3 June 1820. Cobbett, *Autobiography*, pp. 19–21, 102–4. For an instance of sentimentalism on Cobbett's part towards his children, see HSP, Cobbett Papers, Folder 14, Cobbett to James P. Cobbett, 30 October 1819. For Cobbett and fatherhood, see Matthew McCormack, ' "Married men and the fathers of families": fatherhood and franchise reform in Britain', in Trev Broughton and Helen Rogers (eds), *Gender and Fatherhood in the Nineteenth Century* (Basingstoke: Palgrave, 2007), pp. 46–8. Cobbett's family life was far from being the idyll that he often presented it as to the world: George Spater, *William Cobbett: The Poor Man's Friend*, vol. 2 (Cambridge: Cambridge University Press, 1982), pp. 389–90, 518–19.

46 Dyck, *Cobbett*, pp. 31, 69, 102, 78.

47 William Cobbett, *Cottage Economy* (London, 1838), p. 6.

48 The most persuasive and recent account of Cobbett's authorship of the *Soldier's Friend* (which he denied more than once) is Grande, *William Cobbett*, pp. 19–26.

49 Cobbett, *Autobiography*, pp. 25, 53.

50 Mansfield, *Soldiers as Citizens*, p. 6.

51 For an early articulation of Cobbett's oppositional patriotic feeling, see *CWPR*, 6 December 1806 (Letter to Mr Windham). There is now a sizeable body of scholarship which has successfully challenged Linda Colley's argument, advanced in *Britons*, that a patriotic consensus prevailed in Britain during the Napoleonic Wars: Philip Harling, 'The Duke of York affair (1809) and the complexities of war-time patriotism', *HJ*, 39 (1996), 963–84; Stuart Semmel, *Napoleon and the British* (New Haven: Yale University Press, 2004), chapter 6; Anna Clark, *Scandal: The Sexual Politics of the British Constitution* (Princeton, NJ: Princeton University Press, 2004), chapter 6; Katrina Navickas, *Loyalism and Radicalism in Lancashire, 1798–1815* (Oxford: Oxford University Press, 2009).

52 *CWPR*, 25 June 1808.

53 *CWPR*, 11 March 1809.

54 J.R. Dinwiddy, 'The early nineteenth-century campaign against flogging in the army', *EHR*, 97 (1982), 308–31.

55 *CWPR*, 1 July 1809.

56 Grande, *William Cobbett*, p. 61.

57 *Law Report: Court of King's Bench, Friday June 15: The King v. William Cobbett*, reprinted in Leonora Nattrass (ed.), *William Cobbett: Selected Writings*, vol. 2 (London: Pickering & Chatto, 1998), pp. 254–5.

58 Boddice and Smith, *Emotion, Sense, Experience*, p. 11.

59 On the legal apparatus of the state's clamp-down on radicalism, see Philip Harling, 'The law of libel and the limits of repression, 1790–1832', *HJ*, 44 (2001), 107–34; John Barrell, *Imagining the King's Death: Figurative Treason, Fantasies of Regicide, 1793–1796* (Oxford: Oxford University Press, 2006); John Barrell, *The Spirit of Despotism: Invasion of Privacy in the 1790s* (Oxford: Oxford University Press, 2006); Katrina Navickas, 'Political trials and the suppression of popular radicalism in England, 1799–1820', in Michael T. Davis, Emma Vincent Macleod and Gordon Pentland (eds), *Political Trials in an Age of Revolution* (Basingstoke: Palgrave, 2019), pp. 185–212.

60 Spater, *Cobbett*, vol. 1, pp. 130–1.

61 J. Ann Hone, *For the Cause of Truth: Radicalism in London, 1796–1821* (Oxford: Oxford University Press, 1982), p. 197.

62 *King v Cobbett*, pp. 263–74. In the aftermath of the trial and his imprisonment, Cobbett pushed these distinctions even further, excusing his hatred for the people's oppressors as evidence of the depth of his patriotism: 'it is because I love my country, that I hate its oppressors'. HSP, Cobbett Papers, 2129, Folder 13, Cobbett to John Morgan, 17 July 1815.

63 In August 1809, Cobbett relayed to Hunt that his wife had given birth to a stillborn baby and he had feared for his wife's life. HSP, Cobbett Papers, 2129, Folder 10, William Cobbett to Henry Hunt, 28 August 1809. Cobbett felt himself a victim of several years of attempts by the government to blacken his name – 'of exciting in the public mind, an evil opinion of me'. *Ibid.*, Cobbett to John Wright, 19 November 1809. Against this background of mounting anxiety on Cobbett's part, these personal strains may explain why he prevaricated for a time over whether to accept the government's offer of giving up its prosecution of him in return for ceasing his radical journalism. Publicly, Cobbett put on a brave, defiant face, which continued while he was incarcerated: *Ibid.*, Cobbett to Frederick Reid, 23 July 1810. Francis Place, in his later autobiographical writings, uncharitably accused Cobbett of cowardice during this period, and was ashamed of the terror that Cobbett exhibited in the run-up to his trial and of the way he bungled his defence in court. BL, Additional MS 35145, Francis Place Papers, Autobiography, vol. iv, 1809–36, fos 11–13.

64 Spater, *Cobbett*, vol. 1, p. 245.

65 On the problems of identifying emotions from facial expression, see Jan Plamper, *The History of Emotions: An Introduction* (Oxford: Oxford University Press, 2012), pp. 150–61.

66 Cobbett, *Autobiography*, p. 121.

67 HSP, Cobbett Papers, 2129, Folder 11, William Cobbett to Nancy Cobbett, 1 November 1811.

68 Anne Cobbett, *Account of the Family* (London: William Cobbett Society, 1999), p. 40; Navickas, 'Political trials', pp. 187–92. For examples of setbacks and woes, see: HSP, Cobbett Papers, 2129, Folder 11, William Cobbett to Nancy Cobbett, 25 October 1811.

69 TNA, HO 40/9, 'A Letter to the Luddites by William Cobbett', fol. 69; *CWPR*, 3 November 1816, quoted and cited in Robert Poole, *Peterloo: The English Uprising* (Oxford: Oxford University Press, 2020), p. 97.

70 TNA, HO 40/3, Extract of a letter sent from Mr. Weyland Jnr. to Lord Sidmouth, n.d. fol. 34v; Some Particulars as to the nature of meetings held in London, 23 December 1816, fol. 906. Jason McElligott has recently suggested that Cobbett may have been associated with the Cato Street conspiracy, but this seems improbable given the trajectory of his career as a radical reformer. Jason McElligott, 'The men they couldn't hang: "sensible" radicals and the Cato Street conspiracy'; cf. John Stevenson, 'Joining up the dots: contingency, hindsight and the British insurrectionary tradition', both in Jason McElligott and Martin Conboy (eds), *The Cato Street Conspiracy: Plotting, Counter-intelligence and the Revolutionary Tradition in Britain and Ireland* (Manchester: Manchester University Press 2020), pp. 49–63, 34–48.

71 Cobbett, *Rural Rides*, vol. 1, p. 3. For the Six Acts, see Malcolm Chase, *1820: Disorder and Stability in the United Kingdom* (Manchester: Manchester University Press 2013), pp. 44–6.

72 *Hansard*, House of Lords, vol. 41, 9 December 1819, cols 970–1. A similar affective language had been used in 1817 in justifying the Seditious Meetings Act, the suspension of Habeas Corpus and new treason legislation: *Hansard*, House of Commons, vol. 35, 24 February 1817, col. 599; 26 February 1817, cols 725, 753.

73 *CWPR*, 29 April and 18 November 1820.

74 *CWPR*, 6 May 1820.

75 *CWPR*, 18 August 1821; E.A. Smith (ed.), *A Queen on Trial: The Affair of Queen Caroline* (Stroud: Alan Sutton, 1993), pp. 101–2, 114. The best account of Cobbett and the Queen Caroline affair is Grande, *Cobbett*, chapter 5. On the hydraulic theory of emotions, and the problems associated with it, see Barbara H. Rosenwein, 'Worrying about emotions in history', *American Historical Review*, 107 (2002), 821–45.

76 *CWPR*, 29 April 1820.

77 John Gardner, *Poetry and Popular Protest: Peterloo, Cato Street and the Queen Caroline Controversy* (Basingstoke: Palgrave, 2011), p. 171.

78 Grande, *Cobbett*, p. 130; Tim Fulford, *Romanticism and Masculinity: Gender, Politics and Poetics in the Writings of Burke, Coleridge, Cobbett, Wordsworth, De Quincey and Hazlitt* (Basingstoke: Macmillan, 1999), pp. 162–3; *CWPR*, 18 August 1821.

79 Cobbett, *Autobiography*, p. 207.

80 *CWPR*, 11 September 1817, 19 May 1821, 14 August 1824.

81 *CWPR*, 16 July 1804. For Cobbett's racism, see Ryan Hanley, 'Slavery and the birth of working-class racism in England, 1814–1833', *Transactions of the Royal Historical Society*, 26 (2016), 103–23. There are parallels here with what Joanna Bourke has termed 'zero-sum' humanitarianism. In other words, 'If sympathy is allotted to one group ... there [is] a risk that it will be removed from another group.' One of Cobbett's implicit concerns was that there was not enough sympathy to go around. Joanna Bourke, *What it Means to be Human: Reflections from 1791 to the Present* (London: Virago, 2011), p. 94.

82 *CWPR*, 17 July 1824, 3 March 1827, 9 August 1834. On Cobbett and Scotland, see Alex Benchimol, 'Scotland under the Scotch system: narratives of resistance from *Cobbett's Tour in Scotland*', in Grande and Stevenson, *William Cobbett*, pp. 93–106; James P. Huzel, *The Popularization of Malthus in Early Nineteenth-Century England* (Aldershot: Ashgate, 2006), pp. 106, 127.

83 *CWPR*, 5 July 1817. On Foucault, population and emotion, see Nicole Eustace, 'Emotion and political change', in Susan J. Matt and Peter N. Stearns (eds), *Doing Emotions History* (Urbana, Chicago and Springfield: University of Illinois Press, 2014), pp. 175–7.

84 *CWPR*, 12 June 1818, quoted and cited in Chase, *1820*, p. 46.

85 *CWPR*, 6 December 1806, 5 August 1815, 23 March 1816; Dyck, *Cobbett*, p. 28. For similar examples, see *CWPR*, 23 March 1809 (on the false indignation of the government in response to the Mary Anne Clarke scandal), 18 January 1817 and 10 December 1825 (weeping for the fundholders but not the labourers), 3 October 1810 (unnatural craving for money). See also Cobbett's *History of the Protestant Reformation*, which, *inter alia*, deprecates the attempts by the elite to distract the working class from its sufferings by inculcating hatred of 'No Popery'. Matthew Roberts, 'Catholicism and constitutionalism in William Cobbett's English and Irish medievalism', in David Matthews and Mike Sanders (eds), *Medievalism from Below: Subaltern Medievalisms in the Nineteenth Century* (Cambridge: D.S. Brewer, 2021), pp. 19–38.

86 Ruth Mather, 'The home-making of the English working class: radical politics and domestic life in late-Georgian England, c.1790–1820' (PhD dissertation, Queen Mary, University of London, 2016), pp. 45, 49.

87 Cobbett, *Autobiography*, p. 88.

88 HSP, Cobbett Papers, 2129, Folder 10, Cobbett to Anne Cobbett, 10 July 1810.

89 Barbara H. Rosenwein, *Anger: The Conflicted History of an Emotion* (New Haven and London: Yale University Press, 2020), p. 125.

90 While Cobbett despised his enemies, they hated him, and the reason they hated him, in Cobbett's view, was because they feared him. *CWPR*, 2 October 1819.

91 TNA, HO 42/199, Home Office Papers, 'To the Reformers in and near Manchester, by W. Cobbett', fol. 313A.

92 E.g., Cobbett, *Autobiography*, pp. 213, 220. For the ways in which Cobbett's writing defied the vulgar/refined dyad, see Olivia Smith, *The Politics of Language, 1791–1819* (Oxford: Oxford University Press, 1984), chapter 6.

93 Grande, Stevenson and Thomas, *Opinions*, p. 77.

94 *CWPR*, 8 May 1819.

95 For these shifts in popular culture, see Robert W. Malcolmson, *Popular Recreations in English Society, 1700–1850* (Cambridge: Cambridge University Press, 1973). More recently, historians have emphasised the continuities between an older rural popular culture and that of the new industrial towns: Emma Griffin, *England's Revelry: A History of Popular Sports and Pastimes, 1660–1830* (Oxford: Oxford University Press, 2005).

96 *CWPR*, 6 October 1827.

97 Cobbett, *Autobiography*, p. 93.

98 *CWPR*, 24 September 1803. On Cobbett and manliness, see Matthew McCormack, *The Independent Man: Citizenship and Gender Politics in Georgian England* (Manchester: Manchester University Press 2005), pp. 3, 33–4.

99 HSP, Cobbett Papers, 2129, Folder 11, Cobbett to Nancy Cobbett, 6 August 1811.

100 William Cobbett, *A Year's Residence in the United States of America* (London, 1818), para 290.

101 Cobbett, *Autobiography*, pp. 10, 25.

102 Cobbett, *Advice to Young Men*, para 311.

103 HSP, Cobbett Papers, 2129, Folder 11, Cobbett to Nancy Cobbett, 25 October 1811.

104 Cobbett, *Cottage Economy*, p. 17.

105 Grande, Stevenson and Thomas, *Opinions*, p. 203; Plamper, *History of Emotions*, p. 24. Cobbett was certainly familiar with Rousseau's ideas: Dyck, *Cobbett*, p. 43; Spater, *Cobbett*, vol. 1, p. 18.

106 Research by Frank O'Gorman and the History of Parliament has shown that serious election violence of the kind Cobbett encountered at Coventry was unusual, at least in England. Frank O'Gorman, *Voters, Patrons and Parties: The Unreformed Electorate of Hanoverian England, 1734–1832* (Oxford: Oxford University Press, 1989), p. 256; David R. Fisher, 'General elections, 1820–1831', in David R. Fisher (ed.), *The History of Parliament: The House of Commons, 1820–1832* (Cambridge: Cambridge University Press, 2009), www.historyofparliamentonline.org/volume/1820-1832/survey/v-general-elections-1820-1831 [accessed 15 January 2021].

107 Cobbett, *Autobiography*, p. 97; William Cobbett, 'History of the Coventry election', 23 March 1820, reprinted in Nattrass, *Selected Writings*, IV, p. 215.

108 Cobbett only polled 517 votes, as against the 1,474 and 1,422 of the two winning candidates. The fullest account of the election, in addition to Cobbett's own, is T. W. Whitley, *The Parliamentary Representation of the City of Coventry from the Earliest Times to the Present* (Coventry, 1894), pp. 257–62. See also Margaret Escott, 'Coventry', in Fisher, *Commons, 1820–1832*, www.history-ofparliamentonline.org/volume/1820-1832/constituencies/coventry [accessed 15 January 2021].

109 Cobbett, 'History of the Coventry election', p. 220.

110 Colin McGinn, *The Meaning of Disgust* (Oxford: Oxford University Press, 2011), p. 181.

111 Jon Lawrence, *Electing Our Masters: The Hustings in British Politics from Hogarth to Blair* (Oxford: Oxford University Press, 2009), p. 19.

112 *Cobbett's Evening Register*, 8 March 1820.

113 Plamper, *History of Emotions*, p. 119.

114 Cobbett, 'History of the Coventry election', p. 215.

115 *Ibid.*, pp. 216–18.

116 *CWPR*, 29 December 1832. Cobbett had earlier opposed the secret ballot, citing the usual arguments that such sneaking and cowardly behaviour was anathema to Englishmen. Poole, *Peterloo*, p. 107.

117 *Cobbett's Evening Post*, 14 and 16 March 1820; HSP, Cobbett Papers, Folder 15, Cobbett to James P. Cobbett, 12 February 1820.

118 Dyck, *Cobbett*, p. 32.

119 Penny Young, *Two Cocks on the Dunghill: William Cobbett and Henry Hunt* (South Lopham: Twopenny Press, 2009), p. 176.

120 *CWPR*, 14 January and 30 June 1832.

2

Richard Carlile and the embodiment
of reason's republic

In the 1820s and early 1830s the radical freethinker Richard Carlile (1790–1843) was one of the leading radicals of the day. Born in Devon, apprenticed as an artisan tinsmith, he moved to London in 1811 and was radicalised by the post-war social unrest. By 1817 he had established himself as a radical hawker and publisher, and by 1819 a journalist and printer-publisher of seditious and blasphemous texts, a crime which led to his imprisonment in Dorchester gaol for six years. In the late 1820s he set out to make his brand of radical infidelism – republicanism and religious freethought – the basis of a popular movement until he was imprisoned once again for sedition in 1831, this time for allegedly inciting the Swing rioters.[1] Taking his career as a whole, Carlile spent over ten years in prison because of his dogged campaigning for free speech and a free press. 'Few men have suffered more severely, or more unjustly for a conscientious expression of opinion than Carlile', wrote the transatlantic infidel Robert Dale Owen.[2]

Historians have not been too kind to Carlile, and not without reason, but this has resulted in a caricatured portrait of his radicalism. On the one hand, this is the consequence of the rehabilitation of the radical leader Henry Hunt, hero of Peterloo, who found himself at loggerheads with Carlile over ideology – Hunt advocated constitutionalism and reform of the House of Commons, Carlile wanted a republic – and over strategy – Hunt put his faith in ritualised public display and the threatening collective force of large open-air meetings (the mass platform), Carlile in the redeeming power of the printed word and individual moral reform.[3] The latter's radicalism was purist, rational, austere, dispassionate and uncontaminated with populist elements – or so he claimed. While Hunt's supporters gave expression to their radicalism via the effusive, boisterous mass platform and tap room, Carlile's met in 'temples of reason' – bookshops, infidel chapels, lecture halls and prison cells.[4] On the other hand, Carlile has been a casualty of the characterisation of popular radicalism in the 1820s as cleft in two – divided into libertine excess (obscenity and pornography) and moral restraint (improving and respectable). The unambiguous identification of

Carlile with the latter has obscured the affective basis and populist aspects of his radicalism.[5]

As befitted someone who operated in the tradition of transcendent Jacobinism, Carlile's affective politics cut across the public–private divide as well as national boundaries in his quest for a politics of pure reason unsullied with feeling. He was conscious of the way in which political and religious authorities legitimated their hegemony by enslaving the mind as a way of enslaving the body. Carlile challenged this by practising and promoting an embodied affective politics which demystified popular understandings of the passions and prescribed an ascetic regimen that empowered the working classes. Unlike other radicals discussed in this book, he was resistant to the idea that bodies were porous and merged with their environments. As the first section shows, Carlile engaged in a debate about the location of feeling in the body. Far from being an esoteric preoccupation of his that spoke only to his interest in materialism and science, Carlile insisted that the seating of the passions had important political implications. The chapter then moves on to discuss Carlile's *Every Woman's Book*, a book widely known among historians of feminism and sex, but not historians of emotion.[6] Carlile's excursus on this one passion is revealing of his understanding of sex, gender and the politics of feeling. This chapter develops the concept of ascetic radicalism to underscore the affective basis of Carlile's problematic quest for 'pure reason', focusing on the period in which he was a prominent radical leader, c.1819–32. Ironically, for someone who rejected the notion that bodies were defined by space, Carlile's affective politics reached their apotheosis in the prison cell, but for reasons explored in the final section, his transcendent affective politics began to break down in the early 1830s.

'In reason's cause his nervous thoughts combin'd'

Carlile was part of a transatlantic network of radical infidels who were, *inter alia*, debating the nature of the passions as part of their engagement with the bequest of the radical Enlightenment.[7] This debate owed a great deal to one of the leaders from the previous generation of American deists, Elihu Palmer (1764–1806), whose impact on Carlile has not been fully registered by the latter's biographers. It was not just for republishing Thomas Paine that Carlile was imprisoned in 1819, but also Palmer's *Principles of Nature*. It is thanks largely to Carlile that we know anything at all about Palmer's life. Carlile reached out to his American contacts, notably the New York radical freethinkers John Fellows and William Carver, for biographical information relating to Palmer. Fellows supplied him with an unpublished memoir that he had authored of Palmer's life, which in turn Carlile published.[8]

Carlile asked Carver, a British-born New York radical artisan turned vet-
erinarian who had known Palmer, to send him any writings, as well as a
portrait (Figure 2.1).[9] Carlile then produced an engraving, the only image of
Palmer to survive. At first glance, Palmer is a model of composure, restraint
and respectability, even in the face of his disability: he had lost his sight,
and very nearly his life, to the yellow fever epidemic that swept through
Philadelphia in 1793. Here was the personification of pure reason.

What is interesting for the historian of emotion is not the engraving itself
but the poetic lines that Carlile appended, most likely penned by himself.
Having begun with the assumption that Palmer's literal blindness enabled
him to see further, intellectually – not an uncommon argument in descriptions of disability around this time,[10] the register changes from reason to
feeling, or rather to reason-feeling: 'In reason's cause his nervous thoughts
combin'd'. For a radical who was allegedly in pursuit of 'pure reason', this
is an odd declaration as it implies the composite and dialectic nature of
thought and feeling. This may have been a nod by Carlile to some of the
arguments about the passions put forward by Palmer in his most influential work, *Principles of Nature* (1801), arguments that Carlile would later
develop in his own affective politics. Palmer's subtitle is also revealing:
A Development of the Moral Causes of Happiness and Misery. This is an
apt summary of how Carlile conceived his own stated political goals. One
of Palmer's main propositions was that humans had been endowed by their
creator with reason and could, therefore, restrain their passions to maximise well-being. Palmer also alleged that religion inflamed the passions;
that the Bible was an immoral work which excused base passions; and that
humans in their conceit depicted God and his servants as creatures of passion. Palmer took deism to the borders of atheism, not least by denying the
existence of an immaterial and indestructible soul, and there is no doubt
that this played a part in Carlile's conversion to atheism in the early 1820s.[11]

It would be easy to dismiss Carlile's poetic homage to Palmer's affective
politics as little more than atypical poetic licence. But this was not an
uncharacteristic statement of his. Carlile participated in scientific and moral
philosophical debates about the location, function and pliability of the passions. This was not a random or esoteric set of preoccupations. In questioning religious truths, freethinkers drew on scientific learning and medical
knowledge as well as philosophical treatises. Artisans and autodidacts, like
Carlile, were invariably bricoleurs who drew on a diverse body of knowledge, often derived from scattered sources, access to which they felt had
been denied by elites. Democratising knowledge, especially that which furthered materialist attacks on Christianity, was an integral part of radical
infidelity, and this extended to the human body. Lack of knowledge about
the human body, including the passions, had allowed religious and political

ELIHU PALMER,

Copied from the best Likeness that appeared in America.

The darkness drear obscured his visual ray,
His mind, unclouded felt no loss of day;
In Reason's cause his nervous thoughts combin'd
Flow to the world, and harmonize mankind.

Engraved for & Published by R. Carlile, 84, Fleet St London.

Figure 2.1 Elihu Palmer, published by Richard Carlile (c.1820).

elites to oppress the people.[12] Carlile was especially scathing of those radicals and reformers who only focused on political reform to the exclusion of combatting the errors of religion, which furthered the hegemony of a political and religious elite: 'mental slavery is the sure and certain ground in which to establish bodily slavery'.[13] To put it another way, Carlile would have taken as axiomatic the assumption, advanced as part of the recent 'bodily turn' in the history of emotions, that 'the body is never pure soma: it is configured in social, cognitive, and metaphorical worlds'.[14] This is not to suggest that bodies can be reduced to text; rather, that the way in which people experience and use their bodies, including feelings, is determined by power hierarchies. As Carlile reasoned, the purpose of religious authorities was to 'render man unhappy in mind, and to reduce him to a state of mental degradation, by preaching up a changing and capricious God, on whom he has to depend for future happiness'. This was pernicious because it stripped the people of any agency in securing their own happiness. Worse still, clerics directly benefited from this slavery: 'they also make the body miserable by depriving it of the fairest fruits of its labour, to support themselves in indolent luxury'.[15] Only by destroying priestcraft could mental, and then bodily, slavery be ended. Like Owenite socialists who shared his religious infidelity, Carlile often conceptualised his politics not as the pursuit of pure reason – at best, that was a vehicle towards a particular goal, at worst an unachievable desideratum – but as the 'science of happiness'.[16] Also akin to Owenism, Carlile's aim was not to banish feelings, but to calibrate them – through manipulation of the environment and the development of reason – to maximise human happiness. This might entail suppressing some of the baser passions, but equally it might necessitate unleashing others, notably love.

Carlile's understanding of the passions was indebted to several sources and influences, some of which are easier to discern than others because of his explicit engagement with then. One possible influence was the English philosopher and itinerant John 'Walking' Stewart, whom Carlile called the progenitor of some of his ideas.[17] But other than including extracts from his lectures, some of which included discussion of the passions, Carlile did not comment. Interestingly, he extracted from Stewart's lectures his discussion of Pope's famous dictum 'Reason is the card, but passion is the gale', which Nicole Eustace has used to explore the relationship between emotion, power and social status in colonial North America.[18] Stewart pronounced this axiom 'the moral law of nature'.[19] Other possible influences on Carlile's understanding of the passions include Socrates, Pythagoras, Seneca, Confucius and Gibbon, whose writings on the passions were also extracted, again without comment.

A major influence on Carlile's thinking about the passions was phrenology, the practice of reading psychological traits from the size and shape of the human skull. Dubbed by Carlile 'an infidel science', phrenology grew in popularity on both sides of the Atlantic in the early nineteenth century.[20] He was familiar with the seminal work of the German phrenologists Drs Gall and Spurzheim, whose works and lectures are frequently referenced in Carlile's periodicals, though it was neither uncritically nor fully embraced by radical infidels. Carlile's own understanding of it was mediated through his engagement with the controversial surgeon Sir William Lawrence; but there was more to his interest in phrenology than mere opportunism.[21] Phrenology also furnished confirmation of the materiality of mind; in other words, the absence of a divinely created immaterial, immortal soul, which distinguished Carlile's thinking about feelings from the prevailing view about the passions. The human mind is 'a compound of sensations', he declared. Sensations were impressions and impulses 'made by external objects on the nerves and their fluids, a trace of which is immediately imprinted on the brain', a view he appears to have derived from the rational mechanical theory of the popular scientist Sir Richard Phillips.[22] The result is feeling: 'Thus, we find excitement produces anger, joy, sorrow, pleasure, pain, crying, laughing, grief, sympathy, love, hatred, revenge, and other passions and sensations, entirely upon electrical principles.'[23]

Bodily politics

But where exactly did Carlile locate the passions? In a letter to the Quaker prison reformer Elizabeth Fry, in which he rebuked the Quakers for confusing sensation with spirit, he was more emphatic about their location:

> The brain has been called the seat of sensation; and so it may be, generally speaking, for it is the root of the nerves. The nerves are fed from the brain with that fluid which pervades them; but the brain has no particular qualities separate from being the root of the nerves. Physiologists have attributed too much to the brain.[24]

At this point, he distanced himself from Gall and Spurzheim because they had, in his view, erroneously made the brain the centre of human character, before concluding 'The nerves are the seat of the passions'. Carlile then turned his fire on the romantic disposition of locating feelings in the heart, which, he countered, was little more than a mechanical pump.[25] He returned to this theme just over a year later and judged it to be 'an exceeding great mistake, to suppose that the heart is the seat of the passions. All its pulsations and agitations are mere motions of the blood, and not from any nervous principle in the heart.'[26] Another year hence, Carlile was joking with one correspondent that ' "The age of chivalry is gone!" No more than the buttocks has the heart any thing to do with courage.'[27] In this formula-tion, feelings are outputs, distinguished from sensations which are inputs: 'I clearly trace mind to sensation, and sensation to body', which is acted upon by external stimuli which, in turn, produces sensation.[28] Thus, in truth, Carlile's understanding of feeling transcended the mind-body dualism then prevalent: 'mind and body is one and the same thing'.[29]

This had political implications in his battle not just with sentimental radicalism but also religious authority. Ejecting passions from the heart was an important part of Carlile's rejection of sentimental radicalism; seat-ing the passions in the heart implied that feelings were beyond control, which contradicted the assumptions of ascetic radicalism. Locating feeling throughout the body in the nerves and not just in the brain restored some bodily agency to those whose minds were enthralled to religious authority and who believed that only a Christian life offered any prospect of discip-lining the passions; the inference being that the mind was the creation and property of a divinely created soul. Carlile countered this by asserting that 'the mind is wholly material; for the mind is a compound of all these sensa-tions and is improved and increased by action, by exercise, by strengthening the moral powers, and by controuling [sic.] the immoral powers'.[30] Further, seating feeling in the body was also connected to Carlile's libertarian pro-ject of demystifying knowledge around passions such as love. By stripping away overly sentimentalised understanding of love and by combating the taboo culture of repression, guilt and fear created by religious authority – in short, by freeing both the mind and the heart – love, desire and sex could be approached rationally as a set of natural bodily feelings.[31] Whatever its scientific veracity, we can see that Carlile had a complex understanding of feelings, and that he dissented from the emerging view that the passions were located in the brain, or the traditional and sentimental view of the heart.[32] Indeed, in some respects he anticipated the laboratory-based science of emotion that emerged in the late nineteenth century which made the body (though not, in Carlile's case, the brain) the key to emotion.[33]

Surprisingly, Carlile did not subscribe to a universalist notion of the passions – that everyone had the same capacity for feeling. True, he appears to have accepted that all humans had the same *potential* capacity for feel-ing, as did Paine and Palmer. Carlile implies potential universality in his attacks on slavery and the notion that white men were superior to black, in his attack on social and political hierarchy, and in his pleas for cosmo-politan fraternity between nations.[34] But this was qualified by his brand of ascetic radicalism along with some conservative preconceptions about gender and sex. To take the first of these, Carlile took the view that only through the improving of one's mind and morals would the 'animal sensa-tions' become 'more fine and more numerous'. It followed that those who either refused or were denied the opportunity to do this, felt differently. This led him to conclude that if feelings are outputs, those outputs are not just the product of sensations as allowance had to be made 'for a difference in the materials worked upon', or what he termed elsewhere nervous organisation.[35] This is not that radically different from the understandings of the passions that issued from moral philosophers and theologians in the eighteenth century: Isaac Watts and Thomas Cogan, for example, asserted that the passions were influenced by a whole range of situational factors, including age, health, temperament, custom, education, habit and prejudice.[36] It was only a short step from this to the next proposition that the passions were malleable; or to use Carlile's precise formulation, passions could be 'moulded', a view which he appears to have derived in part from his reading of Seneca.[37] For Carlile this was confirmation about the location of the passions. He relayed a story he had heard of how a pregnant white woman had produced a black child just by repeatedly looking at a picture of a black person displayed in her room. 'To me this seems direct proof, that the nerves are the seat of the passions ... for it seems both natural and rational, that the sensations of the mother should be communicated to the infant in the womb' – an interesting leap to say the least.[38] Passions were also contagious. An angry mother, Carlile averred, would be sure to produce that character upon her child. While nervous organisation and health was important, so, too, was example.[39]

According to this understanding, Carlile reasoned, a person who routinely practises keeping their passions under control will be less likely to succumb to them when provoked. He was explicit on this point when it came to his conduct in prison where, because of his practise at composure, he never gave his goading gaoler the satisfaction of letting him 'work ... me into [a] temper'.[40] Robert Dale Owen, who shared Carlile's views about the potential ability of humans to control their passions, remarked on Carlile's composure which he observed first-hand when he visited him in the Giltspur Street Compter prison: 'He converses calmly if not cheerfully; and his resolution seems unbroken.'[41] This psychological mindset was intimately bound up with Carlile's brand of ascetic radicalism. As discussed in the introduction, asceticism has connotations of austerity, self-denial, stoicism; in short, a mental state free of feeling in the face of suffering such as Carlile's calm unbending resolve in response to his imprisonment, or his refusal to back down and cease publishing blasphemous and seditious works when faced with opposition from the authorities. As Carlile said when facing prosecution in August 1819, 'I will not be intimidated'; in other words, his ascetic mindset negated feelings of timidity.[42]

But on closer inspection, asceticism is inseparable from pain and suffering which is not surprising given that its origins are to be found in early

Christian ethics and spirituality. For the Christian ascetic, pain is not only
something deliberately sought out but can also be accompanied by feelings
of pleasure.[43] While it would be perverse to say that Carlile found prison
pleasurable, there is no denying that he derived a certain level of satisfaction in refusing to yield to his oppressors. As he taunted the Society for
the Suppression of Vice, the body which had instigated legal proceedings
against him for blasphemy in 1818–19:

> I can assure the Vice Society that I smile to myself, and have the most agree-
> able feelings when I reflect how much they have contributed to strengthen my
> attack on the common fraud of religion. I feel that I am quite another being to
> what I should have been, had I been left alone and not prosecuted.[44]

A biographical article in Carlile's periodical *The Prompter* (possibly penned by
himself) observed that 'Imprisonment to him does not seem a punishment'.[45]
Granted, some of this may have been Carlile whistling to keep his spirits
up – certainly, he suffered from periods of melancholy in prison. But even
conceding this becomes problematic if we accept William Reddy's concept
of emotives – emotion words not only describe affective states, but the act
of uttering them can also be intensifying and reinforcing.[46] So if Carlile was
whistling to keep up his spirits, we need to allow for the possibility that this
may have altered his affective state (on which more below).

Prison provided Carlile, somewhat paradoxically, with a safe space in
which to continue his campaigning and writing. It was only when this was
infringed during the period when his family were allowed to lodge with him
in Dorchester gaol that he found prison stifling. 'I write with a room full
of children', he complained in July 1824. 'Having Mrs C. and the children
here, and a noise to which I have of late been so little accustomed to, I find
a difficulty to get through my ordinary pen and ink work.'[47] The period
following his liberation in November 1825 was much more unsettling and
psychologically harrowing for him due to the constant threat of the bailiffs,
creditors and the collapse of his marriage.[48] Although Dale Owen expressed
reservations about the wisdom of Carlile's 'violent expression of opinion' as
a tactic which had 'provoked the anger of the government', he nonetheless
praised him for his indomitability: 'It requires, to resist the oppression of
brute force, not so much men of cultivated intellect as of strong nerves and
unflinching courage; men who will speak plainly and suffer coolly.'[49] For
all that prison was meant to be, in Carlile's term, a 'repository of reason',
feeling rules were an integral part of the 'radical sub-culture' identified by
recent research on the life of imprisoned radicals.[50]

Someone who was not taking to his reimprisonment coolly in 1831 was
Carlile's close associate, the mercurial Reverend Robert Taylor. As Carlile
lectured his histrionic friend, it was precisely because Taylor was not

accustomed to this regimen of affective restraint that his captors got the better of him: 'You say Walter the gaoler insults you – that is your fault. It is not in the power of men to insult me ... there can only be insult where there is a disposition to court it.' Having scolded Taylor, he then concedes that 'I know that reason is one thing and passion another, and neither one nor the other can be commanded', but as the thrust of his rebuke implies, feelings can be manipulated with practice: 'cool methodical warfare' was required not further displays of 'excitement'. Waxing to his theme of the micro-politics of conflict and survival in prison, Carlile boasted that he made his gaoler 'fear me simply by a power of looking at him ... I conquered him by virtue'. His final advice to Taylor was: 'You must reason with your-self and write down laws for your own guidance in prison. You will do this coolly and this will keep you cool.'[51] The implication here was that Taylor had transgressed the feeling rules of the prison cell as a space of radical reason prescribed by Carlile. The latter would cite as the cause of his separation from his first wife, Jane, her 'indomitably violent and ill-tempered ... domestic outrages', from which imprisonment, by his own admission, provided 'great relief'.[52] Clearly, he took seriously transgressions of the feeling rules he policed. A preoccupation with the 'excess of temper' was a concern with radical infidels on both sides of the Atlantic, in large measure because the enemies of freethought depicted infidels as brutish.[53] Whether Carlile was always such a model of restraint is unclear; certainly he seems to have ignored his own advice when he threatened his new gaoler-tormentor in the Giltspur Street Compter with violence, though this appears to have been an unsent letter.[54] Perhaps the act of playing out his violent passion on paper dampened his ardour.

Sex, love and disordered passions

Ascetic radicals like Carlile, and later the London Working Men's Association (discussed in chapter 6), had little time for those whom they deemed to be creatures of base passions. This aversion expressed itself in numerous ways, but the most important was through the practised body: a regimen of different ways in which Carlile prescribed the use of one's body.[55] This regimen was advocated most notably in the *Moralist*, a new serial that he published in the early 1820s, a telling title that hints at the intimate connections that historians of emotion have drawn between morality, feeling and the quotidian. As recent work has underlined, morality is always something that is experienced, and the '*value* of experience is and has always been established by or filtered through what experience *felt* like'. 'In other words, the moral compass exists in the realm of *feeling*.'[56] The *Moralist* was a compendium

of self-improving and ethical prescriptions of bodily practice, largely based
on the reprinting of extracts from a range of thinkers who advocated knowledge, temperance, cleanliness, economy and independence. For example,
those addicted to alcohol knew 'no pleasures, but in the swallowing of those
poisons' which acted as a barrier to 'sensible happiness', Carlile reasoned.[57]
This contempt also informed his self-declared prudery. Commenting on his
rival William Benbow's salacious *Rambler's Magazine*, an exposé of upper-
class debauchery, Carlile dismissed it as 'calculated to incite public curiosity
by their wantonness or excess. Such publications are evidently mischievous
to public morals; for instead of shaming or allaying vicious passions, it is
notorious and natural that they are incentives to such passions.'[58] Contrary
to what his enemies alleged, Carlile clearly drew a line between blasphemy
and obscenity. He frequently distinguished between 'bad' passions – such as
swearing – and 'natural passions', though elsewhere this hierarchy is belied
by a dialectical and relative conception of feeling: 'every distinct passion is
also ... a circle. Love is a comparison of objects, an attachment to one, a
dislike of another, a preference to one of two or more.'[59] The natural passion Carlile devoted most attention to was love. This he conceived as 'not
a passion of the mind, or an artificial passion, such as a craving to exhibit
the distinctions of society; but a natural passion, or a passion of the body,
which we hold in common with every other animal'. He traced love to the
human desire to reproduce, the indulgence of which was perfectly natural,
neither criminal nor a 'sinful pleasure'.[60] What *was* criminal was where the
indulgence was withheld, ostensibly by religious authorities for purposes
of morality, but in reality from a desire to control the minds and bodies of
the credulous. Sexual intercourse was natural and should be enjoyed by all
consenting adults.

But not quite all. For all his advocacy of free love and the right to sexual
pleasure, Carlile did not extend this to same-sex relationships. Such views
were not unusual, even among more romantic radicals who, though they
might dissent from the prudery of ascetic radicalism, viewed sodomy as
incompatible with manly independence.[61] What made this more surprising
in Carlile's case was his declaration in his controversial essay *What Is Love?*
that 'due allowances should always be made for the actions and passions
of those which differ from our own, provided, they injure none design-
edly but themselves'.[62] Here the hierarchy of passions reasserted itself with
sodomy seen as a bad passion. The occasion for his homophobic views was
the public scandal surrounding the Bishop of Clogher in 1822 when he
was caught *in flagrante* with a soldier in the White Lion pub in St. James's.
For Carlile this was grist to his mill of proving just how much religion
debases: 'The gross credulity, effeminacy, and foul passions generated by
religion, is just that species of excitement which must lead to the crime of

Bishoping', the term that Carlile said he would, henceforth, use to refer to sodomy. Carlile politicised this bodily practice as part of his radical attack on a parasitic aristocracy. Such practices, he thundered, were only the preserve of the idle classes: 'An industrious man ... could never harbour such beastly passions, but he would shudder at the bare mention ... of such a thing.' As befitted an ascetic radical, Carlile not only equates abhorrent bodily practices with the sub-human, he also prescribes the appropriate bodily response – a shudder, which functions here as a compound output of disgust and fear.[63] Three weeks later, when news of Lord Castlereagh's suicide broke, allegedly in response to being blackmailed for the 'crime of bishoping', Carlile made essentially the same points again, berating him for his homosexual 'outrage[s] against humanity'.[64] Reactions of moral disgust – defined as reactions to persons or behaviours that transgress social norms – towards acts of sodomy was by the early nineteenth century a well-established response.[65] Carlile used moral disgust – his preferred recourse when attacking base passions – to invert the hierarchy of the social order as part of his radical critique of a corrupt aristocracy by subordinating Clogher and Castlereagh to the level of a brute. Carlile had essentially made the same point during the Queen Caroline affair in 1820 when he claimed that the 'disgusting' behaviour of the King towards the Queen in trying to prevent her from being crowned, taught the people to hate monarchy. This behaviour, he confessed, had brought 'an involuntary tear' to his cheek, and was symptomatic of arbitrary government and the ways in which 'honest industry is robbed to gratify the bad passions of the idle and vicious'. This was the real reason why 'every vein in' Carlile 'had swelled with indignation at ... the filthy tales manufactured' by the Queen's enemies who were without shame.[66]

All this was perfectly consistent with ascetic radicalism, though in the case of the Clogher scandal it made for some strange bedfellows in the shape of those evangelical groups promoting the reformation of manners. Carlile was positively ecstatic that Clogher was a member of the Vice Society.[67] Less easy to square with Carlile's ascetic radicalism, given his feminist sympathies, is the second caveat that he entered regarding feelings: 'there is ... a striking difference in the male and female on that head' 'allowing for a difference in our different sensations'.[68] Unfortunately, this was not an assertion on which he elaborated, but it does suggest a tension in his gender politics, especially because in other respects he subscribed to the view that men and women were equals. But not when it came to feelings. He claimed that women would make better surgeons because they were more tender and as a result would be more attuned to alleviating pain. Further complicating matters is that Carlile's own views shifted. By the time he wrote *What Is Love?* (1825), he was arguing that male and female 'possess the same passions' and 'have the same desires'.[69] On the other hand, he also conceded that not all women are the same in terms of their affective states, which further complicates his sexism. Working-class women were politically and morally superior to upper-class ladies because the latter were 'corrupted with spleen and foul vapour from the perversion and suppression of their natural passions'.[70] In drawing this distinction between women of different classes, Carlile was combining class and gender to further his broader radical critique of aristocracy and the corruption of the idle and parasitic classes. Some of the tensions, then, which previous studies have noted in Carlile's feminism – 'a curious mixture of patriarchal and egalitarian attitudes',[71] in Bush's words – were derived from his understanding of the passions.

In a letter to Elizabeth Fry, Carlile had declared that 'The passions are various; but those which are more frequently called into action are the passions of desire and fear'. In making this declaration he revealed his indebtedness to a long tradition in moral philosophy, derived in part from his reading of Palmer, and one that had been revitalised by utilitarianism in the early nineteenth century.[72] Carlile conceptualised his politics as one that sought to increase human happiness. Elsewhere, he emphasised the affective, utilitarian basis of society: 'Society is instituted by man as an artificial means to increase his pleasurable sensations.'[73] This was inseparable from morality, which he defined as the principle in human action which 'delights to do good, and is pained at the thought of giving pain to others'.[74] Palmer had also argued this in his *Principles of Nature*.[75] Even more revealing was Carlile's assertion to one of his infidel followers, Humphrey Boyle of Leeds, that 'True pleasure cannot be separated from morality', and here, again, he was following in Palmer's footsteps.[76] The context for this assertion was a discussion that the two infidels were conducting through their correspondence (Carlile was still in prison) about societal happiness and the conditions under which it could be increased, or lessened. Restraining base passions was crucial to achieving this objective. As Carlile informed Robert Affleck, one of his Edinburgh supporters, 'I am convinced, that nothing will restrain and control their passions [mankind], but that species of equal power which equal knowledge and equal laws will produce'.[77] This was a shrewd judgement on Carlile's part as it underscored the democratic basis of his affective politics: if progress and increased happiness was the goal, then a precondition for that was a democratic polity.

True to his Paineite credentials, Carlile devoted much more attention to attacking the barriers to happiness than he did in sketching out a positive programme. And here we are reminded of Barbara Rosenwein's suggestion that historians of emotion pay careful attention to what she terms 'emotional repertory', not the just the list of emotion words used by those in the past, but the sequence and coupling of emotions.[78] For Carlile, happiness largely equated to removing fear and constraints which engendered misery. This explains why he devoted very little space – far less than Paine – to outlining ambitious programmes of state-sponsored reform. Unusually among radicals, Carlile was broadly supportive of the ideological thrust of liberal political economy with only a few caveats such as the abuses of the factory system, or support for land reform.[79] He was no socialist. Carlile's was a destructive radicalism, ever-ready with its axe. 'I hate the hypocrisy, the cruelty, that would stifle or disguise a virtuous passion', he began his essay on *What Is Love?* Marriage and the difficulties of divorce was one such barrier as 'love withers under constraint'.[80] To be denied love and the sexual gratification which should accompany marriage was abnormal and damaging. Developing this theme in *What Is Love?*, he reasoned that bachelors and old maids were 'hybrid or sub-animal class; for to be loveless is certainly to have some defect in body or in mind'.[81] Those like Malthus and the advocates of abstinence, Carlile accused of suffering from disordered passions which they wished to inflict on everyone else.[82] As we have seen with his juxtaposition of the natural passion of love with the artificial passion of class distinctions, an irrational political and social order was another such barrier. Thus, Carlile conceptualised the social order in affective terms. But the main barrier as he saw it, just as Paine had, was Christianity. The evolution of Carlile's religious beliefs, from deism to atheism and finally to an allegorical form of Christianity, have puzzled historians, just as they did some of his contemporaries. One of the constants in all this was his attack on organised religion and the ways in which it fostered bad passions among mankind.

In the second half of the 1820s, Carlile periodically exchanged the life of a London journalist, publisher and bookseller for that of an itinerant lecturer. His goal was simple: 'I have but one passion that is predominant, and that is the desire to break down all the superstition and oppressions that are found among mankind.'[83] Though never an accomplished orator, he did gain valuable experience on the lecture circuit and he began to develop a lively style once he gained in confidence.[84] By 1833 when he was preaching his brand of Christian atheism he tellingly referred to himself as the 'messiah of reason', which tried to capture something of the millenarian mood that was sweeping across Britain at this time. Others observed in Carlile 'a growing "messianic ... temperament and conviction" '; hardly the characteristics of an austere radical in pursuit of pure reason.[85] During the infidel tours, he was keenly aware of the role of heightened feeling, two in particular, that were responsible for the crowds he attracted: excitement (by which he meant hatred, horror and disgust among local evangelicals who turned out to accost him or abetted the mob to pelt him) and curiosity.[86]

Like other infidels in pursuit of reason, Carlile could never completely divorce himself from the affective. The American infidel-feminist Frances Wright in her first lecture at the Owenite community at New Harmony, Indiana, reproduced verbatim in Carlile's new periodical *The Lion*, asserted, 'Truth needs not the excitement of passion to be felt'.[87] Pure reason, it turns out, was something that needed to be felt to be understood. The passion Carlile set himself against, above all others, was religious bigotry and intolerance. In his dedication of the second volume of the *Deist* (another periodical he began publishing in 1819), he counselled 'cool and candid examination' of the arguments against the 'quick sensations' excited by his calumniators.[88] But once again, the pursuit of cool reason turns out, on closer inspection, to be an affective experience: a central aspect of the affective politics of radical infidelity was counteracting the fear which surrounded areas such as sex and death, so often used for scaremongering by the clergy.[89] One of Carlile's stated aims in authoring *What Is Love?* was to promote contraception with the aim of making sexual intercourse 'a pleasure independent of the dread of a conception'.[90]

Radical infidels like Carlile went to great lengths to counter the myths of death-bed conversion and the lurid tales of horrific infidel deaths spread by evangelicals.[91] Engaging infidels on the rational plain of philosophical and intellectual debate ran the risk of lending credence to such opinions, especially given the propensity of those like Carlile to use their trials to read verbatim the full texts which had led to prosecution. Hence the recourse by the political elite and their apologists to fear and traducing. Even this was far from effective. As Carlile had the satisfaction of lecturing the Vice Society: 'Make anything a mystery, cry it up as something forbidden, and, directly, you create an appetite for it that would not have been otherwise created. Thus, in every shape, your Vice Society has engendered the passion it affected to suppress.'[92] He rejected accusations that infidels were depraved and creatures of base passions. This assertion was the leitmotif in one of the lesser-known loyalist parodies of 1820, *The Christian House Built by Truth*, prompted by Carlile's trial for blasphemy. Through publishing 'vile books' (such as those by Paine and Palmer), this 'vile mushroom race' (infidels) sought to 'entangle the hearts of the wild and deprav'd'. What turned this loyalist feeling of disgust into utter revulsion was the perverse delight infidels derived from their scepticism. Such profaneness for the spiritual led to the 'despising of the laws' temporal, which induced the masses to revolt.[93] Carlile utterly rejected this specious slander. If infidels were so morally depraved, why had none been brought to the gallows, he asked? This he attributed to the fact that a deist 'places himself under a continual moral restraint, and regulates well his passions'.[94]

Unfortunately, these claims were seriously dented in a high-profile murder case at Leicester in June 1832 when a bookseller, James Cook, murdered a salesman, apparently for no other motive than robbing him of his money. What shocked the public was the gruesome details of the murder: the salesman was beaten to death with an iron rod to the point of extreme disfigurement. During his trial, Cook eventually confessed and attributed the beginnings of his slide into immorality to the reading of Paine and Carlile and to the frequenting of a group of infidels in Leicester, a confession that was seized upon by the press and evangelical Christians.[95] This prompted Carlile to publish a long letter refuting the inference that infidelity led to a disordering of the passions. He began by pointing out that his publications had led to the abatement of 'political excitement' by promoting rational and sober discussion. Second, developing a line of argument he had been marshalling for over a decade,[96] he claimed that it was Christianity that inflamed men's passions and brutalised people with its Biblical tales of killing, violence, vengeance and lasciviousness. It was religious passion that was the cause of so many murders in history, its perpetrators secure in the knowledge that all would be forgiven if they repented.[97] Religion did more than inflame the passions; it licensed them in the name of zeal.[98]

The authorities were, unsurprisingly, unconvinced – and had been since Carlile's trial for blasphemy in 1819. Carlile was condemned, in the words of one outraged loyalist, because 'he gloried in his horrid blasphemies' and was 'without shame'.[99] This was clearly the incorrect response to horror and was viewed as confirmation that infidels were deviants. Such views were also a commentary on the public–private divide. Disbelief was acceptable in private, but in public it was horrible, while using it for political and pecuniary purposes was disgusting and dangerous. It was for this reason that William Wilberforce, arguing the merits with the Sheffield evangelical Samuel Roberts of whether punishing Carlile would attract unnecessary attention to his blasphemy, insisted on the need to use the full force of the law. This, Wilberforce asserted, was necessary to stamp out such 'moral poison' lest it continue to 'seduce the … imaginations' of the people.[100] Wilberforce, along with the Vice Society, knew that simply labelling it disgusting was not enough to combat Carlile's infidelity. After all, the problem with disgust is that it does not always repel – forcing one to turn away – it can also be alluring.[101] As Wilberforce's comments imply, disgust needed to be backed up with fear, in this case fear of punishment to deter others from following in Carlile's footsteps.

Feeling for reason

Carlile's path to 'pure reason' was paved with affective tensions, while it turns out that the destination of 'pure reason' was a state of happiness. In one crucial respect, this feeling for reason did not constitute a fundamental departure from the Paineite tradition. Paine no less than Carlile frequently appealed to feelings in his 'rationalist' writings.[102] Carlile did not conceptualise liberty as an abstract, cerebral concept, but something that had to be felt, and the affective state was pleasure: 'Liberty can only be defined to be a government founded on the will and pleasure of the people.'[103] There is no doubt that Carlile spent the earlier part of the 1820s trying to disassociate himself and his followers from the contaminations of popular culture and irrationality.[104] There was more going on here than simply a capitulation to middle-class liberalism, individualism and respectability, a dubious lens through which to make sense of an ultra-radical.[105] Rather, as we saw in the introduction, this was a reaction to the sentimentalism of the radical response to the Queen Caroline affair of 1820, including Carlile's own tears, though his response to the affair was not quite as diversionary as his biographers have claimed.[106] The affair 'taught people to hate monarchy', or so Carlile thought, and, above all, it underscored the affective basis of tyrannical and despotic rule: 'It is repugnant to despotic feelings to live in affection and concord with those who are considered subjects. To reign by any other means than terror has ever been the disposition of the despot.'[107] Carlile concluded that this feeling was not only the preserve of monarchs, but also families, i.e., aristocracy. Finally, some of the comments that he made during the Caroline agitation concerning marriage and love implicitly anticipated some of the arguments of *What Is Love?* Nevertheless, the wave of sentimentalism that surrounded the Queen's affair had been distasteful to the rational republicanism that Carlile preached: 'the corruptions and delusions of the day required to be attacked with something stronger than squib and pasquinade'; these might annoy or amuse but they were 'ill adapted to convey principles to the mind'.[108]

It was not just the melodrama of the Caroline agitation that troubled him. His quest for pure reason was also meant to be an antidote to 'the folly and madness' that Carlile alleged had led to violent radical episodes such as the Cato Street conspiracy when Spencean radicals had plotted the assassination of the cabinet, a group that he had been close to.[109] This can be interpreted as Carlile's attempt to construct and police a set of feeling rules that prized reason above all else, and he was always on the lookout for transgressions – among foe and friend alike. Carlile used Paine as a weapon in his battles with fellow reformers, berating them for their sentimental and brutish attachment to monarchy and institutional Christianity. In Carlile's

opinion, Cobbett and Hunt – his major rivals as leaders of popular radicalism – were too emotional and predisposed to attack persons rather than
principles.[110] His solution, according to Belchem and Epstein, was ideological purification and physical puritanism – a distillation of pure Paineite
rationalism of 'counter-cultural rigour'.[111] The problem is that when we
view his career over the broader period of 1817–32, the emphasis on 'pure
reason' in the early 1820s appears to be the exception rather than the norm.
Even during the early 1820s, he was never able to fully realise his quest for
pure reason unsullied by feeling because of the many accommodations he
made with popular culture and the 'irrational' that he claimed to abhor, to
say nothing of his frequently falling short of his own stated ascetic standards.

Carlile's personal conduct could belie his stated, tightly bound feeling
rules. One might also wonder just how much he led an ascetic lifestyle in
practice, given his penchant for pies and puddings – by his own admission he had become too corpulent – along with his roving eye for attractive
women. His own relationship with women could fall markedly short of
his feminist manifesto. As we shall see in his relationship with his second
wife, Eliza Sharples, he could be controlling, and his insistence that the
needs of his first wife, Jane, and family be strictly subordinated to the cause
could easily degenerate into a patriarchal dominance and callous neglect.[112]
It was not just his own bodily practices which undermined his asceticism,
but also, more significantly, his political, printing and publishing practices.
Throughout the 1820s, Carlile had been a savvy publisher-editor, quite willing to resort to populist idioms to disseminate his message. This included
satirical humour, which he not only sold and published but also produced.
He might express a personal aversion to the intellectually deadening role
of imaginative literature, but he still published and sold it – not just *Wat
Tyler* but Shelley's *Queen Mab*, Byron's *Cain* and *Vision of Judgement*,
and Voltaire's drama *Saul*.[113] A telling instance of just how much Carlile
seemed to be wrestling to suppress his natural creative and poetic side in
the early 1820s was his response to reading, for the first time, the epitaph
that William Carver had delivered at Paine's funeral in 1809. Carver for-
warded this to him in a letter published in the *Republican*. Having judged
Carver to be a sub-standard poet, and after disclaiming the value of poetry
('I look at rhyming as trifling with common sense ... [and] it has been substituted for reason in exciting the passions', he said on another occasion),
Carlile nonetheless proceeded to publish his own highly poetic epitaph.[114]
He continued to publish and occasionally author poems, sonnets, songs,
ballads, doggerel, squibs, dramas and mock prayers in the 1830s just as he
had in 1817–19: 'Move the heart of the King, O Lord God, to dismiss ...
the Necessary Women! (*necessary for what?*)'. The repetition of the refrain
'Move the heart' in this mock prayer, which occurs many times, underscores

his disdain for religious sentiment by locating it in the heart. This parodic seating of the passions had also appeared in an earlier satire that Carlile produced.[115] Such populist idioms, however, could serve purposes other than titillation for the vulgar masses. Introducing to the readers of the *Lion* some 'doggerel' that he had authored, Carlile owned that 'There are some men ... I think below the merit of a reason, and when I desire to speak of them, I feel, that my contempt will allow me to speak of them only in rhyme'.[116] Reason, it seems, was only for the regenerate – an interesting and convenient way of excusing the resort to feeling.

Dabbling in doggerel, poetry, satirical humour and visual satire were not the only evidence of an enduring populism. We can also see some of this interplay between Paineite rationalism and populist idioms in Carlile's efforts to consolidate the cult of Paine in the 1820s. This encompassed more than simply publishing Paine's work: he also sold portraits, busts, medallions and statues (complete with a coat of arms) of Paine at his shop. Carlile was typically contradictory here: while berating Cobbett's sentimental attachment to the bones of Paine and claiming that the latter's published works was the only monument he needed, he confessed that 'I should like his skull', and he was clearly willing to sell sentimental merchandise, if only to make money.[117] The grandest of Carlile's souvenirs was a three-foot statue of Paine that he had specially commissioned, featuring an illuminated glass globe displaying the United States and accompanied with the inscription 'To reason with despots is throwing Reason away. The best of arguments is a rigorous preparation.' Reason, it would appear once again, was only for the regenerate.[118] Carlile's various premises in Fleet Street, the 'temple[s] of reason' were not quite the space devoid of humour, theatricality and personalisation of politics that he claimed. From as early as 1819 down to the mid-1830s, he was known for displaying provocative images and models in his windows.[119] So provocative, in fact, that he was nearly the victim of iconoclasm from outraged Christians who insisted that he remove the statue of Paine. By the mid-1830s, he was displaying effigies of clerical figures (arm-in-arm with the figure of the Devil) in protest at church rates (Figure 2.2). Eventually the authorities instructed him to take them down. Such blatant displays of blasphemy aroused the ire of militant Christians and the authorities. As Figure 2.2 implies, the double layering of Carlile's affective politics is aptly depicted with the ground floor representing reason and order, and the upper floor feeling and disorder. These exhibits suggest that he knew just how important 'the small area of pavement in front of the shop' could be when used to display visual satire for the deliberate purpose of exciting interest and provoking ire. As Brian Maidment has argued, it was this kind of intrusion – of imagery intruding from the shop windows – into the street which made print shops a source

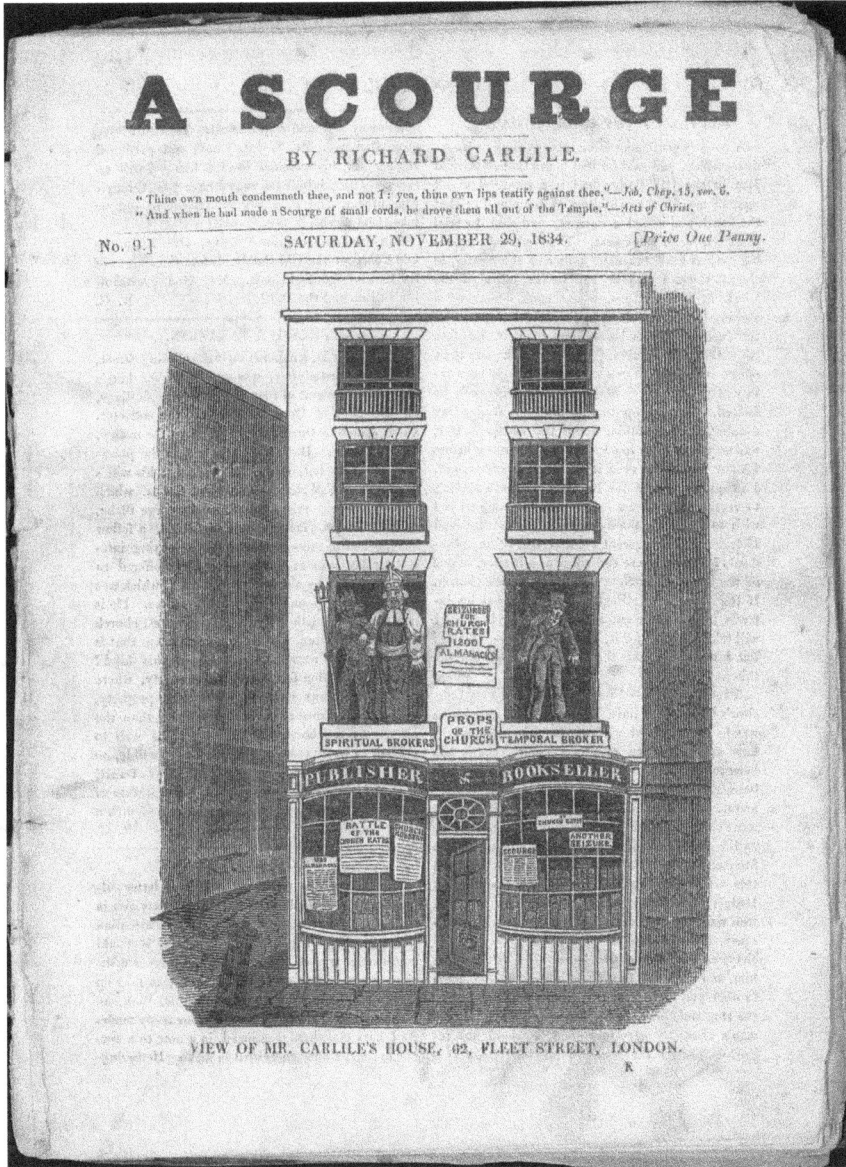

Figure 2.2 View of Mr Carlile's house, 62 Fleet Street, London (1834).

of anxiety for the authorities, a perspective we can extend here to Carlile's radical bookshop: 'I saw at Carlile's window a great many placards exhibited around which a crowd' gathered, reported a spy.[120]

The irony was that during the 1820s when many radical infidel followers were invoking Paine as the litmus test of genuine radicalism, Carlile was beginning to question some of Paine's religious ideas, to the extent that by the late 1820s he no longer enjoyed the status that he once did with him. In the process, Carlile jettisoned deism and embraced atheist materialism. His materialist phase did not last long. Having moved from deism to atheism, he began from the mid-1820s to view Christianity as a perversion of a much older allegory with Pagan roots which stood for the principle of reason 'figured to mankind under various names' – Prometheus, Logos, Christ.[121] Soon Carlile came to the view that Christianity could be purged of its many corruptions and stripped back to the underlying principle of reason. This was a position that was hardly unusual at the time, even though his particular shifts raised some eyebrows.[122]

This move was underlined by the partnership he struck in 1828, emerging for some time, with the eccentric defrocked clergyman Robert Taylor. Taylor's blend of blasphemy and allegorical Christianity, allied to his charismatic oratory and burlesque humour seemed far removed from Paineite rationalism and sober Enlightenment deism.[123] The culmination of this populist turn was the opening of the Rotunda in Blackfriars road as a lecture hall in May 1830, a joint venture between Carlile and Taylor, which would serve as one of the premier hubs of London radicalism between 1830 and 1831. Once again, Carlile alluded to the blend between reason and feeling in his announcement that the Rotunda would be 'the birth-place of mind, and the focus of virtuous public excitement'.[124] It would be easy to dismiss Carlile's partnership with Taylor as little more than opportunistic, but the correspondence between the two men suggests that the bond went deeper than this. While making allowance for his attempts to rescue Taylor from the morose pit of depression into which he had sunk during his imprisonment for blasphemy, Carlile, in a notable display of feeling, told Taylor that 'If you die, we shall not fill the chasm for many years, if all the genius of England were to unite its efforts.' Later in the letter he declared that 'I am more than a brother – I have an estate in your life. I shall lose and not gain an estate in your death.'[125] Such sentimental outpourings were becoming more the norm with Carlile as the 1820s gave way to the 1830s. When he was tried for sedition at the Old Bailey in 1831, he tellingly said that the only crime he was guilty of was extending a 'feeling heart' to the rioting agricultural labourers, a far cry from the austere radical infidel of the previous decade.[126]

This sentimentalism was a harbinger of the feelings that Carlile would display towards Eliza Sharples – 'Isis' as she was named – who took over the Rotunda during his incarceration and would eventually become his second wife (though the marriage was 'moral' rather than legal). The result was that Carlile found his hitherto relatively tightly bound feeling rules under strain, an effect produced in all probability by being genuinely in love, possibly for the first time, having found a soulmate who shared so many of his views. Try as he might to conceptualise his love in philosophical terms and to counsel reason in both himself and Eliza,[127] the contrast with his hitherto restraint was striking: 'I am enamoured with love', he told her, 'I love with all my heart, with all my mind, and with all my soul, and with all my strength'. In a telling aphorism, he likened his state of mind to that of the English constitution: 'In vain have I been endeavouring to find out the charms of [love] ... But no, like the glorious Constitution of England, its charms are lost, are hidden, and the more you become acquainted with either the more anxious are you to run away from both.'[128] Over the coming months when Isis found herself under attack for professions of public infidelity, the stirrings of chivalry further strained Carlile's emotional composure. Recall his advice to Taylor while in prison, and contrast that with Carlile to his own gaoler some three years later: 'if you attempt again to offer me a personal insult, or to address me in any other style than as you would address a gentleman or a good man in or out of prison, I will, on the spot wring your nose for you'.[129] Granted, these were private exchanges, written in the heat of the moment no doubt, but even so this is a different Carlile from the man who had claimed that it was not in the power of anyone to insult him.

Thus, Carlile's politics, already unstable because of the affective tensions and contradictions in his quest for pure reason, were increasingly being undermined by his growing sentimentalism, irritability, intolerance and rancour. There can be no doubt that his emerging mental instability, and eventually partial paralysis, was due in large measure to the mercury 'treatment' he had daily subjected himself to since 1824. Interestingly, when he first began ingesting a daily globule of mercury, he reported how very soon it removed the chronic sciatica pain he had been suffering from for years.[130] Modern studies of prolonged mercury poising list, ironically, 'emotional lability' as a symptom,[131] though whether Carlile suffered from this is impossible to tell. His behaviour certainly became more erratic: he would be charged with assaulting Robert Taylor in 1834, following the collapse of their partnership and friendship.[132] Leaving aside Carlile's mental health, after the Rotunda began to decline in popularity in 1831, his influence began to wane, especially when he found himself at loggerheads with a new generation of radicals over strategy and goals.[133] Some of this was clearly motivated by jealously, and it was nothing new.

Carlile had spent much of the 1820s being jealous of Hunt and Cobbett's influence, a feeling that was entirely mutual. This jealousy was expressed in claims of cowardice, and counterclaims of bravery, which is illustrative of the affective qualities and defects associated with radical leadership. Carlile and Hunt, for example, engaged in a series of public quarrels about who was

most cowardly at Peterloo, both having been on the platform when the yeomanry charged the crowd. Carlile cleverly turned the tables on Hunt, first,
by legitimating his own fear for the safety of the people – 'if any man could
view such a scene without agitation or emotion, he must have been deficient
of common sensibility'. And second, by rounding on Hunt for his express
instruction that the people attend the meeting unarmed: 'Throughout the
whole scene of carnage, I declare solemnly, that I felt nothing so much as a
deep grief to think that so many brave fellows were assembled without the
means of resistance.'[134] By the early 1830s, Carlile was losing this sort of
affective perspicacity, by which time he had transferred his jealousies to a
new generation of radicals, some of whom had initially supported Carlile
but recoiled in disgust at the way he treated his first wife and family.[135]
He was clearly frustrated by the greater successes of the Chartists and the
Owenites.[136] But the more he accused his rivals of irrationality, the more
it rebounded on him: for all his stricture to never trade in personalities, he
found it virtually impossible to practise what he preached.[137]

Ironically, Carlile's rancour and increasing sentimentalism meant that
when he was imprisoned in 1831 and again in the mid-1830s, he was not
able to fully exploit sympathy for his predicament, and by extension the
cause of radical infidelity. As his American friend, the Scottish born Robert
L. Jennings astutely observed in February 1830, sympathy had always been
Carlile's major asset. It was the absence of sympathy in America for freethinkers which Jennings held responsible for the limited progress of infidelity compared to Britain. He told Carlile

> Infidelity is spreading rapidly in this country but we have one great obstacle –
> indirect persecution. In England, the use of force to suppress liberalism elicits
> sympathy and promotes enquiry – but here we have an indirect persecution
> which robs a man of the means of subsistence and thus starves him into hypo-
> critical submission and silence.[138]

The problem for the authorities in Britain was that civil society proved
much less reliable in policing blasphemy than in the USA; hence the repeated
recourse to the law. Once that sympathy was withdrawn, because of Carlile's
irascibility, allied to the fact that the government shrewdly never imprisoned
him again, his career as a radical leader was over, tied as it had been so
closely to the prison cell.

Conclusion

If anyone within nineteenth-century British radicalism aspired to a politics
devoted to the pursuit of reason unsullied by feeling, it was Carlile who

undoubtedly tried to create and practise an austere republican-infidel politics. But that quest for a politics of pure reason was doomed to failure because his conception of political reason was an affective construct based not only on suffering and pain but also certain kinds of pleasure. Even 'reason's republic' required men to have certain kinds of feeling, and here Carlile was merely the latest in a long line of moral philosophers who argued that rationality had to be underpinned by feeling.[139] His ascetic radicalism also failed because of his accommodations with popular culture, and while this might not have been a problem, the fact that he had claimed so insistently in the 1820s to practise the austere republicanism that he preached meant that he was, in his failure to live up to this, hoist by his own petard. Paradoxically, the more Carlile compromised – as demonstrated by the infidel tours and the Rotunda episode – the more popular his brand of radicalism became, but just as he could never fully liberate himself from popular culture, so, too, was he unwilling to abandon the quest for pure reason. Underpinning that quest was also another assumption which prevented his radical infidelism from becoming a mass movement: too many working-class people were creatures of their base passions. 'My passion for reform consists of a desire to see the aggregate of mankind raised above the character and condition of the brute animal world', he declared.[140] But contained within that declaration was the assumption that so many of the masses *were* brutes.

Carlile and his band of rational republicans may have been anti-sentimental, but they were not, could not be, anti-sentiment. For in confronting the mighty power of religion, Atlantic infidels, from Paine and Palmer through to Carlile and Frances Wright, knew only too well that this power rested, in part, on inculcating feelings of awe and fear which would have to be combated in any assault on its temporal power. Removing fear was a central goal of Carlile's affective politics not just in the public sphere but also in the bedroom. Unfortunately, for radical infidels, the 1830s saw a resurgence of Christianity, which also shaped the next generation of popular radicals, many of whom had little sympathy, much less affinity, with freethinkers. Radical Christianity was the order of the day.[141] The case study of Carlile also shows that debates about the location of the passions could have significant political ramifications. In his view, the erroneous seating of the passions in the head or the heart played a part in enslaving mankind. By relocating them in the body, he sought to banish the irrational fears and ignorance that religion and romantics had placed in the head and the heart through false notions of a divinely created immortal soul. 'Man is body, mortal body, and nothing but mortal body', Carlile proclaimed in 1824.[142] This was a view that was shared by another Atlantic infidel, Robert Owen whose affective politics are the focus of the next chapter.

Notes

1 The term 'infidel' began life as a term of abuse directed at deists and freethinkers, but like many pejoratives it was adopted as a badge of pride. The term had also become conjoined with radicalism in politics. This 'double radicalism' not only attacked organised religion but also advocated democratic republicanism. When wielded by its enemies, 'infidel' was meant to incite feelings of horror and disgust, not least because, in Royle's words, the term signified 'anyone who rejected orthodox Christianity and who combined such a rejection with a low social position or an appeal to those in such a position'. Edward Royle (ed.), *The Infidel Tradition from Paine to Bradlaugh* (London: Macmillan, 1976), p. xvi.

2 *Free Enquirer*, 19 November 1828. Even Carlile's enemies were forced to concede how indomitable he was, even in the face of imprisonment, poverty, or both. TNA, HO 64/11, secret service report, December 1827, fol. 37.

3 John Belchem, *'Orator' Hunt: Henry Hunt and English Working Class Radicalism* (London: Breviary, 2012), pp. 5, 114–19.

4 Iain McCalman, 'Popular radicalism and freethought in early nineteenth century England: a study of Richard Carlile and his followers, 1815–32' (Australian National University MA thesis, 1975); James Epstein, *Radical Expression: Political Language, Ritual, and Symbol in England, 1790–1850* (Oxford: Oxford University Press, 1993), chapter 4; Joel Wiener, *Radicalism and Freethought in Nineteenth-Century Britain: The Life of Richard Carlile* (Westport, CT: Garland, 1983), p. 65.

5 Iain McCalman, *Radical Underworld: Prophets, Revolutionaries, and Pornographers in London, 1795–1840* (Oxford: Oxford University Press, 1993), p. 216. Taken together, this historiography has resulted in the marginalisation of Carlile as a faddist crank who had little following. Yet as Michael Bush has recently shown in his study of Carlile's 'zetetic' followers (seekers after rational truth), he attracted a 'considerable following' in the 1820s. M.L. Bush, *The Friends and Followers of Richard Carlile* (South Lopham: Twopenny Press, 2016).

6 This began with an article 'What is love?' published in Carlile's periodical the *Republican*. The article was subsequently expanded and published as *Every Woman's Book*. For a history of the text, see M.L. Bush (ed.), *What Is Love? Richard Carlile's Philosophy of Sex* (London: Verso, 1998 [1826]), chapter 1.

7 E.g., by the late 1820s American freethought periodicals were following Carlile's career closely and often published lengthy extracts from his periodicals. *Republican*, 8 August 1823 (Carlile to William Carver). See also Celia Morris Eckhardt, *Fanny Wright: Rebel in America* (Cambridge, MA: Harvard University Press, 1984), p. 225. The last of Carlile's periodicals to gain any significant popularity, *Isis* (1832), was published in New York as well as London. See also Eric R. Schlereth, *An Age of Infidels: The Politics of Religious Controversy in the Early United States* (Philadelphia: University of Pennsylvania Press, 2013), p. 6.

8 Roderick S. French, 'Elihu Palmer, rational deist, radical republican: a reconsideration of American freethought', *Studies in Eighteenth-Century Culture*, 8 (1979), p. 90. As he did with Paine, Carlile endeavoured to publish the whole

of Palmer's oeuvre: McCalman, 'Popular radicalism', pp. 216–17. For John Fellows, see Christopher Grasso, *Skepticism and American Faith: From the Revolution to the Civil War* (New York: Oxford University Press, 2018), p. 118.

9 *Republican*, 1 and 8 August 1823, 5 November 1824.

10 Acknowledgements to David Turner, Swansea University, for pointing this out.

11 Elihu Palmer, *Principles of Nature* (London, 1819), pp. 40, 107, 141.

12 For Carlile's interest in and understanding of science, see Adrian Desmond, 'Artisan resistance and evolution in Britain, 1819–1848', *Osiris*, 3 (1987), 77–110. See also J.F.C. Harrison, 'Early Victorian radicals and the medical fringe', in W.F. Bynum and R. Porter (eds), *Medical Fringe and Medical Orthodoxy* (London: Routledge, 1987), pp. 198–215.

13 Richard Carlile, *To the Reformers of Great Britain* (London, 1821), p. 18.

14 Joanna Bourke, *The Story of Pain: From Prayer to Painkillers* (Oxford: Oxford University Press, 2014), p. 17.

15 *Republican*, 7 July 1820.

16 *Moralist*, vol. 1, no. 1 (n.d. [1823]).

17 Huntington Library, San Marino, Richard Carlile Papers, RC 423, Richard Carlile to W.V. Holmes, 17 October 1825.

18 Nicole Eustace, *Passion is the Gale: Emotion, Power, and the Coming of the American Revolution* (Chapel Hill, NC: University of North Carolina Press, 2008), chapter 1.

19 *Republican*, 5 May 1826.

20 T.M. Parssinen, 'Popular science and society: the phrenology movement in early Victorian Britain', *Journal of Social History*, 8 (1974), 1–20; John D. Davies, *Phrenology Fad and Science: A 19th-Century American Crusade* (New Haven: Yale University Press, 1955).

21 *Republican*, 27 June 1823, 24 October 1823. On radicalism and phrenology, see Roger Cooter, *The Cultural Meaning of Popular Science: Phrenology and the Organization of Consent in Nineteenth-Century Britain* (Cambridge: Cambridge University Press, 1984), pp. 208, 216.

22 Wiener, *Radicalism and Freethought*, p. 112.

23 *Republican*, 27 June 1823.

24 *Ibid.*, 24 October 1823.

25 *Ibid.*

26 *Ibid.*, 19 November 1824.

27 *Ibid.*, 8 December 1826.

28 *Ibid.*, 12 March 1824.

29 *Ibid.*, 25 November 1825.

30 *Ibid.*, 27 June 1823.

31 *Ibid.*, 24 October 1823, 6 May 1825 and 13 October 1826.

32 Fay Bound Alberti, *Matters of the Heart: History, Medicine and Emotion* (Oxford: Oxford University Press, 2010), pp. 6–7, 14.

33 Barbara H. Rosenwein and Ricardo Cristiani, *What is the History of Emotions?* (Cambridge: Polity, 2018), p. 64.

34 *Republican*, 18 January 1822, 21 May 1824, 8 August 1823. This admission seems difficult to square with Ryan Hanley's description of Carlile as a

racist: Ryan Hanley, 'Slavery and the birth of working-class racism in England, 1814–1833', *Transactions of the Royal Historical Society*, 26 (2016), 120–1.

35 *Republican*, 27 June 1823.

36 Frances Henry, 'Love, sex and the noose: the emotions of sodomy in 18th-century England' (PhD dissertation, University of Western Ontario, 2019), pp. 34–5.

37 *Moralist*, No. 16 (n.d. [1823], on anger).

38 *Republican*, 7 November 1823.

39 *Ibid.*, 21 November 1823. For similar examples of contagion, see *Republican*, 25 April 1823 (Carlile to Judge Bailey).

40 Carlile Papers, RC 323, Richard Carlile to Robert Taylor, 26 July 1831.

41 *Boston Investigator*, 12 October 1832; Robert Dale Owen, *Moral Physiology* (New York, 1831), pp. 13, 33, 39.

42 *Wooler's British Gazette*, 29 August 1819.

43 Rob Boddice, *Pain: A Very Short Introduction* (Oxford: Oxford University Press, 2017), p. 17 and chapter 6.

44 Richard Carlile, *A Letter to the Society for the Suppression of Vice* (London, 1819), p. 6.

45 *Prompter*, 29 January 1830.

46 William M. Reddy, *The Navigation of Feeling: A Framework for the History of Emotions* (Cambridge: Cambridge University Press, 2001), pp. 104–5. For a psychological profiling of Carlile during his imprisonment in the 1820s, see Wiener, *Radicalism and Freethought*, pp. 57–9.

47 HSP, Simon Gratz Autograph Collection, 250A, Case 13, Box 21, fragment of a letter in Carlile's hand, 8 July 1824.

48 The Home Office was receiving regular reports from a spy about the parlous state of Carlile's finances in the late 1820s along with the challenges this posed for his family. Carlile's debts were estimated at £2,000 by the end of 1828: TNA, HO 64/11, secret service report, 11 October 1828, fol. 68.

49 *Boston Investigator*, 12 October 1832.

50 Wiener, *Radicalism and Freethought*, p. 55; Michael T. Davis, Iain McCalman and Christina Parolin (eds), *Newgate in Revolution: An Anthology of Radical Prison Literature in the Age of Revolution* (London: Bloomsbury, 2005), p. x; Katrina Navickas, 'The "bastilles" of the constitution: political prisoners, radicalism, and prison reform in early nineteenth-century England', *LHR*, 83 (2018), 97–123.

51 Carlile Papers, RC 323, Carlile to Taylor, 26 July 1831. For similar boasts by Carlile about his emotional restraint, see *Republican*, 11 July 1823 (reviewing Cartwright's *English Constitution*).

52 Carlile Papers, RC 308, Carlile to Lord Mayor of London, 11 March 1833; Theophila Carlile Campbell, *The Battle of the Press: The Life of Richard Carlile* (London, 1899), p. 17.

53 *Free Enquirer*, 7 January 1829.

54 Carlile Papers, RC 324, Carlile to John Teague, 10 March 1833.

55 For the practised body, see Rosenwein and Cristiani, *What is the History of Emotions?*, chapter 3.

56 Rob Boddice, *The History of Emotions* (Manchester: Manchester University Press, 2018), pp. 192, 202.

57 *Moralist*, No. 2 (n.d. [1823]).

58 *Republican*, 19 July 1822; Wiener, *Radicalism and Freethought*, p. 127.

59 *Isis*, 24 March 1832; *Republican*, 5 July 1822. For similar rebukes of revelry, drunkenness and violence and the base passions they engendered, see *Republican*, 25 April 1823 (prize fighting), 27 June 1823 (Whitsuntide), 9 May 1823 (whipping).

60 *Republican*, 6 May 1825; *Lion*, 3 October 1828.

61 Matthew McCormack, *The Independent Man: Citizenship and Gender Politics in Georgian England* (Manchester: Manchester University Press 2005), p. 209.

62 *Republican*, 6 May 1825.

63 *Ibid.*, 2 August 1822.

64 *Ibid.*, 23 August 1822.

65 Henry, 'Love, sex and the noose', p. 50.

66 *Republican*, 8 December 1820.

67 McCalman, *Radical Underworld*, p. 206.

68 *Republican*, 27 June 1823. For Carlile's feminism and relationship with women, see Iain McCalman, 'Females, feminism and free love in an early nineteenth century radical movement', *LHR*, 38 (1980), 1–25; Angela Keane, 'Richard Carlile's working women: selling books, politics, sex, and *The Republican*', *Literature & History*, 15 (2006), 20–33; Christina Parolin, *Radical Spaces: Venues of Popular Politics in London, 1790–c.1845* (Canberra: ANU Press, 2010), chapters 3, 8.

69 Bush, *What Is Love?*, pp. 24, 57.

70 *Republican*, 21 May 1824.

71 Bush, *Friends and Following*, p. 22.

72 Palmer focused on the relationship between morality, happiness and free-thought in his short-lived periodical *Prospect; or View of the Moral World* (1803–4).

73 *Republican*, 22 August 1823.

74 *Ibid.*, 24 October 1823.

75 Kerry Walters, *Revolutionary Deists: Early America's Rational Infidels* (New York: Prometheus, 2011), p. 198.

76 West Yorkshire Archive Service, Leeds, WYL 623/5/8, Humphrey Boyle Papers, Carlile to Boyle, 3 July 1823.

77 *Republican*, 13 June 1823. For Affleck and the Edinburgh Zetetics, see Gordon Pentland, 'The Freethinkers' Zetetic Society: an Edinburgh radical underworld in the eighteen-twenties', *Historical Research*, 91 (2018), 314–32.

78 Barbara Rosenwein, *Emotional Communities in the Early Middle Ages* (Ithaca: Cornell University Press, 2006), chapter 2.

79 *Lion*, 25 January and 29 February 1828; Malcolm Chase, 'Paine, Spence and the "real rights of man"', *Bulletin of the Society for the Study of Labour History*, 52 (1987), 39.

80 *Lion*, 11 April 1828.

81 Bush, *What Is Love?*, pp. 56–7.

82 *Republican*, 6 May 1825.

83 *Lion*, 29 February 1828.

84 Bush, *Friends and Following*, pp. 358, 363, 366.

85 Philip Lockley, *Visionary Religion and Radicalism in Early Industrial England: From Southcott to Socialism* (Oxford: Oxford University Press, 2013), p. 204.

86 Carlile Papers, RC 584, Deposition of William Smith, 13 May 1830, relating to Carlile's visit to Nottingham, 8 September 1828.

87 *Lion*, 21 August 1829.

88 *Deist*, dedication, vol. 2.

89 Quoted in Bush, *Friends and Following*, p. 39.

90 Bush, *What Is Love?*, p. 75.

91 Schlereth, *Age of Infidels*, pp. 162–4; Laura Schwarz, *Infidel Feminism: Secular, Religion and Women's Emancipation, England, 1830–1914* (Manchester: Manchester University Press 2012), chapter 2.

92 *Republican*, 18 March 1825.

93 *The Christian House, Built by Truth on a Rock; or an Antidote to Infidelity* (London, 1820), pp. 8–9, 16.

94 *Republican*, 12 November 1819.

95 *Public Ledger*, 11 August 1832; *Morning Post*, 11 August 1832; *Bell's Life in London*, 12 August 1832.

96 *Republican*, 31 March 1820 (letter to Hartwell), 12 July 1822 (letter to Reformers calling themselves Christians), 25 April 1823 (letter to Judge Bailey), 16 July 1824 (trial of John Clark); *Lion*, 28 March 1828 (Carlile's response to 'R.P.').

97 *Cosmopolite*, 26 August 1832.

98 *Republican*, 11 April 1823.

99 Anon, *Third Letter from John Nott to his Fellow Townsmen* (Birmingham, 1819), p. 20; M. Adams, *A Parody on the Political House that Jack Built* (London, 1820), p. 11.

100 Sheffield Archives, RP/1/29, Samuel Roberts Papers, William Wilberforce to Samuel Roberts, 24 December 1819. For similar views in the USA, see Schlereth, *Age of Infidels*, p. 99. As Don Herzog has shown, since the 1790s medical idioms – contagion, poison, plague, disease – had saturated loyalist attacks on radicals. Don Herzog, *Poisoning the Minds of the Lower Orders* (Princeton, NJ: Princeton University Press, 1998), p. 97.

101 Rob Boddice, *A History of Feelings* (London: Reaktion, 2019), p. 63.

102 Eustace, *Passion is the Gale*, pp. 439–42; Boddice, *History of Feelings*, pp. 112–15.

103 *Republican*, 8 December 1820.

104 Epstein, *Radical Expression*, pp. 130–41.

105 Belchem, 'Orator Hunt', p. 5.

106 Epstein, *Radical Expression*, p. 132; McCalman, 'Popular radicalism', p. 63, Wiener, *Radicalism and Freethought*, p. 57.

107 *Republican*, 7 July and 1 September 1820.

108 *Ibid.*, 29 December 1820.

109 Wiener, *Radicalism and Freethought*, p. 39. As Wiener notes, Carlile had also advocated recourse to revolutionary violence in 1819–20 following the unprovoked attack on the people at Peterloo, and he was advocated it again during the reform bill episode. TNA HO 64/11, secret service reports, 25 and 27 November 1830, 11 October 1831, fols 130, 134, 252.

110 *Lion*, 25 July 1828.

111 John Belchem, *Popular Radicalism in Nineteenth-Century Britain* (Basingstoke: Macmillan, 1996), p. 51.

112 TNA, HO 64/11, secret service report, 13 August 1827, fol. 7.

113 *Lion*, 14 November 1828; Lord Byron, *Cain: A Mystery* (London: Carlile, 1822). See also the appended catalogue attached to Richard Carlile, *Everyman's Book, or What is God* (London, 1826).

114 *Republican*, 1 August 1823; Carlile Papers, RC 368, Carlile to Holmes, 10 April 1823.

115 *Republican*, 8 October and 5 November 1819; *Lion*, 16 May and 12 September 1828; *Prompter*, 8 January, 26 February, 16 July, 20 August, 17 September, 29 October, 12 November 1831; Carlile Campbell, *Battle of the Press*, pp. 133–4; Richard Carlile, *The Order for the Administration of the Loaves and the Fishes* (London, 1817).

116 *Lion*, 3 July 1829.

117 *Republican*, 8 August 1823. Ian Haywood has interestingly observed that while Cobbett's monument to Paine never materialised, the closest it came – if only on paper – was in the 'republican symbolism of the frontispieces to Richard Carlile's periodical *The Deist*', which 'are the most sublime allegorical tributes to Paine's "immortal" reputation as an Enlightenment thinker'. Ian Haywood, *Romanticism and Caricature* (Cambridge: Cambridge University Press, 2013), p. 118. Carlile, of course, had his own monument to Paine in the window of his shop.

118 *Republican*, 8 October 1819.

119 For another example of Carlile's provocative use of images, see the literal depiction of God he published in the mid-1820s, which he pieced together from descriptions in the Bible and had the audacity to send to the Home Office. Vic Gatrell, *City of Laughter: Sex and Satire in Eighteenth-Century London* (London: Atlantic, 2006), p. 543. This image was so infamous that knowledge of it reached freethinkers in the United States: *Correspondent*, 17 November 1827.

120 Brian Maidment, *Comedy, Caricature and the Social Order, 1820–50* (Manchester: Manchester University Press 2017), pp. 114–15; TNA, HO 40/25, secret service report, 10 November 1830, fol. 211.

121 Richard Carlile, *The Gospel According to Richard Carlile* (London, 1827), p. 4.

122 Carlile's mutations from doubt, deism, atheism to a form of Christianity was much more in line with the trajectories of many American freethinkers such as William Miller (from deist to Baptist minister) and Orestes Brownson

(Presbyterian-Universalist-socialist freethinker-Unitarian). Christopher Grasso, 'Skepticism and American faith: infidels, converts, and religious doubt in the early nineteenth century', *Journal of the Early Republic*, 22 (2002), 465–508.

123 For Taylor, see Iain McCalman, 'Popular irreligion in early Victorian England: infidel preachers and radical theatricality in 1830s London', in Richard W. Davis and Richard J. Helmstadter (eds), *Religion and Irreligion in Victorian Society* (London: Routledge, 1992), pp. 51–67.

124 *Prompter*, 13 November 1830. For the Rotunda as a radical space, see Parolin, *Radical Spaces*, chapters 6–7.

125 Carlile Papers, RC 323, Carlile to Taylor, 26 July 1831.

126 Wiener, *Radicalism and Freethought*, p. 176.

127 Carlile Papers, RC 294, Carlile to Eliza Sharples, n.d. [c.1832]. For Carlile's meeting of Sharples, see Bush, *Friends and Following*, pp. 391–3.

128 Quoted in Carlile Campbell, *The Battle of the Press*, pp. 174–5.

129 Carlile Campbell, *Battle of the Press*, p. 128; Carlile Papers, RC 324, Carlile to John Teague, 10 March 1833.

130 Bush, *Friends and Following*, pp. 46–7.

131 'Mercury poisoning', in Philip Wexler (ed.), *Encyclopaedia of Toxicology* (London: Academic Press/Elsevier, 3rd edn, 2014), www.sciencedirect.com/topics/biochemistry-genetics-and-molecular-biology/mercury-poisoning [accessed 7 July 2020].

132 *Morning Chronicle*, 27 September 1834.

133 Carlile's career was far from over by 1832, but his days as an influential radical leader were behind him. For his later career see Wiener, *Radicalism and Freethought*, chapters 10–12.

134 *Republican*, 12 April 1822. Carlile and Hunt were still arguing over who was cowardly at Peterloo as late as November 1830: TNA, HO 64/11, secret service report, 13 November 1830, fol. 126. Carlile authored and published one of the first accounts of what happened at Peterloo, and the account was deemed sufficiently incendiary that it was sent to the Home Office: TNA HO 42/192, J. Stoddart, enclosing *Sherwin's Political Register*, 20 August 1819, fol. 253.

135 TNA HO 64/11/, secret service report, 23 May 1831, fol. 305.

136 E.g., Carlile Papers, RC 480, Carlile to Thomas Turton, 17 October 1839.

137 Carlile Papers, RC 469, Carlile to Turton, 22 March 1839.

138 Carlile Papers, RC 132, R.L. Jennings to Carlile, 17 February 1830. For a similar observation, see the letter by John Fellows, another of Carlile's American correspondents, to Carlile: *Republican*, 5 November 1824. Eric Schlereth makes exactly this point in his study of the relationship between religion and freethought in the USA: Schlereth, *Age of Infidels*, p. 234

139 Rosenwein and Cristiani, *What is the History of Emotions?*, p. 73.

140 *Lion*, 31 July 1829.

141 Matthew Roberts, 'Posthumous Paine in the United Kingdom, 1809–1832: Jacobin or loyalist cult?', in Sam Edwards and Marcus Morris (eds), *The Legacy of Thomas Paine in the Transatlantic World* (Abingdon: Routledge, 2018), pp. 123–4; Grasso, *Skepticism*, pp. 292–3.

142 *Republican*, 12 March 1824. This was why he was able to offer qualified support for the Anatomy Act of 1832 which, *inter alia*, provided licensed anatomists with a more regular supply of dead bodies, including those of paupers. This was a prospect that filled other radicals, notably William Cobbett and Richard Oastler with horror. Ruth Richardson, *Death, Dissection and the Destitute* (London: Routledge and Kegan Paul, 1988), pp. 169, 100, 373.

3

Robert Owen, harmonic passions and the practice of happiness

Universal happiness was the goal of Robert Owen's 'new moral world' or the 'rational system of society', the names that he and his socialist followers gave to their communitarian system. This world would replace the old immoral world of capitalist competition, private wealth and families, based on the pessimistic Christian view of man's inherent and utter depravity. Owen promised to eradicate bad passions. As he told the inhabitants of New Lanark: 'When these great errors shall be removed, all our evil passions will disappear; no ground of anger or displeasure from one human being towards another will remain; the period of the supposed Millennium will commence, and universal love prevail.'[1] While Owen shared with other radicals the belief that conditions could and should be reordered to bring about happiness for the working classes, he differed from them in terms of how that goal was to be achieved. He had no faith in the redeeming power of democratic politics; such tinkering and cashiering of one set of rulers for another would not bring about the fundamental societal changes that were required. Genuine democracy and happiness could only be realised in self-governing socialist communities based on egalitarian living which replaced competition with co-operation and abolished personal wealth, the private, single family and the institutional power of revealed religion. A total of twenty-nine Owenite communities were established in Britain (nine) and North America (twenty), mostly between the 1820s and 1840s. Each of these communities soon failed due to a combination of differences of opinion on how and when to implement equality and what form that was to take, allied to financial problems, the persistence of various forms of individualism, the lack of necessary skills, to say nothing of Owen's high-handedness and absenteeism.[2] Ironically, the experimental communities collapsed amid rising unhappiness.

Owen's story and the fate of the Owenite communities are well known. From relatively humble beginnings in north Wales (he was born in 1771), by the age of thirty he became the managing partner of New Lanark Mills, the largest cotton spinning factory in Britain, some thirty miles south-east of Glasgow. Over the next two decades, he transformed New Lanark into a model factory run on paternalistic lines with huge profits and, allegedly, happy workers. But Owen was not content to remain a mere factory paternalist, and although the paternalist in him died hard, New Lanark became a springboard for the development of a utopian community. Having failed to seriously interest politicians and clergymen in his projected scheme (a lifelong problem), he went to America in 1824 having learned of how conditions in the United States leant themselves to setting up of alternative communities, several of which had come into existence by the early nineteenth century. Intriguingly for Owen, one was for sale at Harmonie, Indiana, which had been set up by the Rappites, the millenarian followers of the German pietist George Rapp, which Owen bought in 1825. New Harmony, as it was renamed, was transformed into an experimental socialist community. Leaving others to implement his blueprint, Owen continued the itinerant propaganda he had begun in Britain with a view to gaining more support for his scheme, traversing the States and delivering lectures and seeking audiences with influential figures. Retuning to England in 1829, he found himself at the head of an incipient co-operative and socialist movement which had grown up in support of his ideas during his absence in America.

For the next four years, Owen was hailed as a leader of the working-classes, presiding over a militant trades union and co-operative movement which, for a time, supported him. The benevolent, kind-hearted, disarming Mr Owen became a much-loved father figure of the working classes, and even during Chartism's ascendency when the Owenite and Chartist leadership saw one another as rival movements, at the grassroots level there was considerable overlap and joint membership.[3] Owen's working-class followers tried to implement a system of co-operative trading and labour exchange whereby value was based on the amount of labour hours expended on each product rather than the market. With the state clamp-down on trades unionism, culminating in the transportation of the Tolpuddle Martyrs in 1834, Owen and the unions parted company, and Owenism re-emerged as a movement of devoted socialist followers who shared Owen's secular millenarian faith in the inevitable triumph of the new moral world.[4] A vibrant Owenite culture based of fellowship, joy and the inculcation of 'brotherly communal feeling' was created at the grassroots through local 'Halls of Science', as the local Owenite venues came to be known, and through the pages of their periodical the *New Moral World*.[5] Owenism would culminate in the final community of Queenwood in Hampshire which lasted from 1839 to 1845, and following the failure of that community, the movement declined.

If Owen's story is well known, much less has been said about what, exactly, he meant by happiness. As recent work has shown, in the late eighteenth century West, there was a dramatic shift in attitudes towards and understandings of happiness. For the first time, it was now seen as legitimate to pursue happiness. Peter Stearns has viewed this surge in happiness as revolutionary, citing a whole range of factors, notably the Enlightenment and the associated challenge to a particular religious view of the world which believed that one's purpose on earth was to suffer, though as Stearns rightly cautions the happiness surge was not necessarily anti-religious.[6] Joanna Innes has also argued that happiness was politicised in late eighteenth and early nineteenth century Britain as radicals claimed that good government should promote the happiness of the people while mainstream politicians rejected this as it risked promoting anti-social behaviour (with Malthus leading the charge here). But it is not clear from Innes's account what radicals, including Owen whom she mentions in passing, meant by happiness.[7] In contrast to what Innes sees as the dominant view held by the political elite that it was neither possible nor desirable to make everyone happy, Owen believed the opposite because of the wealth countries like Britain were generating.[8] In Owenite formulation, happiness actually meant something quite specific and tended to be used relatively – in short, happiness denoted the absence of negative feelings, and was to be achieved in quite prescriptive ways. Further, we will also see how the feeling of happiness for Owenites was inseparable from its practice. As the first section shows, on the surface Owen appears to be an ascetic radical, but on closer inspection his views on whether feelings were beyond the control of an individual was ambiguous. Owen had an entirely reductive understanding of the passions which led him to turn on its head the prevailing view that negative feelings were the result of bad, immoral character.

Having sketched out the centrality of the passions in Owen's critique of the old moral world, the chapter then moves on to consider how and why Owen believed changing the conditions in which people lived would lead to changes in how they felt. Central here was his belief that happiness would ensue when the passions had been recalibrated and harmonised rather than restrained *per se*, though Owen never satisfactorily resolved the tension between the need to restrain some passions and unshackle others.[9] Although he was never able to completely free himself from Benthamite understandings of happiness (based on hedonism), in contrast to Bentham, Owen's conception of happiness was social rather than individual. While it is difficult to sustain Mark Kaswan's observation that 'the term "happiness" does not appear all that much in Owen's work', there is no doubt that Owen devoted much more attention to how happiness would be achieved rather than with what happiness meant or –crucially – would feel like.[10] Focusing on the tensions and contradiction in Owen's formulation of happiness – and feelings more generally – sheds new light on the reasons why Owenism failed. Given the importance that was attached to happiness and feeling in Owenism, these tensions and contradictions amounted to a fatal flaw.

An ascetic radical?

At first glance, Owen appears to be a quintessential ascetic radical. Fond of the Stoics, especially Seneca, Owen believed that such was the plasticity of human character that it could be made rational or irrational, a commonplace of the Enlightenment that he may have picked up from Godwin, a key influence on the young Owen.[11] Given the right circumstances – the removal of want and careworn anxieties, and through education, habit and discipline – individuals would be able to curb the baser passions of envy, hatred, jealousy and anger. 'Terminat[ing] the bad and inferior passions' was the key to Owenism.[12] As a member of the Queenwood community explained, it was the titles and distinctions of the old world which resulted in 'jealousies and miseries'; while 'equality and mutual consideration' in the new moral world would lead to 'universal love and harmony'.[13] In the view of Owen's radical detractors, the new moral world was designed to suppress feelings of all kinds. Critics such as Robert Southey found it telling that Owen referred to his New Lanark workers as 'human machines' and questioned his insistence that they were happy.[14] Frank Podmore in his biography of Owen, paraphrasing the radical Thomas Wooler's indictment, noted that the new moral world was little more than a 'pauper barracks, where men, women and children would be reduced to mere automata; their feelings, passions and opinions measured out by rule'.[15] But such criticisms, as we shall see, are overstated – not least because Owen's conservative detractors took the opposite view that his system was designed 'to allow unrestrained indulgence in the gratification of the passions'.[16]

Owen's goal was neither to allow free play for all the passions nor to create a joyless, docile workforce of automata, or later, a movement of docile socialist followers. Some popular radicals parted company with him over democratic reform and baulked at his autocratic style of rule, a notable irritant for the future Chartist William Lovett. And there were democratic elements in the trades union movement that rejected Owen's attempts to exert control and spoke out against his overbearing love: 'the sweetest despotism is that of universal love, and this we yield to Mr. Owen; but even that has thorns and briers growing in its path'.[17] This was a shrewd and pointed attack on someone who claimed to be leading his followers to love and happiness. Nevertheless, he was universally respected by the working classes and their radical leaders for the way he tried to raise the dignity of working men:

> Every working man who reads Mr. Owen's essays becomes a new being in his own estimation. He no longer feels himself a mere lump of living mechanism, predestined for the use and abuse of others. He sees that, however degraded he has been made to be, it is possible for him, under new arrangements, to become the equal of those that look down upon him.[18]

This was not an isolated instance of a working man claiming that Owen had changed how they thought and felt about themselves. H.D. Islington, writing in Owen's *Crisis*, emphasised the affective changes he had experienced since becoming an Owenite: 'The change my whole being has undergone since I heard you [Owen], most respected Sir, advocate the people's cause, and teach him the heart-reviving lesion [sic.], to respect himself.' As Islington contemplated this, 'a noble pride swelled within me' and he began to 'feel my own importance'.[19] Historians of radicalism have sometimes struggled to explain how and why working men loved Owen, given his paternalistic and autocratic tendencies, but as Islington and the *Poor Man's Guardian* imply, once we begin to understand the affective basis of that relationship, it becomes clearer. Seen from this perspective, Owenism was designed to readmit the working classes into the category of human, not so much in this case by explicitly contesting the assumption that workers were unfeeling brutes – though that was clearly implied – but more by inculcating a set of empowering feelings anchored in dignity.[20]

Owen was also far less censorious of working-class moral 'failings' such as intemperance than other ascetic radicals, and this brings us to the problem in labelling him as such. In contrast to other ascetic radicals (including Godwin), Owen did not believe that individuals had agency to modify their behaviour, though he was not always consistent on this,[21] including changing how they felt. This view stemmed from his core belief that the character of man is formed for him, not by him.[22] Focusing on the affective dimensions underscores the subtle differences between Owen and Godwin. Although the two men shared an anxiety about the passions and their destructive potential in the public sphere, Owen clearly put greater weight on the determining role of circumstances than did Godwin and Wollstonecraft as the latter pair rejected the deterministic view that humans were entirely or largely helpless victims of their passions. Such a view, they held, was dangerous as it reinforced passivity. Owen did not condemn sensual pleasure for its own sake as did Godwin, a product of the latter's Calvinist upbringing which viewed all feelings as suspicious.[23] Owen certainly shared Godwin's anti-sentimentalism though ironically some of Owen's detractors thought him too sentimental.[24] For all Owen's promise of universal happiness, he never slipped into a sickly sensibility, despair or misanthropy. He did not lose faith in humanity or the certainty that his ideas would eventually triumph.

Thus, Owen was no straightforward ascetic radical. Contrary to what many of his detractors have claimed, he never asserted that man was entirely the creature of his circumstances. Rather man's character was a 'twofold compound' of nature and nature, though he certainly placed the accent on the latter.[25] He was insistent that it was pointless to blame individuals for their moral failings and feelings: 'to apply responsibility or blame to a being so created and enforced to feel, think, and act, is most irrational – not to say insane'.[26] It was an error, and a dangerous and immiserating one, to 'seduce … men to believe that … they can believe and feel as they like'.[27] As one of the fundamental 'laws of human nature' laid down by Owen's Rational Society put it: 'Each individual is so organised that his feelings, and his convictions, are formed for him by the impressions which circumstances produce upon his individual organisation.'[28] Like other radicals, and those especially steeped in the tradition of the Enlightenment, he frequently legitimated his own ideology by equating it with rationality. He lost no opportunity to round on the prevailing view that individuals *were* to blame for their failures and feelings:

> The evil principle which has been instilled into all minds from infancy, 'that the character is formed by the individual', has produced, and so long as it shall continue to be cherished will ever produce, the same unwelcome harvest of evil passions, – hatred, revenge, and all uncharitableness, and the innumerable crimes and miseries to which they have given birth; for these are the certain and necessary effects of the institutions which have arisen among mankind in consequence of the universally received and long coerced belief in this erroneous principle.[29]

Implicit in Owen's reasoning here is a radical inversion of the conventional understanding of the relationship between morality, feeling and behaviour which carefully preserved political and social hierarchies. In this reading, upheld by religious institutions, wrongdoing was attributed to defective character and bad passions. To put it another way, the deviant – which included working-class radicals, trades unionists and other subversives – were unhappy because they were vicious. Owen turned this reasoning on its head by arguing that workers were vicious because they were unhappy: vice and negative feelings were outputs, not causes of human character. As he explained in a lecture at Manchester, 'vice consists in those actions which produce the most misery, and virtue in those which produce the most happiness'.[30] The onus was thus not on individuals to reform themselves, and change how they felt, which for Owen was an impossibility; rather the conditions in which people lived needed to be reformed by farsighted individuals such as Owen.

Students of Owen have frequently noted that much of the religious opposition to his schemes turned on the latter's declaration of moral non-responsibility, but what has largely escaped attention is just how much this turned on feeling. For example, when a public debate took place at Coventry on Owenism between a socialist missionary and a local clergyman, the Rev. Mr Bannister, the latter asked what was to become of conscience in Owen's system: 'Mr Bannister then went on very forcibly to advert to the operations of conscience, and the influence upon the feelings of men, in taking a retrospective view of their conduct, proving thereby that every man felt himself accountable for his own acts.'[31] Bannister accused Owen of trying to reduce man to a machine, a being devoid of feeling, a deeply flawed and dangerous move: man could neither be divested of his feelings or his conscience. For Owen, of course, the conscience of man was defective in the old immoral world, hence the proliferation of base passions.

The cost of the erroneous belief that individuals could change the way they felt was the unleashing of dangerous and destructive passions. As Susan Matt has shown in her study of homesickness in American culture, learning how to manage feelings and the prioritising of particular feelings has been central to the rise of capitalism.[32] Owen and his followers were acutely conscious of the ways in which capitalism was dependent for its survival on inculcating feelings which promoted individualism. The unholy trinity of private property, irrational religion and private family fostered 'the growth of all the evils passions' and produced 'the disunion of mind and feeling among all'. Owen's choice of words here are revealing: the unnatural practices of individualism resulted in a disconnect between mind and feeling, of individuals alienated from their true social selves. The result, he continued, was the calling forth of

> the passions of hatred, jealousy, revenge, pride, anger, ill-will, avarice, conceit, spiritual pride and all manner of uncharitableness, until these feelings and passions of irrationality instigate men to the insane actions of robberies, murders, wars, and to the common practice of injustice, oppression, and cruelties of the most revolting description, making the earth ... a true pandemonium.[33]

Owen was particularly condemnatory of organised religion, especially evangelicalism, because it not only taught that man was inherently sinful – which in his view condoned base passions and their effects – but also for its arrogance in claiming that man, with the aid of religious instruction, could conquer these passions. This led to the delusion that man could feel as he liked, and under the strictures of religious authorities he was compelled to love and hate at their command.[34] Religion 'destroye[d] ... the natural feelings between the sexes' by instituting legalised prostitution in the form of marriage from which there was no escape for the vast majority of sufferers; hence Owen's attack on the artificial institution of marriage (as opposed to equal partnerships based on love).[35] His religious enemies naturally retorted that it was only through their intercession that bad passions were restrained, and that if Owen's system prevailed it would be 'destruction to all those sacred obligations which restrain the viciousness of the human passions'.[36] Owen's indictment of the old immoral world was that it drew people to what he termed the 'seductive passions' such as intemperance and created bad feeling, especially between the classes.[37]

Unlike many other radicals, Owen never sought to deepen or politicise class conflict, opting instead for trying to unite hearts, if not opinions, among all classes, taking as one of his mantras a quotation from the Tory Chancellor of the Exchequer, Nicholas Vansittart: 'If we cannot yet reconcile all opinions, let us endeavour to unite all hearts.'[38] On occasion, Owen berated radicals and socialists in Britain and abroad for fomenting bad feeling between the classes, and this was one reason why his alliance with the trades in the mid-1830s came to an end.[39] Yet as recent work has begun to underline, it is slightly misleading to claim that Owen refused to engage in class politics as he added to the building blocks of an anti-capitalist political economy that was a key strand in working-class radicalism.[40] True, he longed for class harmony rather than conflict, but he also spoke out against the misery that issued from the artificial division of society into three classes.[41] Further, there can be no doubt that his message resonated most powerfully with the working classes. He frequently drew attention to the affective consequences of industrialisation and liberal political economy for the working classes. Owen and the Owenites utterly rejected the distinction drawn by the apologists of liberal political economy such as Nassau Senior who exclaimed: 'It is not with happiness, but with wealth, that I am concerned as a political economist.'[42] Owen sought to re-moralise the economy by condemning the way in which capitalism unleashed base passions: 'Commerce, having for its object money-profit for the individual, has converted the best and finest feelings of human nature into a sordid love of gold.'[43] Elsewhere, he condemned the way in which the principle of selfishness 'steel[ed] the heart of man against his fellows'.[44] A prerequisite for healing the class divide was enlightening the upper classes about the misery that industrialisation was having on the working classes. In contrast to other radicals, Owen rarely resorted to shaming his fellow manufacturers and elite; the emollient laird of New Lanark would never stoop to such shock-tactics. In any case, he seems to have genuinely believed that the upper classes were largely ignorant of the true depths of working-class misery, 'they generally experience sufferings and privations which the gay and splendid will hesitate to believe it possible that human nature could endure'.[45] Was it any wonder that such obliviousness, when coupled with the degradation that labourers felt, led to retaliation?

While he may have refused to inflame class politics, Owen certainly used fear of working-class reprisal to frighten the elite into supporting his plans, especially in the early years when he was campaigning in the shadow of the French Revolution.[46] When unrest returned once again in the late 1830s, he assured the upper classes that the adoption of his principles would 'tranquilise the present agitated state of society'.[47] But even when it came to the politics of fear, Owen was mild compared to his friend Richard Oastler, or in comparison with the enthusiasm of popular revivalism and apocalyptic millenarianism. Thus, it is not quite true – as E.P. Thompson claimed – that 'Mr. Owen, the philanthropist, threw the mantle of Joanna Southcott across his shoulders'.[48] Owen's secular millennium was to be ushered in by calm, self-assured persevering cheerfulness (one of the ways in which the Enlightenment's emphasis on happiness was translated into personal practice) rather than through the apocalyptic, denunciatory invective of a Stephens or Oastler.[49] Tellingly, an Owenite who resigned his membership from the Association of All Classes of All Nations because of the vehement hostility that some of the Owenite lecturers were voicing towards religion, implied that Owen was exempt because of the calm and measured way in which he spoke out against religion.[50] Owen's public speaking style was a cross between a lecture delivered at a Lit. and Phil. Society (the forum which provided him with the first taste of public speaking in Manchester) and a Unitarian sermon, including the feeing rules associated with those spaces: cool, calm, self-assured and disarming, albeit mildly earnest. The radical *Poor Man's Guardian* owned that 'We are sincere admirers of Robert Owen ... We admire the goodness of his heart, his singularly serene temper – a temper so singularly serene, that he appears to breathe an atmosphere of his own beyond the reach of human passions.'[51] Occasionally, it was even suggested that it was because Owen and his followers were so amiable that this made them even more dangerous because beneath the disarming exterior was a pernicious desire to 'destroy the existing race of men'.[52]

His lecturing style has been seen by some historians as rather boring, but contemporary testimony does not always support this. One of the Owenites at New Harmony conceded that Owen was 'not an orator; but he appears to have the power of managing the feelings of all at his will'.[53] Another American correspondent who saw Owen lecture in New Orleans remarked that while 'it is true that his manner is singular [when] collected before an audience', he 'seems more master of himself in that situation ... than I could have supposed possible'.[54] There was no place for intense feelings, other than a gentle sense of millenarian excitement about the reign of happiness that would inevitably follow the implementation of communitarianism. Owen was benevolence, politeness and restraint personified, and this also seems to have coloured his personal relationships as well. G.D.H. Cole claimed that Owen 'became a humanitarian, and lost his humanity' – so obsessed was he with trying to bring about the new moral world that he neglected his family, especially his wife Caroline Dale, and like his mentor William Godwin he was seen by some as a cold, unfeeling man incapable of domestic affection.[55] As we saw with Carlile in the previous chapter, it is surely no coincidence that Owen came to advocate unions based on love and easier divorce when he was becoming increasingly estranged from his wife, who did not share his beliefs. Just how estranged the two had become was evident in 1831 when Caroline died and Owen, despite being in Britain at this time, did not even attend her funeral.[56] But the notion of Owen as a self-obsessed man without feeling is rather overstated: many remembered him as a warm and generous personality especially fond of children. The veteran Charing Cross radical Francis Place recalled that Owen was 'a man of kind manners and good intentions, of an imperturbable temper, and an enthusiastic desire to promote the happiness of mankind'.[57] In short, he was a model of the type of new human being that he expected would emerge from the new moral world.

Practising happiness

'The end of government is to make the governed and the governors happy', Owen declared at the start of the fourth essay of his *New View of Society*, the set of essays that he wrote in 1812 and which would form the foundation of his mature philosophy. 'The government, then, is the best, which in practice produces the greatest happiness to the greatest number', he continued.[58] But what did Owen mean by happiness, and how was this feeling to be realised? Was his conception of happiness Benthamite, as the plagiarism of the famous quotation might suggest? Some have argued that Bentham's principle of utility was the basis of Owen's thinking.[59] The presence of the 'greatest happiness' phrase is something of a red herring here, and in any case, it had become a common place of Enlightenment thinking, featuring, for example, in the work of Beccaria and Helvetius which predated Bentham. Owen certainly knew Bentham as the latter was one of the investors in the New Lanark enterprise, and both men shared a belief that humans were mechanical structures which could be manipulated by legislators.[60] Owen occasionally discussed happiness in terms of the pursuit of pleasure and the avoidance of pain.[61] In this sense, there were traces of a Benthamite notion of utility, though again this principle was older and had featured in Scottish moral philosophy, some of which Owen may have picked up second-hand (though there is no evidence that he subscribed to Hume's theory of the passions). Yet Owen rejected the individualism that was the cornerstone of Bentham's hedonistic understanding of happiness: Bentham 'did not expect each individual to aim at anything other than the maximisation of his own happiness'.[62] By contrast, Owen insisted that an individual's happiness could only be secured through relationships with others which included a duty to ensure the happiness of all; in short, Owen's conception of happiness was social, not individual (on which more below). As Gregory Claeys observes, 'most Owenites also assumed that the chief sources of happiness derived from satisfying the need for sociability rather than from relations to objects'. But once again, Owen was inconsistent here as he often stated that there was now sufficient wealth being generated to ensure everyone's happiness, which implies a materialistic conception of happiness.[63] Further, unlike Bentham, Owen did not believe that individuals were necessarily the best judges of what made them happy.[64] No doubt it was these kinds of differences that Owen had in mind when he wrote to Bentham in 1818: 'However we may differ on some points you may be sure I wish well to whatever is calculated to remove the gross errors which now exist throughout every part of society and which alone keep the population of the world in misery.'[65]

Placing further distance between Bentham and Owen helps us to begin to clarify what Owen did *not* mean by happiness. As with Bentham, Owen and the Owenites, it has been observed, said very little about what they meant by happiness, or indeed feelings more generally.[66] In Owen's case at least, this is not strictly accurate. Reference to the passions and the obstacles to realising happiness featured heavily in his work and in Owenite literature more generally. It is true that, unlike the Fourierists – the rival followers of the French socialist Charles Fourier who also had supporters in Britain and the America – Owen and the Owenites did not elaborate in any systematic way a theory of the passions.[67] Fourier calculated that there were twelve basic passions, the different combinations of which produced 810 personalities. This knowledge could then be used to form new communities – phalanxes – in which those with similar or the same personality types could live together. But if Owenite theories lacked this sort of specificity, it was because they were sceptical about its accuracy. While the Owenites dismissed Fourier's schemes as visionary and impractical, as a number of Owenites and Fourierists conceded, both systems were grounded essentially in a similar understanding of the passions.[68] Fourier believed that the free play of passions would lead to universal harmony, while Owen sought to change the conditions in which people lived so as to recalibrate the passions and restore them to equilibrium. Owen implied that unhappiness in the old immoral world was the result of a disjuncture between convictions and feeling, a disconnection that would be corrected in the new moral world. As he explained in response to a question on how passions would be controlled in his new system when lecturing at Brighton in 1838:

> The will was the result either of convictions or of feelings, and action was the result of the will. In the present system of the world, the convictions of individuals was generally at variance with their feelings. If a man acted upon feeling, and not upon conviction, he generally suffered in consequence; but in the new moral world convictions and the feelings would be one and the same.[69]

In his study of the Owenite William Thompson, Mark Kaswan has suggested that the Owenite notion of happiness should be termed 'eudaimonia' to accurately capture the social understanding of well-being and the condition of life. He contrasts this with Benthamite, individualistic notions of the pursuit of pleasure, which he terms 'hedonism'.[70] But this was not a term used by Owen or the Owenites, and thus it remains of limited conceptual value in defining what Owen meant by happiness, or how he understood feeling more generally. By conflating well-being with happiness – which are not necessarily the same – Kaswan erases the affective specificity of Owenite notions of happiness. Given that he used the words 'happy' and 'happiness', we should stick with these terms and take as our starting point how his use of them differed from how we might define them, rather than add new layers of complexity by using different terms. This seems preferable especially given that 'eudaimonia' traces its derivation to classical Greece where it was 'not well understood as an emotion, or a passion, but rather as a disposition'.[71] Kaswan is on stronger ground, though, when he claims that the Owenite notion of happiness was a reaction to the selfish pursuit of pleasure as licensed by Benthamite hedonism. As we have already seen, Owen also fundamentally rejected the view of the liberal political economists that desire could be fulfilled through capitalist pursuit of profits and consumption of goods. Only a system of co-operation and working for the happiness of all could deliver happiness to an individual.

There can be no doubt that Owen devoted much more attention to how happiness was to be achieved than with defining what he meant by happiness which, at times, extended little beyond a relative notion that what was needed to arrive at this state was the removal of negative feelings. With a breath-taking certainty that anticipated Marx, who famously dismissed the Owenites as utopian, Owen asserted that when his communitarian system had fully established itself, negative feelings that an individual had about himself or others would just wither away (like Marx's state, though also like Marx, he was vague on why and how this would eventuate). As late as 1841, with several failed community experiments behind him, Owen could still declare: 'as soon as the members acquire a knowledge of the principles and their right application to practice, all anger, ill will, and division among them, must cease'. A 'new mode of speaking to, and of, each other', it continued, 'will naturally arise, and harmony and good feeling will be evidence in the countenance, manner, and conduct, of all'. And he was still proclaiming this with the same assurance in 1858, the year of his death.[72] In short, the advent of the new moral world would change how people felt. A large part of this optimism stemmed from Owen's enlightened belief that man was naturally good and sociable, and if his social circumstances were so engineered, irrational feelings would cease to exist. For Owen, the closest he came to offering a positive definition of happiness was in his axiom that truth and harmony were the basis of it – though note, again, the derivative nature of the definition: he focuses mainly on identifying the barriers to truth – religion, harmony, and competition.[73]

It was not just discordance between individuals that led to misery, but imbalance within individuals. As Owen explained, man is a compound being comprising the physical, intellectual and moral. His 'happiness can arise only from the harmony existing between these component parts of his nature'. The paternalist and ascetic radical in Owen ruled out the selfish and gluttonous pursuit of pleasure: 'the highest and most permanent happiness that human nature can experience, arises from all parts of each man's nature being satisfied without being over-excited or over-exerted'.[74] If gratification was 'continued without intermission' the initial pleasure derived would subside and become 'ultimately painful' and enervating (such as alcohol consumption).[75] When Owen commenced his new periodical *The Crisis* in 1833 the prospectus declared that 'We do not mean to offer our readers any of the excitabilities arising from personal contests, or criminal proceedings'; sensationalism would have no place in the new moral world.[76] Owen believed that through changing the social conditions in which men lived and through education, people could be moulded into happy beings, a process which he described through the telling analogy of giving man 'a new heart, and a new mind'.[77] Education was always central to his mission, all the way back to his time at New Lanark where he had introduced his 'Institute for the Formation of Character', the grandiloquent name of Owen's school for both children and adults. It was vital to reach the young before they were ruined by the old immoral world which taught them all the base passions of jealousy, pride and selfishness. Children were also far more malleable than adults: 'children can be trained to acquire any language, sentiments, belief, or any bodily habits and manners, not contrary to human nature'.[78] Children were to be taught with kindness, not with anger and violence, and their curiosity for knowledge was to be kindled and not drilled in via rote-learning.[79] As William Thompson reasoned, it was pointless to expect children to love one another if they were 'surrounded by the hourly example of all the bad passions that afflict humanity'.[80] Education was also important because of the pleasures that it could bring. The most important lesson that Owen wanted children to learn was 'that life may be enjoyed, and that each may make his own happiness consistent with that of all the others'.[81]

The education of children was also linked to the Owenite attempt to abolish the single family. The communal rearing of children was seen as preferable to biological parentage because of the tendency of the latter, at least prior to their reformation in the new moral world, to infect them with their own defective characters.[82] Unsurprisingly, this aspect of the new moral world did not escape the attention of Owen's enemies. 'The socialist "man and wife" are bound only by their sensual passions,' complained the *Kentish Mercury*, 'and their offspring are a sort of spurious orphans.'[83] But education was not just for children, it was to be lifelong in the new moral world, not least because happiness was a practice. This was not just in the sense that it was a feeling which had to be continually cultivated, but, more fundamentally, it was the practice that defined the feeling. True happiness, as we have seen, could not be derived by an individual in the pursuit of pleasure; it could only be achieved by social practice that was communitarian, and it needed to be habitual. This was why emphasis was placed on joy, rational recreation such as singing and dancing in Owenite culture, both inside and outside of the experimental communities. Music and especially singing offered a practical demonstration of harmony, both literally and figuratively. As the Salford branch of Owenites explained, singing generated 'pleasing sensation', not least because 'When our finest affections, mingled with softest and sweetest vibrations shall carry man without his narrow self, and point out the means by which he may make a perfect diapason of all the jarring and conflicting interests of the great family of man'.[84]

Creating feelings of brotherly love, friendship and joy were at the core of the rich branch life of Owenite culture. William King, the Brighton Owenite, saw co-operation as a means of forging new relationships: 'friendly feeling, among the members generally, must not be left to chance and accident. It must be ... enforced as an imperative and paramount duty and obligation.'[85] Politeness was also integral to this culture. As the leader of the Sheffield Owenites, Isaac Ironside, put it, the rich programme of lectures, dances, singing and soirees were a means to counteract the 'bitterness, wrath and malice; envy, hatred and evil speaking' which characterised the life of the town by encouraging people to 'break their bread together and eat it in a singleness of heart'.[86] This was about more than mere entertainment or even mood-setting; it was prefigurative of the affective life of the new moral world. Dancing, singing, tea parties, excursions were 'manifestations of innocent joyousness' designed to 'thaw ... the heart of the coldest misanthrope'. And for the iciest of hearts there was, at least on one occasion, a supply of laughing gas. One way or another, happiness was obligatory.[87]

There was, however, a more controlling and inhibiting side to Owenite branch life which was meant to conduct itself in the image of Owen's cool, calm and rational manner. When news reached the central board of the Rational Society of acrimony in the Whitechapel branch, between the branch leaders and the membership, the board simply resolved that the branch was not abiding by the feeling rules as laid down by Owen:

> That this board are of opinion that in carrying out the principle of government recommended by Mr Owen the executive of the Whitechapel Branch have not

exhibited the kindness of manner which should follow the reception of our principles and that the complaining individuals are not influenced, by a proper feeling in the view which they take of the acts of those to whom the Branch have entrusted the management of its affairs, and this Board recommend the study of the principles to both parties.[88]

Just as happiness was to be enforced, so too, it would seem, was harmony. There was no place for acrimony in the new moral world, which brings us to the tensions and contradictions that were at the heart of Owen's affective politics.

The chimera of happiness

In the fourth essay of *A New View of Society* Owen declared: 'Human nature, save the minute differences which are ever found in all the compounds of the creation, is one and the same in all.'[89] Elsewhere, he extended this maxim into the affective realm, arguing that as all humans were built the same way, each had the same capacity for feeling. But Owen went further than Bentham, and indeed many other radicals, in the conclusion that he drew from this universality by asserting that what constituted happiness was also universal. To put it another way, what made one person happy was the same for everyone.[90] With statements such as this, it is easy to see why some have labelled Owen proto-totalitarian, though such a view is, ultimately, a serious misreading of his aims and methods.[91] At the very least, this is further evidence of the paternalist vein in Owen persisting (revealingly, he defined his paternalism as 'a firm well-directed kindness').[92] The problem was that he was not consistent here, possibly because he was aware of some of the tensions and contradictions that flowed from trying to put into practice this ideal. He was partly able to square this by claiming that differences were only possible in the old immoral world where a combination of nature and nurture, with the emphasis weighted to the latter, had made people different. It logically followed that if conditions were made favourable to all as they would be in the new moral world, then all would think and feel the same and there would be no place for negative feelings. Unfortunately, this did not follow logically inside the Owenite communities.

On occasion, Owen was insistent that his communities were not designed to make everyone the same: 'The diversity of the human race is necessary to the happiness of man', he proclaimed in the *Book of the New Moral World*.[93] And yet, he implied that not only would all be equally happy in the new moral world, but since human nature was universal, what was pleasurable or painful was the same for all. The only exception that he was willing to concede was 'organic disease'. Such was the anticipated transformation wrought by communitarianism that he could not concede that Owenites might think and feel differently. But the fact that rules were written into the constitutions of some of the experimental communities for dealing with differences through arbitration, and in the final resort power to exclude members if they did not mend their ways, implies that Owen was reluctantly forced to acknowledge the possibility of this. Post-mortems into the reasons for the collapse of communities, which invariably cited that the wrong sorts of people had been admitted to the communities, further compromised the view that all would be made to think and feel the same.[94] Once again, Owen tried to square this by urging his followers to exercise forbearance when confronted with displays of base passions. If they only reasoned that the character of man, including his passions, was made for him and not by him, 'they would discover that to be angry or displeased with their fellow-men, was an act of irrationality, and that those poor individuals who have been least favoured by nature, were not objects for their blame or punishment, but for their sympathy'. Elsewhere he defined sympathy as 'expressive of the lively participation of one human being in the joys and sorrows of another'.[95] So far so good, but he prefaced this by instructing his supporters to put aside their angry feelings, which implied that individuals could change how they felt.[96] And yet the universal code of the Rational Society stated that 'No one shall be responsible for feelings and convictions within him, and which to him are the truth'.[97] When Owen returned to New Harmony in the summer of 1826 and was confronted with a community that was splintering and beset with seemingly intractable problems, he accused the inhabitants of bringing the passions of the old immoral world into the new. This contradicted his theory that this was not possible because of the changed circumstances.[98] As far as Owen's enemies were concerned, this was proof positive that he had mistook passions for circumstances; the latter could be changed to the most favourable and yet the base passions would remain because they were an ineradicable element of human nature.[99]

Further contradictions in the affective politics of Owen and the Owenites also present themselves in relation to ideas of gender, race and slavery. On the one hand, radical implications issued from the maxim that human nature was 'one and all the same'. Universal affective capacity was sometimes cited in support of the equality of the sexes, an important feminist current in Owenite thought. A writer in the *New Moral World* asked women to examine carefully the men who ruled them: 'you will see in them beings like yourselves, subject to the same passions, directed by the same impulses ... similar in all respects, save in education and circumstances'.[100] William Thompson similarly asserted that as women were 'equally capable with men of contributing to the common happiness' and 'equally capable of individual enjoyment' they were equal to men.[101] Of the many evils of artificial marriage (the term Owen used to describe marriages sanctioned by the church), he complained that under religion the wife must 'have no will of her own, no opinions, nor any feelings but in accordance with the will, perhaps, a capricious one, of her lord and master'. Thus, conventional marriage alienated women from their true feelings, and possibly also men if they had not married for love. Seeking to put their feminist principles into practice, Owen promised women that through the abolition of artificial marriages and single-family arrangements, relations between the sexes would become natural, based on 'a sincere and genuine affection', and if a point were reached where misery rather happiness existed, they could part legally and amicably.[102]

As Barbara Taylor and Carol Kolmerten have shown, the reality was somewhat different – even in the experimental communities – as women were unable to rid themselves of the patriarchalism of the old immoral world as conventional gender roles reasserted themselves. Many women now found themselves working a 'double day', labouring for the community during the day and undertaking domestic chores at evenings and weekends. Worse still, some mothers were relieved of the one role they yearned for: motherhood, with the community now assuming parental responsibility for the rearing of children, which led to feelings of loss and bitterness.[103] This was registered in the affective politics of Owenism in which the feminist current was undercut by notions of 'women's mission', female purity and domesticity. This undercutting was grounded in gendered notions of feeling, though there was some acknowledgement that these differences may just have been the product of circumstances.[104] The Owenite trades union newspaper *The Pioneer*, for example, observed that woman's 'moral influence ... [acted] as a power check upon the brutish character of the other sex'. Women, the article continued, could 'regenerate the whole morality of love, which [was] the leading passion in the great social intercourse of mankind'.[105] As Carol Kolmerten observes, ultimately, 'Owen, like Godwin, was more interested in marriage and, specifically, in the unhappiness surrounding a marriage where neither party loved each other, rather than in the different roles for women'.[106]

Owen's position on race and slavery was even more contradictory and, ultimately, much less progressive. True, he never appears to have subscribed to the view that blacks or native Americans were in any way inferior to whites; and he certainly did not relegate blacks, the enslaved or native Americans to a 'category outside of the human ... marked out by unregulated and uncivilised emotions'.[107] But he did question whether it was the institution of slavery that made Africans miserable, noting that the inhabitants of Africa were already wild, savage and living in misery.[108] For reasons that are not entirely clear, it was written into the rules of the New Harmony community that persons of colour were not allowed to join; though it was permissible to employ them for assistance. It was left to others, notably Frances Wright, to extend and adapt Owen's communitarian experiment to abolition: Wright established a community at Nashoba, Tennessee, to prepare ex-slaves for freedom by enabling them to pay for their own freedom through labour in the community.[109] Worst of all, though, was Owen's paternalistic view towards slaves, which revealed itself most fully during his visit to Jamaica following the winding up of New Harmony. Like many other British radicals, Owen came to the crass conclusion that many slaves, provided they had good masters, were in a better condition than British workers, 'and are greatly more free from corroding care and anxiety than a large portion of the working classes in England, Scotland and Ireland'.[110] Not only is the statement revealing of Owen's lingering paternalism, it is also indicative of just how cursory and shallow his conception of happiness could be; all that mattered was the underlying conditions – in this case humane planters – not how the institution of slavery made individual slaves feel.

Conclusion

There are many reasons why Owenism failed, in the sense of the collapse of the experimental communities and the survival of the old immoral world, each of which have been highlighted by Owen's biographers and students of the movement. A further factor is that Owen did not have a coherent, sustainable affective politics. Such a conclusion might be accused of bathos, until, that is, we recall just how central feelings were in both the journey towards, and the destination of, the new moral world. The experimental communities set up in Owen's name did not have coherent feeling rules, rent as they were by even deeper and more fatal tensions and contradictions than bedevilled the wider radical movement. Feelings were beyond human control, but in the right hands they could be controlled – even, it would seem, by far-sighted individuals such as Owen who miraculously were able to transcend the determining power of their own circumstances and check their passions. Were the feelings of humanity to be restrained or given free play? Yes and no, neither and both. Rule 13 of the universal code of the Rational Society unequivocally stated that 'Every individual shall be encouraged to express his feelings and convictions', while rule 26 of the general arrangements for the population contradicted this: 'All individuals trained, educated and placed in conformity to the laws of their nature, must, of necessity, think and act rationally' unless 'morally diseased' (a determination to be made by the community leaders).[111] But in true utilitarian fashion, and further underlining the contradictory nature of Owenite affective politics, it was assumed that base passions would simply wither away in the new moral world and individuals, rightly indoctrinated, would police their own passions, though just in case they did not, the community was empowered to inflict sanctions and even expulsion.

As for happiness, on closer inspection this emerges as the inevitable destination of the rational pursuit of truth. As we have seen, Owen – like Marx – was also stronger on the journey towards happiness – of the various obstacles that stood in the way of its realisation – than he was in defining what the destination would look like. He certainly appears to have had little understanding or appreciation of the precariousness and contingent nature of happiness, emphasised in some modern work.[112] Pointing out Owen's under-theorised concept of happiness might be deemed unfair and the product of hindsight. Perhaps, but the mounting failures to successfully implement his new view of society, as one after another of the Owenite communities failed, which it could be argued was evidence of the chimerical pursuit of happiness, never prompted Owen to flesh out, much less interrogate, what he meant by happiness. Indeed, for all his pioneering communitarianism, it is possible than some of these difficulties were the result of conceptual ambiguity and shifting understandings of happiness. His thinking revealed the persistence of an older understanding of happiness as an ethical ideal – a product of living well – rather than the modern understanding of happiness as a feeling that we are more familiar with (if no less problematic).[113] Sometimes he adhered to a Benthamite notion of happiness as the pursuit of pleasure and the avoidance of pain, but on others he rejected this, not least because he did not believe that individuals were always the best judges of what made them happy. Unlike Bentham, Owen did not develop a tool for measuring happiness – Bentham's felicific calculus, though on one occasion he did casually promise that if his system were introduced happiness would increase a hundredfold.[114] As a result, the precise route and meaning of Owenite happiness remained, and remains, tantalisingly elusive. It proved much easier to attack the causes of unhappiness in the old immoral world, a task that made for some strange bedfellows who cast off Owen's cool restraint and tightly bound feeling rules of ascetic radicalism. It is to these sentimental radicals that we now turn.

Notes

1 Robert Owen, 'Address delivered to the inhabitants of New Lanark,' in Gregory Claeys (ed.), *Selected Works of Robert Owen*, vol. 1 (London: Pickering & Chatto, 1993), p. 130.

2 For a list of the Owenite communities, see Donald E. Pitzer (ed.), *America's Communal Utopias* (Chapel Hill, NC: University of North Carolina Press, 1997), pp. 481–2.

3 Edward Royle, 'Chartists and Owenites – many parts but one body', *LHR*, 65 (2000), 2–21.

4 For Owen and millenarianism, see J.F.C. Harrison, *Robert Owen and the Owenites in Britain and America* (London: Routledge and Kegan Paul, 1969), pp. 91–139; W.H. Oliver, 'Owen in 1817: the millennialist moment', in Sidney Pollard and John Salt (eds), *Robert Owen: Prophet of the Poor: Essays in Honour of the Two-Hundred Anniversary of his Birth* (London: Macmillan, 1971), pp. 166–87.

5 Eileen Yeo, 'Robert Owen and radical culture', in Pollard and Salt, *Robert Owen*, p. 96. For the Halls of Science as spaces of working-class politics, see Katrina Navickas, *Protest and the Politics of Space and Place, 1789–1848* (Manchester: Manchester University Press 2016), pp. 200–5.

6 Peter N. Stearns, *Happiness in World History* (New York: Routledge, 2021), chapter 7.

7 Joanna Innes, 'Happiness contested: happiness and politics in the eighteenth and early nineteenth centuries', in Michael J. Braddick and Joanna Innes (eds), *Suffering and Happiness in England, 1550–1850: Narratives and Representations* (Oxford: Oxford University Press, 2017), p. 106.

8 Harrison, *Robert Owen*, p. 68.

9 Anne Taylor's argument that what Owen really meant by happiness was docility is, arguably, overstated. Anne Taylor, *Visions of Harmony: A Study in Nineteenth-Century Millenarianism* (Oxford: Oxford University Press, 1987), p. 65.

10 Mark Kaswan, 'The politics of happiness and the practice of democracy' (PhD dissertation, University of California, Los Angeles, 2010), p. 112.

11 Ian Donnachie, *Robert Owen: Owen of New Lanark and New Harmony* (East Linton: Tuckwell Press, 2000), p. 27. As many of Owen's biographers have concluded, it is difficult to precisely trace Owen's intellectual formation and specifically who and what were the key influences because he never cited his sources. In addition, as a self-made man, he was often dismissiveness of 'book learning'. Frank Podmore, *Robert Owen: A Biography* (London: Allen & Unwin, 1906), pp. 109–10, 121–3.

12 Robert Owen, *Memorial ... to the Lords* (1858), reproduced in Robert Owen, *A Supplementary Index to the Life of Robert Owen: Volume 1A* (London, 1858), p. xviii.

13 TNA, HO 44/38, report on the socialists at Queenwood by Rev. Henry Robert Lloyd, 22 February 1840, fol. 189.

14 Edward Royle, *Robert Owen and the Commencement of the Millennium: A Study of the Harmony Community* (Manchester: Manchester University Press 1998), p. 28; Cornelia Lambert, ' "Living machines": performing and pedagogy at Robert Owen's Institute for the Formation of Character, New Lanark, 1816–1828', *Journal of the History of Childhood and Youth*, 4 (2011), 428. See also James Kirke Paulding, *The Merry Tales of the Three Wise Men of Gotham* (New York, 1826), p. 36.

15 Podmore, *Robert Owen*, pp. 238–9.

16 *Staffordshire Gazette*, 24 August 1839; *Debate on the Evidences of Christianity between Robert Owen and Alexander Campbell* (London, 1839), p. 233.

17 *Pioneer*, 7 June 1834.

18 *Poor Man's Guardian*, 4 April 1835. For Lovett's mixed views on Owen, see William Lovett, *The Life and Struggles of William Lovett in his Pursuit of Bread, Knowledge and Freedom* (London: Routledge and Kegan Paul, 1976), pp. 35–41.

19 *Crisis*, 17 May 1832.

20 For a discussion of the relationship between humanity and emotion, see Joanna Bourke, *What it means to be Human* (London: Virago, 2011), chapter 6.

21 E.g., speaking at Leeds in 1833, he urged workers to 'discountenance intemperance' and 'put an end to angry feelings and causes of division'. *Leeds Times*, 23 November 1833. See also *Crisis*, 13 July 1833.

22 Robert Owen, *A New View of Society* (London, 1813), in Claeys, *Selected Works*, vol. 1, pp. 61–2. Some of Owen's followers were even more explicit on this point: 'That all man's feelings are formed for him, by external objects acting upon his organisation, and its reaction', declared the Rational Religionists: *The Constitution and Laws of the Universal Community Society of Rational Religionists* (London, 1835), p. 18, copy in TNA 40/38, fol. 75.

23 Though Godwin did later begin to concede that feelings were natural and more important than he had initially believed, the rationalist (and Calvinist) in him died hard. See Peter H. Marshall, *William Godwin* (New Haven: Yale University Press, 1984), pp. 24–5, 160, 167, 199–200.

24 Boyd Hilton, *The Age of Atonement: The Influence of Evangelicalism on Social and Economic Thought, 1785–1865* (Oxford: Oxford University Press, 1988), p. 200.

25 Robert Owen, *The Social System* (1826), in Claeys, *Selected Works*, vol. 2, p. 58.

26 Robert Owen, *Memorial to Both Houses of Parliament* (1858), in Owen, *A Supplementary Index*, p. xxvi.

27 *Manchester and Salford Advertiser*, 1 October 1842 (lecture by Owen at Manchester).

28 Co-operative Archives, Manchester, Robert Owen Papers, RO135, Outline of the Rational System of Society.

29 Robert Owen, *Report to the County of Lanark* (1820), reproduced in Owen, *A Supplementary Index*, p. 308.

30 *Manchester and Salford Advertiser*, 1 October 1842.

31 *Coventry Herald*, 18 January 1839.

32 Susan J. Matt, *Homesickness: An American History* (Oxford: Oxford University Press, 2011), p. 7.

33 *Manchester and Salford Advertiser*, 1 October 1842.

34 *Correspondent*, 14 July 1827 (Owen lecturing at Philadelphia); Robert Owen, *The Book of the New Moral World* (1840), p. 47. On Owen and religion, see Robert A. Davis, 'Robert Owen and religion', in Noel Thompson and Chris Williams (eds), Robert Owen and His Legacy (Cardiff: University of Wales Press, 2011), pp. 91–112.

35 Owen, 'Introduction', in *Supplementary Index*, p. iv. On Owen, Owenism and marriage, see Barbara Taylor, *Eve and the New Jerusalem: Socialism and Feminism in the Nineteenth Century* (London: Virago, 1984), chapter 6.

36 *New Harmony Gazette*, 20 September 1826; *New Moral World*, 8 February 1840 (report of Bishop of Exeter attacking Owenites in House of Lords).

37 Robert Owen, *Observations on the Effects of the Manufacturing System* (1815), in Claeys, *Selected Works*, vol. 1, p. 114.

38 Co-operative Archive, RO153, Prospectus of a New Weekly Paper, *The Crisis*.

39 W. Hamish Fraser, 'Robert Owen and the workers', in John Butt (ed.), *Robert Owen: Prince of Cotton Spinners* (Newton Abbot: David & Charles, 1971), p. 91; BL, Additional MS 46344, John Burns Papers, Robert Owen to Thomas Allsop, n.d. [1848].

40 Ben Maw, 'Robert Owen's unintended legacy: class conflict', in Thomson and Williams, *Robert Owen*, pp. 155–73.

41 *Manchester Times*, 31 August 1833 (Owen's Address to the Productive Classes of Great Britain and Ireland).

42 Quoted in Harrison, *Robert Owen*, p. 74.

43 Owen, *Supplementary Index*, p. 108.

44 *Ibid.*, p. 41.

45 Owen, *New View of Society*, p. 98.

46 Robert Anderson, '"Misery made me a fiend": social reproduction in Mary Shelley's Frankenstein and Robert Owen's early writings', Nineteenth-Century Contexts, 24 (2002), p. 422.

47 Robert Owen, *An Outline of the Rational System of Society* (Leeds, 1840).

48 Thompson, *The Making*, p. 787.

49 On Enlightenment and cheerfulness, see Peter N. Stearns, 'Modern patterns in emotions history', in Susan J. Matt and Peter N. Stearns (eds), *Doing Emotions History* (Urbana, Chicago and Springfield: University of Illinois Press, 2014), p. 29.

50 International Institute of Social History, Amsterdam, Minutes of the Central Boards of the Association of All Classes of All Nations 1838–1840, letter from Mr Hawkes Smith, 7 March 1839, item 340.

51 *Poor Man's Guardian*, 12 March 1835.

52 *Radical Reformer*, 10 December 1831.

53 Quoted in Rowland Hill Harvey, *Robert Owen, Social Idealist* (Berkeley: University of California Press, 1949), p. 106.

54 *Correspondent*, 29 February 1828.

55 G.D.H. Cole, *The Life of Robert Owen* (London: Frank Cass, 1930), p. 237. Owen once wrote to his wife, 'To know that you are well is the greatest pleasure I have, except to hear that you are happy, as that includes something still more than health', though admittedly this was in 1813 before his public career had really commenced. Podmore, *Robert Owen*, p. 94, 176, 179. For Godwin's lack of feelings, see Corinna Wagner, *Pathological Bodies: Medicine and Political Culture* (Berkeley: University of California Press, 2013), p. 85.

56 Donald E. Pitzer, 'The new moral world of Robert Owen and New Harmony', in Pitzer, *America's Communal Utopias*, p. 92.

57 BL, Additional MS 27791, Francis Place Papers, Narrative of Political Events in England, 1830–35, vol. III, fol. 264. For other examples of Owen's mildness and politeness, see *Correspondent*, 29 February 1828 (report of Owen's lectures at New Orleans); George Flower, *History of the English Settlement in Edwards County, Illinois* (Chicago, 1882), p. 282; Anon, *R. Owen at New Lanark* (Manchester, 1839), p. 14, copy in TNA HO 44/38, fol. 462A.

58 Owen, *New View of Society*, p. 77.

59 Max Beer, *A History of British Socialism*, vol. 1 (London: Allen & Unwin, 1953), p. 163; E.P. Thompson, *The Making of the English Working Class* (New York: Vintage, 1963), pp. 780–1.

60 Royle, *Robert Owen*, p. 7.

61 E.g., Robert Owen, *Catechism of the New Moral World* (London, 1840), pp. 2–3; Co-operative Archive, RO135, Outline of the Rational System of Society, rule XII.

62 John Dinwiddy, *Bentham* (Oxford: Oxford University Press, 1989), p. 29.

63 Gregory Claeys, *Citizens and Saints: Politics and Anti-Politics in Early British Socialism* (Cambridge: Cambridge University Press, 1989), p. 112; cf. Owen's Address to the Productive Classes of Great Britain and Ireland, August 1833, *Manchester Times*, 31 August 1833.

64 Kaswan, 'The politics of happiness', p. 113.

65 Robert Owen to Jeremy Bentham, 8 February 1818, in Stephen Conway (ed.), *The Correspondence of Jeremy Bentham*, vol. 9 (Oxford: Oxford University Press, 1990), p. 160.

66 Kaswan, 'The politics of happiness', p. 112.

67 For Fourier and the Fourierists in France, see Pamela Pilbeam, *French Socialists Before Marx* (Teddington: Acumen, 2000), and in Britain, see Richard K.P. Pankhurst, 'Fourierism in Britain', *International Review of Social History*, 1 (1956), 398–432.

68 A series of articles on Fourierism were published in volume 8 (1840) of the *New Moral World*, see in particular: 24 October 1840 (article by Goodwyn Barmby), 28 November 1840 (letter by 'A Young Socialist'). See also *New Moral World*, 21 September 1839 ('Socialism in France'), 9 November 1839 ('Fourierism').

69 *Operative*, 9 December 1838 ('Robert Owen on the Resurrection').

70 Kaswan, 'The politics of happiness', p. 319.

71 Rob Boddice, *A History of Feelings* (London: Reaktion, 2019), p. 44.

72 *New Moral World*, 19 June 1825; Owen, *Supplementary Index*, p. xxvi.

73 Owen, *Book of the New Moral World*, p. xvi.

74 *Ibid.*, p. 14.

75 Co-operative Archive, RO135, Outline of the Rational System of Society, rules XV–XVI.

76 Co-operative Archive, RO153, *Crisis* prospectus.

77 Owen, *Supplementary Index*, p. 132.

78 Owen, *New View of Society*, p. 35.

79 Marshall, *William Godwin*, p. 167.

80 Quoted in Harrison, *Robert Owen*, p. 145.

81 Quoted in Harold Silver, 'Owen's reputation as an educationalist', in Pollard and Salt, *Robert Owen*, p. 66. For Owen and education, see also Francis J. O'Hagan, 'Robert Owen and education', in Thompson and Williams, *Robert Owen*, pp. 71–90.

82 Owen, *New View of Society*, p. 58. It is noteworthy, though, that when socialism re-emerged as a popular movement in the late Victorian period, this collectivised approach to family life and child-rearing was largely dropped – even during Owen's time this had been controversial. On late Victorian socialism, children and emotion, see Stephanie Olsen, *Juvenile Nation: Youth, Emotions and the Making of the Modern British Citizen, 1880–1914* (London: Bloomsbury, 2014), chapter 2.

83 *Kentish Mercury*, 16 May 1840.

84 *New Moral World*, 30 July 1836. On Owenism and music, see Harrison, *Robert Owen*, p. 51; Lorna Davidson, 'A quest for harmony: the role of music in Robert Owen's New Harmony Community', *Utopian Studies*, 21 (2010), 232–51; Kate Bowan and Paul A. Pickering, *Sounds of Liberty: Music, Radicalism and Reform in the Anglophone World, 1790–1914* (Manchester: Manchester University Press), p. 308.

85 *Brighton Co-operator*, 1 November 1828, quoted and cited in Yeo, 'Owen and radical culture', p. 86.

86 *Sheffield Iris*, 4 November 1843. For a similar observation, see *Reasoner*, 27 October 1852, quoted and cited in Edward Royle (ed.), *The Infidel Tradition: From Paine to Bradlaugh* (London: Macmillan, 1976), p. 75.

87 *New Moral World*, 8 June 1839.

88 International Institute of Social History, Amsterdam, Minutes of the Central Board Meetings of the Rational Society, 1843–45, Book No.2, 18 October 1844.

89 Owen, *New View of Society*, p. 84.

90 See, for example, Owen, *Catechism of the New Moral World*, pp. 2–3.

91 Claeys, *Citizens and Saints*, pp. 119–20.

92 Owen, *New View of Society*, p. 47.

93 Owen, *Book of the New Moral World*, p. 16

94 Co-operative Archive, ROC135, Outline of Rational System of Society, fifth 'fundamental fact', and rules XXVIII–IX. See also Harrison, *Robert Owen*, p 188, 192.

95 Robert Owen, *Lectures on the New State of Society* (London, 1835), p. 205.

96 *Leeds Times*, 23 November 1833. See also *Crisis*, 13 July 1833 (Owen's Sunday lecture at the Charlotte Street Institute).

97 Co-operative Archive, ROC135, Outline of Rational System of Society, universal code of law, rule VII.

98 Paul Brown, *Twelve Months in New Harmony* (Cincinnati, OH, 1827), p. 31.

99 Paulding, *Merry Tales*, p. 37, 43, 58–9, 80, 139; *Economist*, 4 August 1821 (letter from Philadelphus).

100 *New Moral World*, 2 September 1843.

101 London Co-operative Society, Articles of Agreement, rule VIII, reproduced in John Gray, *A Lecture on Human Happiness* (London, 1825), appendix, p. 6.

102 Robert Owen, *Lectures on the Marriage of the Priesthood of the Old Immoral World* (Leeds, 1840), pp. 24, 12.

103 Taylor, *Eve and the New Jerusalem*, chapter 8; Carol A. Kolmerten, *Women in Utopia: The Ideology of Gender in the American Owenite Communities* (Syracuse: Syracuse University Press, 1998), chapter 3.

104 *New Moral World*, 9 August 1845 ('Syrtis').

105 *Pioneer*, 26 April 1834, quoted in Christy M. Gretsinger, 'Oblivion: an analysis of the decline of feminism within the Owenite movement' (University of Maryland MA thesis, 2013), p. 58.

106 Kolmerten, *Women in Utopia*, p. 20. For a more optimistic assessment of the role of women in Owenite communities, see Pitzer, 'Robert Owen', pp. 118–9.

107 Rob Boddice, *The History of Emotions* (Manchester: Manchester University Press 2018), p. 99.

108 *Poor Man's Guardian*, 3 January 1835. It appears that Owen was more complimentary of native Americans, claiming that they were, in some respect, superior to whites, though that was in the context of trying to convert them to his system: Caroline Dale Snekeker (ed.), *The Diaries of Donald Macdonald, 1824–1826* (Indianapolis: Indiana Historical Society, 1942), pp. 216–17; Joel Hiatt (ed.), *Diary of William Owen* (Indianapolis: Bobbs-Merrill, 1906), p. 43.

109 *New Harmony Gazette*, 1 October 1825. For Wright and Nashoba, see Celia Morris Eckhardt, *Fanny Wright: Rebel in America* (Cambridge, MA: Harvard University Press, 1984), chapter 5.

110 *British Co-operator* (1830), pp. 93–4, quoted and cited in Podmore, *Robert Owen*, pp. 339–40.

111 Co-operative Archive, ROC135, Outline of Rational System of Society, universal code of law, rule XIII, general arrangements for the population rule XXVI.

112 Sara Ahmed, *The Promise of Happiness* (Durham, NC: Duke University Press, 2010).

113 Darrin M. McMahon, 'Finding joy in the history of emotions', in Matt and Stearns, *Doing Emotions History*, pp. 108–9.

114 Robert Owen, *Address to the Inhabitants of New Lanark* (1820), in Claeys, *Selected Works*, vol. 1, p. 131.

4

Gothic King Dick: Richard Oastler and Tory-radical feeling

This and the next chapter serve as a sustained counterpoint to ascetic radicalism by shifting the focus to the second of the two forms of affective politics which characterised popular radicalism – sentimentalism. The present chapter re-examines the relationship between Richard Oastler, the 'Factory King', and his northern working-class supporters in the 1830s and early 1840s. A land steward at Fixby Hall on the outskirts of Huddersfield, he forged his kingdom by playing leading roles in the campaigns for factory reform and opposition to the New Poor Law of 1834. When the Chartist Henry Vincent was touring the West Riding of Yorkshire in 1837, he was struck by Oastler's popularity: 'We visited Dick Oastler ... Oastler is here called the King – he is perfectly idolised by the people.'[1] While earlier studies have done much to elucidate the issues which formed the central planks in his platform, very little attention has been paid to *how* Oastler crafted his public persona or to the modes of communication and tropes he employed. As with other radicals in this book, the role of intense feeling in Oastler's rhetoric though noted – 'tear-wringing melodrama', in the words of J.T. Ward – has not been the subject of detailed analysis.[2] In the absence of this, a crucial element in his popularity has been obscured.[3] Various models have been proposed by historians to make sense of Oastler, notably the gentleman leader, Tory paternalism and evangelicalism, but he does not quite fit any of them.[4] Hybridity, that key Gothic characteristic which had enormous subversive potential, was at the heart of his public persona.[5]

This chapter offers an alternative framework for interpreting Oastler's popularity, that of Romanticism, and more specifically its dark cousin, the Gothic. The Gothic was an influential and enduring aesthetic in early Victorian popular culture, and one that Oastler registered powerfully.[6] The word aesthetic is especially apt here when we recall that its literal definition relates not to beauty but sensation, and in the case of the Gothic, an excess of feeling.[7] The Gothic was highly accessible to the masses, as demonstrated by the rise of 'penny dreadful' novels, the enduring popularity of sensational crime broadsides and chapbooks along with Gothic novels themselves which were widely advertised in the popular radical press.[8] Thus Oastler's affective politics – the intense theatricality, melodrama and sentimentalism – would have been familiar. As the feminist theorist Sara Ahmed has argued, 'emotions *do* things ... they align individuals with communities ... through the very intensity of their attachments'.[9] The intense feelings that were at the heart of Oastler's Gothic self-presentation served as a catalyst for popular political mobilisation. The chapter begins by reinterpreting key episodes in Oastler's public career as a moral crusader for the working-classes by using the Gothic lens to highlight the aesthetic framing of his ideology. Focusing on the affective dimensions of Oastler's politics, in particular his sentimentalism, sheds new light on why he and other Tory-radicals largely failed to achieve their political objectives in the 1830s and 1840s. In his analysis of the political culture of late eighteenth-century France, William Reddy defined sentimentalism as 'the novel view of emotions as a force for good in human affairs, and on the enthusiasm for emotional expression and intimacy'.[10] As we shall see, while this definition works extremely well for Oastler and his supporters, as far as his many enemies were concerned this was a dangerous form of affective politics which ought to have no place in the public sphere.

A Gothic biography

It is unfortunate that we know so little about Oastler's intellectual and cultural formation; all that exists are occasional insights, drawn chiefly from retrospective autobiographical musings. We cannot be certain about what he read during his youth and early adulthood. His *Fleet Papers* – the periodical he edited while in prison in the early 1840s – suggests that he had more than a passing familiarity with Romantic and Gothic literature, including Shakespeare, the proto-Gothic Graveyard Poets, and the Lake Poets.[11] Yet the index of his Romanticism can hardly be limited to his explicit referencing of the Romantic canon; rather, it was the narrative devices he employed, his manner of speaking and writing, and, above all, the way he expressed feeling that reveals the traces of a Gothic aesthetic in Oastler's cultural stylistics. As one would expect of a popular politician, those cultural stylistics were akin to the penny dreadful genre, with its Gothic and melodramatic aesthetic, of heroes and villains, and good versus evil locked in creative tension. Melodrama, a central characteristic of the Gothic, was an 'intense emotional and ethical genre' and was widely employed by advocates of factory reform and critics of the New Poor Law.[12]

It is important not to read such an enduring genre as the Gothic out of its historical and cultural context as it was not homogeneous, stable or continuous.[13] The Gothic had evolved by the early Victorian period, with the Victorian incarnation much more domesticated than its eighteenth-century forebear. The figures, spaces and themes were no longer fantastic and exotic, but 'disturbingly familiar: the bourgeois domestic world or the new urban landscape'. In part a reaction to the rise of interest in sensational crime, a more materialistic, secular and scientific culture, the Gothic was 'appropriated to represent the new social problems' of the Victorian period. A special focus was the social consequences of industrialisation and urbanisation – what has recently been termed 'Industrial Gothic' (discussed in the final section of this chapter). The modern Gothic genre, inaugurated by Horace Walpole's *Castle of Otranto* (1764), tended to re-emerge at moments of crisis, when writers became fascinated with experiences that were outside the established bounds of normality such as the terror of the French Revolution or the anomie and alienation associated with the new urban-industrial landscape.[14] It was from this melange that Oastler crafted his cultural stylistics and through which his audiences made sense of that projection.

Oastler's career could easily have been taken from the plot of a Gothic novel, and nowhere more so than the date on which his career as a popular tribune commenced. On 28 September 1830, he was converted to the cause of factory reform by candlelight at the home of his friend, the Bradford manufacturer John Wood. The guilt-ridden Wood unburdened himself late into the evening with horrific accounts of the evils of the factory system, about which Oastler claimed to be completely ignorant prior to this disturbing and harrowing revelation. The next morning, at 4am, Oastler entered Wood's bedroom, to find him reading the Bible by candlelight. As Oastler recalled:

> On my advancing towards the side of his bed, [Wood] turned towards me, reached out his hand and in the most impressive manner pressing my hand in his he said: 'I have had no sleep tonight. I have been reading the Book and in every page I have read my own condemnation. I cannot allow you to leave me without a pledge that you will use all your influence in trying to remove from our factory system the cruelties which are practised in our mills.' I promised I would do what I could ... I felt that we were each of us in the presence of the Highest and I knew that that vow was recorded in Heaven.[15]

The exchange between the two men was one of heighted feeling and prophetic of the register in which the future campaign would be waged. When Oastler inaugurated the popular movement for factory reform with his famous letter published in the *Leeds Mercury*, provocatively titled 'Yorkshire slavery', he signalled the importance that intense feelings would play. The first line contained the phrase 'No heart responded with truer accents to the sounds of liberty' than his when he heard the boast that it was the pride of Britain that no slave could exist on her soil. Oastler punctured that boast by a highly sentimental account of the 'scenes of misery' that 'thousands of our fellow-creatures' were being subjected to in the factories in 'a state of slavery more horrid than are the victims of that hellish system "colonial slavery"'.[16] Unlike Cobbett, Oastler did not seek to reclaim the white working-class for humanity by asserting their superiority to blacks, but like Cobbett he did adhere to a hierarchy of suffering in making the controversial claim that white factory workers suffered more than the enslaved. We will return to this letter later in the chapter.

Like many Gothic characters, Oastler revelled in the transgressive: a zealous humanitarian Churchman who refused to fit the mould of evangelicalism; a paternalist who emphasised the need for workers to organise and lead themselves; a defender of the English constitution who incited workers to take up arms and whose toryism licensed his radicalism, and the intense feelings he expressed and elicited. Feeling was the plane on which Oastler, the Tory, met with working-class radicals: 'ultra Tory as he is in name, [Oastler] possessed genuine Radical feelings', declared the Leeds radicals.[17] Religion was clearly an important element in Oastler's affective politics as a source of strength and bond of feeling: 'my nerve is strengthened when I remember two of our company are above', he told Thomas Daniel(s), the secretary of the Manchester Short-Time Committee, when reflecting on the death of two colleagues from cholera. 'Oh Daniels', he continued, 'you know I love you all – let us get nearer and nearer to God in this business [factory reform]'.[18] At first glance, this expression of love appears odd in a letter between two fellow campaigners for factory reform. But it is illustrative of the way in which Oastler used declarations of affection – often linked with religious rhetoric and imagery – to bridge the gulf between the gentleman leader and the working class (Daniels was a cotton spinner).[19] This declaration of love is also a reminder that there was a more tender side to sentimental radicalism, which is easy to lose sight of given the intensity with which its adherents appealed to a set of negative feelings when attacking the enemies of the working classes. Oastler brought the kind of evangelical fervour – itself a form of sentimentalism – to his campaigns that had characterised the abolition movement, in which he had cut his campaigning teeth as a young man.[20] It is possible that some of this sentimentalism owed something to his connections with Methodism, a form of religious enthusiasm accompanied by 'sighs, tears, trembling, and weeping'.[21] His parents had been Methodists, and his father a friend of John Wesley who had blessed Oastler as an infant. Oastler was fond of invoking Wesley. But unlike his friend and ally, the Reverend Joseph Rayner Stephens, Christianity was only one dimension of Oastler's affective politics. There was more to him than an Old Testament prophet, as his speeches tended to be far bloodier, more monstrous and much less restricted to the Bible than Stephens's rhetoric, as the next chapter shows.

One of the more Gothic episodes in Oastler's biography is the protracted conflict he endured with his employer, Thomas Thornhill, the absentee squire of Fixby Hall. And once again, it is an episode that reveals the importance and place of feeling in Oastler's politics. In the absence of Fixby's rightful heir, Oastler assumed the role of squire himself, a usurpation financed by amassing large debts. Ultimately, the breach between the two men was the result of a clash of ideologies – liberal political economy versus moral economy: Thornhill insisted that his steward run the estate merely as a profitable enterprise; while Oastler the paternalist refused to run it solely for 'pounds, shillings and pence' as he disparagingly complained. To run an estate on these lines was callous, a charge that Oastler would also level at the factory masters and architects of the New Poor Law.[22] As he stated during the height of the anti-Poor Law agitation, what Oastler wished for on the estate was for 'the rich and the poor to mingle together in fond and affectionate society'.[23] This affective bond on the landed estate was the cornerstone of Oastler's sentimental vision for wider society, in which paternalism from above and deference from below were conceptualised, not in the sordid language of economic interest, but filial love. While squire and steward were able for a time to patch up their differences, by 1838 Thornhill, under pressure from Oastler's political enemies, dismissed him and sued for the debt. The Factory King's supporters smelled a rat and believed him to be the victim of 'passion and misrepresentation' in the shape of a cruel and vindictive employer who, at the behest of the factory masters and poor law officials, was determined to ruin him.[24] Like Godwin's literary creation Caleb Williams, Oastler experienced the psychological torment of the vagaries of the law. Months passed and eventually turned into years (just over two-and-half in total from the date of his dismissal to his imprisonment) as Thornhill played cat-and-mouse with his former steward, serving him with papers, then seemingly letting the issue lapse, only to serve him again.

Thornhill's behaviour towards his ex-steward was seen as symptomatic of a wider degeneration of the aristocracy: 'oh! What a falling off there is in the breed!', Oastler seethed.[25] Famed for his gigantic size, Thornhill was so large that a semi-circle had to be cut out from his dining table so that he could sit and eat. He was an absentee landlord, whose life was devoted to the London season, the turf and to eating. His gluttony represented horrific excess, a debauched and tyrannical gentleman, lacking in personal restraint, and of overwhelming power determined to crush his former steward. Oastler visualised this decay and excess for his readers by issuing a portrait of Thornhill to accompany his *Fleet Papers*, which accentuated his corpulence.[26] While Oastler himself did not resort to verbal insults of Thornhill's size, some of his supporters did: 'plethoric' and 'overgrown' being two choice adjectives.[27] Elsewhere, Thornhill was equated with awesome nature. In a poem by one of his supporters, Oastler was likened to 'A prostrate oak, nearly a thousand years old, blown down by the hurricane, in Fixby Park'. Thornhill was a 'rough unfeeling blast'. Uprooted from his natural environment and deprived of sustenance – including the 'fond ivy … about thy withering root' the oak eventually died, for whom the 'morning dew weep[ed]' and grieved, a reference to the tears which were shed by Oastler and by the tenants of Fixby when he was forced to leave, following his dismissal as steward.[28] When 'open warfare' had commenced between the two men, Oastler began to reveal secrets about his former employer's youthful indiscretions: 'Suppose I had cheated him of a few thousand pounds', he mused to his successor,

> I never cheated a woman out of his wife, and then made hundreds of tenants sweat to fortunize two Bastards!! Oh, my dear sir, Mr Thornhill little knows the anxiety which his youthful 'dissolute habits,' have caused to my dear father [who had preceded Oastler as steward], myself and hundreds of his tenants![29]

Again, Oastler hints at the psychological torment inflicted by a dissolute and parasitic aristocracy which resulted in the tangible bodily suffering of the tenantry who are forced to sweat. The question of who lacked restraint the most – Oastler in his tirades, Thornhill in his aristocratic gluttony, and subsequently the insatiable greed of the manufacturers – was a leitmotif in Oastler's affective politics.

Suffering (for) humanity

> I have this moment returned from beholding one of those awful scenes – so grand, so terrific – which force man to acknowledge the existence and the power of that Being whose 'is the sea,' because 'He made it;' a scene which feeble man can never contemplate without reverence and awe. I have been standing on the beach, when a mighty storm was raging, … As I stood listening to the howling of the wind, the roaring of the waves, and watching the raging of the ocean, I thought – just so furiously is man now raging against his fellow man.[30]

The above narrative, a scene from Oastler's account of his holiday in north Wales following his dismissal in the autumn of 1838, is just one of many examples of Romantic and sublime imagery in his language. The narrative is also characteristically laden with feeling: awe, terror, rage and fury, which stand proxy for the conflict in British society. Oastler railed against 'system' – pre-eminently liberal political economy and Malthusianism.

As he confided to a friend in 1839: 'I think I can say truly – there is no man to whom I wish ill. But there are Systems, which I would willing[ly] die to destroy'.[31] To exercise any kind of restraint – affective or otherwise – in the war against these systems was tantamount to complicity: 'To have been cool, calm, and unmoved by such circumstances, would have required a colder heart than mine', he recalled.[32]

For Oastler, liberal political economy was underpinned by the 'ruling passion of selfishness', a manifestation of 'cold-blooded tyranny'.[33] He conceptualised selfishness as a passion, connecting it with 'cruel avarice'. Tyranny and vindictiveness were also passions in his view.[34] Liberal political economy – the legitimating ideology of the New Poor Law and the factory system – was predicated on unfeeling. Speaking at a mass meeting on Hartshead Moor in May 1837, Oastler asked how any individual 'having a heart in his bosom to throb with the natural affections and feelings of his species' could support the New Poor Law.[35] Yet there was a contradiction here: unfeeling (callousness) implies an absence of feeling, whereas cruelty denotes, at best, a wilful disregard of the suffering caused through one's actions, and at worst, deriving pleasure from causing pain. Thus, strictly speaking, it was not the callousness but the cruelty of the architects of political economy that Oastler lambasted with the latter charge having greater accusative impact because it implied that the enemies of the working class had feelings, but chose to withhold feelings of sympathy (for reasons which will be explored in the final section).[36]

Tyrannical factory owners and poor law commissioners were castigated as 'satanic monsters'.[37] These monsters literally turned the upper classes into the undead: 'they have been struck dumb – their senses are frozen'. Similar to the accusations that we saw Cobbett level in chapter 1, Oastler links the charge of unfeeling with deadened or hardened senses, which inverts the charge of inhumanity visited on the poor by some as a way of defending the factory system and a cruel poor law. Oastler advanced the claims of the poor to be readmitted to humanity by juxtaposing that claim against the inhumanity of the elite. He appealed to the operatives as 'men of feeling' and quoted the line from Byron's *Don Juan*, 'The drying up of a single tear has more of honest fame, than shedding seas of gore'.[38] Like many reactionary and radical Romantics, Oastler attacked the destructive consequences of unchecked individualism; his worldview is prelapsarian and anti-Enlightenment: 'the demolition of our liberties ... has progressed under the gilded theory of "enlightened and liberal philosophy"'. So far this is little more than a paraphrasing of Rousseau, but with the final sentence Oastler strikes a Gothic chord: 'The mind is enslaved by this delusion, and prepares the body tamely to succumb to oppression and injustice.'[39] Enlightenment might enliven the mind, but it deadens the body.

Figure 4.1 Richard Oastler, by Benjamin Garside (1837).

Some of Oastler's extraordinary hold over northern workers undoubtedly stemmed from his bodily presence and practice. This was partly physical: he was well above average height (over six feet tall), 'proportionally large of limb and shoulder' with stentorian lungs, in the opinion of Tom Trollope, son of the novelist Frances Trollope, whom the pair had encountered during their travels collecting material for Frances's factory novel *Michael Armstrong*.[40] Francis Place similarly remarked that Oastler was 'a man of great animal power', a characteristically damning choice of words by Place who was suspicion of Oastler's hold over northern audiences.[41] Oastler also used his own body in ways that visualised and accentuated his inner feelings. Tom Trollope wrote of Oastler's mouth, 'The scornful curl of those lips was terrible', doubly accentuated in the Garside oil painting of Oastler (Figure 4.1) with the red coloured lips and translucent skin tone.[42] A description of him three months after his departure from Fixby in the *Morning Chronicle* noted that 'His complexion is ghastly pale', an outer reflection of the inner torment he was enduring on account of his dismissal and unemployment, a form of personal suffering on behalf of the suffering working class.[43]

This was not the first time that Oastler had broadcast his personal suffering to legitimise his claims to speak for the oppressed. Another occasion which he made much of was a violent meeting in support of the candidacy of his coadjutor and friend, Michael Thomas Sadler, who stood for Leeds at the 1832 general election. On one occasion, Oastler's coat was torn when supporters of rival candidates clashed with Sadler's. For months afterwards he proudly adorned the coat at public meetings as a symbol of his unflinching courage in the face of personal abuse.[44] This clever use of material culture, especially at large outdoor meetings when many of those attending could not hear what was being said by Oastler and others, was a declaration of suffering without words (to paraphrase Paul Pickering on class without words) and further transcended the boundary between the gentleman leader and the working classes by reminding those present that Oastler had also been a victim of the violence as well as the crowd.[45]

There is no doubt that Oastler relished this sort of opposition, and that it emboldened him: 'I am delighted to think they hate me and my cause', he confided to Thomas Daniel.[46] In contrast to the restraint of ascetic radicalism, there was no attempt to sublimate raw feeling; hatred was met with hatred, and gloried in: 'I hate Whig politics with a most perfect hatred.'[47] Tellingly, Oastler spoke of 'sinless anger' to legitimise its underpinning of the factory movement.[48] Excusing his impassioned language in a letter to Lord Ashley, a parliamentary champion of factory reform, Oastler begged 'Oh, my lord, do excuse me; I must write as I feel'.[49] Similarly, negative feelings were invested with legitimacy and retributive agency. While 'hope might refuse to glance across' the 'awful chasm in society ... despair, maddened by hatred and revenge, would dare the leap'.[50] If 'reason and religion' could not effect redress, then it would be left to 'the fury of a whirlwind of malice personified in an ocean of blood'.[51] Unsurprisingly, Oastler's enemies deprecated the use of such language. The *Leeds Mercury* rebuked Oastler for calling factory owners 'monsters' and 'devils', 'diabolical' and 'infernal', likening him to a 'Fire-king or salamander, whose element is flame'.[52] The proprietor-editors of the *Mercury*, Edward Baines, Senior and Junior, were soon bearing the brunt of Oastler's ravings. Not content with hurling Cobbett's famous quip that Baines Senior was 'the great liar of the North', Oastler resorted to the language of Gothic monstrosity: 'His complexion is Yellow, – his phiz is leering, – his breath (from weekly doses of *Mercury*) is very stinking', a graphic politicisation of the senses to elicit feelings of disgust.[53]

To like-minded Chartists such as Feargus O'Connor, who were also seeking to mobilise radical supporters by expressing and eliciting intense feeling, Oastler was a consummate performer of great skill. W.R. Croft recalled of the King that 'his large audiences ... would alternately tremble with fear, be roused to anger and hate, or melted to tears under the spell of his irresistible eloquence'.[54] Joseph Rayner Stephens remarked of his friend, 'The amazing readiness and rapidity with which his pen can record the stirring emotion of his ever-active mind is truly astonishing'.[55] The use of the word 'emotion' is striking here and characteristic of the period. If the term was being used to describe Oastler's affective life – what we might recognise today as an emotional state, then this begs the question, why does the word emotion appear in the singular and not the plural? Further, if the writer *had* been referring to Oastler's affective life, then the word 'passion(s)' or 'sentiment(s)' would have been used, as was customary at this time. As we have seen, Oastler spoke of passions – the 'ruling passion of selfishness' – and like others, he also used the word passion as a verb rather than an adjective: Thornhill, 'was in a most furious, frenzied passion' with him, Oastler informed his readers.[56] But he never used the word 'emotion' in the modern sense when referring to feelings, and neither did his friend Stephens. The use of the word 'emotion' by the latter appears to denote outward movement – e-motion; in other words, Oastler's pen captures what literally comes out of his mind, a definition consistent with other usages of the word at this time, and one that had its origins in the Latin word *motio*.[57] Elsewhere – the occasion of his release from prison – Oastler interestingly counterpoised emotion with feeling, the former denoting the outward expression of the latter.[58] We might note, too, that the word 'emotion' was also used at this time to describe the audible and visible response of audiences to stirring speeches, or conversely, groans and hisses at the mention of political enemies. Thus, it is no coincidence that it was a word frequently used in this way in reports of speeches by Oastler and Stephens.[59]

Oastler's enemies did not view such e-motion as measured in the slightest, and it was his very facility in manipulating the passions of the people that unnerved them. As the campaign for factory reform unfolded and Oastler grew bolder in his denunciations, allied to a bitterly fought general election contest at Leeds in 1832, he was increasingly cast as a deranged villain. *The Leeds Mercury*, organ of the northern manufacturing interest, began to suggest that he was unbalanced and prone to 'silly ravings' and 'Pandemonium fervour'.[60] His speaking and writing style was ridiculed for its lack of restraint – a classic(al) charge levelled against the Gothic. Oastler's enemies portrayed him as crazed, less than human, 'as a brute, as an assassin ... as a fanatic, and as a mad bull'.[61] The Whig Lord Brougham exclaimed, 'it was difficult to believe that any being in human form could utter such sentiments, in such language', yet another aspersion which sought to relegate Oastler beyond humanity.[62] Some of his initial supporters recoiled from the incendiarism of his public rhetoric: by 1841 Lord Ashley remarked of the Factory King that 'his feelings are too powerful for control'.[63] There is a parallel here with the cultural alarmism that greeted penny dreadful and Gothic literature in some elite circles: such sensationalism was dangerously subversive. If penny dreadfuls promoted crime,[64] Oastler's speeches promoted violence against property and even person. While some recent accounts have cast doubt on the genuineness of Oastler's inflammatory rhetoric, the Home Office and the legal officers of the Crown were in no doubt about the fears and anxieties that he evoked in the propertied classes. As he boasted in a private letter to his friend and fellow factory reformer, John Fielden, his objective was to 'make the [child] murderers tremble'.[65]

The authorities were especially anxious over the malign influence that Oastler exercised over the young and impressionable.[66] In the eyes of his enemies there was something distinctly feminine in Oastler's histrionics, a characteristic often levelled at the Gothic genre itself, just as it was also levelled at radicals for inflaming the passions. Both charges served to reinforce a gendered notion of citizenship as the exclusive preserve of the rational, calm (elite) male.[67] The tears that were so frequently shed at Oastler's meetings, the trembling of the audience, allied to his putative mad ravings, were all seen as dangerous manifestations of unrestrained passion. In the shadow of the French Revolution, weeping in public came to be identified as childish, effeminate and foreign. Oastler would not have baulked at the suggestion that he was able to turn on the waterworks at will during his meetings, but he would have vehemently rejected the aspersion that they were crocodile tears. It was the act of contemplating the suffering of factory children and of workhouse inmates that moved him and audiences to tears. As Thomas Dixon has argued, 'It is particular beliefs about the world, rather than mere physiology, that turns on our tears'.[68] Even among his friends, Oastler was noted for his tears. Stephens was struck by the fact that when Oastler witnessed the love the working classes of Ashton-under-Lyne bore for Stephens, it moved him to tears.[69] This particular instance is also evidence of what Dixon has termed the interactive and social nature of tears: 'tears are strongly associated with attachment and separation' and act as a 'kind of liquid social bond'.[70] Thus, Oastler's tears were an affective means of bonding with his working-class supporters.

These affective bonds were further underlined during Oastler's period of incarceration in the early 1840s. The gifts that he received from his supporters to ease his time in prison frequently moved him to tears. But these tears were not just the liquid expression of an enduring bond, they also demonstrated to his enemies that prison had not deadened his senses. After weeping in response to receiving a plum-cake, Oastler addressed his captor directly: 'Although I am a prisoner, Mr Thornhill, my heart is not yet hardened.'[71] Oastler's friends, too, could perceive this weeping as feminine. On witnessing his oratory for the first time, Feargus O'Connor observed: 'He has the face of a philanthropist, the mind of a philosopher, and the heart of a woman.'[72] Oastler's widely remarked sentimentality – of his tears and trembling, which frequently formed part of his platform performances – was also of a piece with this sort of commentary.[73] There is a parallel here between Oastler and the impact he had on audiences, especially women, and the fears that greeted the rise of the sentimental novel in the late eighteenth century 'that could, reputedly, reduce women to passionate wreckage'.[74] Some of the women involved in the anti-Poor Law movement, such as the Elland radical Mary Grasby who knew Oastler, readily conceded that one of the reasons why women had more of a stake in resisting the New Poor Law was because 'their feelings were more susceptible and the pangs of being separated from those to whom they had been used to look for support, and from the children of their own bearing were more severe, she believed, than it was possible for men to feel'. This was a subtle politicisation by a working-class woman of the sentimentalised domesticity espoused by Oastler, which implied that women were uniquely placed through their bodies to contest the putative rationality of the male authors and implementers of the New Poor Law.[75] The influence of Oastler – whom Grasby thanked at the end of her speech – was further registered in her opening statement: 'The New Poor Law was not concocted by men, but by fiends in the shape of men.'[76] The gendered dichotomies of female/emotion and male/reason were also reinforced by medical 'science', which equated nervous sensibility with effeminacy.[77] From Oastler's perspective, this 'feminised' mode of treatment was a riposte to the masculinised discourse of politics, statistics and abstractions. As Mary Poovey has argued in relation to the social-problem novel (which explored the social consequences of urban-industrialism between the 1830s and 1850s), the normative abstractions, calculations and aggregates that were the very stuff of political economy had the effect of erasing feelings. In reaction to this, the social-problem novel deployed a mode of representation that personalised these abstractions, not least by focusing on feelings as a way of eliciting sympathy in the reader.[78] A similar calculation lay behind Oastler's tears.

It was not just Oastler's tears that were a regular feature of his public interventions; he also frequently remarked on the tears shed by the victims of the factory system, and here they served another purpose. His famous letter to the *Leeds Mercury*, discussed earlier, made several references to tears: 'The very streets which receive the droppings of an "Anti-Slavery Society" are every morning wet by the tears of innocent victims at the accursed shrine of avarice'. Oastler's letter to the *Leeds Mercury* must surely rank as one of the most sentimental outpourings in popular politics during the whole nineteenth century. Through participating in the latter stages of the abolitionist movement, he had seen first-hand the power of sentimentalism.[79] The 'poor infants' who were forced to work in the factories, principally girls, were friendless and 'unpitied'. What made the 'cold-blooded avarice' of the factory masters hypocritical is that many were zealous abolitionists. Oastler's purpose was to shame the masters and the abolitionists: 'listen to the cries and count the tears of these poor babes'. It is worth emphasising that he was not addressing the victims of factory slavery, but the perpetrators who formed one of the main groups who read the *Leeds Mercury*. His objective was 'to rouse the hearts of the nation' by pricking the social conscience of provincial middle-class opinion by exposing, shocking, shaming and embarrassing the factory masters – 'Britons, blush while you read it!'. The repeated references to tears were meant to induce pity, sympathy and guilt just as the cult of pathos did which underpinned the 'condition of England' novels.[80]

Turning to Oastler's discourse, his favoured mode was the written address in the form of a public letter. Epistolary was a genre that had been made famous by Romantic and Gothic authors. G.D.H. Cole was, perhaps, a little unfair in his observation that 'the pen was not Oastler's natural weapon', if only because of the stir his celebrated letter on 'Yorkshire slavery' created, to say nothing of the numerous piercing insults he hurled. An instance of the latter was his description of the shareholders of the *Bradford Observer*: *A Letter to those Sleek, Pious, Holy, and Devout Dissenters Messrs. Get-all, Keep-all, Grasp-all, Scrape-all, Whip-all, Gull-all, Cheat-all, Cant-all, Work-all. Sneak-all, Lie-well, and Company*.[81] The venom, scorn and sarcasm on display here was characteristic of sentimental radicalism.[82] Not only were Oastler's contributions to radical newspapers in the form of letters but his own *Fleet Papers* were always epistolary. The form of these letters is just as revealing as their content, and the same point can be made about his speeches. Although Oastler is obviously the authorial voice, he deploys the kinds of distancing techniques characteristic of the Gothic genre, notably framed narratives (purportedly written by someone else, or ventriloquised, for example). Other examples of framed narratives include Oastler's letters and speeches on factory reform and the New Poor Law, which invariably contain corroborating testimony, even if the identity of the victims are anonymised for their protection, from accounts of 'factory cripples' to the gruesome accounts of doctors detailing the bodily horrors inflicted by the factory system and workhouse. These functioned not only as proof of the evils of the factory and workhouse regimes, but also challenged the claims of Oastler's enemies that his accounts were incredible, prone to much exaggeration and hyperbole. It also served to underscore the collaborative basis of the campaigns that he led, symbolised by the Fixby Hall Compact of June 1832, when he entered into an alliance with the workers and their radical leaders in pursuit of factory reform.

Oastler was driven by an obsession with unmasking the enemies of the working class and revealing their true monstrosity, which was hiding behind professions of humanity, philanthropy and religiosity. It is this Gothic motif of unmasking which dominates his public letters. To the Cragg Dale factory masters, Oastler responded: 'Your deeds of *Darkness* and of *Death*, shall now be brought to *light* ... *Oh 'twill* as you say, "be a day of rejoicing," to unmask *Falsehood*'.[83] Those enemies are frequently portrayed as hideous monsters who wore masks to hide their true selves. 'You know', Oastler taunted Baines about the Dissenters, 'that under their sleek YOllow Mask, they wear very forbidding countenances. They have large leering green eyes – such wide mouths – and such long sharp teeth – and then such thin-nipped keen looking noses – that it is no wonder people are disgusted at their Portraits'.[84] Again, the language of monstrosity is used to intensify feelings of disgust, while the pun on the word yellow (the party colour of the Liberals) alludes to the hollowness and unfeeling body of the Liberal Dissenters.

Fixby Hall became a centre of information storage and retrieval as Oastler amassed material relating to his campaigns, from parliamentary 'blue books', statistics, newspaper clippings, transcribed testimony for the purposes of defeating the villainous factory owners and poor law officials. Two such volumes appear in the background of the famous Garside portrait of Oastler (Figure 4.1), an engraving of which was issued by the *Northern Star*, one entitled 'White slavers', the other by 'Marcus', the sensationalist *Book of Murder*. The latter, published in 1839, took Malthusian principles to the extreme by suggesting that pauper children should be exterminated. The book was possibly penned as a satirical attack on the New Poor Law; less plausibly, it was a neo-Malthusian plea to be taken literally – as Oastler and Stephens claimed.[85] The identity of 'Marcus' has remained a mystery. It is possible that Oastler, or Stephens, or both, had a hand in this book – if only in the preface: the style is certainly consistent with their writing even to the level of typographical features, notably frequent capitalisation and emphatic punctuation.[86] As George Jacob Holyoake observed of Oastler, he 'was an emphatic man, and wrote, spoke, and thought in capitals. His ideas, like his letters, were all underlined'.[87] But even if Oastler was not the literal author of the *Book of Murder*, there can be no doubt that his melodramatic and sensational rhetoric had inspired the author. The *Book of Murder* is an impeccably Gothic text: there is authorial distancing – no one knew who wrote it; it is a framed, composite narrative based on the stitching together of two pamphlets with the addition of an introduction; and its status as a text is ambiguous – is it fact or fiction? Is it prophetic? Its subject matter is also recognisably Gothic: the unveiling of a diabolical scheme for ridding society of surplus population – the 'painless' gassing of children. This 'theory of painless extinction' further underlined the cold and unfeeling nature of political economy and especially Malthusian utilitarianism which creates an ethical shelter for mass infanticide.[88]

The sounds, sights and spaces of bondage

The sites where Oastler's affective politics were played out were more than just dramatic backdrops, they were recognisably Gothic spaces: the country estate (not quite complete with a ruined castle, but a hall that was initially dilapidated) of hallowed antiquity; the dystopian 'dark Satanic mills' and foreboding workhouses – sinister gothic spaces *par excellence* where the most horrific acts take place. Fixby eventually turned from being a delightful dream to a hellish nightmare: 'it was not likely that I should fancy, as its beauties entwined themselves around my heart, that they were only weaving a net, which should afterwards ensnare me here'.[89] Even his enforced holiday in north Wales takes on a distinctly Gothic twist. In one of his letters to the Chartist *Northern Star*, he included a description of a funeral he attended (an unusually gloomy way to spend a holiday, even by Oastler's sombre standards). He dwelt in particular on the grieving widower whose 'breast heaved, tears gushed from his reddened eyes – they rolled down his manly cheeks. It was not for me to remain unmoved, midst such a scene.' Recalling the graveyard poets, Oastler mused 'I am always fond of church yard thoughts'. He later confessed in the *Fleet Papers* that one of his favourite pastimes was to 'ramble in the country churchyard, and read the rustic epitaph'.[90] The church was, of course, 'Gothic, old, and rustic'.[91]

Oastler's removal from the northern fastness of Fixby, to the brooding mountainous terrain of Wales and thence eventually to prison, almost parallels the shift within the Gothic genre itself: from an eighteenth-century preoccupation with external, remote and fantastical spaces to a Romantic, and subsequently Victorian, reconfigured Gothic which was much more

Richard Oastler
12 Coffee Gallery Fleet Prison Dec. 9 1840.

Figure 4.2 Engraving of Richard Oastler from the *Fleet Papers* (1841).

domesticated, internalised and 'real' in the form of psychological torment.[92] He exploited the propaganda value of his imprisonment by sitting for a prison portrait (Figure 4.2), prints of which were sold with the *Fleet Papers*, named after the London prison where he was incarcerated. Though not quite Gothic-style arches, the architecture and the closed blinds are clearly meant to convey the dungeon-like existence of his confinement, though he has lost neither his dignity nor his gentility: not only is he well dressed, but his relaxed deportment – with legs crossed and flowing coat (almost cape-like) – with pen in hand signals his patient determination to continue campaigning. Illumination *will* issue from the prison cell.

On numerous occasions, protesting a little much, Oastler issued defiant reports to Thornhill that prison had not altered him, and contrasted his own freedom with that of his former employer: 'My mind, no locks and bolts can restrain ... You are in closer confinement than myself: *your* mind is held in chains by pride and misrepresentation – *mine* is as free as the breezes of heaven.'[93] Oastler could also have been putting on, what has been termed in studies of contemporary prison life, an 'emotional mask' to conceal his vulnerability, not least because elsewhere he conceded that his psychological state was far from serene.[94] Indeed, he conceived of the prison-cell as an institution designed to purge excessive negative feelings. As he relayed to Thornhill, until the anger which he bore towards his former master and others had abated, he must remain incarcerated.[95]

Oastler's conceptualisation of prison was not framed in relation to his own incarceration, but that of the working classes in two other prison-like spaces: the factory and the workhouse, two institutional locations of the 'Industrial Gothic'. Both institutions were envisaged as mighty, oversized and overwhelming, which drew working people in and compelled them to do things that were against their will. Akin to the castles of Gothic literature, mills and workhouses were seen as dangerous places where a range of horrific atrocities took place out of sight. Oastler portrayed factories and workhouses as both sublime and horrific, sublime in that factories and the new workhouses were places outside the bounds of normality, and they were novel, awe-inspiring and potentially terrifying sites that interrupted and intruded upon a harmonious landscape. After describing an otherwise Arcadian vision from a mountain top in north Wales, complete with its 'venerable and renowned castles', Oastler lamented that 'the devil has planted two footsteps [new workhouses] in this paradise'.[96] The antithesis to this dystopia was the country estate run on paternalistic lines and the labourer's cottage: 'The night may be dark and the prospect gloomy: but the cottages of the poor are like stars of light, spangling amidst the surrounding gloom.'[97]

These juxtapositions were at the centre of Oastler's ideology – between the artificiality of modern, urban industrial society and the naturalism of pre-industrial society – spaces which were ordered by very different feeling rules. Many of his letters include detailed descriptions of landscape and geography which emphasise the affective dimension: 'My mind is naturally formed to enjoy such scenes', he said of the Vale of Clwyd.[98] One of his stock devices was the dream (another key Gothic trope) – an imagined space which he used to add to the feeling of dislocation, alienation and the horror wrought by the factory system and the New Poor Law.[99] Nick Groom has argued that '"apparition narratives" anchored the metaphysical in human experience and both personal and communal testimony, and thereby challenged … down-to-earth mechanistic and materialist thinking', such as liberal political economy which left little room for feeling.[100] In his first letter to the Duke of Wellington, Oastler relayed a singular encounter he had experienced when walking through the hills close to Fixby. Ruminating on the 'congregated mass of wretchedness' that was the lot of the poor, he 'wished for an isolated case, on which to contemplate'. At that moment, he recalled: 'I either saw, or else I thought I saw, a man. I won't be sure, that what I saw was real; but it appeared to me so very plain, and is after all, so really like what is passing around us, I will relate it as a fact.' The Gothic ambience is further underlined by Oastler's spectral description of the man, reminiscent of the creature in *Frankenstein*:

> He was very tall, but very thin. His bones were large and long – wrapped up in folds of skin, – of flesh he had none. His eyes were sunk … his lips were white and parched; his cheeks were hollow – their bones projected, just like his chin … He was the sad remains of a strong, athletic Englishman.

Part ghost – 'his soul had not departed' – the figure was skeletal, driven to madness by destitution and the shame of being compelled to send his children into the local mill, where one of them dies a horrible death. The man is reduced to begging and is now consumed only by the desire for revenge against those he holds responsible for his plight. As Oastler and the man sat conversing, various characters passed them – T.B. Macauley, Joseph Hume, Poulett Thompson, Edward Baines, all apologists for liberal political economy – who prescribed quack remedies. When the Whig Lord Brougham passed, he kicked the old man and called him 'pauper'. This induced rage and the old man pursued Brougham, and the man himself became a monster, much as Dr Frankenstein's creation does, and exacts his revenge: 'It was not long before I saw and heard his work of death. – the shrieks were horrible, – the flames terrific.'[101] As the graphic description of this pauper suggests, Oastler was sensitive to the bodily experience of poverty and the ways in which it destroyed psychologically as well as corporeally.

Above all, it was the impact that factories and workhouses had on the bodies and minds of the working classes that weighed most heavily on Oastler. Violence, torture, murder, rape, abduction along with the emphasis on pain, torture and death, are key concerns of the Gothic, and each featured heavily in his lurid accounts of factory slavery and work-house internment.[102] On occasion he explicitly likened the factory lords to vampires: addressing the fathers of factory children, he asked 'could'st thou believe thou wert but fattening a vampire, to feed upon thine own child's blood?'[103] On another occasion, he credited political economy with calling into existence a vampire which drained the lifeblood of agriculture and manufacture.[104] The increasing propensity to discuss capitalism and capitalists in vampiric terms by the mid-nineteenth century owed some-thing, no doubt, to depictions of vampires as cold to human feeling.[105] While the vampire often featured occasionally in Oastler's speeches and letters, he frequently employed a more generic monstrous idiom.[106] He also likened factory owners and poor law officials to blood-suckers and canni-bals who 'feast on death'. 'Infants blood must be the food' of the avaricious and insatiable factory lord.[107] Thus, it was not Oastler who suffered from disordered passions but the greedy lovers of gold who, ruled by their insati-able appetites, were reduced to the level of a beast or a monster.[108] Worse still, the government were complicit and ate further – via taxation – into the already emaciated working-class body which Oastler contrasted with the 'bloated' bodies of officialdom. This rhetoric was a clever inversion of the charge that workers were outside of the human category. Once again, Oastler attacked what he viewed as the inherent lack of restraint associ-ated with capitalism and liberal political economy: the only competition the capitalist 'had to dread was the cannibalism of their own selfish appetites, which induced them to cut and cut away their profits, and thus cut off the sinews of their children' – literally in the case of the growing number of 'factory cripples' whose bodies had been mutilated and deformed by exces-sive labour when young.[109]

Oastler was only too painfully aware that disability was central to the factory-based system, just as it was to the Industrial Revolution more broadly, as recent work attests.[110] Graphic descriptions of bodily deformity were a recurring refrain in his gruesome narratives, and served as proof of the evils of the factory system: 'There is something awfully affecting in the contemplation of a Factory Cripple', he opined.[111] What struck him in particular was the warped affective response of the masters towards the victims of industrial accidents and lifelong toil: 'the cruel mockery of their oppressors, who pretend to be just, and humane, and benevolent, but who pass them by with scorn contempt'.[112] Oastler's choice of language could be unmistakably Gothic here: the 'factory monster … slowly wastes their health and strength, destroys their symmetry'.[113] He even commissioned a sketch of one factory cripple, Michael Hopkins, and printed it as one of the few images in his *Fleet Papers*.[114] The 'naturalness' of capitalist competition is further undermined by Oastler's description of it as an 'incubus' – a male demon who rapes sleeping women – which further hints at the factory reformers' anxiety for vulnerable girls.[115] Once again, akin to the horrific creation of Dr Frankenstein, the factory cripple is 'forced to hide himself from the gaze of others, because of his deformity', the response of society is 'universal abandonment of these poor, miserable creatures'.[116] In parading the bodies of the factory cripples, Oastler was forcing the factory owners to gaze upon their horrific creation.

But it was not just their bodies that he feared for, but their immortal souls. Treated as little more than brutes, a new race of factory children was multiplying who were being denied the opportunity to live Christian lives: there was precious little time for religious instruction and the filial bonds that should have inculcated love and devotion were being sundered by the economic necessity of parents sending their children out to work:

> How many thousand cases are there, where little girls and boys never see their parents, but with weary drowsy eyes? ... How hard the fate of the poor factory slave! Born to a world of woe – the avaricious monster seizes them even in the springs of life, – deprives them of the sportive joys of childhood, and immures them, even from their infancy, in these 'modern hells!'[117]

Deprived of love and subjected to cruelties in the workplace, children were brutalised by the system and having been denied a Christian education when these brutes died, Oastler feared that they would not be saved but condemned to an afterlife of eternal purgatory.[118] In short, the factory worker would join the ranks of the undead, the Gothic (and Christian) liminal space *par excellence*.

The tragedy was that the economics of survival turned working-class parents into exploiters of their own offspring. The New Poor Law, by forcing children into the lesser evil of factory work, or, worse still, cast off by their parents as orphans, 'transformed the affectionate mother into a selfish murderer, and the doating [sic.] father into a roaring beast of prey'.[119] The law, it seems, had the power to alter the affective state of parenthood. Once in the factory, the real threat to working-class women was not some imaginary wayward aristocratic youth, bent on sowing his wild oats – a figure whom many working-class women were unlikely ever to encounter – but those who exerted authority over them in their everyday working lives.[120] Exploitative factory owners and poor law guardians (often the same figures) wielded absolute power and their victims were tortured, raped and murdered. They were cannibals who devoured the bodies of helpless workers. The capital of cannibalistic factory production was Manchester where, Oastler relayed to the readers of the *Northern Star*, 'every brick is cemented with the blood and upheld by the wasting sinews of little, innocent, English, free-born infant *slaves!*'[121] Thus, the very landscape and fabric of the factory and workhouse permeated working-class bodies.

Far from being bounded and autonomous, the bodies of the working class were porous and merged with the environment of the factory and workhouse.[122] These places dehumanised their victims, and disidentified their souls as they became mere appendages, numbers, automatons unfit for citizenship: in short, unthinking and unfeeling brutes. In the factory and workhouse, bodies were no longer self-contained but merely conduits in a network of (capitalist) exchange, the circulating medium little more than traffic in blood: 'The exorbitant taxes which we are obliged to pay ... and every other abuse, must and ought to be paid and borne out of the blood, bones, and sinews of our infantile population!'[123] Presenting the victims of the factory system as dehumanised was, however, something of a double-edged sword as it reinforced the perception that the working classes were outside of the category of human, and thus, like the enslaved black in this callous (and racial) reading, not deserving of protection. 'The law-makers of the present age, whether Whig or Tory, have imbibed the Utilitarian notion, that men are mere things, without rights or feelings', Oastler complained – summarising in one sentence, almost, the entire basis of his affective politics.[124] This threatened Oastler's objective of reclaiming the factory workers and paupers for humanity. As Rob Boddice has observed,

> those who are relegated by the powerful to a category outside of the human ... have their non-human or sub-human status marked out by an inferiority of emotions. This might mean ... a dulled disposition that is incapable of tender emotions that have tended to be the self-definition of civilised beings.[125]

Oastler made this argument when attacking the New Poor Law, which treated the poor as if they were devoid of 'natural, social [or] domestic feeling'.[126]

Nothing underscored the pauper's status as outside the category of human than the Anatomy Act of 1832, and its proleptic linkage with the New Poor Law. Under the terms of these acts, bodies of unclaimed paupers were sold to the surgeon for dissecting.[127] For Oastler, as for many of the humanitarian objectors to the Anatomy Act, this was tantamount to legalised body-stealing, with the workhouse masters and other officials now taking the place of the body-snatchers as it was alleged that some officials were selling corpses for profit. This was rendered all the more nefarious because the avowed objective in passing the Anatomy Act was to bring an end to the trade of the body-snatchers and thus 'quiet the disturbed feelings of the people'.[128] Less well known is Oastler's linking of the factory system with the body snatchers in the early 1830s, at a time when body-snatching had made local and regional news in the West Riding due to the discovery of a body on a coach at Leeds bound for an Edinburgh surgeon.[129] Oastler's friend and mentor Michael Thomas Sadler had made opposition to the Anatomy Act part of his 1832 election campaign at Leeds.[130] The cavalier attitude of the factory owner to his workforce, with its high mortality rates – 'the slaughter-house system', was tantamount to 'Burking', Oastler reasoned – the eponymous slang term used to describe the deliberate murder of victims to supply corpses for dissection. Oastler occasionally invoked the sensational trial of Burke and Hare which took place over the winter of 1828–29 to mount an attack on the traffic of dead pauper bodies licensed by the Anatomy Act.[131] This linkage was one of many examples he used to shock his audiences with accounts of the horrors of the factory and workhouse systems.

Of equal if not more importance than shock was shame, the central role of which was foregrounded by Oastler in his letters on factory slavery, as previously discussed.[132] Oastler shocked audiences with visceral accounts of workhouse diets containing poison, of starvation diets, and of barbarity in factories by brandishing before his audiences an example of the 'strap' used by overlookers to discipline recalcitrant children and even producing on one occasion the scalp of a girl which had been caught in a driving belt.[133] The shock value of these accounts was deepened by synaesthetic descriptions of the sights, smells and sounds that permeated working-class bodies in factories and workhouses, and which served to sharpen the imaginative senses of Oastler's hearers/readers.[134]

It is no coincidence that gruesome and graphic descriptions of slavery were central to the anti-slavery movement, in which Oastler had participated. Like the abolitionists, Oastler used auditory triggers and visual props to let audiences hear and see the sounds of bondage, to shock and shame.[135] As he explained on one occasion, the purpose of these devices and exposures was to shame: 'I thought that very shame ... would have driven the cruel, unfeeling, inhuman, barbarous tyrant (whether master or overlooker,) to alter his mode of treatment, and would have induced him to consider that factory children were of the human family.'[136] The affective politics on display here is significant. Oastler conceives of shame as a tool for combating callousness and cruelty, and ultimately a vehicle for readmitting factory children to the category of human. Horror – in the form of exposing the evils, cruelties and dreadfulness of the factory system and the new workhouses – also served a similar affective purpose. The problem with shame, as Peter Stearns has recently pointed out, is that it tends to paralyse and generate counterproductive anger or aggression in the accused, especially among dominant and powerful interests. Further, Stearns also notes the propensity for shame to decline with modernisation, due to the replacement of honour codes (the traditional abnegation of which was a core element of shame) with the passion for the love of gain (capitalism and liberal political economy).[137] Oastler's cultural stylistics and affective politics were ultimately undone by contradictions and tensions of this kind.

Conclusion

There can be no doubt that Oastler's affective politics exhibits virtually all of the hallmarks of sentimental radicalism. Extremes of feeling, the tendency to couch his political rhetoric and practice in terms of feeling, based on the assumption that feelings ought to be a force for good in politics.[138] Akin to the Gothic novel, his affective politics were based on a searching examination of the role that feeling played, and ought to play, in a polity. Sentimentalism was not just a rhetorical device used to appeal to his audiences and build support for his campaigns, though it certainly did this. It was also a calculated riposte to the growing ascendancy of liberal political economy which, in his view, was predicated on banishing feeling from political and social affairs through the creation of an ethical shelter for capitalists and their apologists. Not only was this immoral and callous, but it concealed within it a cluster of negative feelings: greed, contempt (for workers), fear (of the workers), and hatred towards those, like Oastler, who called them out. The problem was that sentimentalism, as Reddy has shown, as a basis for politics is deeply problematic and too often contains the seeds of its own destruction. The emotional over-heating – evident here with the ever-emboldening of Oastler's rhetoric, culminating in his injunction to workers to take up arms against the factory owners and poor law officials – lost him valuable support from those like Wood, and eventually led to his imprisonment. The Gothic aesthetic employed by Oastler also compounded this over-heating as the genre was associated with 'sensory over-stimulation'.[139] Oastler's problem, as with other sentimental radicals, was that he felt too much – at least in the eyes of his growing band of enemies. This could overwhelm listeners/readers with conflicting feelings of disgust and sympathy, with the propensity to act on the latter disabled by the former feeling. Whatever sympathy the factory masters and architects of the Poor Law may have felt towards workers and paupers was, in part, nullified by what they viewed as Oastler's histrionics on the grounds that 'the sufferer's lamentations [were deemed] to be disproportionate'.[140] Ironically, for someone who was trying to shame the factory masters and their defenders out of their ethical shelter – which enabled them to campaign, without any sense of hypocrisy or guilt, against chattel slavery but not white slavery – Oastler's affective politics resulted in the advocates of liberal political economy retreating even further into that ethical shelter.[141] As we saw with shame, the extremes of feeling expressed by Oastler was also counterproductive, provoking anger and resentment in those he was trying to induce to mend their ways. It is no coincidence that when reform came – in the shape of the Factory Act of 1847, and the rolling back on some aspects of the New Poor Law – it was largely the achievement of more moderate men. When Oastler emerged from prison in 1844 and returned to campaigning it was widely remarked how the old fire, which had animated his earlier career, had gone and he never again commanded the popular support and influence he had previously enjoyed.

Focusing on the affective politics of Oastler also points to a deeper flaw in the Tory-radicalism that he and others like him espoused. It was because of its sentimentalism and emotional over-heating that Tory-radicalism ultimately failed. Like Mary Shelley, Oastler reached for the Gothic aesthetic as a way of cloaking his radicalism – as a protective act of distancing and obscuring. It was never quite clear what he was, politically speaking, and in this respect there is some similarity with other ambiguous leaders such as Ernest Jones and G.W.M. Reynolds, who in some respects Oastler anticipated. For example, the theme and genre of Jones's famous poem 'The Factory Town' (1847), with its 'vision of modern industry as a fiery hell' and new urban Gothic motifs, had been staple features of Oastler's affective politics since 1830, as had the notion of an unfeeling nobility.[142] But just as Oastler's affective politics contained the seeds of their own destruction, so too was the Gothic genre an unstable base. The Gothic, it has been argued, 'carried its own ideological risks, for, as a genre residing in the protean nature of language and symbolic form, it did not lend itself to absolute mastery or control'.[143] The problem was that his affective politics were perceived as too serious and shrill, and it was a problem that also beset the affective politics of his close friend, the Reverend Joseph Rayner Stephens, albeit for different reasons, as the next chapter suggests.

Notes

1 People's History Museum, Manchester, John Minikin/Henry Vincent Papers, LP/VIN/1/1/4, Henry Vincent to John Minikin, 4 September 1837.

2 J.T. Ward, *The Factory Movement, 1830–1855* (London: Macmillan, 1962), p. 65. A partial exception is the work of Janette Martin who has examined Oastler's oratory, including a brief discussion of his capacity to move audiences to tears, along with the highly choreographed celebrations of his release from prison: Janette Martin, ' "Oastler is welcome": Richard Oastler's return to Huddersfield, 1844', in John Hargreaves and E.A. Hilary Haigh (eds), *Slavery in Yorkshire: Richard Oastler and the Campaign against Child Labour in the Industrial Revolution* (Huddersfield: Huddersfield University Press, 2012).

3 This explains why previous accounts have struggled to explain that popularity. As Cecil Driver conceded, in what is still the only substantial biography of Oastler (published as long ago as 1946): 'The explanation of the extraordinary hold Oastler was to exercise over these northern workers is not easy to formulate.' Cecil Driver, *Tory Radical: The Life of Richard Oastler* (New York: Oxford University Press, 1946), p. 126.

4 Matthew Roberts, 'Richard Oastler, toryism, radicalism and the limitations of party, c.1807–46', *Parliamentary History*, 37 (2018), 250–73. On the difficulties in labelling Oastler an evangelical, see Boyd Hilton, *The Age of Atonement: The Influence of Evangelicalism on Social and Economic Thought, 1795–1865* (Oxford: Oxford University Press, 1988), p. 97; Robert Gray, *The Factory Question and Industrial England, 1830–1860* (Cambridge: Cambridge University Press, 1996), p. 57; John Belchem and James Epstein, 'The nineteenth-century gentleman leader revisited', *Social History*, 22 (1997), 174–93 (at 180).

5 Fred Botting, *Gothic* (London: Routledge, 1996), p. 14.

6 Conventionally, the Gothic was seen as distinct from Romanticism, but more recently the two have come to be viewed as having a shared kinship. See Emma McEvoy, 'Gothic and the Romantics', in Catherine Spooner and Emma McEvoy (eds), *The Routledge Companion to Gothic* (London: Routledge, 2007), p. 20. Oastler's biographers have not been unaware of these facets, but they have not been explored systematically: Driver, *Tory Radical*, p. 4; Gray, *Factory Question*, p. 53; Patrick Joyce, *Visions of the People: Industrial England and the Question of Class, 1848–1914* (Cambridge: Cambridge University Press, 1991), p. 34.

7 Rob Boddice, *The History of Emotions* (Manchester: Manchester University Press 2018), p. 172.

8 Martha Vicinus, *The Industrial Muse: A Study of Nineteenth Century British Working-Class Literature* (London: Croom Helm, 1974), chapter 1. For advertisements for Gothic fiction in the radical press, see: *London Dispatch*, 17 September and 25 December 1836 (advertisements by John Limbird); *Operative*, 11 November 1838 (advertisement for The Romancist and Novelist's Library); *Northern Star*, 22 November 1838 (advertisement by D. Green); *Charter*, 30 June 1839 (advertisement by William Dugdale).

9 Sara Ahmed, 'Affective economies', *Social Text*, 22 (2004), 119.

10 William M. Reddy, *The Navigation of Feeling: A Framework for the History of Emotions* (Cambridge: Cambridge University Press, 2001), p. 146.

11 *FP*, 11 November 1843, 6 November 1841, 24 June 1843, 24 August 1844.

12 Sally Ledger, *Dickens and the Popular Radical Imagination* (Cambridge: Cambridge University Press, 2007), pp. 7, 79–92; Peter Gurney, *Wanting and Having: Popular Politics and Liberal Consumerism in England, 1830–70* (Manchester: Manchester University Press, 2015), chapter 2; Rohan McWilliam, 'Sweeney Todd and the Chartist Gothic: politics and print culture in early Victorian Britain', in Sarah Susan Lill and Rohan McWilliam (eds), *Edward Lloyd and His World: Popular Fiction, Politics and the Press in Victorian Britain* (Abingdon: Routledge, 2019), pp. 198–215.

13 Angela Wright, *Britain, France and the Gothic, 1764–1820* (Cambridge: Cambridge University Press, 2013), p. 15; James Watt, *Contesting the Gothic: Fiction, Genre and Cultural Conflict, 1764–1832* (Cambridge: Cambridge University Press, 1999).

14 Botting, *Gothic*, chapter 1; David Punter and Glennis Byron, *The Gothic* (Oxford: Wiley, 2004), pp. 26–30.

15 Driver, *Tory Radical*, p. 41.

16 *Leeds Mercury*, 16 October 1830.

17 *Leeds Patriot*, 23 April 1831.

18 Yale University, MS 782/7/1/15, Cecil Herbert Driver Papers, Oastler to Thomas Daniel, 1 August 1832.

19 For Daniels, see P.P. 1831–2 [706], *Select Committee on Bill for Regulation of Factories*, p. 323. For similar declarations of love, see Driver Papers, Oastler to Daniels, 23 August 1832.

20 Samuel Kydd, *The History of the Factory Movement from 1802 to the Enactment of the Ten Hours Bill in 1847*, vol. 1 (London, 1857), p. 90.

21 Thomas Dixon, *Weeping Britannia: Portrait of a Nation in Tears* (Oxford: Oxford University Press, 2015), p. 70. For instances of Oastler invoking Wesley, see: *A Report of the Proceedings and Speeches of a Public Meeting held in the Primitive Methodist Chapel, Oldham, 14 March 1835* (Oldham, 1835), p. 6; Richard Oastler, *Speech Delivered at a Public Meeting held in Huddersfield Market Place, 18 June 1833* (Leeds, 1833), pp. 11–12; Richard Oastler, *A Letter to those Sleek, Pious, Holy and Devout Dissenters* (Bradford, 1834), p. 2.

22 BL, Additional MS 41748, Oastler-Thornhill MS, Oastler to Thornhill, 26 January 1835, fol. 6.

23 *Manchester and Salford Advertiser*, 13 January 1838.

24 *FP*, 26 June 1841. Alfred Power, the Assistant Poor Law Commissioner, hinted as much in a letter to the Home Office: TNA HO 73/54, Power to Home Office, 6 June 1838, fol. 132v.

25 *NS*, 25 September 1838.

26 *FP*, 26 June 1841. This image was a reproduction of a sketch by 'H.B.' [John Doyle]: 'Two personages of great weight on the turf', 1829; Huntington Library, California, RB240387, vol. 1, p. 20. As Corrina Wagner has shown, the link between gluttony and aristocratic excess was a well-established trope in radicalism by the early nineteenth century: Corinna Wagner, *Pathological Bodies: Medicine and Political Culture* (Berkeley: University of California Press, 2013), chapter 5.

27 *NS*, 22 January 1842. As Christopher Forth has argued, 'corpulence in itself was not enough to condemn a person as profligate. Rather, it had to be accompanied by morally questionable behaviour that allowed critics to propose that such misdeeds were in fact legible on the body.' Christopher E. Forth, *Fat: A Cultural History of the Stuff of Life* (London: Reaktion, 2019), p. 98. The body of George IV would be an earlier example of this legibility. John Gardner, *Poetry and Popular Protest: Peterloo, Cato Street and the Queen Caroline Controversy* (Basingstoke: Palgrave, 2011), pp. 163–5.

28 'E.P.', 'To a Prostrate Oak', copy in WYAS, Bradford, DB27/C1/20/4; *NS*, 1 September 1838.

29 BL, Additional MS 41748, Oastler to Ramsbotham, 3 September 1838, fol. 18.

30 *NS*, 17 November 1838.

31 LSE, Thomas Allsop papers, COLL 0525/4, Oastler to Henry Mott, 21 October 1839.

32 W.R. Croft, *The History of the Factory Movement, or Oastler and His Times* (Huddersfield, 1888), p. 106.

33 *FP*, 9 September 1843; *Leeds Times*, 27 April 1837.

34 *FP*, 5 and 19 February 1842, 22 October 1842, 25 November 1843, 27 August 1842.

35 *Manchester and Salford Advertiser*, 2 May 1837.

36 On the distinction between cruelty and callousness during this period, see Rob Boddice and Mark Smith, *Emotion, Sense, Experience* (Cambridge: Cambridge University Press, 2020), p. 12.

37 TNA, HO 73/52/61, Alfred Power to Home Office, 9 December 1837, fol. 407; Richard Oastler, *Mr. Oastler's Three Letters to Mr. Hetherington* (1836), p. 3.

38 Richard Oastler, *Exposition of the Factory System* (Leeds, 1831), broadside in Columbia University, New York, Seligman Collection, 1831e Oa73.

39 *FP*, 14 January 1843.

40 Thomas Adolphus Trollope, *What I Remember*, vol. 2 (London, 1887), p. 11.

41 BL, Additional MS 27820, Francis Place papers relating to Working Men's Associations, fol. 150.

42 Trollope, *What I Remember*, vol. 2, p. 12.

43 *Morning Chronicle*, 5 January 1839.

44 Driver, *Tory Radical*, p. 185; Driver papers, Oastler to Daniels, 2 September 1832.

45 Paul A. Pickering, 'Class without words: symbolic communication in the Chartist movement', *Past and Present*, 112 (1996), 144–62.

46 Driver Papers, Oastler to Daniels, 17 September 1832.

47 *FP*, 13 February 1841.

48 Richard Oastler, *A Letter to those Mill-Owners who Continue to Oppose the Ten Hours Bill* (Manchester, 1836), p. 5.

49 Oastler to Lord Ashley, 17 April 1835, quoted and cited in Edwin Hodder, *The Life and Work of the Seventh Earl of Shaftesbury*, vol. 1 (London, 1886), p. 215. For similar examples, see Ward, *Factory Movement*, p. 187.

50 Richard Oastler, *Infant Slavery* (Preston, 1833), p. 4.

51 *Poor Man's Guardian*, 20 June 1835.

52 *Leeds Mercury*, 3 December 1831.

53 Richard Oastler, *A Letter to a Run-A-Way M.P.* (Leeds, 1836), p. 1. For similar use of smell to accentuate feelings of disgust, see Ward, *Factory Movement*, p. 174.

54 Croft, *History of the Factory Movement*, p. 98.

55 *NS*, 21 April 1838.

56 *NS*, 10 October 1840.

57 Rob Boddice, *A History of Feelings* (London: Reaktion, 2019), p. 88.

58 *FP*, March 1844.

59 *NS*, 17 November 1838 (meeting at Wigan), 29 November 1838 (Newcastle), 16 February 1839 (Stalybridge); Joseph Rayner Stephens, *The Political Pulpit* (London, 1839), pp. 4, 5, 12, 13, 14, 24.

60 *Leeds Mercury*, 10 December 1831; *Driver, Tory Radical*, p. 77; Driver papers, Oastler to Daniels, 2 September 1832.

61 *Leeds Intelligencer*, 29 April 1837.

62 Ward, *Factory Movement*, p. 89.

63 *British Labourer's Protector*, 5 October 1832; Hodder, *Life of Shaftesbury*, vol. 1, p. 342.

64 Rohan McWilliam, 'The French connection: G.W.M. Reynolds and the outlaw Robert Macaire', in Anne Humphreys and Louis James (eds), *G.M.W. Reynolds: Nineteenth-Century Fiction, Politics, and the Press* (Aldershot: Ashgate, 2008), p. 45.

65 John A. Hargreaves, ' "Treading on the edge of revolution?" Richard Oastler (1789–1861)', in Hargreaves and Haigh, *Slavery in Yorkshire*, p. 202. TNA, HO 73/52/61, Alfred Power to Poor Law Commissioners, 9 December 1837, fols 394–421; HO 73/54/, Power to Poor Law Commissioners, 6 June 1838; John Rylands Library, Manchester, John Fielden papers, FDN/4, Oastler to Fielden, 11 June 1836.

66 TNA, HO 73/54/81, 'Poor Law commissioners' Report on Public Opinion, 28 December 1838', fol. 337v.

67 Carol Margaret Davison, *Gothic Literature, 1764–1824* (Cardiff: University of Wales Press, 2009), pp. 2–3; Michael T. Davis, 'The mob club? The London Corresponding Society and the politics of civility in the 1790s', in Michael T. Davis and Paul Pickering (eds), *Unrespectable Radicals? Popular Politics in the Age of Reform* (Aldershot: Ashgate, 2008), p. 24.

68 Dixon, *Weeping Britannia*, p. 110.

69 *Operative*, 6 January 1839.

70 Dixon, *Weeping Britannia*, p. 8; G.J. Barker-Benfield, *The Culture of Sensibility: Sex and Society in the Eighteenth Century* (Chicago: University of Chicago Press, 1992), p. 67.

71 *FP*, 30 January 1841.

72 *Twopenny Dispatch*, 28 August 1836.

73 For instances of Oastler crying in public, see Richard Oastler, *Damnation! Eternal Damnation to the Fiend-Begotten, 'Coarser Food' New Poor Law* (1837), p. 11; *FP*, 30 January 1841, 7 August 1841, *NS*, 1 September 1838.

74 Boddice, *History of Emotions*, p. 93; Barker-Benfield, *Culture of Sensibility*, pp. 326–30.

75 I am following here the feminist critiques of male authored and policed notions of rationality and objectivity. See Carolyn Pedwell and Anne Whitehead, 'Affecting feminism: questions of feeling in feminist theory', *Feminist Theory*, 13 (2012), 119.

76 *NS*, 17 February 1838.

77 Janet Oppenheim, *'Shattered Nerves': Doctors, Patients, and Depression in Victorian England* (New York: Oxford University Press, 1991), pp. 141, 149.

78 Mary Poovey, *Making a Social Body: British Cultural Formation, 1830–1864* (Chicago: University of Chicago Press, 1995), pp. 132–3.

79 Tabish Khair, *The Gothic, Postcolonialism and 'Otherness'* (Basingstoke: Palgrave, 2009), p. 95.

80 *Leeds Mercury*, 29 September 1830, 16 October 1830; Dixon, *Weeping Britannia*, p. 153; Matthew Roberts, 'Tory-radical feeling in Brontë's *Shirley* and early Victorian England', *Victorian Studies*, 68 (2020), 34–56.

81 Richard Oastler, *A Letter to the Shareholders of the Bradford Observer* (Bradford, 1834); G.D.H. Cole's *Chartist Portraits* (London: Macmillan, 1941), p. 102.

82 Richard Oastler, *A Well Seasoned Christmas-Pie* (Bradford, 1834), p. 36.

83 Richard Oastler, *To the Factory Masters in Cragg Dale* (Huddersfield, 1833), broadside in Goldsmiths'-Kress, Oastler and the Factory Movement Collection, no. 563(4); Fielden papers, FDN/4, Oastler to Fielden, 11 June 1836.

84 Richard Oastler, *The Huddersfield Dissenters in a Fury* (Leeds, 1835), 5. For similar examples see, *NS*, 27 October 1838 (Oastler's letter); *Northern Liberator*, 8 December 1838 (Oastler's letter); *NS*, 6 January 1839 (Oastler speaking at Manchester); *Champion*, 3 February 1839 (Oastler speaking at Huddersfield).

85 John Knott, *Popular Opposition to the 1834 Poor Law* (London: Croom Helm, 1986), pp. 237–43. As Knott points out, there were, in fact, two pamphlets by 'Marcus': a first edition that was published in 1838 made no mention of either infanticide or painless extinction, both of which were included in the second edition.

86 *Operative*, 20 January 1839.

87 G.J. Holyoake, *Life of Joseph Rayner Stephens: Preacher and Political Orator* (London, 1881), p. 83.

88 I have defined ethical shelter in the introduction. See also Josephine McDonagh, *Child Murder and British Culture, 1720–1900* (Cambridge: Cambridge University Press, 2003), p. 102.

89 *FP*, 2 January 1841.

90 *FP*, 7 August 1841.

91 *NS*, 27 October 1838.

92 For this transformation, see Botting, *Gothic*, chapters 5–6.

93 *FP*, 17 July 1841.

94 Ben Crewe, Jason Warr, Peter Bennett and Alan Smith, 'The emotional geography of prison life', *Theoretical Criminology*, 18 (2014), 56–74.

95 *FP*, 25 June 1842.

96 Oastler, *Oastler's Three Letters to Hetherington*, p. 1.

97 Oastler, *Right of the Poor*, p. 38.

98 E.g., Richard Oastler, *Eight Letters to the Duke of Wellington* (1838), pp. 16–18; *NS*, 20 October 1838, 3 and 17 November 1838.

99 E.g., *FP*, 2 January 1841, 16 January 1841, 13 February 1841.

100 Nick Groom, *The Vampire: A New History* (New Haven: Yale University Press, 2018), pp. 57, 65.

101 Oastler, *Eight Letters*, pp. 19–33.

102 Groom, *The Gothic*, p. 32.
103 Oastler, *Christmas-Pie*, p. 4.
104 Oastler, *Eight Letters*, p. 170.
105 Groom, *Vampire*, p. 109.
106 *FP*, 16 January 1841.
107 *FP*, 2 January 1841.
108 *London Dispatch*, 8 January 1837.
109 *Leeds Intelligencer*, 15 December 1831.
110 David M. Turner and Daniel Blackie, *Disability in the Industrial Revolution: Physical Impairment in British Coalmining, 1780–1880* (Manchester: Manchester University Press 2018).
111 *FP*, 6 March 1841.
112 *FP*, 26 February 1842.
113 *FP*, 13 March 1841.
114 *FP*, 26 February 1842.
115 *Leeds Intelligencer*, 26 April 1832, 24 March 1831, 15 December 1831.
116 *FP*, 6 and 13 March 1841.
117 *Leeds Intelligencer*, 29 March 1832.
118 *NS*, 27 October 1838.
119 *Manchester and Salford Advertiser*, 13 January 1838.
120 Clark, *Struggle for the Breeches*, pp. 216–17; Jutta Schwarzkopf, *Women in the Chartist Movement* (Basingstoke: Macmillan, 1991), p. 45.
121 *NS*, 5 May 1838.
122 For the distinction between bounded and porous bodies, see Barbara Rosenwein and Riccardo Cristiani, *What is the History of Emotions?* (Cambridge: Polity, 2018), p. 62.
123 *Leeds Intelligencer*, 24 March 1831.
124 *FP*, 14 January 1843.
125 Boddice, *History of Emotions*, p. 99. See also Nicola Eustace, *Passion is the Gale: Emotion, Power, and the Coming of the American Revolution* (Chapel Hill, NC: University of North Carolina Press, 2008), pp. 70–2.
126 Oastler, *Damnation*, p. 15. See also Debbie Lee, *Slavery and the Romantic Imagination* (Philadelphia: University of Pennsylvania Press, 2002).
127 Ruth Richardson, *Death, Dissection and the Destitute* (London: Routledge and Kegan Paul, 1988), pp. 200, 266; Robert G. Hall, 'Hearts and minds: the politics of everyday life in Chartism, 1832–1840', *LHR*, 74 (2009), 31.
128 *FP*, 1 May and 15 June 1841.
129 Another similar case had been reported at York in 1829: *The Dreadful Effects of the Resurrection in Yorkshire* (1829), copy of a broadside in BL, 74/1870.c.2(567).
130 Richardson, *Death*, p. 195; *Braford Observer*, 3 November 1836.
131 *Leeds Intelligencer*, 2 February 1832.
132 *Leeds Mercury*, 30 October 1830.
133 Mark Hovell, *The Chartist Movement* (Manchester: Manchester University Press, 1970 [1918]), p. 89.

134 E.g., *FP*, 4 December 1841 (Oastler to Thornhill). For synaesthetics and the Gothic, see Grace Kehler, 'Gothic pedagogy and Victorian reform treatises', *Victorian Studies*, 50 (2008), 440.

135 Boddice and Smith, *Emotion, Sense, Experience*, p. 45.

136 *FP*, 23 April 1842.

137 Peter N. Stearns, *Shame: A Brief History* (Urbana, Chicago and Springfield: University of Illinois Press, 2017), pp. 5, 50.

138 Reddy, *Navigation of Feeling*, p. 146.

139 Kehler, 'Gothic pedagogy', p. 447.

140 Boddice, *Science of Sympathy*, pp. 8–10.

141 It was precisely in relation to the selective humanitarianism of the abolitionists – in campaigning against chattel slavery, but not white slavery – that Thomas Haskell coined the concept of an ethical shelter: Thomas L. Haskell, 'Capitalism and the origins of the humanitarian sensibility, Part 1', *American Historical Review*, 90 (1985), 352.

142 For a discussion of Jones's poem, see Taylor, *Ernest Jones*, pp. 84–6. See also Ledger, *Dickens*, p. 155.

143 Luke Gibbons, *Gaelic Gothic: Race, Colonization, and Irish Culture* (Galway: Arlen House, 2004), p. 80.

5

His Satanic Majesty's chaplain: J.R. Stephens and the prophetic politics of the heart

Few gentleman radical leaders came close to rivalling the sentimentalism of the Reverend Joseph Rayner Stephens, and no name was more calculated to elicit feelings of dread and disgust among the propertied classes in the late 1830s. One of his enemies, the Manchester Liberal John Easby, dubbed Stephens 'a base mercenary ... his Satanic Majesty's chaplain'. Stephens exulted in depravity and glorified 'in the vilest strains of indecency', the product, Easby conjectured, of 'a splenetic and envenomed heart'.[1] A renegade Wesleyan minister who had resigned in 1834 on account of his zealous advocacy of the separation of church and state, Stephens took most of his Ashton-under-Lyne and Stalybridge congregations with him and became pastor of the independent 'Stephenites'. This was no minor secession: by August 1834, there were upwards of 800 Stephenites across Ashton, Stalybridge, Hyde and Oldham, divided into fifty classes with twenty-two local preachers. The last time a local religious census had taken place in Ashton – in 1829 – there had only been 1,000 Wesleyans.[2] By the late 1830s, Stephens had established himself as a self-styled 'political preacher', and from his pulpit had become the foremost leader of the factory reform and anti-Poor Law movements in north-west England and, like his friend Oastler, beyond. The outpouring of intense feeling was the dominant and recurring refrain in his sermons. The chronicler of the factory movement, Samuel Kydd, recalled that Stephens 'knew how to appeal to the affections of the poor' and that 'he would appeal to the affections of the heart'.[3] A reporter for the hostile *Stockport Advertiser* was of the opinion that: 'Never did I hear such strong, masculine, fervid, impassioned ... language really terrific to hear'.[4] The waspish Francis Place thought him 'a fanatic possessing great command of language and great power of declamation', who 'paid little or no regard to the feelings of any but those he wished to command, and these were the working people'. He was, Place continued, 'obeyed & most adored by the multitudes'.[5]

While it is no longer possible to claim, as G.D.H. Cole did in 1941, that 'Joseph Rayner Stephens has not fared well at the hands of the historians',[6] the role of feelings in his politics, though often remarked upon, has never been taken seriously by historians. There was more to his cultural stylistics than Romanticism and melodrama; in contrast to Oastler, Stephens was a much less recognisably Gothic figure.[7] The early twentieth-century historian of Chartism Mark Hovell tellingly wrote of Stephens's 'unreasoning sentimentalism', a judgement that placed Hovell in the proto-Fabian tradition begun by Francis Place which damned Stephens, Richard Oastler and Feargus O'Connor for their impassioned advocacy of physical force.[8] The implication here is that Stephens's speeches were ravings, the product of an unstable mind, a charge frequently levelled at him by his enemies. As this chapter will argue, it would be more accurate to speak of Stephens's *reasoned* sentimentalism or refined sympathy: not only was it a calculated response, but it was also a logical extension and transference of his religious beliefs and feelings to the political sphere. Unfortunately for Stephens, this transference, as we shall see, transgressed the feeling rules of Methodism, or emotional regime to use Reddy's concept. Stephens's biographers have presented him as self-consciously operating in the Biblical prophetic tradition, leavened by Romanticism, but surprisingly much less has been written about how his political preaching was shaped by his Methodism.[9] By drawing on recent work which has explored the relationship between Methodism and emotion, it becomes clear that while Stephens may have resigned from the Connexion, his 'heart-religion', as Methodism has been termed, remained intact.[10] It was this cluster of religious feelings, seated in the heart, which underpinned his political preaching.

Have nothing to do with sects or parties was one of Stephens's injunctions to his congregation; independency in matters of politics and faith was his mantra. As the second section suggests, it was the affective consequences of surrendering to party and church that Stephens singled out as the greatest evil of 'belonging' in matters of faith and politics. Although some recent accounts have been more cautious,[11] there is a long tradition of inaccurately labelling Stephens a Tory in the 1830s, a product, in part, of the same retrospective rereading of his earlier career in light of his later closer affinity with Tories that we saw with his friend and ally Richard Oastler. Tory-radical is little better given its origins as a term of abuse; labels such as Tory-radical or Christian radical obscure more than they reveal.[12] Tory strands there may have been but feeling and temperament kept him outside Peel's Conservative Party. The final section of the chapter brings together Stephens's faith and politics, tracing the affective dimensions of his leadership of the factory and anti-Poor Law movements. For all its undeniable appeal with working-class audiences, Stephens's violent sympathy for the victims of the factory system and the hated new workhouses frightened and alienated the propertied classes with the result that he was imprisoned for eighteen months in 1840–41, thus bringing an end to his brief meteoric career as a political preacher, which lasted less than three years.[13]

'Heart religion' and the place of feeling

Joseph Rayner Stephens was born in 1805, the son of a Wesleyan minister. He was educated at Woodhouse Grove Methodist boarding school, Leeds, and then Manchester Grammar. After a brief period as a teacher in Hull, he entered the Wesleyan ministry in 1825, and was ordained the following year. He then undertook missionary work in Sweden, before returning to England where he was appointed to the Cheltenham circuit in 1830. Two years later, he transferred to the Ashton-under-Lyne circuit, the district in which he would spend the remainder of his life (he died in 1879).[14] Raised in an impeccably Methodist household, Stephens was inducted into a religious connexion that had its origins in the enthusiasm of the evangelical revival. Noted for its effusiveness of feeling, Methodism was characterised by a style of impassioned preaching which appealed to the hearts of the people. Like other forms of evangelical religion at the time, Methodism was known as 'heart-religion'. This was also a reflection of where, anatomically, evangelicals located feeling and faith, though there was nothing unusual in this as the heart had long been identified as the seat of the self, feeling and soul.[15] While it was never the stated intention of John Wesley and his disciples to appeal solely to feeling – to view it as such is to see the movement entirely through the eyes of its enemies – as Phyllis Mack has shown there was 'an acceptance of the limits of reason in understanding religious truths'. This meant that 'emotion, not intellect, was the touchstone of religious and philosophical truth'.[16]

Given the deliberate appeal to feelings with a view to cultivating a particular kind of sensibility, it is no exaggeration to label Methodism an emotional regime. Reddy defines an emotional regime as: 'a normative order for emotions … which require individuals to express normative emotions and to avoid deviant emotions'.[17] Hence the importance that Methodists placed on the need to 'master "bad feelings" like anger or envy while nurturing "good" feelings such as compassion or tenderness'. The right ordering of feeling was of crucial importance to Methodists because their 'ability to feel correctly and to help others feel correctly determined the health' of their own soul. 'At the same time', Mack continues, the Methodists tried to attune themselves to the flow of emotion moving between the individual and others. In part, this was because the movement was also a product of the age of sensibility in which 'the ability to feel and to share another's feelings was viewed as a sign not of uncontrolled enthusiasm or loss of integrity, but of refined sympathy'.[18] Stephens was clearly shaped profoundly by this 'heart religion'. In one of his addresses he asked, what is religion?

> The string by which the earth is hung on Heaven – the golden hand by which the soul is, as it were, tied to God. God sheds his love abroad in our hearts and that love leads us in all things so to act as becometh godliness. Religion, Godward, is the worship of a holy heart.[19]

The anonymous author of *The Factory Lad, or the Life of Simon Smike*, an exposé of the cruelties of factory life based on the testimony of those like Stephens, singled out the latter's 'vital religion: – the religion of the heart' as a wellspring of his humanitarian crusade on behalf of the oppressed.[20]

There was, however, a tension at the heart of Methodist theology between passivity and agency. The religious discourse of the Atonement which emphasised Christ's suffering implied that the 'goal of the sufferer was passivity and acceptance' – one of the hallmarks of pietism. At the same time, it was incumbent on the believer to protect one's health and aid the afflicted, including the poor, which implied agency.[21] As we shall see, this was a tension that Stephens would ultimately resolve in favour of the latter. For Methodists, then, there was certainly a place for intense feelings, but it was to be directed towards the spiritual plane, not the profane, and here they were following the teachings of St. Augustine.[22] Thus, it was perfectly acceptable – indeed desirable – that a preacher would appeal to the feelings of audiences by stimulating and controlling 'waves of passion', always careful to direct such waves upwards. As John Kent notes, Wesley and the early Methodists 'had never responded to the condition of the poor in a political manner'; rather, in deploring poverty they had encouraged charity.[23] By the time that Stephens entered the Wesleyan ministry in the mid-1820s, the Connexion had expended a great deal of effort in setting its face firmly against radical politics and protest, on the grounds that it was the duty of the Christian to support the existing, providential, order. In practice, this gave the Connexion strong Tory sympathies, not least because of its support for the principle of religious establishments which upheld Christian values.[24]

It was in relation to the question of church and state that Stephens broke with the Wesleyans in 1834. What is remarkable about this episode is just how much it revolved around the *place* of feeling, an aspect which has not been accorded the significance it merits by Stephens's biographers.[25] Stephens openly flouted Connexion policy by playing a prominent part in the local campaign for the disestablishment of the Church of England by becoming secretary of the Ashton-under-Lyne Church Separation Society. He was soon reported to his local superiors in the Manchester District, before whom he appeared for the first stage of his 'trial' but, refusing to back down, he was suspended and his case was traversed to Conference, the governing body of the Connexion. Censured and refusing to desist, he tended his resignation. On the surface, the episode appears as little more than a straightforward conflict over policy: Wesleyan official policy was, in line with its toryism, to support religious establishments; Stephens saw the matter differently, and as a young man of deep principle refused to yield. A closer look reveals that this was not just a conflict over policy, though that was certainly the plane on which Stephens expected to be tried. The year before his case came up, Conference had warned against 'too warm an interest' in political affairs which 'do not immediately concern our Connexion'.[26] In drawing up the charges against Stephens, a similar emphasis was placed on feeling and it was not just his role as secretary that offended but the speeches he had delivered in favour of disestablishment: 'The speeches of Mr Stephens are directly at variance with the sentiments of Mr. Wesley and the Conference, and are distinguished by a spirit highly unbecoming of a Wesleyan minister.' Further, he had disturbed the 'internal tranquillity' of the Connexion by the part he had played in the 'aggressive proceedings' of the Church Separation Society. Jabez Bunting, the dictatorial Wesleyan leader who acted as judge in the trial, also spoke of how Stephens had 'violated the peaceable and unsectarian spirit of Wesleyan Methodists'.[27]

At issue here was not just what Stephens had said in his speeches, but the *way* he had delivered them and, crucially, *where* they had been delivered. Much of this revolved around the place of the pulpit. One of the charges against him was that he had used the pulpit in his Wesleyan chapel to announce to his congregation that there was a petition in the vestry in favour of disestablishment, which he encouraged them to sign. But arguably, what outraged the hierarchy was not what Stephens said in his pulpit, but the impassioned speeches he was delivering elsewhere. By making impassioned speeches in favour of disestablishment, Stephens had transgressed the boundaries of the Methodist emotional regime: passion was fine in the pulpit, but not outside of it. And here we need to be mindful of how different emotional regimes relate to one another, and the scope for navigation between them (what Reddy terms emotional navigation).[28] As we have seen, the leaders of Wesleyan Methodism were acutely conscious of the broader political emotional regime in which they operated and knew only too well that the political establishment was still anxious about displays of intense passion. In failing to delimit his displays of passion to the circumscribed pulpit, Stephens had, in effect, failed to navigate successfully between the different emotional regimes, and thus he experienced emotional suffering from the goal conflicts between official Wesleyanism and his own beliefs (on which more in a moment). In becoming a political preacher, he had committed the sin of trying to expand the boundaries of the emotional regime to incorporate secular affairs, but this the Wesleyan hierarchy would not countenance. Identical charges would be levelled at him when he began to make impassioned speeches in favour of factory reform and opposition to the New Poor Law. Bunting rebuked him for his obstinacy and unwillingness to express 'regret' for the 'embarrassment' he had created for his brethren.[29] The implication here was that Stephens was failing to demonstrate the right kind of feelings, which compounded the initial charge of untethering his passions from the pulpit and directing them to the profane.

One final detail of Stephens's trial is noteworthy. During the initial hearing at Manchester, John Bowers, a preacher from the Stockport circuit who was present, relayed to Bunting what had transpired. The Manchester District leaders were exasperated over Stephens's refusal to offer any meaningful defence of his action. This was deliberate on his part because he wanted his case traversing to Conference so that he could provoke a debate on the position of the Wesleyans towards religious establishments. Bowers found Stephens's behaviour 'inexplicable'. When Stephens refused to accede to the injunction that he abstain from any further involvement in campaigning for disestablishment, Bowers was struck by his affective state: 'This was not said in a tone of contumacy or defiance, but with deep, and (undeniably) unaffected emotion. He wept profusely.'[30] His tears may have been outward evidence of what Reddy terms 'emotional suffering' – the suffering that results from goal conflicts between the emotional discipline imposed by the regime against conflicting desires such as freedom.[31] It is possible that Stephens was shedding crocodile tears, though this seems unlikely, not least because his principled stand had also strained his personal relationship with his father, who was then a prominent figure in the Wesleyan hierarchy. Adding further to his difficulties was that his father was every bit as conservative as Bunting, and so the son's battle with the Connexion spilled over into his family life.[32] Stephens's conduct at Conference was seen as inexplicable and self-defeating, but approaching the episode from the history of emotions makes it more understandable. Although his tears were shed at the district hearing rather than at the second stage of the trial at Conference, the treatment he received in both arenas must have been deeply painful for him. As William J. Abraham has written of Methodist internal politics, 'Being mistreated by one's Annual Conference is as painful as being betrayed by one's biological family'.[33] The disappointment for Stephens was that Conference very deliberately refused to let the trial expand into an open debate about the merits or otherwise of religious establishments: the resolutions and Bunting's summing up shut this down by claiming that disestablishment was contrary to the sentiments of John Wesley. Yet Stephens claimed (not without some justification) that this was untrue.[34] In so refusing, Stephens's position was untenable, and this was why his adversaries shifted the focus towards feelings, because here they felt on safer, less controversial ground. It was no coincidence that all this occurred at a time when the Connexion hierarchy were fighting wars on several fronts from malcontent Methodist reformers demanding greater ecclesiastical democracy. Not for the last time in his career as a political preacher Stephens had been censured for his misplaced passions, of religious enthusiasm run amok.

Evangel of retributive toryism?

With his seemingly inexplicable behaviour and misdirected passions, rumours began to circulate that Stephens was mentally unbalanced, a malicious accusation that dogged sentimental radicals as we saw in the previous chapter. Even Stephens's father thought his son 'daft' for entering politics.[35] The usual charges levelled at gentleman radicals were voiced: he was not all that he seemed; he was an unprincipled popularity-seeker whose violent rhetoric served no other purpose than to excite and dupe the masses into donating their hard-earnt pennies to pay for a dissolute life as a political agitator. The inspector sent by the Home Office to interview Stephens during his imprisonment even doubted whether he had any religious beliefs at all, which seems wide of the mark.[36] As for conning the working-class out of their money, it is true that Stephens was largely dependent on the financial support from his congregations, but when working-class members started to lose their jobs because of their support for him, he shared his stipend with them.[37] The chronicler of Methodism Benjamin Gregory attributed Stephens's recklessness to his youth and to the period of isolation he had endured as a missionary in Sweden, where he had been stationed in the late 1820s. In Gregory's view, Stephens was 'by temperament and habit, hot, heady, hazardous, restless and intractable' and these 'powerful weaknesses had been nurtured into revolutionary passions' during his time as a solitary missionary in Sweden. Correctly, Gregory also noted that Stephens had formed friendships with 'adventurous men of genius' during this period of life.[38] Most notable was the French liberal Catholic Montalembert with both men, perhaps, nurturing in the other the beginnings of the romantic temperament and commitment to reform that would characterise their later careers. Years later, Stephens wrote to Montalembert and recollected their youthful ardent love of liberty along with their 'mutual love of poetry, metaphysics and moral philosophy'.[39] Upon his return to England this circle was enlarged by men of 'romantic natures', including the novelists Harrison Ainsworth and Samuel Warren, whom Stephens had known since his schooldays with the trio taking a keen interest in amateur dramatics.[40]

Stephens was clearly shaped by continental Romanticism. He could read several European languages, including German, and he also studied British dialects and Anglo-Saxon.[41] It has escaped Stephens's biographers that it is possible he may have spent some time in Germany in the period between his departure from Sweden in November 1829 and his appointment to the Cheltenham circuit in the summer of 1830.[42] When he was interviewed at the behest of the Home Office during his incarceration in 1840, the notes stated that he had spent a period of time in Germany.[43] He clearly read German literature. Not only did he translate German pietist poetry, he also translated poems by the incipient romantic Johann Gottfried Herder – 'one of our favourites, when we were young' – and wrote several senti-mental poems himself.[44] German pietism appears an unlikely wellspring of Stephens's affective politics due its quietist and inward-looking tendencies. Yet some German pietists who reacted against these quietist precepts were progenitors of Romanticism by prioritising intense feeling and imagination in religion as well as the imperatives of moral action.[45] Stephens's time in Sweden, during which he learned to speak not only Swedish but also Danish and Finnish, had sparked an interest in northern literature and the ancient sagas.[46] He was also familiar with Scandinavian Romanticism, in particular the Swedish lyrical poet Karl August Nicander and the Finnish-Swedish poet Frans Mikael Franzén, some of whose work Stephens translated.[47] His literary output has been judged unfavourably, but Stephens was no dilet-tante when it came to metaphysics, literature and the dramatic arts. It seems likely that his encounter with Romanticism served to accentuate the senti-mentalism which had been implanted in him by exposure to heart-religion. As Fay Bound Alberti has observed, 'the feeling heart was crucial to the Romantic project and provided evidence of creativity and the divine'.[48]

It was Stephens's encounter with Romanticism that made him such a restless spirit as far as Wesleyanism was concerned. The trial of 1834 and the carving out of the role of 'political preacher' forced him to confront the limitations of Wesleyan Methodism. For all that he tried to legitimate his political preaching by claiming that he was simply restoring Methodism to the pristine purity of John Wesley, this failed utterly to convince his supe-riors. The broader movement of evangelicalism offered few wellsprings for the political preacher, either. In any case, Stephens was at odds with various aspects of evangelicalism. Notwithstanding their espousal of vital religion, evangelicals also emphasised moral rectitude and self-restraint, a reac-tion, in part, to the excesses of Romanticism, but mainly, as Boyd Hilton puts it: 'Because they made a fetish of salvation by faith, evangelicals were obliged to elevate the passions, but they were also afraid of them, a tension they sought to resolve by inventing over-elaborate rules of conduct.'[49]

Having resigned from the Connexion in 1834, Stephens took full advan-tage of his freedom as pastor of the secessionists who broke with him at Ashton and Stalybridge to flesh out his role as political preacher. But it was no longer the cause of disestablishment that preoccupied him. Some four years residence in the centre of a cotton district had opened his heart to the oppression of the new factory system, witnessing first-hand the devastating effects that it was inflicting on the working-classes, some of whom were members of his congregations. By 1836, he had become the Lancashire Oastler, not just on account of his advocacy of far-reaching factory reform but also due to his vehement hostility to the New Poor Law of 1834. From a theological point of view, Methodism certainly provided Stephens with some justification for his social gospel: the accent placed on love of God and one another, and care for the poor, and it also rekindled some of the fervour, excitement and sentimentalism of early Methodist preaching. But this was only really by way of amplifying what E.P. Thompson termed the 'democratic spirit' within Methodism 'which struggled against the doctrines' of the connexional hierarchy.[50] In Stephens's case, his encounter with Romanticism appears to have also amplified the emphasis on feeling and agency as opposed to reason and passivity, thus disturbing the delicate equilibrium at the heart of Methodism.

It was not just Romanticism that supplied Stephens with the means to accent intense feeling in his political preaching. As virtually all his biographers have noted, he identified strongly with the Prophetic tradition in the Bible, and there is little point here in recapitulating the many and varied ways in which he donned the mantle of an Old Testament Prophet.[51] But revisiting the Prophetic tradition, from the perspective of the history of emotions, illuminates why and how that tradition shaped his affective politics. The word 'prophet' comes from the Hebrew and means one who speaks God's message. The authority of the prophet derives from God, and it is to Him, and only Him, that the prophet is responsible.[52] A deponent from Leigh, Lancashire, who attended a lecture by him in November 1838, informed the magistrates that Stephens began speaking 'by quoting scripture: "Vengeance is mine saith the Lord", and then stated that he believed God had raised him up as an instrument to assert or protest the people's rights against their oppressors'.[53] He told his listeners that his mission was to bring England's rulers back to the laws of God as a basis for government, reminiscent of Wesley's canonical sermons which began with the dangers of abandoning the written law of God. This was a calling. As Stephens confessed: 'I wish not to live by excitement ... I am not a public man by nature or by choice ... but ... I can and will endeavour to be where conscience calls me.'[54] By conceiving himself as a prophet, Stephens and his hearers drew strength, courage, hope and, above all, empowerment. 'We must feel that God will give us the power ... and we must set our hearts upon employing that power', he told his Stalybridge congregation.[55] As with Methodism, Stephens's prophetic message was meant to bring reassurance. There is a sense in which the prophetic tradition provided him with his own ethical shelter. As he was only communicating a message from God, he could not be held responsible for his impassioned rhetoric, including his violent denunciations of the enemies of the working class and recommendation that the people arm themselves in readiness for violent conflict with their enemies. As he told his congregation at Ashton in March 1839, 'If I have said strange things, words which made the people shudder; words which made the land … shake and tremble; the words have not been mine … [t]he mouth of the Lord hath spoken it'.[56]

While noted for their impassioned speech, as religious scholars have pointed out, prophets did not base their appeal solely on feeling, but also faith, reason and the ethical conduct of the prophet himself. Stephens often denied that he appealed to base passions. He claimed to speak 'in cool blood; I speak the language of truth and soberness' and cautioned his audience not to misread his impassioned rhetoric: 'Though I am a man of strong words, they are not hastily adopted.'[57] This was also why he went to great lengths to cultivate an image of himself as a man of spotless character, who in his 'natural' and preferred environment of the home was 'mild mannered' and a loving father (Stephens had two daughters by his first marriage).[58] In other words, he projected an image of the refined man of feeling. As his enemies knew only too well, this made him even more vulnerable to accusations of personal scandal, and it was precisely on that front that some of the Chartists at Ashton attacked him. Dr Peter McDouall, the Chartist doctor, spread the rumour that Stephens had sexually harassed the sister of Bronterre O'Brien, a charge that Stephens vehemently denied and, according to Feargus O'Connor, was invented by O'Brien because he was jealous of Stephens's influence.[59] The ethical conduct of a prophet was important because they drew 'their conclusions from the moral behaviour of the people around them'.[60] Their main concern was not with the behaviour of the righteous and the poor but the rich, corrupt and tyrannical rulers who inflict suffering. In exhorting the fallen to return to the word of God, the prophet is a moral guardian. What shocked Stephens was the complicity of his co-religionists and others in the perpetuation of the evils of factory slavery and the harshness of the New Poor Law. He attributed this to a turning inwards by the propertied classes and a deliberate attempt to shut themselves away from the suffering around them, what he termed a retreat 'into the innermost recesses of [their] luxurious and selfish heart[s]'. Mere legislation could have no effect unless there was a genuine change among hearts and minds. 'An Act of Parliament cannot change the hearts of the tyrants … unless their hearts were changed, and your hearts changed, what could the law do?'[61] Like Oastler, Stephens was determined to breech the ramparts of the ethical shelter constructed by the propertied classes.

The prideful pursuit of riches, 'the insatiable avarice', violence and oppression of the rich had resulted in 'poverty, without guilt'. Poverty was recast as a crime and was 'inflicted without mercy' until death, 'a more compassionate enemy than mammon', ended the suffering of the poor.[62]

Liberal political economy had, in effect, anaesthetised the rich and powerful from feeling the pain of poverty and suffering. 'Pray, then, for the spirit of God to be poured out', Stephens pleaded, 'pray that God would strike with the hammer of his word, and break this national heart of stone'.[63] As he asked in one of his sermons, condemning the speech from the throne which opened parliament, is there 'one word of sorrow for the people, one word of regret ... is there one tear of pity from the maiden eye of youthful royalty? No, the queen's eye has been forbidden to weep; the queen's heart has been forbidden to feel.'[64] Unsurprisingly, Lord John Russell, then Home Secretary, was singled out by Stephens as 'the most cold-blooded, hard-hearted murderer that ever existed in the world'.[65] It did not escape Stephens's attention that the author of the *Book of Murder*, which advocated the extermination of every additional child born to a poor family who already had two children, had recommended death by gassing as a 'humane project of "painless extinction" '.[66] Like Oastler, Stephens also highlighted the hypocrisy of the middle classes in their sympathy for the plight of enslaved blacks and their refusal to see factory labour as a form of slavery. In doing so, he implied that it was easier to feel sympathy for the distant and abstract victim rather than the immediate, an inversion of the younger David Hume's conception of sympathy.[67] As Stephens's sermons began to attack this hypocrisy, he lost the well-heeled members of his congregations.[68]

But this was not just a class issue, of Stephens defending the working class against cruel and tyrannical capital. Also at issue was the way in which he was challenging the fundamental Methodist, and indeed Protestant, tenet of justification by faith alone, which for many Methodists was contrary to the teachings of Wesley who had warned of the temptation to '"buy salvation" by good works'.[69] In one of his sermons, Stephens used a bodily metaphor to emphasise faith *and* works, and to legitimate political preaching:

> I contend that law and religion can never be separated. If you attempt to dissociate or disunite them, it is like attempting to dissociate and disunite the soul from body ... The body without the spirit is dead; faith without works is dead; religion without politics is dead; the one is the body, the other is the soul.[70]

The connection he drew here between religion and politics raises the question of his party politics. Was he a Tory, or a Tory-radical? He never self-identified as a Tory in the 1830s and 1840s; in fact, he was averse to the label, an aversion which was no doubt increased by the tory proclivities of the Wesleyan hierarchy. He was an independent who freely attacked Tory, Whig and radical, and bemoaned the 'rancorous spirit of party' fomented, in his view, by inciting 'party passions'. The image of the lonely prophet, shunned by respectable society, burdened with God's message, also reinforced this independence. This independence stemmed from a deep aversion to the affective consequences of tying oneself to the dictates of party. 'In religion and politics it is all one. You must either bend or be broken,' he reasoned. In surrendering to the dictates of party, partisans were cowardly and because they never stopped to question and reason for themselves, they grow ever more 'pig-headed'. Only fidelity to Christ, he urged, furnished courage, independence and open-mindedness (Stephens conveniently ruled out the possibility that fidelity to Christ might be construed in the same way as partisanship): 'Christ's followers are freemen. The love that is within them from on high casteth out fear.' In a characteristically heartfelt Methodist sentiment, he concluded with the injunction 'If you would benefit your country you must begin each man with his own heart', for that was the surest way to effect God's will. 'The word of God thrown open before a sound understanding, which works as bidden by a lowly, guileless, loving-heart will lead you in the right way in all things.' He looked forward to a time when party distinctions would cease and be replaced with 'good neighbourship and brotherly love'. In doing so, he caught the popular mood for independent politics at this time, to which his radicalism and toryism were firmly subordinated. Stephens was no more the prophet of Chartism than he was 'the evangel of retributive Toryism'.[71] When Chartism emerged in 1838–39 he made it clear that his alliance with the Chartists was tactical: he had entered the movement on his own terms and for his own reasons, namely to secure an improvement in the conditions of the working classes. Although he had supported universal manhood suffrage and continued to do so even after he denounced the Chartists, Stephens refused to sign up to the other five points of the People's Charter. During his trial in 1839 he attacked the Chartists in an attempt to save himself – an apostasy that some never forgave, especially on the heels of McDouall's allegations of sexual impropriety.[72]

The laws of the fleshy tablets of the heart

In the mouth of Stephens, whatever remained of his Methodism was no 'chiliasm of despair', as E.P. Thompson famously described the tendency in the movement which preached passivity and acceptance of suffering.[73] Rather, his heart religion was meant to promote political and social action in this world. While there was undoubtedly an apocalyptic and millenarian vein running through his speeches, this invariably took the form of warning the tyrannical and unjust to mend their ways lest they incur God's avenging wrath.[74] Similarly, he did not instruct the working classes to wait patiently and passively for the second coming; they were to arm themselves and battle with God's enemies, and though like other advocates of physical force he could be ambiguous and shift his position, on other occasions he called for violence against persons as well as property. This, he claimed, was perfectly justified as the Bible condoned slaughtering of tyrants.[75] As Mike Sanders has argued, there was a deeper ambiguity in Stephens's theological notion of insurrection which affirmed 'the right of armed resistance to oppression but insists that the time for fighting, though close, has not yet arrived'.[76] By drawing on Romanticism and the prophetic tradition, Stephens fashioned an affective politics that built on and radicalised religious enthusiasm in ways that resonated powerfully with northern working-class audiences in whose hearts he was said to reign.[77]

Stephens's sermons and political speeches were characterised by intense displays of passion. Space was an important aspect of his affective politics, and to the affective experience of his listeners. Holding meetings outdoors was no mere exercise in practicality – of having no one else to meet because of the size of audience or the refusal of civic authorities to grant access to public buildings. Rather, these real spatial constraints were transformed into affective enablers: 'I love to meet you' outdoors, he began his sermon in Ashton marketplace on 3 March 1839, because 'it always seems to me that the mind of man is fresher and the soul larger, and the heart more full of hope and joy when thus we come together'. These scenes were 'exceedingly beautiful, as well as affecting'.[78] As Katrina Navickas has argued, the mass platform was about more than space, or even a show of numbers to intimidate the authorities, as important as those considerations were. The experience was also meant to inculcate feelings of empowerment, uplift and elation, some of which came from the speeches.[79] It was no coincidence, Stephens continued, that they met outside because the buildings of organised religion had been closed off to the people on account of the mean-spiritedness and hostility towards the poor. The problem with the extant churches and chapels was that because of innovations such as pew rents, the need for Sunday 'best' attire, they were no longer spaces which brought the classes together in brotherly love. On the contrary, when the poor did attend these places their feelings were of resentment, envy and contempt for the hypocrisy of the employing classes. Churches were meant to be spaces for 'loving each other … promoting each other's happiness … by the exchange of mutual affection'.[80]

Stephens's independent chapels, and even more so his outdoor itinerant preaching in open spaces (as well as Ashton marketplace, similar meetings took place at Primrose Hill, Shepherd and Shepherdess Fields and Kennington Common in London), constituted what Reddy has termed an 'emotional refuge': 'A relationship, ritual or organisation (whether informal or formal) that provides safe release from prevailing emotional norms and allows relaxation of emotional effort, with or without an ideological justification, which may shore up or threaten the existing emotional regime.'[81] Akin to the revivalist preaching of Wesley and Whitefield a hundred years before – a parallel that Stephens explicitly drew, the latter's sermons were responded to with the same affective fervour by the assembled crowds: 'Many appeared to be completely overwhelmed with their feelings, while tears of gladness stole down the cheek.'[82] Just how Stephens knew that these were tears of gladness is unclear. Oastler made a similar remark when he attended a factory reform demonstration in Stephens's fiefdom of Ashton in December 1836: sitting alongside his friend, Oastler observed 'many a tear of joy was seen to trickle down the cheeks of fathers and mothers, whose worn-out haggard looks betokened that they were bred to factory labour, and thus knew the horrors to which their sons and daughters must submit ... they looked, and wept in hope'.[83] It is possible that some of these tears may have stemmed from guilt – of parents having to rely on the wages of their children employed in factories, or from genuine worries about how families were to make ends meet if children ceased working in factories. But as far as Stephens and Oastler were concerned these tears were emotional outpourings of the affection felt by the working class towards them, another instance of tears as 'liquid social bond' between leaders and followers. These tears along with other visible and audible emotional expressions were seen as sentimental barometers that both men used to gauge the traction of their campaigns and popularity.[84]

But even emotional refuges have their rules, and Stephens did not give free rein to uncontrolled feeling on these occasions; though his detractors would claim otherwise. Far from manifesting uncontrolled feeling, his politics were a form of refined sympathy which formed the basis of a positive, disciplined moral energy – a formulation that was central to Methodist views of emotions.[85] In a revealing phrase, he referred to his campaigns as 'moral warfare'.[86] As Rob Boddice has argued, morality and feeling were conflated in the early nineteenth century, a conflation that emerged from a long tradition of ethics which held that feeling, not reason, was the source of morality. 'We measure feelings by actions, by the practices they produce. We label a moral action sympathetic and thereby define, by tracing backward, the sympathetic impulse.'[87] For Stephens, the factory system and New Poor Law was deeply immoral – at variance not only with the laws of God, but also natural feelings. The chronicler of the factory reform movement Samuel Kydd, who knew Stephens from the campaign, recalled of his oratory:

> He was an orator, a logician, and knew how to appeal to the affections of the poor. It was his habit to raise himself, step by step, to an altitude of reasoning which all could see; he would then strike out in bold and homely Saxon

against his opponents; depict in thrilling words the sufferings of the oppressed, and having pointed to the victims, he would appeal to the affections of the heart, asking 'If the poor had not feelings, sympathies, and love for their kind and country.' Mr Stephens was never more thoroughly 'at home' than when talking of the gambols of children, the affections of mothers, the duties of manhood; by appealing to the innermost working of the heart of each, he concentrated the sympathies of all.[88]

In the view of Stephens, it was this sympathy which licensed his strong rhetoric. 'Gentlemen! I speak freely, because I feel acutely', he told the electors of Ashton in 1837.[89] It was crucial for Stephens's credibility to authenticate his testimony of working-class suffering; and feeling was central to establishing that authenticity. As he told a London audience in 1839, 'it was impossible for anyone who had not dwelt with the people, and visited and communed with them in their heart of hearts as he had done, to have the least conception of the heartless and remorseless tyranny to which the victims of the factory system were subjected'.[90] He was also quick to contrast the relative comfort he experienced in prison compared to that endured by the workers in factories and workhouses, singling out the psychological impact, especially on children: fretting, pining, broken, hopeless, broken-hearted.[91] At the same time, Stephens also drew attention to how he, too, had suffered persecution and, ultimately, imprisonment for battling on behalf of the oppressed people. Thus, sympathy – based on mutual suffering – formed yet another social bond between Stephens and his followers in a way that democratised the relationship between gentleman leader and working-class follower.[92]

Nevertheless, Stephens knew he had to tread a careful line; hence his insistence that he did not appeal to base passion. It was a shrewd move on his part to publish his sermons, which, in addition to spreading his message much further afield, also pre-empted the accusation – sometimes levelled at extempore sermons – of unbridled enthusiasm. Committing them to paper brought a semblance of order, coherence and measure (though it is unclear whether Stephens actually read from a script or whether the published versions were more restrained).[93] He also went to great lengths to fashion a reasoned sentimentality that brought together reason and feeling as indivisible – and, occasionally, in ways that imbricated his sentimental radicalism with ascetic radicalism. Again, the heart was central: this was the nexus where reason and feeling met. Stephens referred to this nexus as the 'fleshy tablets of your heart' to denote the place in the human body where the laws of God were inscribed, a phrase with Biblical provenance (Proverbs 3:3 and Jeremiah 17:1), a popular refrain with radicals as it signalled not only the divine origins of rights but also imparted a sense of righteousness and militant defiance when those rights were transgressed.[94] In justifying his and the working class's resistance to the New Poor Law, he explained how 'The feelings of the hearts could not be brought to square with the understanding of that bill', as if the terrain of feeling was the plane on which government was to be assessed. The heart was not just a moral compass for guiding and assessing politics, it was also the wellspring of political feeling itself. In a pastoral address written during his incarceration, he entreated his followers to 'live and enjoy the truth'. 'Out of the heart the mouth will then speak with power ... There is no eloquence like that of a heart glowing with the warmth of its own pure and holy feeling.'[95] To withhold one's heart from God, was to close one's mind. Interestingly, Stephens centred his relationship with the working class in his heart. In one of his prison letters he concluded 'Give my heart's best love to all ... You [his supporters] live in my heart'.[96] Each of these statements, all written after he had left the Wesleyan church, are indicative of the ways in which the Methodist cult of the heart still shaped his political preaching.

Further evidence of the importance that Stephens attached to restraint was his insistence that his working-class supporters live respectable, disciplined lives, lest they furnish their enemies with moral ammunition that workers were little better than unfeeling brutes. Thus, even Stephens's affective politics were not untouched by asceticism. Just as Wesley had, Stephens urged the workers to practice frugality, temperance and cultivate a loving domesticity, which entailed keeping women and children away from the workplace, all based, on a 'highly sentimentalised view of the working-class family' and chivalric masculinity.[97] If the working class did display traits of brutality, then it was the product of the harsh environment in which they were situated. Were the present factory system to be abolished, and more time afforded to recreation and mental improvement, he told an audience at Bury, then 'the moral condition of the Factory Labourers, generally, would be improved'.[98] 'The factory system has deprived you [mothers and children] of almost all natural affection', he thundered from his pulpit. To illustrate this charge, Stephens relayed the following 'testimony':

> I know it for a fact, on the testimony of several medical men, of irreproachable character and worthy of credit, that in score and scores of instances when they have been called in to attend women in childbed in these factory districts the mother herself, as soon as she has become aware that the child is loosened from her, has bid the doctor – BEGGED the doctor to take no pains to keep the child alive. (Great emotion.)[99]

'Great emotion' functions here as the outward, audible and visible manifestation of inward feeling. Stephens certainly understood emotion in this way: as he declared at a meeting in support of the Glasgow Cotton Spinners' strike in 1838: 'I have forborne to express my feelings by any outward token of emotion.'[100]

Feelings on trial

The factory system was literally rewriting the bodies and brains of working-class women, not least by deadening their senses. But Stephens was playing a dangerous game here: while the image of working-class women as hardened and unsexed by the brutalities of the factory system was clearly being deployed for its shock value, it ran the risk of confirming elite prejudices about the working class as sub-human. During his trial at Chester Assizes in August 1839 he emphasised the damage that the factory system was doing to working-class families by destroying natural, loving relationships between husband and wife, parent and child. The result was that the working-class household 'became divided against itself … for those who ought to be natural, who ought to have natural feelings, affections, and regard, and sympathy for one another, become like unnatural brute beasts, burning in lust, hatred, revenge, uncharitableness'.[101] In a similar way, he dwelt on the psychological impact of working-class suffering. 'Many of you are suffering want, the hardest of all our sufferings, because least of all under our control.' 'When hunger becomes widely spread,' he continued, 'when it eats into whole neighbourhoods and knaws [sic.] the heart of an entire nation, there is an end of all endurance.'[102] It is noteworthy that Stephens conceptualises hunger not just as physical want, but as a feeling that also eats at the heart, the effect of which is to diminish patience. By highlighting the affective dimensions of suffering, he was not just seeking to license working-class violence towards their enemies, he was also drawing attention to the humanity of the workers who have the same capacity for feeling as their social betters. His expanded definition of hunger was a riposte to the prevailing view that hunger was a condition to be endured because it was unavoidable and only fell on morally flawed individuals; if the workers were morally flawed it was through no fault of their own.[103]

Focusing on the actual needs of the people, and on the affective aspect of those needs, enabled Stephens to mount a more persuasive and relevant campaign for redressing the people's grievances. Abstract theory and narrow claims to political rights, he countered, would only bring about 'mere change in the framework of our outward institutions'. This was why he always underscored in his speeches to Chartists the positive affective changes – notably an improvement in the mood and confidence of the working classes – which would flow from granting to the workers democratic rights: 'happy firesides for good labour' as he put in a speech at Bradford.[104] His speech at the great Chartist demonstration on Kersal Moor in September 1838, when he famously defined universal manhood suffrage as a 'knife and fork question', is well-known to historians of Chartism. Less well-known are the affective changes he laid out in his speech that he expected to issue from the enactment of manhood suffrage, and, in fact, belie his earlier statement that the vote was only a means to a bodily end of securing the workers good conditions. Not only would the vote afford the working man 'the enjoyment of all the blessings of life', but:

> Universal suffrage which he wanted was that knowledge in the mind, that principle in the heart, that power in the conscience, and that stalwart strength in the right arm, that would enable the working man to meet his master, and stand boldly, and upright upon his feet, without the brand-mark of a bonds-man upon his brow, and without the blush of shame and slavery upon his cheek. (Tremendous cheers.)[105]

As these extracts from Stephens's speeches suggest, he was acutely attuned to the micro-politics of class interaction – of the quotidian ways in which working-class subordination was felt. As these positive affective changes which would flow from the enactment of the People's Charter imply, it would be a mistake to assume that he dealt only in negative feelings. On the contrary, the anger, resentment and outrage that he and the people harboured towards the propertied classes and the government stemmed from the want of love and compassion, and it was the purpose of these negative feelings to bring about a restoration of this 'right feeling and God-like love to man'.[106] Much of this derived from Stephens's reading of Genesis which emphasised the goodness of the world created by God, and included the argument that sensual pleasures and proper reward for labour were divinely ordained. Hence his insistence that life should be 'sweet'.[107] The bodies and souls of the workers, he insisted, did not belong to their employers; they were the property of the workers, a gift from God.[108] And God, he insisted, 'has laid down one and the same law to all'. Thou shall love thy neighbour as thyself and do unto others what thou would have him do unto thee. This 'is the law for the king's heart and the heart of the husbandman'.[109] All were equal in the sight of God because he had implanted the same feelings, and by extension capacity for feeling. This ' "law of love" in the good old book', as he termed it, was the fundamental axiom of Stephens's affective politics.[110] What enraged him was that the working class had been met with scorn and contempt.[111] It was this which had, understandably, inflamed 'the unbridled passions of an insulted and suffering people'.[112] Was it any wonder that the masses were resorting to violence to resist the New Poor Law, under which families were to be separated on entry into the work-house to prevent them from further procreating? This, Stephens asserted, made 'marriage a mockery and offers brutal violence to the holiest feelings of our nature'.[113] He pleaded for a return to love and sympathy, and it was the absence of these right feelings which underpinned the hostility between the classes. The rich:

[S]eem eaten up with fear, lest those, whom they ought by kind treatment to have inspired with affectionate respect, should, in their blind rage and by some sudden effort of their united strength, avenge themselves for the wrongs that have been done to them by a general and indiscriminate onslaught upon all, who are better off than themselves. The poor hate the rich as their oppressors, the rich dread the poor because they well know how sorely they have wronged them, and how much reason they have therefore to take vengeance on those who have brought them to their present pitch of wretchedness, whenever the time is in, and the means of wreaking their pent-up fury are put into their hands. No state can be more dreadful, more appalling than this.[114]

The above represents one of the fullest statements by Stephens not only of the centrality of feeling in the politics of his day but also of the particular combination of feelings that were operative in the relations between the classes.

While Stephens asserted that he had only preached the word of God, however impassionedly, the propertied classes and the government were not convinced and accused him of fomenting 'bad feeling' between the classes.[115] John Easby, the Manchester Liberal who dubbed him the 'Satanic Majesty's chaplain', excused his own vehemence and lack of restraint in attacking Stephens on the grounds that the latter did not 'possess the semblance of the feelings of a man'. 'My heart loathes and my better feelings turn with disgust from your putrid fame', Easby concluded, subtly subverting the emotional conventions which dictated restraint in the public sphere.[116] Not for the first time in his career as a political preacher was Stephens being censured for his medium rather than his message, and for the space in which he spoke. 'The scenes which occur in your chapel,' Easby declaimed, 'beggar description ... [w]hen you are pandering to the vilest passions of human nature.'[117] The indictment brought against Stephens for sedition in 1839 foregrounded the ways in which he had 'captivated' the people by his 'wild and furious appeals to their passions, rather than by the calm discussion of alleged grievances'. One of those who gave evidence against him made this point precisely: 'he cannot recollect the exact language he made use of at the various meetings, but by his addresses he caused considerable excitement in the neighbourhood'. The charges brought against Stephens are also revealing (as are similar charges against other popular agitators) for the emphasis that was placed on the way in which the feelings of the law-abiding citizens (read property owners) were effected: 'it will be recollected that one of the great evils arising from a system of agitation endured perhaps for too long, is to alarm the peaceable inhabitants'. Stephens had disturbed the public peace with the intention to 'terrify and alarm'.[118] The indictment continued to highlight the fear that underpinned this sense of alarm, and to attribute to that fear the refusal of many to come forward with evidence against Stephens. In other words, one – if not *the* – central issue at stake in the conflict between 'agitators' (itself a revealing label for radical leaders) and the state was the feelings of the propertied classes: with questions of law – and life and death in the cases of those convicted of treason – resting on little more than the subjective states of feeling one is reminded just how unequal and arbitrary the law could be when dealing with political opposition.

As Katie Barclay has argued in relation to treason and sedition in Ireland, this 'ability to evoke seditious feeling in others reflected the broader cultural understanding of emotion and particularly the belief that emotion was a transferable entity. Emotion appeared to be a force of its own that could drift and infect people (like a disease).' Sedition, Barclay concludes, was construed as 'uncontrolled enthusiasm'.[119] Elsewhere, Stephens was accused by Charles Mott, one of the commissioners sent to the north of England to implement the New Poor Law, of 'inflammatory language' and creating 'lawless excitement'.[120] The authorities drew a direct causal link between his language and unrest. As a deponent from Leigh, Lancashire, told the magistrates, 'until the arrival of Stephens the people and township were always peaceable ... but on account of the inflammatory and exciting language, used by Stephens it has caused a disaffection and insubordination' among the people who were now arming.[121] Though it was never proven, a factory at Ashton belonging to James Jowett was burnt and completely destroyed in suspicious circumstances in December 1838 – at the height of Stephens's incitements, and so he was blamed.[122] Given the repeated threats made by him that if the New Poor Law was introduced into Ashton the whole district would be ablaze, and that the fire at Jowett's was evidence of divine vengeance on the unrepentant sinner, it is easy to see why. Stephens wondered 'what must be the feelings of lucifer Jowett when he beheld the devouring element consuming his substance, did no fear assail his unjust, his cruel black heart ... did no fears pierce his callous heart?'[123] On 27 December 1838, Captain Clarke, one of the local magistrates, reported to the Home Office that Stephens's arrest had produced, unsurprisingly, 'a great feeling of safety'.[124]

What really concerned Mott was the adulation and devotion that Stephens commanded with the masses, with the implication that it was this love which had led many of them to arm. In the same letter in which he had complained of his inflammatory language, Mott enclosed a portrait of Stephens then circulating in the north-west of England (Figure 5.1). The portrait 'will give you some idea of the pains which are taken to puff this man into notice', Mott wrote. 'The gun and the pike in the hands of the young man, and the attack upon the "Bastile" in the background, need no explanation', he continued.[125] The Bastile, always with one l, was the term used by factory reformers and anti-Poor Law protestors for factories and workhouses, and Mott was clearly aware of the threat of violence that was

Figure 5.1 Thomas Paine Carlile's portrait of Joseph Rayner Stephens, printed by W. Clark (1839).

being implied. This portrait – in contrast to others in circulation – underlined Stephens's status not just as a gentleman 'friend of the people' but one who belonged to the people.[126]

On the one hand, Stephens is presented as the loving, respectable and protective father of the people. He was the guardian of children, not quite literally in this case as the age of the two flanking individuals is ambiguous, but then the factory reform movement was premised on the assumption that the factory system had eroded the distinction between adults and children through the over-employment and the exploitation of the latter.[127] On the other hand, it is the two flanking individuals who take on the role of the loving and protective subjects defending their father, a timely posture as it turned out as Stephens was awaiting his trial when Mott sent this portrait to the Home Office. An impressive campaign was underway to raise a subscription to pay for his legal defence, which amounted to £1,000 by March 1839. Contrary to Mott's judgement that the pike and Bastile needed no explanation, the image is hardly one of unambiguous threat, no doubt deliberately. The pike in the boy's hand looks more like a ceremonial one – often used as banner poles or to mount caps of liberty just as the girl is doing. The object in the boy's right hand is also unclear: it could be a broom or a gun. Neither is it clear whether the assembled crowd is attacking the bastille or just staging a demonstration (hence the presence of banners). The presence of laurel leaves – which form the crown above Stephens's head – and the olive branches which surround the portrait – are also ambiguous. While laurel was a symbol of triumph, historically associated with military victories, olive branches were signs of peace. In reality, then, the affective message of the portrait is far from clear, though it is noteworthy that the authorities were in no mood to draw such fine distinctions. Mott was not the only one sending copies of the portrait to the Home Office. Hamlet Gretton, a resident of Duckinfield – the district where Stephens resided – informed them that he viewed the thousands of copies of the portrait which were circulating as 'indicative of a very bad feeling among the poor working class of the community'.[128]

As a result of his fiery rhetoric and prophetic denunciation of the people's enemies, allied to the adulation of him by the working-classes of northern England, Stephens frightened and alienated the propertied classes. Easby accused him of sundering the bond of sympathy and mutual interest that once existed between masters and men: he had 'banished domestic happiness – and plunged the whole district into one hateful mass of rancour, hatred, discord and heart-burnings. There is not one particle of generous blood flowing within the veins of Stephens'.[129] Stephens, along with Oastler and the radical cotton lord John Fielden, had taken the decision in July 1836 to escalate their campaign against the factory masters by using fear as well as reason. The problem with this, as Michael Edwards has pointed out, was that 'the appeal to fear had to be maintained and increased if it was to achieve its end'. By December 1838, the authorities had had enough and moved against Stephens. Like the French revolutionaries, Oastler and Stephens fell prey to the kind of emotional overheating which was unsustainable and, from a certain point of view, counterproductive in alienating the manufacturers and government. The orthodox Wesleyan newspaper *The Watchman* naturally inveighed against 'the rash and insane opposition of Messrs Oastler and Stephens and others'.[130] Again like Oastler, Stephens was quick to condemn the factory masters and architects of the New Poor Law as shameful and to brand anyone who was remotely complicit as guilty: 'The Churchman is guilty – the Dissenter is guilty – the Whig, as the prime mover, is guilty – the Tory, for aid, is guilty – the Radical is guilty for having supported' the New Poor Law Bill.[131] Reaching even further depths of condemnation of those who refused to lend assistance in resisting the implementation of the New Poor Law, Stephens thundered:

> May God Almighty's curse – his most terrible vengeance – rest on the head of every man who now hears me; may the curse of Christ dwell in the heart of every woman who now hears me, who does not her utmost to stem so horrible an iniquity; may the Almighty's curse rest on your children, and on their children to the third and fourth generation.[132]

Conclusion

Even more than was the case with Oastler, the particular combination of feelings that were at the heart of Stephens's affective politics – guilt, shame and fear – alienated the propertied classes and left them securely in their ethical shelters. In other words, there was failure of sympathy on behalf of the propertied classes. In the view of his enemies, Stephens excelled in the disproportionate. When he resigned from the Wesleyan Methodists in 1834, his independent chapel and his itinerant preaching, often outdoors (reminiscent of the early Methodist preachers) functioned for a short time as emotional refuges, spaces where he was relatively free to develop his impassioned political preaching. But the refuge and emotional liberty which ensued were short-lived with the propertied classes and the state assuming the policing role of the Wesleyan hierarchy, taking it to new heights of emotional suffering as far as Stephens and his supporters were concerned: we have seen very clearly just how high the emotional stakes were as evidenced by the politicisation of feeling by the state and its legal apparatus. Thus, Stephens fell foul of two emotional regimes in quick succession, the effect of which was to end this most dramatic episode in his life as a minister. Though his career was far from over, he would never regain the popularity and impact that he had commanded in the late 1830s. Ironically, he found himself condemned for the same reason as the first Methodist preachers a hundred years before: a fanatical style of preaching which inflamed the passions of the credulous. For Stephens and his followers, the impassioned rhetoric was a manifestation of their heartfelt sensibility, a sensibility that was shaped profoundly by Methodism and Romanticism which spoke of the thinking as well as feeling heart.

As Stephens opened his farewell sermon just before his trial, he hoped that his congregation would find his words 'to be the outward and visible body of the inward and spiritual mind, to convey to your understanding, and to carry down into your hearts the meaning of those things'.[133] Despite what his enemies said, he was always careful to repel the charge that his affective politics were grounded only in the passions, a charge, it has to be said, not easily or convincingly repelled. Indeed, he tried to transcend the emerging dichotomy between reason and feeling that was being drawn in ever sharper etches by the advocates of liberal political economy who had little sympathy for affective politics that were engraved on the fleshy tablets of the heart. Because of its inability to melt the icy-heart of liberal political economy, the 'cult of the heart', as it has been termed elsewhere, was unable to heal the divisions between the classes, and thus remained a class-based politics.[134] For all its reliance on gentleman leaders, sentimental radicalism would always remain much more class-conscious than ascetic radicalism. As the next chapter shows, some ascetic radicals by the 1840s attempted to use feeling to heal the class divide, though without much success in the short term.

Notes

1 John Easby, *J.R. Stephens Unveiled* (Manchester, November 1837), p. 4.
2 Robert G. Hall, 'Work, class, and politics in Ashton-under-Lyne' (PhD dissertation, Vanderbilt University, 1991), pp. 76, 280.
3 Alfred [Samuel Kydd], *The History of the Factory Movement*, vol. 1 (London, 1857), p. 97.
4 *Stockport Advertiser*, 10 January 1839.
5 BL, Additional MS 27820, Francis Place papers, historical narrative relating to working men's associations, vol. II, fols 150–1.
6 G.D.H. Cole, *Chartist Portraits* (London: Macmillan, 1941), p. 78. There is a good biography, written by a Methodist minister: Michael S. Edwards, *Purge this Realm: A Life of Joseph Rayner Stephens* (London: Epworth Press, 1994). There is also, in the words of Cole, an 'exceedingly bad' (*ibid.*, p. 361) biography of Stephens by G.J. Holyoake, *Life of Joseph Rayner Stephens: Preacher and Political Orator* (London, 1881). For Stephens's religious beliefs and how this informed his political preaching, see Dale Johnson, 'Between evangelicalism and a social gospel: the case of Joseph Rayner Stephens', *Church History*, 42 (1973), 229–42; Eileen Yeo, 'Chartist religious belief and the theology of liberation', in James Obelkevich, Lyndal Roper and

Raphael Samuel (eds), *Disciplines of Faith: Studies in Religion, Politics and Patriarchy* (London: Routledge, 1987), pp. 410–21; Eileen Groth Lyon, *Politicians in the Pulpit: Christian Radicalism from the Fall of the Bastille to the Disintegration of Chartism* (Aldershot: Ashgate, 1999), chapters 4–5; Mike Sanders, '"God's insurrection": politics and faith in the revolutionary sermons of Joseph Rayner Stephens', in Joshua King and Winter Jade Werner (eds), *Constructing Nineteenth-Century Religion* (Columbus, OH: Ohio State University Press, 2019), pp. 65–80. For Stephens's relationship with the Chartists, see Thomas M. Kemnitz and Jacques Fleurage, 'Joseph Rayner Stephens and the Chartist movement', *International Review of Social History*, 19 (1974), 211–227.

7 Cf. Patrick Joyce, *Visions of the People: Industrial England and the Question of Class, 1848–1914* (Cambridge: Cambridge University Press, 1991), pp. 33–4. See also Dorothy Thompson, *The Chartists: Popular Politics in the Industrial Revolution* (New York: Pantheon, 1984), p. 75.

8 Mark Hovell, *The Chartist Movement* (Manchester: Manchester University Press 1918), p. 188. For this reading of Hovell, see Malcolm Chase, 'Packed tightly with the strong meat of history and political economy': Mark Hovell and histories of Chartism', *Bulletin of the John Rylands Library*, 94 (2018), 43–57.

9 Even Edwards's biography has little to say about this, to the extent that his earlier assessment of Stephens still appears valid: 'Secular historians underestimated or misunderstood his Methodist background; Methodist historians ... have denied any Methodist responsibility for his post-1834 activities.' Michael S. Edwards, 'The resignation of Joseph Rayner Stephens', *Proceedings of the Wesley Historical Society*, 36 (1967), p. 16.

10 Phyllis Mack, *Heart Religion in the British Enlightenment: Gender and Emotion in Early Methodism* (Cambridge: Cambridge University Press, 2008).

11 Edwards, *Purge this Realm*, p. 36; Bob Hayes, '"Joseph Rayner Stephens has not fared well at the hands of the historians": a reappraisal on the bicentenary of his birth', *North-West Labour History*, 30 (2005), 17–20; Jörg Neuheiser, *Crown, Church and Constitution: Popular Conservatism in England, 1815–1867* (Oxford: Berghahn, 2016), chapter 5.

12 For the Tory/Tory-radical interpretation of Stephens, see Hovell, *Chartist Movement*, p. 89; Cecil Driver, *Tory Radical: The Life of Richard Oastler* (New York: Oxford University Press, 1946), pp. 314–15; J.T. Ward, 'Revolutionary Tory: the life of Joseph Rayner Stephens', *Transactions of the Lancashire and Cheshire Antiquarian Society*, 68 (1958), 97–116; David Walsh, *Making Angels in Marble: The Conservatives, the Early Industrial Working Class and Attempts at Political Incorporation* (London: Breviary, 2012), passim. For the tendency to reread Stephens's politics in the 1830s in light of his subsequent career, see Johnson, 'Between evangelicalism'. For Stephens as a Christian radical, see Groth Lyon, *Politicians in the Pulpit*, chapters 4–5.

13 Brief though it was, it would be a mistake to underestimate the impact Stephens had. Even Francis Place appreciated this, noting how Stephens eclipsed the popularity of the great Chartist leader Feargus O'Connor in 1838 and early

1839 among the northern working class: BL, Additional MS 27820, Place papers, fol. 267.

14 For biographical details, see Eileen Groth Lyon, 'Stephens, Joseph Rayner (1805–1879)', *Oxford Dictionary of National Biography* (Oxford: Oxford University Press, 2008).

15 Fay Bound Alberti, *Matters of the Heart: History, Medicine and Emotion* (Oxford: Oxford University Press, 2010), pp. 6–7, 14.

16 Mack, *Heart Religion*, pp. 15–16.

17 William M. Reddy, *The Navigation of Feeling: A Framework for the History of Emotions* (Cambridge: Cambridge University Press, 2001), pp. 124–5.

18 Mack, *Heart Religion*, pp. 15–16, 210.

19 *Stephens' Monthly Magazine*, April 1840.

20 Anon., *The Factory Lad, or the Life of Simon Smike Exemplifying the Horrors of White Slavery* (London, 1839), p. 71.

21 Mack, *Heart Religion*, p. 210.

22 Stephen Pattison, 'Mend the gap: Christianity and the emotions', *Contact*, 131 (2011), 5.

23 John Kent, *Wesley and the Wesleyans* (Cambridge: Cambridge University Press, 2002), p. 28.

24 David Hempton, *Methodism and Politics in British Society, 1750–1850* (London: Routledge, 1984), pp. 179–85 (quote p. 185).

25 The full details of the controversy and the trial were covered in the *Christian Advocate*, edited by Stephens's younger brother, John, who, as a Wesleyan reformer, was only too happy to devote column inches to his brother's campaign. These articles were collected and published as *The Case of the Rev. J.R. Stephens, Wesleyan Minister* (London, 1834).

26 Edwards, *Purge this Realm*, p. 9.

27 Benjamin Gregory, *Side Lights on the Conflicts of Methodism* (London, 1898), pp. 153–4.

28 Reddy, *Navigation of Feeling*, p. 129.

29 Gregory, *Side Lights*, p. 155.

30 John Bowers to Jabez Bunting, 29 April 1834, in W.R. Ward (ed.), *Early Victorian Methodism: The Correspondence of Jabez Bunting, 1830–1850* (Oxford: Oxford University Press, 1976), pp. 60–1.

31 Reddy, *Navigation of Feeling*, pp. 122–5.

32 Gregory, *Side Lights*, p. 150.

33 William J. Abraham, *Methodism: A Very Short Introduction* (Oxford: Oxford University Press, 2019), p. 38.

34 *Christian Advocate*, 3 November 1834. For Wesley's ambivalence, see David Hempton, *The Religion of the People: Methodism and Popular Religion, c.1750–1900* (London: Routledge, 1996), p. 83.

35 Holyoake, *Life of Stephens*, p. 57.

36 TNA, HO 20/10, Prison Correspondence and papers (interviews of Chartist prisoners, 1840–41), fol. 8v.

37 *Cleave's Gazette of Variety*, 12 January 1839.

38 Gregory, *Side Lights*, p. 150.

39 Edwards, *Purge this Realm*, p. 25.

40 Gregory, *Side Lights*, p. 150.

41 Edwards, *Purge this Realm*, pp. 2, 77.

42 Edwards notes in his biography that Stephens's 'whereabouts from November 1829 to the summer of 1830 is unknown'. Edwards, *Purge this Realm*, p. 6.

43 TNA, HO 20/10, Prison Correspondence, fol. 8r.

44 *Stephens' Monthly Magazine*, January, February and April 1840; *Champion*, 23 February 1850; *Ashton Chronicle*, 25 November 1848, 13 January 1849.

45 Isaiah Berlin, *The Roots of Romanticism*, ed. Henry Hardy (London: Pimlico, 2000), pp. 36–8.

46 An enthusiasm he shared with his younger brother, George Stephens, who would go on to become professor of literature at Copenhagen University.

47 *Ashton Chronicle*, 14 October 1848, 31 March 1849. For Scandinavian Romanticism, see the special issue 'Romanticism in Scandinavia', *European Romantic Review*, 26 (2015).

48 Bound Alberti, *Matters of the Heart*, p. 8.

49 Boyd Hilton, *A Mad, Bad and Dangerous People? England, 1783–1846* (Oxford: Oxford University Press, 2006), p. 179; Boyd Hilton, *The Age of Atonement: The Influence of Evangelicalism on Social and Economic Thought, 1785–1865* (Oxford: Oxford University Press, 1988), p. 95; Johnson, 'Between evangelicalism', p. 238.

50 E.P. Thompson, *The Making of the English Working Class* (London: Gollancz, 1980), p. 46.

51 E.g., Hovell, *Chartist Movement*, p. 89; Groth Lyon, *Politicians in the Pulpit*, p. 182. The fullest treatment of Stephens as a prophet, and of how that tradition shaped his speeches, is Michael Taylor, 'Joseph Rayner Stephens, political preacher' (PhD dissertation, University of California, Los Angeles, 1966).

52 Michael P.V. Barrett, 'Introduction to the prophet books', in Joel R. Beeke (ed.), *The Reformation Heritage: KJV Study Bible* (Grand Rapids, MI: Heritage Books, 2014), p. 953.

53 TNA, HO 52/37, Examination of William Coward, 1 December 1838, fol. 97.

54 Holyoake, *Life of Stephens*, p. 227.

55 J.R. Stephens, *The Political Pulpit* (London, 1839), p. 17.

56 Stephens, *Political Pulpit*, p. 29.

57 *Christian Advocate*, 7 November and 26 September 1836.

58 Holyoake, *Life of Stephens*, p. 227; Edwards, *Purge this Realm*, pp. 77, 106.

59 TNA, HO/20, Prison Correspondence, fol. 8v; NS, 10 May 1845.

60 Klaus Koch, *The Prophets: Volume One, The Assyrian Period* (London: Fortress, 1982), pp. 2, 4, 19.

61 Stephens, *Political Pulpit*, p. 12.

62 Joseph Rayner Stephens, *The Political Preacher* (London, 1839), pp. 7, 27.

63 Stephens, *Political Pulpit*, p. 11. For similar accusations of coldness, see *Stockport Advertiser*, 15 April 1836.

64 Stephens, *Political Pulpit*, p. 2.

65 *Ibid.*, p. 8.

66 *Ibid.*, p. 17.

67 *Manchester and Salford Advertiser*, 23 January 1836. For Hume's conception of sympathy, see John Mullan, *Sentiment and Sociability: The Language of Feeling in the Eighteenth Century* (Oxford: Oxford University Press, 1988), pp. 29–49.

68 Hall, 'Work, class, and politics', p. 76.

69 Thompson, *Making of the English Working Class*, p. 403.

70 Stephens, *Political Preacher*, p. 20.

71 Driver, *Tory Radical*, p. 315.

72 *Stephens' Monthly Magazine*, January and March 1840; Ward, 'Revolutionary tory', p. 103; *Stephens' Monthly Magazine*, January 1840; Hall, 'Work, class, and politics', p. 130, n. 121.

73 For a critical overview of this debate, see Hempton, *Religion of the People*, chapter 9.

74 E.g., *NS*, 5 January 1839.

75 TNA, HO 40/38, Examination of William Boardman, fol. 656.

76 Sanders, 'God's insurrection', pp. 76–7.

77 *NS*, 26 January 1839 (Carlisle).

78 Stephens, *Political Pulpit*, p. 17.

79 Katrina Navickas, *Protest and the Politics of Space and Place, 1789–1848* (Manchester: Manchester University Press 2016), pp. xii, 65.

80 Stephens, *Political Pulpit*, p. 19.

81 Reddy, *Navigation of Feeling*, p. 129.

82 Stephens, *Political Pulpit*, p. 18.

83 *London Dispatch*, 8 January 1837.

84 Thomas Dixon, *Weeping Britannia: Portrait of a Nation in Tears* (Oxford: Oxford University Press, 2015), p. 8.

85 Mack, *Heart Religion*, p. 26.

86 'Stephens' vindication', copy in TNA, HO 40/38, fol. 634.

87 Rob Boddice, *The Science of Sympathy: Morality, Evolution, and Victorian Civilisation* (Urbana, Chicago and Springfield: University of Illinois Press, 2016), pp. 4–6. See also Barbara H. Rosenwein, *Anger: The Conflicted History of an Emotion* (New Haven and London: Yale University Press, 2020), p. 118.

88 Kydd, *History of the Factory Movement*, vol. 2, p. 97.

89 *True Sun*, 12 June 1837.

90 *NS*, 11 May 1839.

91 *Stephens' Monthly Magazine*, January 1840.

92 Boddice, *Science of Sympathy*, p. 3.

93 Taylor, 'Joseph Rayner Stephens', p 139. As Taylor notes in his linguistic analysis of Stephens's speeches, the published sermons show 'closer care in preparation, though they lack the same feeling of audience immediacy found in the newspaper speeches, with their inclusions of exclamations and cheers inserted in the text' (p. 229).

94 Stephens, *Political Pulpit*, p. 65.

95 *Bradford Observer*, 18 May 1837; *Stephens' Monthly Magazine*, January, February and March 1840.

96 *Stephens' Monthly Magazine*, January 1840.

97 Taylor, 'Joseph Rayner Stephens', p. 233; Malcolm Chase, *Chartism: A New History* (Manchester: Manchester University Press 2007), p. 34; G.J. Barker-Benfield, *The Culture of Sensibility: Sex and Society in the Eighteenth Century* (Chicago: University of Chicago Press, 1992), pp. 75–7.

98 *Bolton Chronicle*, 5 March 1836.

99 Stephens, *Political Pulpit*, pp. 4–5. Stephens's fellow north-west Tory-radical Matthew Fletcher was even more emphatic on the effect of the factory system: 'He had long since said, that if this system was continued through two or three generations more, the unhappy beings employed in it would lose the very form of humanity.' *Charter*, 17 March 1839.

100 *NS*, 17 March 1839.

101 Stephens, *Political Pulpit*, p. 90

102 *Stephens' Monthly Magazine*, April 1840.

103 For this view of hunger in the nineteenth century, see James Vernon, *Hunger: A Modern History* (Cambridge, MA: Harvard University Press, 2007). See also Carl J. Griffin, *The Politics of Hunger: Protest, Poverty and Policy in England, c.1750–1840* (Manchester: Manchester University Press, 2020).

104 *Bradford Observer*, 18 October 1838.

105 *NS*, 29 September 1838.

106 *Stephens' Monthly Magazine*, February 1840.

107 Sanders, 'God's insurrection', pp. 70–2.

108 Edwards, *Purge this Realm*, p. xii.

109 *Stephens' Monthly Magazine*, April 1840.

110 Holyoake, *Life of Stephens*, p. 118. See also *NS*, 2 December 1837. See also Yeo, 'Chartist religious belief', p. 412.

111 'Stephens' vindication'.

112 TNA, HO 40/38, Examination of Robert Ripley, 22 December 1838, fols 651–2.

113 Edwards, *Purge this Realm*, p. 47.

114 *Stephens' Monthly Magazine*, October 1840.

115 TNA, HO 40/38, William Bentley to Home Office, 17 December 1838, fol. 611. See also the speech of Lord Brougham in the House of Lords which attacked Stephens for creating a feeling of alarm. *Hansard*, Lords, 20 March 1838, col. 1043.

116 As Nicole Eustace has shown, 'calculated display of emotion could subtly yet substantially further assertions of dominance'. Nicole Eustace, *Passion is the Gale: Emotion, Power, and the Coming of the American Revolution* (Chapel Hill, NC: University of North Carolina Press, 2008), p. 82.

117 Easby *Stephens Unmasked*, pp. 3, 6, 7.

118 TNA, TS 11/1030, The Queen against Joseph Rayner Stephens, fol. 6.

119 Katie Barclay, 'Sounds of sedition: music and emotion in Ireland, 1780–1845', *Cultural History*, 3 (2014), 63, 65.

120 TNA, HO 73/55, Correspondence between Home Office and Poor Law Commissioners, fol. 192v.

121 TNA, HO 52/37, Examination of Thomas Cleworth, 1 December 1838, fol. 96.

122 Chase, *Chartism*, p. 39.

123 TNA, TS 11/1030, Queen vs. Stephens, fol. 13.

124 Edwards, *Purge this Realm*, p. 60.

125 TNA, HO 73/55, Mott to Home Office, fol. 192v.

126 Matthew Roberts, *Chartism, Commemoration and the Cult of the Radical Hero* (Abingdon: Routledge, 2020), pp. 17–19.

127 Colin Creighton, 'Changing conceptions of children's rights in early industrial Britain', in Nigel Goose and Katrina Honeyman (eds), *Childhood and Child Labour in Industrial England* (Farnham: Ashgate, 2013), pp. 231–54.

128 TNA, HO 40/53, Hamlett Gretton to Home Office, 26 March 1839, fol. 89.

129 Easby, *Stephens Unveiled*, p. 8.

130 Edwards, *Purge this Realm*, pp. 70, 75.

131 *NS*, 3 February 1839.

132 *NS*, 5 January 1839.

133 Stephens, *Political Pulpit*, p. 97.

134 I am thinking here of Patrick Joyce's neologism, the 'cult of the heart', which he formulated to emphasise the common humanity (and cross-class identities) of the working- and middle-classes in mid-Victorian England. See Patrick Joyce, *Democratic Subjects: The Self and the Social in Nineteenth Century England* (Cambridge: Cambridge University Press, 1994). Miles Taylor makes a similar distinction in his analysis of Jones's poetry: 'Jones's early Chartist poetry and oratory was thus distinctive for their evangelical tenor and Gothic, melodramatic sense of history, rather than their appeal to class solidarity.' For Stephens (and for Oastler, for that matter) this is a false distinction. Miles Taylor, *Ernest Jones, Chartism, and the Romance of Politics, 1819–1869* (Oxford: Oxford University Press, 2003), p. 95. Cf. Hall, 'Work, class, and politics', p. 136.

6

William Lovett and the battle for asceticism in early Chartism

This chapter returns to the theme of ascetic radicalism through a case study of the London radical artisan William Lovett. Born in Cornwall in 1800 into humble circumstances, Lovett's life was a long struggle in the 'pursuit of bread, knowledge and freedom'.[1] For much of the twentieth century, he featured prominently and positively in accounts of the Chartist movement as the author of the People's Charter and the leading figure in the organisation under whose umbrella that celebrated document emerged, the London Working Men's Association (LWMA, est. 1836). A member of a select group of metropolitan artisan radicals who prioritised peaceful and constitutional strategies and tactics, which counselled the working class to demonstrate their moral fitness for the franchise through respectability and education, Lovett's moral-force politics resonated powerfully with the Fabian gradualism of Chartism's early historians who claimed him as a progenitor. As Lovett's more discerning biographers have reminded us, the image of him as the rational man of peaceful protest is, in part, a retrospective attempt by Lovett in his autobiography to excise a crucial decade in his life – the 1830s – when he had, at least verbally, been much more threatening than he later cared to admit. The youthful intemperate Lovett was incompatible with the emerging Fabian view of Chartism which attributed the failure of the movement to its hijacking by unprincipled and dangerous demagogues who threatened physical force, pre-eminently Feargus O'Connor.[2] What has escaped the attention of historians is just how much the rivalry and divisions between Lovett and O'Connor were rooted in a debate about the nature and place of feelings in Chartism.

By using Lovett as a case study, this chapter explores how Chartists politicised feeling, focusing mainly on the early years of the movement in the 1830s, an under-explored aspect of the Chartist experience. In Lovett's case, his politicisation of the passions was not just an important part of Chartism's battle with its external enemies; debates about the nature and place of feelings were also central to the internal politics of the movement. Building on recent work on space and place in popular politics, this chapter shows how the affective politics of Chartism, and specific feeling rules, were associated with particular spaces, notably the pub, coffee shops and the mass platform.[3] Particular attention is paid to the ascetic radicalism of Lovett and the LWMA as a way of contributing to recent work which has rehabilitated the notion of moral-force Chartism by showing how there was much more to this than the pursuit of peaceful and constitutional strategies and tactics.[4] Lovett's asceticism has not gone unnoticed by his biographers, but the pivotal affective basis of this remains unexplored.[5] Moral-force Chartism was a worldview grounded in a particular understanding of feeling. The third section of the chapter returns to the seminal work of William Reddy on emotional regimes and refuges, and uses these concepts to re-examine the fortunes of the first Chartist Convention (1839), a key organisation in early Chartism in which Lovett served as secretary. The chapter concludes by showing, briefly, how the intense affective experience of 1839 repeated itself in the second and third peaks of Chartist mobilisation in 1842 and 1848, despite the best efforts of those like Lovett to prevent 'emotional overheating' and build cross-class alliances.[6]

Putting passions in their place

No Chartist penned a lengthy philosophical treatise on the passions. But some did reflect explicitly on the nature of feeling, while many more contributed to these definitions implicitly on a day-to-day basis through their language. As we have seen in previous chapters, the word 'emotion' was seldom used, and when it was it denoted outward expression of inward feeling. In a report to Lovett of his missionary work for the Chartist Convention, William Cardo took the emotions of his audiences as outward evidence that they had been sufficiently moved and would convert to the cause of the People's Charter.[7] The Scottish Chartist John Fraser, under the cover of a letter to Lovett, felt able to express more freely his feelings regarding the (il)legal persecution of the Glasgow Cotton Spinners in 1838: 'This is a painful agonising affair, my brain burns, and my heart sinks within me at the innocent suffering of these men.'[8] Anatomically, Chartists tended to locate feeling in the heart, though as Fraser's description of his affective state suggests this was not in isolation from the cerebral or – connectedly – the bosom. 'Now, quick beats the heart with thrilling emotion', the Barnsley Chartist William Ashton wrote from his prison cell in October 1840.[9] Again, this is entirely typical of the period. Passion and 'passions' may have been used much more widely by Chartists to describe affective states, but this, too, could be problematic. Passion was seldom used in a neutral way. Passion was often associated with more negative, evil propensities in contrast to affection which denoted more virtuous feelings, a typology with a long genealogy.[10] The Chartist lecturer John Watkins made a similar point when he observed 'Sentiment is a kind of weaker passion'.[11]

While such usage of the language of feeling might appear descriptive and neutral, it was also used to carve out and legitimate distinctive political positions within the movement. Lovett juxtaposed the rational and respectable Chartism espoused by the LWMA with that of Feargus O'Connor who made 'furious appeals to the passions of the multitude'.[12] The affective politics of Lovett and the artisans of the LWMA was shaped by the tradition of rational radicalism, the origins of which can be traced back to puritanism, and even further back to stoicism. This was similar to Carlile's ascetic radicalism, with its emphasis on republicanism and freethought, though in the case of Lovett and the LWMA (like Owen) they were much more indebted to the rational Dissent of William Godwin and Mary Wollstonecraft.[13] Reacting against the sentimentalism of the late eighteenth century, this pair had rejected the deterministic view that humans were helpless victims of their passions; such a view, Godwin and Wollstonecraft held, was dangerous as it denied individual agency. Humans needed to control their passions through the exercise of individual rational will, which would lead to the acquisition of disciplined habits.[14] All this was grist to the mill for self-improving, respectable moral-force Chartists like Lovett. Deploying Wollstonecraft's critique of 'mere gothic grandeur', Lovett dismissed the irrationality of 'gothic ignorance', with its romantic preoccupation with historical precedents, baubles, pageants and 'military spirit'. Such preoccupations were 'brutalizing and degrading'.[15] In place of this Gothic irrationality, moral-force Chartists sought to re-establish an age of reason. In January 1839, the LWMA moved a resolution declaring that 'all appeals to the passions of the multitude tending to excite to violence and disorder can only be productive of evil'.[16] If workers could not govern their passions, how could they be expected to govern the country?

Charging his opponents with appealing to 'the passions rather than to the intellect' was one of Lovett's favourite ripostes and was the cornerstone of his ascetic radicalism.[17] He was one of the few Chartists who reflected explicitly on the nature of the passions in his blueprint for the rebirth of the movement, *Chartism: or a New Organisation of the People* (1840), and most fully in *Social and Political Morality* (1853) and *Elementary Anatomy and Physiology* (1853). The latter two books were a characteristic attempt by an artisan radical to democratise and demystify science and medicine.[18] The tripartite division of man into the intellectual, the moral and the animal, which Lovett sketched in *Elementary Anatomy*, had long been adhered to by him, derived in part from his fascination with phrenology. Lovett associated the passions with man's 'animal propensities', and he believed that it was imperative, lest man become a slave to his passions or 'lower feelings', that he continually keep these propensities in check by cultivating the intellectual and moral faculties. For all its bogus status as a pseudo-science, some of the conclusions that students of phrenology reached anticipate modern biocultural approaches to the emotions. To quote David Stack, 'Lovett's analysis was built upon the phrenological linking of form and function – hardening membranes indicating the exercise of the animal passions'.[19] In other words, failure to check the passions led to damaging physiological changes, and vice versa. As with Carlile so with Lovett: he also conflated morality with right feeling: 'We have to cultivate our *moral* nature, which, directed by intellect, will enable us to control our appetites and passions.'[20] Hence the importance that he attached to education, temperance, 'rational' recreation and restraint. As Lovett reasoned in relation to the consumption of alcohol, 'The immediate effect of alcohol on the brain is to excite the passions into activity and weaken the power of self-control', eventually reducing 'man below the level of the brute'.[21] Reduced to these levels, working men were not worthy objects of sympathy, let alone the vote, because they behaved like animals under the impulse of passion. At best they were objects of pity, at worst, disgust.

Although Lovett's most extended treatment of the passions post-dated his career as a Chartist, it is worth noting just how far he had already travelled in becoming an ascetic radical by the mid-1830s, a development that would not be especially noteworthy were it not for the fact that he had spent the early 1830s as a committed Owenite. It is true that he, like many other radicals during this period, did not draw hard-and-fast distinctions between different movements, and saw no incompatibility in multiple memberships. A police spy, commenting on meetings at which Lovett and other future leaders of the LWMA had been present in 1832, noted that Lovett had recently become a follower of Robert Owen.[22] Although Lovett retained a commitment to the social system advocated by Owen as the only system that could, ultimately, redress working-class grievances, he clearly rejected Owen's view that feelings were beyond the control of individuals.[23] Lovett's ascetic radicalism was always far less ambiguous than Owen's.

There can be no doubt of the centrality of feeling in what many at the time and since have come to regard as the fatal fault-line in Chartism: between advocates of moral force (peaceful) and physical force (violence, or the threat of). Lovett sought to widen this gap, and further distance himself from physical force in his autobiography. As spy reports to the Home Office in the early 1830s attest, the pre-Chartist Lovett was regarded as a 'dangerous man' who frequently made 'inflammatory speeches' and urged workers to arm themselves (for defensive purposes).[24] This youthful ardour was entirely redacted from Lovett's autobiography. Nevertheless, this distancing was not entirely after the fact – as early as November 1831 he spoke out against offensive physical force – and was rooted in the different temperaments and cultural stylistics of those like Lovett and O'Connor, widely attested to. In 1836 Lovett claimed that the fusing of his brand of Owenism with the ultra-radicalism of the reform movement in the early 1830s had led to a reduction in the 'violence of feeling'. And by August 1839, he already had a reputation for 'coolness and temperance'.[25] Lovett was able to cite in evidence of his moral-force credentials at his trial in 1839 excerpts from addresses he had authored in the two years prior to his arrest.[26] What really irked Lovett, and by extension other moral-force Chartists, about O'Connor was that they claimed he had the ability to 'calm … down the boiling passions of th[e] infuriated multitude'. Far from exercising this control, O'Connor abused his power to the opposite effect.[27] Implicit here was the assumption that feelings can be switched on and off, and not just in the hands of influential icons like O'Connor. The whole thrust of moral-force Chartism, like Cobbett and Carlile's ascetic radicalism, was that people not only had the same capacity for feeling but they also had the ability to discipline their passions, and nowhere was this more necessary than with the base, lower passions. This was one of the reasons why moral-force Chartists valued education, especially of the young. Lovett's vision of education was no Gradgrindian vision of rote-learning imparted through 'fears of the rod'. Children were to be nurtured by teachers with 'kindness of disposition', further evidence, in part, of his association with Owenism in the 1830s.[28] Lovett shared Carlile's warning that habituating children to cruelty and revenge stimulated 'passions that may ripen into crime', as well as making for weak citizens who were too easily swayed by the legislators … who appealed to the passions.[29]

As the reference to lower or base passions implies, Lovett clearly adhered to a taxonomy of feeling that was hierarchical, with the lower feelings being negative such as hatred, fear and jealousy. The animal propensities 'prompt us to indulge our appetites and gratify our passions, too often to the injury of ourselves and others; and which too frequently cause us delight in revenge, cruelty, destruction, and crime', he cautioned.[30] And here the self-improving, restrained moral-force Chartist was following in the footsteps of the Stoics. The *National Association Gazette*, organ of the successor body to the LWMA, quoted the stoics on the imbecility and childishness of anger, for example.[31] The *Chartist Circular*, organ of Scottish moral-force Chartism, in an article on 'National Curses', decried the 'love of power' as 'an instinctive passion', and cautioned that: 'No passion gains more by indulgence'. Lovett made the same point: the more we give way to our passions, the more powerful and destructive they become.[32] Thus, neo-stoicism was certainly a notable feature of ascetic radicalism and can be read as assertion of autonomy.

It would be a mistake, however, to assume that Chartism, even earnest moral-force Chartism, was aiming for some approximation to Stoic *apatheia* (and even the Stoics and their lineal descendants had not always been clear about which feelings to value, which to suppress).[33] Rather, following in the footsteps of influential medieval theologians and early modern philosophers, they tended to draw distinctions between the passions and virtuous affections, as we saw with Lovett's taxonomy.[34] Despite Lovett's claims that his own politics was based solely on reason, he was no automaton as the highly sentimental account of his courtship with his future wife, Mary, attests as does their companionate, happy marriage.[35] But it was not just in the private sphere that he expressed intense feelings. He appears to have seen no contradiction between the restrained ascetic radicalism that he preached and the intense bitterness of his attacks on those like O'Connor, though others were alive to this contradiction.[36]

Lovett was, however, capable of expressing nobler feelings, such as the poetic address he delivered at a meeting in December 1836 to celebrate the progress made in securing a free press: 'Strong are the thoughts that now our bosoms sway – Holy the cause we celebrate today.' Most of the poetic address was devoted to invoking the memories of the radical greats in the Chartist pantheon of heroes: 'And this the truth that makes the bosom swell at thought of the great peasant-patriot [William] Tell ... With boiling blood and bleeding hearts we bend over the bitter tale.'[37] During his Owenite phase, he remarked that the 'distress of the working classes made the heart bleed', and he called on all men 'to unite hand and heart' to end working-class poverty.[38] Lovett was always sensitive to the injured feelings of the working classes in consequence of state brutality or callousness. At his trial for sedition in 1839 he excused the violence of those who had rioted in the Bull Ring at Birmingham on the grounds that the unconstitutional act of the magistrates in calling on the Metropolitan Police to suppress peaceful protest had added to the 'outraged feelings of the multitude'.[39] As the veteran radical Francis Place observed of Lovett: 'His feelings for his fellow workmen are intense.'[40] Earlier in the same history of radicalism, Place observed that Lovett was

[A] man of melancholy temperament, soured with the perplexities of the world, he was however an honest hearted man, possessed of great courage and persevering in his conduct, in his usual demeanour he was mild and kind, and entertained kindly feelings towards every one whom he did not sincerely believe was the intentional enemy of the working people, but when either by circumstances or his own morbid associations he felt the sense he was apt to indulge of the evils and wrongs of mankind he was vehement in the extreme.[41]

It is possible that the increasing accent that Lovett and the LWMA placed on restraint and reason by the late 1830s owed something to Place's influence, whose own journey from the dissipations of youth and gratification of the animal propensities to respectable rationality was grounded in an ascetic radicalism that also accented restraint. There is certainly a parallel in the temperament of the two men: Vic Gatrell's description of Place as one of laughter's enemies, a reflection of his 'priggish humourlessness, earnestness and vanity about his own distinction' could easily, if uncharitably, be applied to Lovett.[42] But it is difficult to trace the precise extent and nature of the relationship between Place and Lovett: as Tom Scriven has shown, Lovett appears to have turned a blind eye to John Cleave's sexual indiscretions, despite prompting by Place to disown him.[43] Lovett and the LWMA were always much more independent than the O'Connorites claimed; Lovett, for example, did not subscribe to Place's Malthusianism.[44]

In Lovett's case, at least, his mature ascetic radicalism was rooted in a longstanding earnestness which had been inculcated in him as a boy and youth by his Methodist mother and brief dalliance with the Bible Christians. But he soon revolted against the hypocrisy and 'miserable interpretations' of man's utter depravity. Christianity, in Lovett's view, ought to promote 'brotherly kindness'. He conceptualised his radicalisation in the 1820s following his move to London as an affective experience, 'my mind seemed to be awakened to a new mental existence; new feelings, hopes, and aspirations sprang up within me'.[45] He frequently appealed to the nobler, positive feelings. In a published address in support of the Canadian rebels, during their struggles against the British government in 1837–38, he urged his fellow working-class countryman to 'arouse the feelings' of sympathy, fraternity and love for their Canadian brothers under oppression.[46] As the above example of Lovett's construction of his own political reason suggests, the dichotomy that he posited between reason and feeling was polemical and designed to constitute and legitimate his moral-force Chartism. We should also be wary of the binary posited between reason and passion in the ascetic radicalism of those like Lovett when much that was passed off as reason could be seen as disgust – at the adulation of the masses for O'Connor, for example. Lovett also taunted O'Connor for his shameless lack of courage: while he lost no opportunity to goad the masses into violence, when violence did break out, he was nowhere to be seen.[47]

Captivating the senses; informing the mind

How did Chartists politicise feelings, and what role did they play in the movement? Chartists, as with radicals of the previous generation campaigning in the shadow of the French Revolution, were sensitive to the accusation of unleashing baser passions. This was one of the other reasons why those like Lovett emphasised reason to the point of obsession. The return of mass unrest in the 1830s and 1840s saw the re-denigration of angry passions in elite circles.[48] In the febrile and frenetic political atmosphere surrounding the reform bill in 1830–32, one of the ways in which the conservative elite had tried to delegitimise the popular campaign for mass enfranchisement was by claiming that ordinary people were creatures of their passions and, if enfranchised, they would destabilise the political system.[49] The young impassioned Lovett had somewhat unwittingly contributed to this fear; hence, his subsequent ascetic radicalism can be seen, at least in part, as a riposte to this charge. The political debate which had taken place in the 1790s for the 'righteousness of anger' was replayed: the enemies of Chartism tried to demonise the movement as wild fury which had unjustly frightened the law-abiding population; Chartists countered that their anger was just indignation.[50] The fear which Chartists engendered through their threatening language and intimidating behaviour was evidence of the brutish nature of the working classes. What stamped the working class as brutish was their lack of refined sensibility. Refuting these charges was crucial to the Chartist strategy of demonstrating the fitness of the working class for enfranchisement. A caustic article in the Tory *Blackwood's Edinburgh Magazine* asked rhetorically of the working classes: 'And have they evinced, by the prudence with which they regulate their own passions ... that they are adequate to the duties of self government?'[51] Unsurprisingly, the author concluded that they had not. While refuting these accusations was never the exclusive preserve of moral-force artisans like Lovett, they were arguably more sensitive to this charge. As skilled working men who prided themselves on their respectability they went to greater lengths to refute them. Feelings of dignity and honour were intimately bound up with artisan notions of independence and self-esteem.[52]

Displaced, frustrated or degraded artisans such as Lovett, who struggled to acquire and be fully admitted to an honourable trade – cabinetmaking in his case, which was a 'non-aristocratic' craft – were especially sensitive to charges of unfeeling brutishness. Even by the time that Lovett entered middle age at the height of his career as a radical leader he was still a struggling artisan.[53] It would be a mistake, though, to reduce his affective politics, or indeed the man generally, to his artisan status. Not only was the category of artisan ambiguous, but Lovett was just as much at war with the brutish behaviour he encountered among some of his fellow artisans as he was with the wider working class.[54] Working men were beginning to feel, the LWMA newspaper noted approvingly, 'that they are not created as mere machines ... They have an interest in the enjoyments and the beauties of this world – they are created with capacities and affections to appreciate and love.'[55] Some Chartists may have drawn Biblical sanction for the universalist assumption that all had the same capacity for feeling: James V which was popular with the Chartists, and requested as the basis for sermons during the Church sit-ins of 1839 contained the line, in verse 17: 'Elias was a man subject to like passions as we are.'[56]

The 'cult of domesticity' that was part of ascetic radicalism and indeed the wider Chartist movement, with its emphasis on temperance, self-improvement, rational recreation and self-restraint as well as domestic affections stemmed just as much from a desire to demonstrate that working-class men were not creatures of their baser passions than it did from a ploy to keep women in their subordinate places.[57] 'Dear are our families to us, dear our homes; our feelings are as human as your own', the Northern Political Union informed the middle classes.[58] Chartist women, too, legitimated their intrusion into the public political sphere on the basis that working-class women had the same affective capacities as upper-class women, including the Queen.[59] Lovett extolled the virtues of companionate marriage, and in a further nod to Wollstonecraft he drew attention to the importance of educating women, though the vestigial patriarchalism in him envisaged this as husbands instructing wives for the purpose of making them fit instructors of children. Nevertheless, Lovett counselled 'kindness and affections' by husbands to their wives 'to make them our equal companions in knowledge and happiness' and not 'mere domestic drudges, and ignorant slaves of our passions'.[60] Wives, in turn, would curb the baser passions of their husbands, which – just as we saw with the tensions in Carlile's gender politics – implied that Lovett believed that men and women felt differently.[61]

Though not necessarily the preserve of ascetic radicals within Chartism, one of the functions of Chartist poetry was to demonstrate that the working class were sensitive and had a 'refined sensibility'.[62] Even those who did not have literary ability could demonstrate their sensibility through education and rational recreation. For Lovett both were central and lifelong interests for which he campaigned. While education would discipline the passions, rational recreation – music, dancing, singing, tea parties – would inculcate a refined sensibility that fused enjoyment with restraint, a legacy of his Owenism. Promoting education and rational recreation were the central goals of Lovett's National Association in the 1840s. Beyond the National Association, he also campaigned for the opening of galleries and museums on Sundays to facilitate access for working men. The exclusion of the working class from these otherwise elitist spaces had dire affective consequences – sensual enjoyment. If the masses 'were encouraged to admire the beauties of nature, to cultivate a taste for the arts and sciences, to seek for rational instruction and amusement, it would soon be found that their vicious habits would yield to more rational pursuits'. Ever the radical politician, Lovett's paean to rational recreation culminated in the benefits that would be conferred on the political sphere. Once taught to appreciate beauty and throw over vicious habits, 'man would become the friend and lover of his species ... and be better qualified to enjoy happiness in any future state of existence'.[63]

Lovett's ascetic radicalism was associated with particular spaces – the parlour, reading room, coffee house and lecture hall. By contrast, it was averse to other spaces, notably the bluster of the mass platform and taproom. Gammage, the first historian of Chartism and himself a former Chartist, wrote approvingly of the LWMA's eschewal of passionate politics. As he wrote of Lovett's close friend and long-term co-campaigner, Henry Hetherington: 'His meetings were generally held within doors: indeed, anywhere else they would, in more senses than one, have been out of place.'[64] The same could easily be said of Lovett. Lovett, too, preferred indoor meetings, and he was averse to the cultural politics of the mass platform – though it is telling that when he did mount the public platform 'he expressed his feelings more robustly'.[65] In the view of moral-force Chartists, ascetic radicalism was a much more secure foundation on which to build a movement than the 'useless excitement' of the mass platform and its impassioned oratory.[66] The latter soon burnt itself out and played into the hands of the movement's enemies who were always on the look-out for evidence of the over-excitable masses. Reflecting on the failures of early Chartism, Lovett lamented the 'wasted glorious means of usefulness in foolish displays and gaudy trappings, seeking to captivate the sense[s] rather than inform the mind'. 'Our public meetings,' he continued, 'have on too many occasions been arenas of passionate invective ... rather than public assemblies for calmly deliberating.'[67]

For Lovett and his fellow ascetic radicals, there was one space above all others that was to be avoided: 'the contaminating influences of public-houses and beer-shops – places where many of their meetings are still held, in which the passions are inflamed and the reason drowned'.[68] By the early nineteenth century, the convivial public sphere of tavern culture which had acted as a site of Enlightenment in the late eighteenth century, had declined and came to be associated, *inter alia*, with boisterousness and bodily excess.[69] But it was a space from which even ascetic radicals struggled to fully extricate themselves. Pubs remained one of the most important spaces for popular radicals to meet in, especially in working-class districts where they acted as centres of convivial and associational space. Yet in some places there was a discernible trend away from them in the 1840s as Chartists tried to 'raise the Charter from the pot-house' by building or renting their own dedicated buildings.[70] The example of the pub is a good one for complicating Reddy's binary model of regime/refuge, a binary that has been challenged by historians of emotion and space.[71] On the one hand, the pub was one of the few communal spaces to which the working class and the Chartist had free access, and there is no doubt that it could serve in working-class districts as an emotional refuge where workers could express their feelings freely. On the other hand, as moral-force Chartists like Lovett clearly appreciated, the pub could also be a space in which workers literally drowned their sorrows and dulled their senses, which had the effect of turning the pub into a space that shored up the dominant emotional regime, a possibility that Reddy does acknowledge can happen with some emotional refuges.[72] Ironically, for a movement which had, as its fundamental goal, the ending of mass suffering, the short-term alleviation of pain through drink ran the risk of undermining the movement. Ascetic radicals, in any case, countered that alcoholism would lead to greater pain in the long term. Thus, there was a tension within ascetic radicalism between the need for pain – as a spur to radical action – and the alleviation of it as a goal of the movement, a tension aptly captured by the original religious meaning of asceticism, though in this case pain is conceived as politically, rather spiritually, useful.[73] As Lovett explained in *Social and Political Morality*, 'self denial and self sacrifice' were necessary prerequisites for promoting the 'happiness of our race'.[74] The goal of ascetic radicalism was 'the happiness of every human being', but this would not be achieved solely by ending 'class legislation' through democratic reforms. It was also necessary to put one's own house in order and live a moral life.[75]

It is no surprise, therefore, that Lovett's preferred space was the coffee shop, which underscored his metropolitanism and elitism; as Navickas points out 'coffee houses of the Habermasian public sphere and the assembly rooms of the "urban renaissance" were minor venues compared with the ubiquity of the pub'.[76] But Lovett and his fellow LWMA leaders revelled in this minor venue: 'I would prefer to go to a coffee-house to any other place', he informed a fellow radical (who turned out to be a spy).[77] This aversion to pubs and the associated culture of festivity and hedonism that went with them was no retrospective airbrushing by Lovett. While some of his fellow members of the LWMA *had* been more comfortable with this culture as Tom Scriven has shown, Lovett was rarely among them. He was far more prudish, for example – even by the austere standards of Richard Carlile and Francis Place.[78] His early days as a radical in the London of the late 1820s and early 1830s was spent largely in coffee shops in and around Holborn where he moved without any sense of contradiction between the different brands of radicalism on offer: republican, deist, Owenite socialist, co-operation, parliamentary reform, and the campaign for a free press. Only rarely did he venture outdoors, much less speak on the mass platform.[79]

Emma Griffin has recently and correctly pointed to the importance of participating in associational culture as a key formative experience for Chartists, and Lovett was certainly no exception.[80] But equally important was the space in which many of these associations took place – coffee shops, or rooms adjoining them. Tellingly, it was not mutual improvement associations that Lovett singled out as the key factor in bringing about the moral progress made by the working classes during his lifetime, but coffee shops and eating houses, the relative absence of which during his youth accounted for the drunkenness, dissipation and pugilism which characterised London low-life. The coffee shop, by contrast, was a polite space where informed discussion could take place; indeed Lovett completely elides the distinction between coffee shops and debating places, places he recalled that 'I was very fond of attending' – a reminder that radicalism was not always associated with negative feelings – either in terms of what made workers become radicals or their affective experience as a radical activist.[81] This is not to suggest that coffee shops were spaces which necessarily restrained radicalism: the government spy who branded Lovett a 'dangerous man' had formed his impression mainly from attending meetings at the coffee shops run by William Benbow and John Cleave.[82] But any warmness of sentiment was the product of heartfelt ardour rather than alcohol. When the Owenite co-operative venture he was involved in failed, Lovett turned the premises into a coffee house, with a dedicated space for conversation separate from the reading room where 'fellow labourers … can converse freely on all subjects they deem essential to their welfare, unattended with that unpleasant restraint so necessary in a room solely devoted to reading'.[83] This venture soon failed, but Lovett reflected 'I now look back upon those two years of my life with great pleasure and satisfaction' because he learned much and it facilitated radical education.[84] Though he gravitated away from socialism back to radicalism he never entirely shed his Owenism: like Owen, Lovett took the view that the competition which was inherent in capitalism was responsible for unleashing all the evil passions of 'envy, hatred, jealousy'.[85]

One of the tensions in the ascetic radicalism of Lovett and the LWMA was the implication of finding brutishness among the working classes. Historians of Chartism have long emphasised the elitism of the LWMA with its selective appeal to 'the intelligent and influential portion of the working classes'. Only those workers who resisted 'mere sensual and brutalising enjoyments' were deemed moral and worthy of membership of the LWMA, and by extension citizenship.[86] On the other hand, the problem with ascetic radicalism, as Feargus O'Connor was quick to observe, was that making reason and restraint the criteria for working-class enfranchisement ran the risk of setting up the workers to fail.[87] Yet there was a way for ascetic radicals to acknowledge that some workers were slaves to their passions without compromising the case for enfranchisement, though it was only occasionally conceded: if the working classes were creatures of their passions, then it was the product of the harsh environment in which they were situated – a similar concession that they shared with sentimental radicals like Oastler and Stephens. In any case, granting political rights to the workers, it was countered, would check the baser passions.[88] Even Lovett, in an uncharacteristic admission that he and his fellow Chartists may have used intemperate language, excused any talk of physical force on the grounds that 'when the eye dwells on the extremest [sic.] poverty trampled on by severe repression, the heart often forces a language from the tongue which sober reflection would redeem'.[89] As his choice of language suggests, Chartists often conceptualised hunger not just as physical want, but as a feeling that also eats at the heart: historical evidence for contemporary 'biopsychosocial' understandings of pain 'in which the body and mind are bound up with social factors that add up to our collective pain experiences'.[90] Locating feeling in the heart was also another way of underscoring the equality of working men with the enfranchised propertied classes: workers, too, had feelings, and seating those feelings in the heart rather than the head served as a riposte to the counter-assertion that workers were less refined because of their lack of education. Once again, ascetic radicals had to tread a fine line because they were never willing to locate feeling exclusively in the heart. As we have seen with Lovett, he was quick to berate his fellow workers if they divorced feelings from reason and did not exercise control over their passions. This tension would pose serious problems for Chartism as the next section shows.

Sentimental conventions

The General Convention of the Industrious Classes, to give the Chartist Convention of 1839 its full name, has featured prominently in accounts of early Chartism, not least because it was the movement's only national, co-ordinating body at this stage, composed of 'elected' representatives from the localities. The brainchild of Thomas Attwood's Birmingham Political Union, though one that had a long pedigree in radicalism, its ostensible purpose was to superintend the presentation of a mass petition to parliament, praying for the enactment of the People's Charter.[91] Almost immediately from its first meeting in early February in London, it became embroiled in debates about strategy and tactics: should the convention confine itself to the organisation of the petition, or should it propose a raft of 'ulterior measures' to be enacted if (and almost certainly, when) parliament rejected the petition? By summer 1839, advocates of intimidation had gained the upper hand, but this did not stop the Convention from collapsing amid continuing divisions within it, allied to an inability or unwillingness to enforce the ulterior measures. Lovett was elected secretary of the Convention, and he and his fellow

LWMA members did their utmost to try and pack the Convention with their members for the seats allocated to London, and with some initial success.[92] Their objective was to exclude those ultra-radical elements like the London Democratic Association and allies of O'Connor who made 'furious appeals to the passions of the multitude'.[93] But Lovett and the LWMA soon lost control, partly because of their own shortcomings which were arguably just as responsible as the 'physical force swagger' of O'Connor and company.

While the failure of the Convention to successfully lead Chartism has come in for some heavy criticism from contemporaries and historians alike, the reasons for its failure have remained elusive, beyond, that is, citing the not insignificant legal and financial constraints under which it operated. But explanations based on 'inefficient organisation' can only be made to explain so much.[94] Given the constraints under which it operated, the Convention was an impressive display of professionalism and mobilisation and not just at its commencement when it contained several middle-class representatives who were, in any case, always in a minority and most were soon to depart in disgust at the physical force rhetoric of other members. The Convention dispatched missionaries to the localities to mobilise the people; sent detailed questionnaires designed to provide it with knowledge of the conditions of the working classes; formed committees to tackle particular problems and make recommendations; and through the indefatigable organisational energies of Lovett, it received hundreds of letters requesting information or updates on the progress of Chartism in the localities. Lovett was soon overwhelmed and there can be no doubt that this led to a breakdown of communication between centre and locality, a breakdown that would have repercussions for the Convention's affective politics.[95] Similarly, explanations that cite the divisions between the advocates of physical and moral force (underpinned by class divisions in older accounts) are also limited because the 'purist' advocates of moral force were soon purged from the Convention.[96] In any case, most Chartists within and without the Convention were somewhere in between these two extreme poles – 'Peaceably if we may, forcibly if we must' was the rallying cry of the vast majority. Even Lovett, still too often inaccurately presented as the moral-force Chartist *par excellence*, refused to condemn violence outright and, as he had done during the Reform Bill crisis, he urged the people to arm in self-defence.[97]

What follows will suggest that the affective politics of the Convention played a significant part in its eventual failure, and by extension Chartism's failure in 1839. Historians and contemporaries have not been unaware of the role of heightened feeling in the affairs of the Convention: 'Chartists' emotional investment in the Convention was immense', notes Chase.[98] Though he ascribes little explicit explanatory power to them, Gammage emphasised the role of feelings, especially when discussing the Convention's demise (though he opted for the fatal divisions between advocates of phys-ical and moral force as the main factor). The purpose of the Convention was 'to speak the feelings, the thoughts, and the sentiments' of the people; 'after the promises which had been made, and the hopes that had been excited, there was no alternative but to resort to the ulterior measures'; 'A portion of that body were too timid and sluggish, another portion too hasty and precipitate … A considerable number were either vacillating between the fear of danger on the one hand, and the taunts of cowardice on the other', Gammage recalled.[99] Lovett, too, as we shall see, gave feelings a prominent place in his explanation of why the Convention failed.

The parallel between the Chartist Convention and the National Assembly and Convention in the French Revolution of the 1790s has not gone unnoticed; indeed, the group of physical-force militants, associated with G.J. Harney and the London Democratic Association, in the Chartist Convention were styled as Jacobins and publicly gloried in the names of Robespierre and Marat.[100] The parallels and similarities multiply even further when we draw on William Reddy's theory of emotions which he applied to a case study of revolutionary France in the 1790s.[101] True, there are obvious differences: Britain in the late 1830s was not France in the 1790s. The Chartists were not faced with the task of forming a govern-ment and defeating a ruthless and violent alliance of enemies, both domestic and foreign. Nevertheless, like the French National Assembly, the Chartist Convention was also riding a wave of intense feeling, created and deep-ened, in part by the Convention, which simultaneously licensed that wave, but ultimately undermined it. The dilemma for the Convention was how to mobilise support in the country, which invariably took the form of impas-sioned speeches outside the Convention to create excitement, and at the same time restrain and dampen this heightened feeling to put pressure on the government but without giving any hostages to fortune. The result was an increasing bifurcation of what happened within and without the Convention: it is no coincidence that a number of those Chartists who had reputations for impassioned rhetoric were much more moderate and cau-tious in the Convention than they were on the mass platform. Harney, as befitted the transcendent Jacobin, was the exception that proved the rule; but he was rebuked for these outbursts.[102] Even otherwise hostile obser-vers were struck by the sober, sombre conduct of the Convention dur-ing its deliberations, testament, in part, to the feeling rules established by Lovett.[103] This helps to explain the almost pathological insistence by those like Lovett that the Convention should be bound by clear and elaborate rules; hence the obsession with procedure, terms of reference, drafting reso-lutions and counter-resolutions, even down to empowering the chairman to 'check … any irrelevant or improper language'.[104] The intention of those like Lovett was that the Convention would eschew anything that might be construed as unrestrained feeling, and they lost no opportunity to censure more extreme members who were determined, in the words of the LWMA member William Carpenter, to 'mar the object of the Convention' by going 'back to those parts of the country, where they had succeeded by their mass appeals to the passions'.[105] Although they clearly had other motives in withdrawing from the Convention, the delegation from the Birmingham Political Union also cited their revulsion at the 'brutal passions' displayed by more extreme members of the Convention.[106] Tellingly, when passions did become inflamed in the Convention, the moral-force Chartists began holding their own informal meetings at a coffee house in the evening away from the 'physical force party'.[107]

Unsurprisingly, some of the most sentimental outpourings issued from the London Democratic Association, the Jacobin body associated with Harney. David Cater set the tone shortly after the inauguration of the Convention. Writing in Bronterre O'Brien's *Operative*, he asked 'who is the man that has pretensions to natural sympathy and parental affection [and] can endure the affliction of mind by knowing that his father or mother' had been confined to a workhouse. Who could contemplate the regime of 'starvation, misery, wretchedness … in … [the] poor-law murdering house, and not instantly come forward to assist us in our noble and righteous struggle for Universal Suffrage'.[108] Cater continued to describe the intense feelings he felt when surveying the state of other members of his impoverished family. The physical force Chartist Peter McDouall struck a similar sentimental note in his address to his Ashton-under-Lyne constituents: 'How strongly then must the heart of the Englishman beat? How will the heart of the man swell? With what indignant emotion the soul of the patriot must be filled, to see a people … reduced to the brink of despair.'[109]

Although this type of sentimentalism undoubtedly played a significant part in raising feelings of excitement and hope, it was not fatal to the prospects of the Convention, at least not directly. What was much more damaging were the many reports which localities sent into the Convention that, caught in a sentimental spiral of their own, reported that all was well. The Convention papers – the letters that came into Lovett as secretary – can roughly be divided into three categories: procedural (sending money, asking for missionaries), reports from missionaries, and – a category that historians have largely ignored – exhortations. The latter, and to some extent the reports from missionaries, could be very sentimental. The Hull Working Men's Association exhorted the Convention as early as 20 February 1839: 'Go on, as you have hitherto done, and you cannot fail' to rouse the working class.[110] A day later, the Chartists of Canterbury assured the Convention that the dispatch of a missionary would allay fears and feelings of doubt among the Chartists of the district who would then be ready to heed the call.[111] Reaching further heights of sentimentalism, the Chartists of Bridgeton, Scotland, 'contemplate with pleasure the rapid progress the cause of freedom is making'. The Convention 'have excited both our admiration and esteem ... and we can candidly assure you, you have secured our unqualified confidence'. The enemies of the movement 'may treat our petitions with scorn and contempt', but 'the omnipotent power of the people will not be defeated'. '[F]ear not, but we will be among those who will fly to the rescue, then shall the whole barrier be levelled like the frail embankment before an Autumnal flood.'[112] The Chartists of Sutton-in-Ashfield reported that such was the overwhelming 'moral feelings', 'in no place is there more unanimity with regard to the principles of the Charter for 19/20 of the population are in favour of them'. So optimistic were the impoverished framework knitters of this part of Nottinghamshire that it was making their suffering bearable.[113] At Kilmarnock, the delegate Hugh Craig informed Lovett that 'The people of Ayrshire are in high spirits and feel unbounded confidence in the Convention'.[114]

Even in hitherto benighted places, it was reported that the arrival of missionaries converted the people to the cause of the Convention. In hindsight, what was more worrying were the exhortations which assured the Convention that it could do no wrong, invariably expressed as confidence, crucial currency in any political transaction.[115] The atmosphere of excitement, anticipation and hope, which reached a crescendo with the simultaneous mass meetings held over Whitsun, was further stoked by the melodramatic appeals in broadsides, a genre long associated with sensation: 'Men of Birmingham! Arouse! Arouse! And rally round the Standard of your Holy Convention; Your God, your Country, calls aloud for your support; Now or Never; or be Slaves doomed to everlasting toil & misery'.[116] Notwithstanding the timidity of the Birmingham Political Union delegation, beneath that level of middle-class leadership, sentimentalism was clearly present: the Duddeston Radical Reformers greeted the inauguration of the Convention 'with heartfelt and boundless joy'. Warming to its theme, victory was assured: 'Whilst in every town and hamlet the hope and confidence that beam in the eyes of every radical reformer are sufficient evidence that it [the Convention] possesses their undivided fealty.'[117] Paradoxically, complaints from some localities that the Convention had wasted time and allowed the initiative to pass to the authorities added to the frustration from without and sense of urgency within the Convention.[118] Small wonder that the Convention felt duty bound to proceed to the recommendation of 'ulterior measures' in its Manifesto, published on 14 May 1839. Having put the manifesto to the people in a series of questions – would the people strike for a month, withdraw all their savings from the banks, abstain from excisable articles, and arm themselves in self-defence? – the Chartist *Western Vindicator* exclaimed: 'At the meetings to which the above questions have been put the people have answered AYE! We emphatically say, that the NAY to the above, by whoever raised, will be powerless!'[119] As late as September after the Convention had all but collapsed, O'Connor – ever ebullient – was still reassuring delegates that such were the determined feelings of the men of the north that no hazards would stand in their way.[120]

As Malcolm Chase astutely observes, 'This almost habitual inflation of support for Chartism was having two deleterious effects. First it stoked the optimism' of the more impatient and intemperate delegates. Second, 'it exacerbated the fears of the more cautious that the mood of the country was potentially spiralling out of control and their belief that it was the Convention's responsibility to restrain it'.[121] To explain why and how this had happened we need to return to Reddy. The problem with the Chartist Convention is that it did not constitute a stable emotional regime, in part because of its origin in the wider Chartist movement which, by Reddy's definition, was an emotional refuge, and the Convention found it virtually impossible to reconcile these roles, not least because one presupposed affective restraint, the other excess. Chartism certainly provided its members a 'safe release from prevailing emotional norms',[122] in this case by allowing the working class to assert their humanity as feeling subjects and to propose an alternative political economy that secured happiness to all people, not just elites. However, if Chartism was an emotional refuge, then it, too, was beset with tension if not instability between the advocates of restraint and excess. All emotional refuges contain the seeds of regimes – this much Reddy acknowledges, yet he is largely silent on how this transformation takes place, or, crucially, why this transformation sometimes fails. Arguably, the missing dynamic in Reddy's model is space. The very basis of Chartist mobilisation in the run up to, and during the existence of, the Convention was sentimentalism, excitement, confidence and hope. This was fine out on the platform and in the period preceding the Convention when there was no real responsibility to lead, though there is no denying that physical force Chartists were caught in what Reddy terms 'the grip of one of those sentimentalist spirals ... in which expression of intensity elicited increased intensity'.[123]

But with the inauguration of the Convention, Chartism was catapulted into a very different space and context: an elected, constituted sovereign body – not for nothing was the Convention seen by some as an 'anti-parliament', a rival to the authority of parliament.[124] Sentimentalism and excitement without undermined the ability of the Convention to act dispassionately within, despite the best efforts of those like Lovett. The fatal flaw of sentimentalism and excitement without was that it obscured from view the seriously deficient state of Chartist organisation and readiness in the localities to implement the 'ulterior measures', principally the 'sacred month' (a general strike). As the Salford Chartist R.J. Richardson complained to the Convention in July, 'The reports of the state of the country I am sorry to see have been greatly exaggerated'.[125] Just as befell the French revolutionaries, it was much easier and more satisfying to revel in the outpouring of sentiment rather than the practicalities of organising resistance, and Lovett must bare his share of responsibility for this failure as he was the key link between the centre and localities.[126] So much had rested on the intangible feeling of confidence that the Chartist rank and file invested in the Convention, but when the delegates began to prevaricate in July over strategy – notably the climb down from a month-long to a three-day strike – confidence evaporated and confusion reigned. All this had happened on the terrain of feeling.[127] Gammage berated the Convention's decision to proceed to ulterior measures, 'a conviction of such preparedness should be founded on better evidence than their attendance at public meetings, and cheering in the moment of excitement the most violent and inflammatory orator', a view shared by Lovett.[128] In the end, the Convention remained a liminal emotional space, caught between regime and refuge.

It could be argued that the fate of the Convention was sealed when its restraining secretary was himself arrested for recommending the people arm in self-defence. Unsurprisingly, this was the view of Lovett himself, though that is, perhaps, to attribute too much influence to him during a period in his life when he, too, was showing signs of heightened feeling.[129] When the Convention relocated to Birmingham in May 1839, in part as a measure of self-protection – the authorities were closing in around the Convention and the delegates were increasingly anxious if not fearful – and so the body moved to a place where it was assumed it would command greater popular support, thereby assuaging the prevailing anxiety. But tensions soon began to mount in Birmingham. By July crowds were meeting daily in the Bull Ring, which soon turned riotous due to the provocation of the crowd by the decision of the local authorities – which included none other than members of the Birmingham Political Union – to request assistance from the Metropolitan Police who were duly sent by rail from London.

As far as Lovett was concerned this represented an unconstitutional infringement of the rights of citizens to protest peacefully in a move that smacked of continental gendarmerie. Following a violent clash between police and crowd, at Lovett's behest the Convention issued a resolution condemning the authorities. He was indignant, 'feeling most strongly that a great injustice had been afflicted', stating that 'I thought the people were justified in repelling such blood-thirsty and despotic power by every and any means at their disposal'.[130] Compared to some of the rhetoric of the more physical force-inclined Chartists, this was relatively mild, but the authorities were in no mood to draw fine distinctions and so Lovett, as the sole signatory of the resolutions, and John Collins as the Chartist responsible for printing them, were arrested. It was testament to Lovett's courage and convictions that he insisted being the sole signatory of the resolutions to protect other members of the Convention, several of whom had, in any case, already been arrested. Ironically, for reasons explored in the final section, Lovett found himself on trial for 'being a person of a wicked, seditious, and disaffected mind and disposition' who had 'excite[d] diverse liege subjects of our Lady the Queen, to violate, resist, and oppose the laws of the realm'. Lovett, too, was, in the words of Attorney-General, guilty of 'inflam[ing] the angry passions of men'. His defence – that what he had written was not libellous because those 'momentary feelings' were honestly felt with no malice of forethought –failed to convince the jury.[131] He was sentenced to one-year imprisonment in Warwick gaol.

Cross (class) feelings in later Chartism

When the Ulster radical landowner Sharman Crawford wrote to Lovett in September 1837 to thank him for an invitation to attend a dinner, he confided just how much the LWMA had impressed him: 'I never met any association where conduct impressed me with a higher feeling of approval and respect ... I saw a firmness of purpose combined with moderation of expression and conduct.'[132] This was exactly the kind of approval Lovett craved, as it was part of his enduring goal of demonstrating the fitness of his fellow workers for citizenship, and for building bridges with upper-class reformers like Sharman Crawford. Lovett singled out the middle classes whose 'favourable opinion' they had secured until 'the violent ravings about physical force, by O'Connor, Stephens, and Oastler, scared them from our ranks'.[133] There is no doubt that Lovett's assessment of why Chartism failed in 1839 furnishes striking further evidence for Haskell's notion of an 'ethical shelter', into which the scared the middle classes had run for safety and justification for rejecting the demands of the Chartists. Lovett would essentially make the same point again in 1842 and 1848: on the morning of the great Kennington Common meeting in April 1848, for example, he counselled restraint, peace and moral conduct.[134] The 'ethical shelter', it is worth recalling, is a mental space which provides comfort while doing nothing; in other words, an exemption from moral responsibility, in this case redressing the grievances of the working classes.[135] As the quintessential middle-class radical Richard Cobden complained in April 1839: 'The Chartists have by their insane ravings & their continued appeal to brute-force in the absence of reason frightened the *shopkeepers* for the present.'[136] This ethical shelter, then, was a crucial element in the pathologising of Chartism 'from above'.[137]

Once again, sympathy had been trumped by fear and disgust.[138] From the perspective of the Chartists, the dismissal that they had met with inflamed their feelings – as Lovett emphasised at his trial. Of course, we cannot reduce outbreaks of Chartist violence – as at Birmingham during the Bull Ring riots, the Newport rising in November 1839, or the Orange Tree Conspiracy of summer 1848 – to angry, wounded feelings which had been stoked by intemperate physical force rhetoric, but this affective dimension was certainly a factor.[139] As one of the members of the Convention – Charles Neesom – charged those who had used such rhetoric, 'they had excited the hopes of the people', only to pull back from any decisive action.[140]

As with so many fundamental strategic questions in Chartism, the Chartists never really succeeded in resolving the affective dilemma of riding the wave of popular feeling; that is, how to simultaneously appeal to feeling, including the deliberate inflaming of the passions, and yet at the same time discipline that ardour. In Lovett's mind there was no such dilemma: inflaming the passions was to be avoided at all costs. The blueprint for this was the book that he co-wrote with John Collins while in Warwick gaol, *Chartism: A New Organisation of the People*, though because of their lowly class status, the two men were not able to turn their prison cells into relatively comfortable spaces for the creation of a democratic counter-culture. The initial indignities and privations Lovett suffered in prison were enough to scare and degrade any man – imprisoned with common felons, stripped naked and his hair shaved by a prisoner, and his wife was only allowed to visit twice – let alone a man who prided himself on his respectability. In the petition that he and Collins submitted to the government protesting their imprisonment and treatment they understandably complained of this brutalising 'indignity'. Lovett had little difficulty in evoking feelings of disgust through graphic and sensory description of the poor conditions in which they lodged, as well as through the various attempts to reduce them to the level of brutes by making them eat raw bacon and egg and by withholding cutlery and crockery. While his treatment did improve somewhat thereafter, Lovett was still subjected to many privations: the number of letters he was able to send were limited and their content screened, a constraint he described as 'restrictions in writing my feelings'.[141]

Unsurprisingly, the risks of appealing to the passions was something Lovett accented much more strongly in the organisations he was involved with throughout the 1840s following his release from prison in July 1840. Recall Lovett's Address of the National Association: 'We felt anxious to redeem by reason what had been lost by madness and folly', the first meetings of which took place, predictably, in a coffee house.[142] Not for the first time was a radical leader appealing to reason as a way of denigrating his political rivals, in this case O'Connor and the National Charter Association. The preoccupation of Lovett with feelings was part of their strategy of putting as much distance as possible between them and O'Connor, and in the process constituting the very notion of moral-force Chartism which was based on a particular set of feeling rules. The problem with ascetic radicalism, as we have seen, is that it was vulnerable to the charge of elitism and invalidating the raw feelings and moral failings of workers who were prevented by their dire circumstances from meeting Lovett's tightly bound feeling rules, and who found some comfort in 'mere sensual enjoyments'. It was precisely these charges that O'Connor brought against this kind of ascetic radicalism during the so-called 'new move' of 1841 when Lovett restated and expanded his ascetic radical agenda.[143]

Moral-force Chartists like Lovett were acutely sensitive to charges that they had unnecessarily inflamed working-class feelings, and following the setbacks of 1839 there were moves to try and heal the divisions between middle-class reformers and working-class Chartists. Lovett was a leading proponent of these attempts at reconciliation in the 1840s and once again his affective politics became tied to a particular space with a set of prescriptive feeling rules – the National Hall in Holborn, home of the National Association. Akin to the Owenite Halls of Science, this was to be a rational space for promoting education, wholesome recreation, the meeting of the sexes on equal terms and cross-class harmony. As Lovett's longstanding friend and radical colleague Richard Moore tellingly put it, the National Hall acted as a space in 'which a sound rational nucleus of reformers might appeal to and gather strength from their fellow men, and by a reserved and tolerant deportment increase the good feelings already beginning to exist between the middle and working classes'.[144] Lovett fought hard and successfully to ban alcohol from the premises while controversial topics, such as religion, were banned lest the atmosphere of cordial feeling was disturbed.[145]

Lovett was no middle-class collaborator (at least not before the late 1840s), but his working-class consciousness did not preclude working with sympathetic middle-class radicals.[146] Ever since the Reform Bill days, he had always welcomed the assistance of any reformer who was willing to lend assistance. Yet there was to be no dictating of terms by the latter as he demonstrated abundantly when he torpedoed the Complete Suffrage initiative of Joseph Sturge in December 1842. His reason for doing this was that the middle-class delegates insisted, as the price for proceeding, the dropping of the People's Charter on the grounds that the latter was too tainted in the eyes of more moderate middle-class reformers. In a rousing defence of the People's Charter which bordered on sentimentalism, and won the effusive support of Feargus O'Connor who was also in attendance, Lovett made clear that it was more than just a document. Over the last few years since its publication its advocates had 'suffered' for it as victims of execration, imprisonment, transportation and even death. While he acknowledged that some Chartists had unduly inflamed the passions, Lovett countered that he had condemned them and he hoped that the conduct of the Chartists at the various conferences held to further complete suffrage was evidence of their 'calm and rational manner'.[147] In short, the Charter had become what Sarah Ahmed has termed a 'sticky' emotional object, that is 'objects saturated with affect', which act 'as sites of personal and social tension'. The value of this approach is that, in shifting the circulation of feeling from person to object, it recognises that the same object may elicit different feelings in different people, and that conflict between these different feelings acts to heighten the intensity of an emotional experience. In other words, 'shared feelings are not about feeling the same feeling, or feeling in common'.[148]

The mistake that O'Connor made when he found Lovett to be an unexpected ally at this meeting in torpedoing Complete Suffrage was to assume that they felt the same. While the defence of the Charter induced feelings of defiance, fraternal suffering and collegial loyalty even to the point that he outstretched the hand of forgiveness to Lovett, the latter associated Chartism with a much more negative set of feelings including bitterness and malice towards O'Connor. For O'Connor, the People's Charter was largely a symbolic representation of the movement's goals and the collective power of the people, and his emotional investment in it was much less intense than it was for Lovett (only reluctantly had O'Connor initially adopted it as the focus of the movement – his first feeling had been one of suspicion).[149] For Lovett, who had actually authored the document (with some help), his personal pride as well as love for the principles enshrined were at issue. Not for the first time or the last, Lovett and O'Connor felt differently – even when, on the surface, it appeared they felt the same. Lovett now found himself largely isolated, having alienated both O'Connor and the middle-class reformers. He retreated further and further into his ascetic radicalism, which, in the long term, affectively paved the way for the mid-Victorian rapprochement between working-class radicalism and middle-class liberalism, a goal that Lovett had been working towards since the early 1840s.[150] Even in the late 1830s, though extremely cautious of upper-class radicals bearing gifts, he had agreed to co-operate with another charismatic Irishman, Daniel O'Connell. For reasons explored in the final chapter, Lovett would come to loathe O'Connell almost as much as he did O'Connor.

Notes

1 William Lovett, *The Life and Struggles of William Lovett in his Pursuit of Bread, Knowledge and Freedom* (London: Macgibbon & Kee, 1976).

2 For these characterisations of the historiography, see Dorothy Thompson, *Outsiders: Class, Gender and Nation* (London: Verso, 1993), chapter 1; Malcolm Chase, *The Chartists: Perspectives and Legacies* (London: Merlin, 2015),

chapter 2. On Lovett's intimidatory rhetoric in the 1830s, see Joel Wiener, *William Lovett* (Manchester: Manchester University Press, 1989), pp. 2, 19, 61–2, 74.

3 Katrina Navickas, *Protest and the Politics of Space and Place, 1789–1848* (Manchester: Manchester University Press, 2016).

4 Colin Skelly, 'The origins, nature and development of moral force Chartism, 1836–1850' (PhD dissertation, University of York, 2005); Tom Scriven, *Popular Virtue: Continuity and Change in Radical Moral Politics, 1820–70* (Manchester: Manchester University Press, 2017).

5 Wiener, *Lovett*, p. 6; Scriven, *Popular Virtue*, p. 75.

6 The role played by feeling in demarcating the boundaries between Chartism and rival movements is explored in the next chapter which focuses on the relationship between Chartism and Daniel O'Connell.

7 BL, Additional MS 34245A, Correspondence of the General Convention of the Industrial Classes 1839, William Cardo to William Lovett, 14 March 1839, fol. 129.

8 BL, Additional MS 78161, William Lovett papers, John Fraser to Lovett, n.d., fol. 21.

9 *NS*, 17 October 1840. For similar examples, see 29 July 1848; 26 September 1840 (Miss Muir); *Northern Liberator*, 21 December 1839 (editorial).

10 Thomas Dixon, ' "Emotion": the history of a keyword in crisis', *Emotion Review*, 4 (2012), 339; Thomas Dixon, *From Passions to Emotions: The Creation of a Secular Psychological Character* (Cambridge: Cambridge University Press, 2003), pp. 21–2, chapter 2.

11 *NS*, 30 July 1842.

12 *London Dispatch*, 25 February 1838; *NS*, 25 September 1841.

13 For Carlile's influence on Lovett and the future moral-force Chartists, see Iorwerth Prothero, *Artisans and Politics in Early Nineteenth-Century London: John Gast and His Times* (Folkestone: Dawson, 1979), pp. 276–81.

14 Rob Boddice, *A History of Feelings* (London: Reaktion, 2019), p. 118. Godwin would later reject the excessive rationalism of his puritan inheritance and assert the primacy of feeling over reason as the most useful and proper determinant of human behaviour. Rowland Weston, 'Politics, passion and the "puritan temper": Godwin's critique of enlightened modernity', *Studies in Romanticism* 41 (2002), 448. For the influence of Godwin and Wollstonecraft's (affective) politics on the Chartists, see Scriven, *Popular Virtue*, pp. 90–6; Matthew Roberts, 'Romantic memory? Forgetting, remembering and feeling in the Chartist Pantheon of Heroes, 1790–1840', in Matthew Roberts (ed.), *Memory and Modern British Politics: Commemoration, Tradition, Legacy, 1789 to the Present* (London: Bloomsbury, forthcoming).

15 *London Dispatch*, 1 October 1837; Library of Birmingham, Wolfson Centre for Archival research, William Lovett Collection, Ms 753, vol. 2, 'Glorious Meeting of the Unrepresented' (February 1837), fols 26–7. Lovett also registered his indignation at being precluded from personally presenting a petition to the Queen because he did not possess 'court dress' by dismissing the latter requirement as a form of 'Gothic ignorance'. Lovett, *Life and Struggles*, p. 102.

16 BL, Additional MS 37773, Working Men's Association Minutes, 2 January 1839, fol. 135. For similar examples, see Lovett, *Life and Struggles*, 209.

17 Lovett, *Life and Struggles*, pp. 134, 159, 210.

18 J.F.C. Harrison, 'Early Victorian radicals and the medical fringe', in W.F. Bynum and R. Porter (eds), *Medical Fringe and Medical Orthodoxy* (London: Routledge, 1987), pp. 198–215.

19 David Stack, 'William Lovett and the National Association for the Political and Social Improvement of the People', *HJ*, 42 (1999), 1041. See also Scriven, *Moral Politics*, pp. 87–9.

20 William Lovett, *Social and Political Morality* (London, 1853), pp. 32, 35; William Lovett and John Collins, *Chartism: or a New Organisation of the People* (London, 1840), p. 78; BL, Additional MS 37774, Minutes of the National Association, 12 October 1841, fol. 1v.

21 William Lovett, *Elementary Anatomy and Physiology* (London, 1853), p. 143. See also Brian Harrison, 'Teetotal Chartism', *History*, 58 (1973), 193–217.

22 TNA, HO 64/12, secret service reports, 22 May 1832, fol. 96.

23 Co-operative Archive, Manchester, Robert Owen Papers, ROC /12/29/1, Lovett to Owen, 3 March 1836.

24 TNA, HO 64/11, secret service reports, July, 26 October and 22 November 1831, fols 420, 427, 440; HO 64/12, 22 May 1832, fol. 97. Lovett had already acquired a reputation as a stubborn and outspoken man of principle by refusing to serve in the militia on being balloted, an act of defiance that led to the distraining of his household furniture in lieu of his refusal to pay the fine. *Ballot*, 18 September 1831; *British Statesman*, 16 April 1842.

25 *Ballot*, 6 November 1831; BL, Additional MS 27791, Francis Place Papers, Narrative of Political Events in England, 1830–35, vol. III, fol. 248; HO 44/52, secret service reports, 25 August 1839, fol. 178.

26 *The Trial of W. Lovett, Journeyman Cabinet-Maker for Sedition* (London, 1839), p. 13; Wiener, *Lovett*, pp. 51, 78.

27 R.G. Gammage, *History of the Chartist Movement, 1837–1854* (London: Merlin, 1969 [1854]), pp. 7, 100.

28 *Charter*, 31 March 1839; Lovett, *Life and Struggles*, pp. 117–18; Lovett and Collins, *Chartism*, p. 90. See also Brian Harrison, 'Kindness and reason: William Lovett and education', in Gordon Marsden (ed.), *Victorian Values* (London: Routledge, 1990), pp. 13–28.

29 Lovett, *Social and Political Morality*, p. 70.

30 Lovett, *Elementary Anatomy*, p. 123.

31 *National Association Gazette*, 25 June 1842. For the Stoics and emotions, see R. Sorabji, *Emotion and Peace of Mind: From Stoic Agitation to Christian Temptation* (Oxford: Oxford University Press, 2000).

32 Lovett, *Elementary Anatomy*, p. 124.

33 Barbara H. Rosenwein, *Anger: The Conflicted History of an Emotion* (New Haven and London: Yale University Press, 2020), p. 44, 48.

34 Dixon, 'Emotion', p. 339; Dixon, *Passions to Emotions*, chapters 2–3.

35 Eileen Janes Yeo, 'Will the real Mary Lovett please stand up?': Chartism, gender and autobiography', in Ian Dyck and Malcolm Chase (eds), *Living and Learning: Essays in Honour of J.F.C. Harrison* (Aldershot: Scolar Press, 1996), pp. 163–81.

36 Brian Harrison, 'William Lovett and education', *History Today*, 37 (1987), 17.

37 *London Dispatch*, 11 December 1836.

38 *Cosmopolite*, 28 April 1832.

39 *Trial of Lovett*, p. 9.

40 BL, Additional MS 27791, Francis Place Papers, narrative of political events, vol. III, fol. 241.

41 *Ibid.*, vol. III, fol. 66.

42 Vic Gatrell, *City of Laughter: Sex and Satire in Eighteenth-Century London* (London: Atlanta, 2006), p. 583; Wiener, *Lovett*, p. 6.

43 This also underlines the need to disaggregate the members of the LWMA: as Tom Scriven has shown in relation to Henry Vincent, at least some of those who looked outwardly respectable indulged privately in ribaldry. One suspects that Lovett would have been horrified had he read Vincent's bawdy and sensual correspondence with his cousin John Minikin. Tom Scriven, 'Humour, satire, and sexuality in the culture of early Chartism', *HJ*, 57 (2014), 170.

44 The best account of Place's quest for respectability, and an implicit recognition of the role played by feelings in this, is Michael Mason, *The Making of Victorian Sexuality* (Oxford: Oxford University Press, 1994), pp. 20–35. For Lovett's rejection of the Malthusian belief that over-population was the cause of working-class distress, see his speech at the Co-operative Congress of 1832: *Cosmopolite*, 28 April 1832.

45 Lovett, *Life and Struggles*, pp. 18, 29–30.

46 *Ibid.*, pp. 90, 125, 230.

47 *Ibid.*, p. 198.

48 Andrew M. Stauffer, *Anger, Revolution, and Romanticism* (Cambridge: Cambridge University Press, 2005), pp. 1, 174; Stefan Collini, 'The idea of "character" in Victorian political thought', *Transactions of the Royal Historical Society*, 35 (1985), 29–50.

49 E.g., *Hansard*, House of Lords, 11 April 1832, vol. 12, cols 214, 264; House of Commons, 3 March 1831, vol. 2, col. 1296.

50 E.g., *NS*, 7 December 1839 (An Ultra-Radical). The view that there were two kinds of anger – a bad one equated with rage and fury, and a good one that was therapeutic and, salutary – had gained ground in the Middle Ages, and was developed and reinforced by the moral philosophy of Hume and Adams in the eighteenth century. Rosenwein, *Anger*, chapters 7–8.

51 Anon, 'The Chartists and universal suffrage', *Blackwood's Edinburgh Magazine*, 46 (September 1839), p. 296.

52 James R. Farr, *Artisans in Europe, 1300–1914* (Cambridge: Cambridge University Press, 2000), p. 6.

53 So poor were Lovett's employment prospects in this trade – which he had never really enjoyed – that following his release from prison in 1840 he set himself up as a bookseller and later as a teacher as well as taking on various secretaryships to boost his income. Wiener, *Lovett*, pp. 59, 77, 97.

54 Lovett, *Life and Struggles*, p. 25. For the ambiguities of artisans, see Iorwerth Prothero, *Radical Artisans in England and France, 1830–1870*

(Cambridge: Cambridge University Press, 1997), pp. 2–3, 17–19; Iorwerth Prothero, 'Chartism in London', *Past and Present*, 44 (1969), 82–5.

55 *Charter*, 10 November 1839. For similar declarations of affective universalism, see *Chartist Circular* (Scotland), 25 January 1840 (article on Major Cartwright).

56 Eileen Yeo, 'Christianity in Chartist struggle, 1838–1842', *Past and Present*, 91 (1981), 110–11 n.5, 130.

57 Either way, it made Chartist men like Lovett complicit in a hegemonic masculinity based on a sentimental view of the family and a chivalric masculinity underpinned by the male breadwinner wage and the exclusion of women from the workplace. Note the scorn in Lovett's comment, written in 1853, 'A man must indeed have lost all self-respect to allow himself and his offspring to be dependent on a wife's labour'. As ever with Lovett, one detects the disapproval of the self-satisfied artisan towards those less fortunately placed than himself. Certainly, the Lovett of the 1830s and early 1840s could not have written this. His own ascent up the artisanal ladder had been far from easy, and there were episodes when he had clearly relied on the labour of his wife to support them. William Lovett, *Social and Political Morality* (London, 1853), p. 93; Yeo, 'Will the real Mary Lovett please stand up?', p. 175; cf. Anna Clark, 'The rhetoric of Chartist domesticity: gender, language, and class in the 1830s and 1840s', *Journal of British Studies*, 31 (1992), 62–88. For hegemonic masculinity, see Ben Griffin, 'Hegemonic masculinity as a historical problem', *Gender and History*, 30 (2018), 377–400.

58 TNA, HO 40/42, 'To the middle classes of the north of England', July 1839, fol. 207. For similar declarations, see Lovett, *Life and Struggles*, p. 111; Collins and Lovett, *Chartism*, p. 68.

59 *NS*, 12 October 1839 (Female Radical Association of Keighley).

60 Lovett, *Life and Struggles*, pp. 31, 111; Lovett and Collins, *Chartism*, p. 60. The fullest statement of Lovett's views on marriage is in his *Social and Political Morality*, pp. 83–109 (esp. p. 92).

61 Stack, 'William Lovett', p. 1043.

62 Ian Haywood, 'The literature of Chartism', in Juliet John (ed.), *The Oxford Handbook of Victorian Literary Culture* (Oxford: Oxford University Press, 2016), p. 83.

63 Lovett, *Life and Struggles*, p. 47.

64 Gammage, *History of the Chartist Movement*, p. 7.

65 Wiener, *Lovett*, p. 47. For the mass platform as a space, see Navickas, *Protest*, pp. 52, 238.

66 R.B. Pugh, 'Chartism in Somerset and Wilshire', in Asa Briggs (ed.), *Chartist Studies* (London: Macmillan, 1959), p. 190. On the role of feeling in Chartist oratory, see Brian Harrison and Patricia Hollis (eds), *Robert Lowery: Radical and Chartist* (London: Europa, 1979), p. 96; Janette Martin, 'Popular political oratory and itinerant lecturing in Yorkshire and the North East in the Age of Chartism, c.1837–60' (PhD dissertation, University of York, 2010), pp. 185–7.

67 Lovett, *Life and Struggles*, p. 204.

68 Address of the National Association, October 1841, reprinted in Patricia Hollis (ed.), *Class and Conflict in Nineteenth-Century England, 1815–1850* (London: Routledge & Kegan Paul, 1973), p. 227.

69 Ian Newman, *The Romantic Tavern: Literature and Conviviality in the Age of Revolution* (Cambridge: Cambridge University Press, 2019), pp. 31–2.

70 Navickas, *Protest*, pp. 32–5; Sam Griffiths and Katrina Navickas, 'The micro-geography of political meeting places in Manchester and Sheffield, c.1780–1850', in Alida Clemente, Dag Lindström and Jon Stobart (eds), *Micro-Geographies of the Western City, c.1750–1900* (Abingdon: Routledge, 2021), p. 199.

71 Roy Kozlovsky, 'Architecture, emotions and the history of childhood', in Stephanie Olsen (ed.), *Childhood, Youth and Emotions in Modern History* (Basingstoke: Palgrave, 2015), pp. 95–118.

72 William M. Reddy, *The Navigation of Feeling: A Framework for the History of Emotions* (Cambridge: Cambridge University Press, 2001), p. 129.

73 For an excellent discussion of these kinds of tensions, see Rob Boddice, *Pain: A Very Short Introduction* (Oxford: Oxford University Press, 2017), chapters 2 and 6.

74 Lovett, *Social and Political Morality*, p. 32.

75 *Prospectus and Rules of the Working Men's Association* (London, 1836), p. 1; *The Rotten House of Commons* (London, 1836), p. 7.

76 Navickas, *Protest*, p. 32.

77 Lovett, *Life and Struggles*, p. 67.

78 Scriven, *Popular Virtue*, chapter 1, cf. p. 48; Michael Mason, *The Making of Victorian Sexual Attitudes* (Oxford: Oxford University Press, 1994), p. 124.

79 TNA, HO 64/11, secret service reports, 9 April and 20 October 1831, fols 288, 425.

80 Emma Griffin, 'The making of the Chartists: popular politics and working-class autobiography in early Victorian Britain', *EHR*, 129 (2014), 578–605.

81 Lovett, *Life and Struggles*, pp. 26, 29, 51. For the affective dimensions of coffee shops and the public sphere, see Brian Cowan, 'In public: collectivities and polities', in C. Walker, K. Barclay, and D. Lemmings (eds), *A Cultural History of the Emotions in the Baroque and Enlightenment Age* (London: Bloomsbury, 2019), pp. 155–72.

82 TNA, HO 64/11, secret service reports, 26 October 1831, fol. 427.

83 *Poor Man's Guardian*, 25 January 1834.

84 Lovett, *Life and Struggles*, p. 71.

85 *Crisis*, 28 April 1832 (Lovett speaking at the Co-operative Congress).

86 BL, Additional MS 37773, Working Men's Association Minutes, 27 December 1836, fol. 33v.

87 Malcolm Chase, *Chartism: A New History* (Manchester: Manchester University Press 2007), pp. 159, 171.

88 *Northern Liberator*, 1 September 1838 (editorial); *Chartist Circular* (Scotland), 12 October 1839.

89 Lovett, *Life and Struggles*, p. 156. For similar affective readings of poverty, see *NS*, 25 May 1844 (Address of Glasgow Chartists); *Weekly Record*, 20 September

1856, reprinted in Hollis, *Class and Conflict*, p. 227. For Chartism and hunger, see Peter J. Gurney, ' "Rejoicing in potatoes": the politics of consumption in England during the "hungry forties" ', *Past and Present*, 203 (2009), 99–136.

90 Boddice, *Pain*, p. 2.

91 Chase, *Chartism*, p. 35; T. M. Parssinen, 'Association, convention and anti-parliament in British radical politics, 1771–1848', *EHR*, 87 (1973), 504–33.

92 David Goodway, *London Chartism, 1838–1848* (Cambridge: Cambridge University Press, 1982), pp. 24–5.

93 Lovett, *Life and Struggles*, p. 142.

94 Kenneth Judge, 'Early Chartist organization and the Convention of 1839', *International Review of Social History*, 20 (1975), 370–1.

95 D.J. Rowe, 'The Chartist Convention and the regions', *Economic History Review*, 116 (1969), 58–74; Judge, 'Early Chartist organization', p. 387. Nevertheless, J.T. Ward's judgement of the Convention seems wide of the mark: 'It finally realised the futility of its own pompous and exaggerated claims to represent the working classes.' J.T. Ward, *Chartism* (London: Batsford, 1973), p. 131.

96 Thomas Milton Kemnitz, 'The Chartist Convention of 1839', *Albion*, 10 (1978), 169; Dorothy Thompson, *The Chartists: Popular Politics in the Industrial Revolution* (New York: Pantheon, 1984), p. 68.

97 David Large, 'William Lovett', in Patricia Hollis (ed.), *Pressure from Without in Early Victorian England* (London: Arnold, 1974), pp. 115–16.

98 Chase, *Chartism*, p. 59.

99 Gammage, *History of the Chartist Movement*, pp. 105–6, 156.

100 *London Democrat*, 20 April 1839.

101 Reddy, *Navigation*, chapter 6.

102 Fraser, *Dr. John Taylor*, p. 51. For Harney in the Convention, see Matthew Roberts, *Chartism, Commemoration and the Cult of the Radical Hero* (Abingdon: Routledge, 2020), p. 88. For other instances of moderation within, excess without, see Brian Harrison, 'Chartism, liberalism and the life of Robert Lowery', *EHR*, 82 (1967), 508.

103 Chase, *Chartism*, p. 60.

104 *Rules and Regulations of the General Convention* (Lambeth, 1839), p 7.

105 *Charter*, 28 April 1839.

106 C.M. Wakefield, *The Life of Thomas Attwood* (London, 1885), pp. 343–4.

107 Lovett, *Life and Struggles*, p. 170.

108 *Operative*, 24 February 1839.

109 *Ibid.*, 17 March 1839.

110 BL, Additional MS 34245A, Hull Working Men's Association to Convention, 20 February 1839, fol. 52v.

111 BL, Additional MS 34245A, Richard Hawes to Lovett, 21 February 1839, fol. 55v.

112 BL, Additional MS 34245A, Bridgeton Radical Association to Convention, 27 February 1839, fol. 69.

113 BL, Additional MS 34245A, John Tomlinson to Lovett, 1 April 1839, fols .84–5.

114 BL, Additional MS 34245A, Hugh Craig to Lovett, 5 March 1839, fol. 98.

115 E.g., BL, Additional MS 34245A, Matthew Scott to Convention, 16 March 1839, fol. 130; William Cardo to Lovett, 14 March 1839, fol. 128; John Richards to Lovett, 22 March 1839, fol. 128v; Judge, 'Early Chartist organization', p. 380.

116 BL, Additional MS 27835, 'Men of Birmingham', n.d. [late February 1839], fol. 100. On the generic properties of broadsides, see Martha Vicinus, *The Industrial Muse: A Study of Nineteenth Century British Working-Class Literature* (London: Croom Helm, 1974), chapter 1.

117 BL, Additional MS 34245A, Henry Hawks to Lovett, 2 April 1839, fol. 193.

118 Robert Sykes, 'Physical-force Chartism: the cotton district and the Chartist crisis of 1839', *International Review of Social History*, 30 (1985), 213.

119 *Western Vindicator*, 1 June 1839.

120 TNA, HO 44/52, secret service reports, 2 September 1839, fol. 212.

121 Chase, *Chartism*, p. 66; see also Sykes, 'Physical-force Chartism', 227.

122 Reddy, *Navigation*, p. 129.

123 *Ibid.*, p. 289.

124 Parssinen, 'Association', p. 527.

125 BL, Additional MS 34245B, R. J. Richardson to Convention, 21 July 1839, fol. 53. For similar confessions that reports of preparedness had been greatly exaggerated, see Sykes, 'Physical-force Chartism', 218 n.47.

126 Reddy, *Navigation*, p. 193.

127 Judge, 'Early Chartist organization', pp. 393–5.

128 Gammage, *History of the Chartist Movement*, p 110; Lovett, *Life and Struggles*, p. 185.

129 Lovett, *Life and Struggles*, p. 172.

130 *Ibid.*, p. 220; *Charter*, 14 July 1839.

131 *Charter*, 11 August 1839; *Trial of Lovett*, pp. 3, 11, 14.

132 Lovett Collection, Ms 753, vol. 2, William Sharman Crawford to Lovett, 22 September 1837, fol. 170.

133 Lovett, *Life and Struggles*, pp. 142–3.

134 *London Evening Standard*, 10 April 1848.

135 Rob Boddice, *The Science of Sympathy: Morality, Evolution, and Victorian Civilization* (Urbana, Chicago, and Springfield: University of Illinois Press, 2016), pp. 8–10; Thomas Haskell, 'Capitalism and the origins of humanitarian sensibility, part 1', *American Historical Review*, 90 (1985), 339–61.

136 Richard Cobden to William Tait, 2 April 1839, reprinted in Anthony Howe (ed.), *The Letters of Richard Cobden: Volume I – 1815–1847* (Oxford: Oxford University Press, 2007), p. 163.

137 Robert Saunders, 'Chartism from above: British elites and the interpretation of Chartism', *Historical Research*, 81 (2008), 463–84.

138 On the problematic nature of sympathy as a basis for popular politics, see Matthew Roberts, 'Tory-radical feeling in Charlotte Brontë's *Shirley*, and early Victorian England', *Victorian Studies*, 63 (2020).

139 See, for example, the remarks of the black Chartist William Cuffay on the causes of the Newport rising: *Charter*, 1 December 1839. See also David J.V. Jones, *The Last Rising: The Newport Insurrection of 1839* (Oxford: Oxford University Press, 1985), p. 84.

140 TNA, HO 44/52, secret service reports, 28 August 1839, fol. 186.

141 BL, Francis Place Collection, set 55, William Lovett to Mary Lovett, 17 Oct. 1839, fol. 92; *ibid.*, Petition of William Lovett and John Collins, fols 5–6. For Lovett's harrowing experience of prison, see Scriven, *Popular Virtue*, pp. 75–7, and chapter 3 more generally for Lovett's ascetic political strategy in the 1840s. See also Katrina Navickas, 'The "bastilles" of the constitution: political prisoners, radicalism, and prison reform in early nineteenth-century England', *LHR*, 83 (2018), 97–123.

142 Lovett, *Life and Struggles*, p. 209; BL, Additional MS 37774, Minutes of the National Association, 12 October 1841, fol. 1. For the National Association, and Lovett's later career, see Stack, 'William Lovett'.

143 *NS*, 3 April 1841.

144 BL, Place Newspaper Collection, Set 55, Richard Moore to Francis Place, 11 December 1841.

145 Wiener, *Lovett*, pp. 84, 103. For the feminist ideas and gender politics of the National Association, see Kathryn Gleadle, *The Early Feminists: Radical Unitarians and the Emergence of the Women's Rights Movement, 1831–51* (Basingstoke: Macmillan, 1995), pp. 75–82.

146 Iorwerth Prothero, 'The London Working Men's Association and the "People's Charter"', *Past and Present*, 38 (1967), 171.

147 William Lovett Collection, Ms 753, vol. 1, Report of the Proceedings of the Birmingham Complete Suffrage Union, April 1842, fol. 266. In Lovett's defence, he only objected to the peremptory way in which the Sturgites rejected the Charter; he made it clear that he was willing to withdraw his opposition provided that the conference consider both the Charter and the plan drawn up by the Sturgites side by side. *British Statesman*, 7 January 1843; *NS*, 31 December 1842.

148 Sara Ahmed, *The Cultural Politics of Emotion* (2nd edn, Edinburgh: Edinburgh University Press, 2014), p. 18.

149 James Epstein, *The Lion of Freedom: Feargus O'Connor and the Chartist Movement, 1832–1842* (London: Croom Helm, 1982), p. 109. My reading of Lovett's emotional investment in the People's Charter has been influenced by Kathryn Temple, '"Mixed emotions": love, resentment and the Declaration of Independence', *EHCS*, 2 (2018), 34–51. Interestingly, the People's Charter itself is a model of ascetic radicalism – restrained, mechanical and though not devoid of feeling (in the introduction Lovett wrote, for example) it contrasts markedly with the intense feelings of resentment which characterised the petitions that Chartists submitted to parliament.

150 Scriven, *Popular Virtue*, p. 177.

7

Daniel O'Connell, Feargus O'Connor and the politics of 'anger'

In August 1841, a Chartist who signed himself only as 'H.G.' from Ashton-under-Lyne wrote to the Irish Chartist Peter Brophy, then living in Dublin. After briefly congratulating Brophy and the Irish Chartists for the progress their movement was making in Ireland, 'H.G.' then launched into a tirade against Daniel O'Connell, the leader of Catholic Ireland: 'a damnable traitor has [sic.] that old diabolical Dan is'. Warming to his theme, O'Connell was a 'villain', a more despicable 'anamal [sic.] of any that either walks or crawls on the face of the earth'. Reaching his crescendo, 'I think for mine own just that he is worse than the very Devil himself'.[1] Chartist invective of this kind directed towards O'Connell was not unusual; and O'Connell for his part returned with equal vehemence. But if O'Connell was, as Chartists often suggested, a figure to be contemptuously dismissed, why did they devote so much time and energy to hating him? Part of the reason for this is that O'Connell's campaign to repeal the Act of Union of 1800 and Chartism were rival movements and more alike than either cared to admit. As a result, Chartists and Repealers took every opportunity to put as much distance as possible between themselves.[2]

More importantly, there is the question of why Chartists were *so* hostile to O'Connell, a question that has never been fully explored by historians who have been content to ascribe this enmity to a disagreement over goals, strategies and tactics, or to the personal feud between the two Irish 'Os', O'Connell and the Chartist leader, Feargus O'Connor. Once allies in the House of Commons as Irish radical MPs, O'Connor had parted company with O'Connell over the latter's refusal to press for an all-out parliamentary assault for the repeal of the Act of Union, with O'Connell preferring to bide his time and try and secure concessions from the Whigs. But this is only part of the story; whatever the reasons for the anger, the anger was important in and of itself. After all, O'Connell was far from being the only politician who was openly critical of the Chartists, and he was not alone in being accused of apostasy as we saw with Joseph Rayner Stephens.

Further, what appears to be anger on the surface is soon revealed to be a whole cluster of feelings that Chartists associated with O'Connell: loathing, hatred, disgust, shame, and perhaps above all, indignation – each of which meant different things, had different degrees of intensity and were expressed variously. As Thomas Dixon has recently argued, the feeling of anger is especially slippery for historians of emotion, not just because of the usual problems associated with trans-historical categories, but also because anger is part of a 'family of fury' – from rage to indignation, each of which are affectively distinct as well as culturally specific. These problems are compounded by a presentism which assumes a similarity between present-day notions of anger and what is identified by historians as anger in the past.[3] This is especially problematic for the purposes of the present chapter which adopts a functionalist approach towards the feeling of anger. In other words, how can we explore what purpose Chartist anger towards O'Connell served if, in fact, anger may not be the right word to describe this cluster of feelings? Part of the solution to this, as we have seen many times throughout the course of this study, is to pay careful attention to the affective language used by those in the past to mitigate some of this presentism, though a degree of the latter will remain, indeed has to remain if we are to 'recognise cultural formations that have resemblances to each other' and avoid 'drowning in relativism'. To avoid both the pitfalls of resorting to a trans-historical conception of anger on the one hand, and drowning in relativism on the other, we can usefully employ Dixon's portmanteau 'family of fury' and recognise that:

> [E]motional states are composites made up in intricate ways from words, categories, narratives, metaphors, images, moral beliefs, religious attitudes, visual representations, bodily responses, behaviours, public performances, subjective experiences, feelings and testimonies.[4]

This chapter explores what purpose this cluster of negative feelings served for Chartists, and why it was expressed in the way that it was, and, in doing so, illustrates just how interconnected were English and Irish politics during this period. Further, it uses the case study of the fraught relationship between the Chartists (and O'Connor in particular) and O'Connell to explore some of the tensions between the sentimental and the ascetic within popular radicalism. Both were quick to arrogate to themselves the affective high-ground of restraint and rationality, but these claims were often belied by the impassioned way in which they were expressed in the cut and thrust of political conflict. Paying close attention to the concatenation of feelings that O'Connell aroused in Chartists can tell us much about the role played by feeling in popular movements around issues such as mobilisation, building identity and resisting enemies. At the same time, the expression of these feelings was carefully controlled. By the time that O'Connell had become the most hated figure in British popular politics, the Chartists were careful to distance themselves from their portrait of O'Connell's affective politics, which they went out of their way to ridicule as weak, irrational and out of control. The British political elite and their supporters were only too ready to tar both men and their movements with the brush of irrationality, finding little to separate them. Worse still, it was alleged by these that 'the letting loose of the fierce passions of the uninstructed and indigent population' on either side of the Irish Sea dangerously fed on one another.[5] In the process we will see how, once again, claims of reason and rationality were no less undergirded by feeling than were passions.

The chapter begins by showing how the reasons for Chartist enmity towards O'Connell, and the ways in which that enmity was expressed, were much more complex than previous accounts have suggested. The second section focuses on the series of open letters that O'Connor addressed to O'Connell, first published in 1836, and subsequently serialised in the *Northern Star* in 1838–39, as these constitute the most comprehensive Chartist indictment of O'Connell's public career.[6] O'Connor's *Letters* are interpreted as a form of Gothic epistolary, similar to that employed in relation to Oastler in chapter 4, in which O'Connell stands condemned for his sentimental excesses. New light is cast on the leadership styles and affective politics of O'Connor and O'Connell, which are shown to be strikingly similar, especially in terms of the Romantic and sentimental aesthetic on which both men drew. Perhaps surprisingly, as the final section shows, Chartist enmity towards O'Connell seldom manifested itself in the form of either anti-Catholicism or anti-Irish feeling, two baser forms of Gothic 'othering' which one might assume – given the overwhelmingly Protestant and British basis of Chartism – to have been present. For a variety of reasons – ideological, strategic and affective – Chartists chose not to evoke these negative feelings.

Potent enchanter of the passions

By the late 1820s, Daniel O'Connell had established himself as one of the foremost leaders of British popular politics. At a meeting at the Rotunda in November 1830, Henry Hunt singled out O'Connell as the only MP 'who would do justice to the people'.[7] With the success of Catholic Emancipation to his name (secured in 1829), against all the odds, O'Connell had used the leverage of the extra-parliamentary Catholic Association movement to force the English parliament to end the civil disabilities that branded Catholics second-class citizens. Here was a practical and successful demonstration to English radicals of how popular movements could sway parliament. True,

O'Connell had seriously damaged his reputation among radicals when he consented to the disenfranchisement of the forty-shilling freeholders as the price for emancipation, with Cobbett leading the charge against him. By the late-1830s O'Connell had compounded his betrayals of the radical cause: his alliance with the hated Whigs government; his *volte face* over factory reform (allegedly the result of a £1,000 bribe from the factory masters); support for the New Poor Law; and hostility to trades unionism. These betrayals were partly and briefly forgiven (though not forgotten) because of the part he played in the birth of Chartism by attending some of the inaugural meetings of the LWMA. But no sooner had O'Connell allied himself with the LWMA, he publicly renounced his support of Chartism, citing the physical force ravings of O'Connor, Oastler and Stephens. He would spend the next five years denigrating physical force Chartism for its appeal to the base passions of the mob, rarely conceding that not all Chartists could be tarred with the same brush.[8]

O'Connell's failure to discriminate incensed moral-force Chartists like Lovett, James Moir, and William Pattison in Scotland. During a public debate on O'Connell's political career at the Glasgow Lyceum in June 1840, Pattison challenged the veracity of O'Connell's claim that it was fear of physical force which had led him to desert them. This feigned fear was nothing more than a cover to justify his alliance with the Whigs. If O'Connell had spoken out against physical force at the outset, Pattison continued, it would have been diffused, and in failing to do so, he had played 'a dishonest and cowardly part'.[9] In addition to the damage done by the physical force ravings of O'Connor and company, Lovett held O'Connell equally responsible for driving away middle-class support with his scaremongering 'till at last the best feelings of some of the best men in our ranks were carried to a point beyond which reason cannot extenuate'. Lovett drew a causative link between O'Connell's attacks and the rising power of O'Connor: O'Connell's frightening off the middle classes, who now 'regard us with horror' had left Chartism in the hands of the extremists. This was why Lovett attributed most of the blame for O'Connor's assault on Lovett's ascetic radicalism in 1840–41 (the 'new move' episode discussed in the previous chapter) to O'Connell's perfidy.[10]

Precisely because O'Connell was such an important and influential politician, it was imperative that Chartists responded to his many attacks. These counter-attacks were articulated through highly sentimental language: O'Connell's actions were repudiated as betrayal, apostasy and seen as shameful and satanic.[11] At a broad cultural level, this could be seen as one of the many manifestations of melodrama, a central popular aesthetics as discussed in earlier chapters.[12] The aesthetic framing of the Chartist imagination, it could be said, dealt in such Manichean opposites as good and evil, heroes and villains. The problem with this model, if taken to its extreme, is that it comes dangerously close to denying agency to individual actors: in this reading, Chartists were simply caught up in the narrative of heroes and villains, hapless victims of a trope used by cunning leaders, such as O'Connell and O'Connor, to instil loyalty and conformity. Perhaps, but such a view takes us back to the erroneous assumption that Chartist hatred of O'Connell was little more than O'Connor's feud writ-large, a view which has persisted in the historiography.[13] It also implies that Chartist anger towards O'Connell was less than genuine, which would be a clear mis-reading of the evidence. The fact is that the reasons for that anger were much more prosaic, though no less compelling. O'Connell's own career as a hugely successful platform orator, with his ardent, melodramatic lan-guage and theatrical style, demonstrated the mobilising potential but also the pitfalls of appealing to the passions. With quips like 'the landlords' venison was moistened with the widow's tear, and their claret was dyed with the orphan's blood', O'Connell could be as Romantic as any senti-mental radical.[14] The Irishman Richard Lalor Sheil, who had campaigned alongside him, tellingly referred to O'Connell as a 'potent enchanter of the passions'.[15] Chartists themselves were fully alive to this aspect of his character. His 'public existence', the Dumfries and Maxwelltown Working Men's Association observed, 'originated with, and has been kept up by, appeals to the passions of men'.[16] Lovett voiced similar objections to those 'who, like Mr O'Connell, have appealed to the passions rather than to the intellect of men'.[17]

Juxtaposing their own restrained affective politics with O'Connell's pas-sionate abandon was one of the ways in which Chartists sought to deflect the charge of fomenting 'dangerous democratic passions', in the words of the Tory *Yorkshire Gazette*.[18] It is striking that in many official com-munications – between local magistrates and the Home Office, the indict-ments of Chartists and O'Connell himself for sedition in 1843 – as well as in the hostile press, Chartists and Repealers were accused of 'furious and truculent appeals ... to the passions of the ignorant and deluded fol-lowers'.[19] Magistrates and wealthy citizens spoke of the terror, fear and intimidation that they felt in their districts when confronted by thousands of Chartists. Not for nothing did one official broadside warn Chartists of 'illegal excitement'.[20] The Attorney General was at pains to emphasise in the trials which followed the 'Plug Plot' riots of 1842 – the mass wave of strikes in the summer of that year in which Chartists were heavily involved at a local level – that it was not necessary for physical violence to have taken place, just the threat of it, for the law-abiding citizens of the commu-nities to feel intimidated.[21] O'Connell, similarly, was accused against the background of the monster repeal meetings held in 1843, of winding up the expectations of the Irish peasantry: 'their feelings have been wrought upon, and their passions lashed into fury'.[22] When O'Connell was brought to trial at the end of the year, it was for inciting a 'wild and reckless passion for some active warfare against the Queen'.[23] Just as we need to be on our guard when radicals arrogate reason to themselves and irrationality to their rivals and opponents, so too must we be sceptical about the use of that dichotomy by the authorities. The affective underpinning of reason – in this case fear – confounds that dichotomy, but it was a conceited juxtaposition that was fundamental to the authority of the state and its policing of dissent.

Taken to its extreme, one could argue that attempts to assert such control constituted a denial of working-class right to feeling. As Stearns and Stearns have argued, 'The attempt to control anger is, after all, unquestionably a form of social control'.[24] From this perspective, we can see working-class movements like Chartism as representing a reassertion of that right to feeling, and to express feelings in the public sphere. The Chartists were aware of this denial as evidenced by the repeated assertion that working-class people were not unfeeling brutes. In a letter to the editors published in the ultra-Chartist *London Democrat*, 'Philopatris' asserted that 'Dame Nature has bestowed the same kind indulgences upon the whole human race … all pretty well have the same taste for pleasure and recreations; all pretty well have the same sensitive feeling and inward repulsiveness at an infliction of injustice'.[25] A correspondent in the *Northern Star* complained of how the leaders of the Newport rising were 'designated in the public prints as unfeeling brutal monsters, but see the stifled emotion of the soul; and anon, the big tear trickle down the cheek'.[26] 'A Sonnet' by 'Iota' reflecting on the first anniversary of the Newport rising, published in the Chartist *Advocate and Merthyr Free Press*, framed the clash between the Chartists and the authorities on that fateful day which had left some twenty Chartists dead, as an affective dialogue of the deaf. The Chartists had marched on Newport, not with 'murderous intent to slay', but to display and make known their feelings: 'so that a frown,/Of their dread countenances when roused to ire … might have accomplished all,/Their honest ends'. The brutal treatment they met from the military – an act publicly condoned by O'Connell who boasted that some of the soldiers had been Irishmen – and the wider response of the authorities in the aftermath signalled that the working class person was nothing more than a machine: 'an Android … A machine in the human form, which, by certain springs performs some of the natural motions of a living man'.[27] Other Chartists turned the tables and claimed that it was, in fact, their enemies who were unfeeling – 'iron-hearted despotic rulers'.[28]

Yet all this presented what, should be, by this stage of the book, a familiar challenge: workers had a right to express themselves,[29] but *how* was this to be done in such a way that did not give hostages to fortune? We saw in the previous chapter how Lovett sought to walk this tightrope via his ascetic radicalism, and although this was a dilemma that proved especially burdensome for moral-force Chartists, it was also registered by the wider movement. We also saw in the last chapter that this need for restraint gained added urgency in the period following the debacle of the collapse of the first Chartist Convention in the autumn of 1839, which led to a greater accent on ascetic radicalism. Many Chartists had grown increasingly uneasy about the affective politics of the nascent movement, including the 'over-reliance on spectacle [which] diminished (or even destroyed) Chartism's claim to be a rational movement'.[30] The renegade Church of Scotland minister Patrick Brewster, leader of the Scottish moral-force Chartists, accused the advocates of physical force of appealing to the 'lowest and worst feelings' of the working classes. Perhaps not coincidentally, Brewster was an ally of O'Connell.[31]

At this point it is worth repeating that feelings are not just bodily reflexes but are also part of the mind and have their own rationality. As Thomas Dixon puts it, emotions are 'embodied judgements about the world rather than mere physiological feelings. Disgust, fear and envy are forms of belief, construing their objects as dirty, dangerous or desirable, respectively.'[32] Further, feelings result from utilitarian judgements about whether something is likely to be good or harmful, pleasurable or painful, and the way those feelings are elicited, felt and expressed is culturally constructed and historically contingent.[33] From the Chartist perspective, anger towards O'Connell was in some respects beneficial and was an instrumental device for securing specific ends. In other words, it was not an atavistic outburst, but a chosen, calculated response – and one potentially and perfectly consistent with the dictates of ascetic radicalism (expressing the right feelings in the right place). It is telling that the affective relationship between the Chartists and O'Connell revolved, at least in part, around honour. As Ute Frevert has observed: 'Insulting an individual or a group is synonymous with shaming them. It means taking away their honour and dignity, injuring or damaging their integrity. ... Humiliation, as psychologists and social scientists argue, holds strong emotional power.'[34] This can help to explain why Chartists resorted to a series of public acts for the purposes of shaming and humiliating O'Connell, such as burning his portraits.[35]

By venting their anger at O'Connell, the Chartists were attempting to repel the threat that he posed. Anger, it has been argued, is a defence mechanism that helps to define and defend the self from attack.[36] In part this may be true, but anger is much more than this, and such a trans-historical view implies that anger is biological. As we have already seen in the discussion of Dixon's research, anger is, in fact, a portmanteau term for several feelings, while its political and rhetorical usefulness and appropriateness is a function of its situatedness and contextual mutability. For Chartists, this was about more than just keeping an odious individual at arm's-length; it was also about defending the integrity of 'whole-hog' Chartism from the 'instalment' men as O'Connor derisively termed those radicals who were willing to accept less than the full demands contained in the People's Charter, such as household suffrage instead of universal manhood suffrage. 'It is the instalment principle, so much vaunted by the vilest political hypocrite that ever existed – Daniel O'Connell.'[37] This also helps to explain why in expressing their anger towards O'Connell, feelings of disgust and revulsion were often to the fore: 'The villainy, the hypocrisy of O'Connell, in trying to destroy O'Connor's character, because he (O'Connor) has of late used physical-force expressions, is disgusting', fumed the Chartist newspaper the *True Scotsman*.[38] This was to construe O'Connell as repellent and the use of disgust is used to exaggerate the distance between O'Connell and the democratic desideratum of Chartism. Cobbett had adopted an identical position – and language – in 1825 and again in 1829 when attacking O'Connell's willingness to sacrifice the forty-shilling freeholders. Vilifying O'Connell served to keep one pure, to define one's self against a compromiser.[39]

The depth and intensity of Chartist anger was also a reflection of the fact that O'Connell symbolised the wider betrayal of the middle class, which was such an important affective element in Chartism. This began with Catholic Emancipation. As the Manchester Chartist Edward Nightingale put it, 'By that Bill the rich were corrupted, and the poor betrayed'.[40] The catalogue of betrayals since the Reform Act revealed only too clearly that O'Connell was beholden to the Whigs and their middle-class Liberal supporters – an alliance that the 'schoolmaster' of Chartism, Bronterre O'Brien, dubbed the 'Whig-O'Connell-Monied-Class-Conspiracy'.[41] What O'Connell failed to grasp was just how hated the Whigs were by the British working class by the late 1830s; on the other hand, one may counter that British radicals failed to appreciate just how hated the Tories were in Ireland. Just as O'Connell believed that concessions could be wrung from the Whigs, so some Chartists looked, on occasion, to the Tories as allies, most notably Richard Oastler who hated O'Connell more than the Chartists did (a feeling that was entirely mutual): 'I have just learned that Daniel O'Connell is in a tremendous rage at me', Oastler gleefully informed the readers of the *Northern Star* in March 1840.[42] Oastler alleged that it was the malice O'Connell bore towards O'Connor that accounted for the vindictiveness of the Whigs towards the Chartists, a charge that was part of Oastler's wider conspiracy theory (popular with Tories) that, because they were beholden to O'Connell for his support, the Whig government was in reality 'the O'Connell government'.[43] O'Connell for his part was branding Chartists 'Tory Chartists' by the time of the 1841 general election for their refusal to support Whig candidates, a treachery that O'Connell was determined to punish by instructing Repealers to expel from their organisations those with Chartist sympathies.[44] Thus, the friction between Chartists and O'Connell was to some extent the result of mutual affective deafness and the result was a failure of the fundamental maxim that my enemy's enemy is my friend. The net result was that the affective bounds of ascetic radicalism were occasionally breeched as both sides entered passionate recriminations.

Once Chartism had formally established itself as a movement, O'Connell soon added to his catalogue of betrayals. He came out in support of the resignations of the Birmingham Political Union delegates from the first Chartist Convention, who were overwhelmingly middle class: indeed, their resignations were construed as playing into the hands of O'Connell and the Whigs. A further act of betrayal came when O'Connell swung his support behind the Anti-Corn Law League.[45] Even more offensive to the Chartists was the hard line he took during the Chartist trials of February–March 1840 when he tactlessly declared that he was 'perfectly satisfied the sentences passed upon the Chartists were not too heavy for their offences'. Although he had regained a modicum of respect for the part he played in petitioning the government for the commutation of the death sentences passed on the Newport rebels, this was more than wiped out when he absented himself from a crucial division in the House of Commons on the National Petition for the release of Chartist prisoners.[46]

The feelings of betrayal, hatred and disgust were so strong among Chartists because English radical expectations of O'Connell had been high (possibly too high) – he had achieved the impossible in 1829; thus when the betrayal came it was so much harder to bear. Several studies of popular radicalism, from E.P. Thompson to more recent accounts, have emphasised the somewhat exaggerated importance that was attached to leadership in Chartism.[47] We can see something of this in O'Connell's (and the LWMA's) attacks on O'Connor, Oastler and Stephens. One response, of course, was to reject virtually any kind of leadership – as the LWMA claimed to, the latter conceiving adulation of leaders as the supreme act of irrationality.[48] Yet the LWMA was the exception that proves the rule. The affective investment in radical leaders was no less intense; we know this from personal testimony, such as working-class autobiographies, and from the outpourings of adulation that greeted figures like O'Connor and O'Connell. For example, the Carlisle Chartist William Farish, a handloom weaver, recalled of O'Connor that 'he never ceased to entertain a sort of lingering love for the burly Hibernian', in part because of the 'heart he threw into his work'.[49] A culture that prized leadership so highly was always going to judge fallen heroes harshly: the bigger the reputation, the bigger the fall: *corruptio optimi pessima*. As modern psychologists have clearly shown, the betrayal of 'what's right' by leaders can have a profound psychological impact on followers, especially in the context of defeat.[50] By entering into an alliance with the Whigs, and through his subsequent betrayals, O'Connell was perceived to have stabbed the workers in the back. Had he remained loyal to the Chartists, it was alleged, the movement would have been successful. This betrayal symbolised the growing ideological divisions between liberalism and radicalism. As the Manchester Chartist Edward Nightingale put it in an open letter to O'Connell: 'In short, you are an *Irish Patriot* and an English *Liberal*; two distinct characters, but of equal infamy.'[51]

If we shift perspective from the Chartists to O'Connell, feelings were no less central in the latter's equally careful constructed affective politics. There is no doubt that he exaggerated the danger posed by the Chartists to cover his own retreat from radicalism as a way of building bridges with his new allies, the Whigs. It was also a way of silencing those English conservative Catholic leaders like the Earl of Shrewsbury who accused O'Connell of trying to introduce Irish 'political excitement' into England which, in their view, endangered the recent gains of Catholic Emancipation.[52] O'Connell knew only too well that while sentimentalism worked well in Irish popular politics; a certain degree of asceticism would be required in England. As Chartists frequently retorted, O'Connell had often spoken the language of physical force, despite his many protestations that his own organisations counselled 'calm' and 'dispassionate' advocacy. He attempted to square the sentimental-ascetic circle by presenting himself (not very convincingly as far as the Chartists and his English enemies were concerned) as exercising a major restraining influence on Irish popular protest. As he boasted in 1841, 'popular excitement is of so exasperated a character that they will rush into insurrection unless my influence checks and controls them'.[53] By the mid-1840s, O'Connell's claim to have restrained popular passions was, in the eyes of the British state, utterly belied by his relaunch of the repeal agitation. When O'Connell was eventually arrested in 1844, he was indicted for 'exciting a spirit of ill-will against the Government' and of 'exciting animosity, jealousy, and ill-will between different classes of Her Majesty's subjects, and more especially exciting those feelings in Ireland against Her Majesty's subjects in England'.[54] Once again, feelings were on trial, and in a way that underlined how the state saw the Repeal agitation and Chartism in identical affective terms: both stood condemned for exciting popular passion. The irony was that when, in the early 1840s, O'Connell switched his attention back to the extra-parliamentary arena in Ireland, he was worried about the growing popularity of Chartism in Ireland. Although it never came close to rivalling his Repeal movement, Chartism was a larger movement than most historians have been willing to concede, hence O'Connell's bitter invective against the Chartists.[55] The Ulster radical landowner William Sharman Crawford, a Chartist sympathiser, fell foul of O'Connell's jealousy: 'how odd that a man of his superior rank in intellectual argument should appear to feel any jealousy of me who has no pretence or desire to enter into any competition with him for public favour', Sharman Crawford confided to his son.[56] Sharman Crawford, like Lovett subsequently, knew his man: O'Connell would brook no ultra-radical rival in his fiefdom who challenged his alliance with the Whigs, and like O'Connor, Sharman Crawford found Irish politics closed off to him. In contrast to the relatively retiring character of Sharman Crawford, O'Connor went for all-out assault against O'Connell as the next section shows.

Political Frankensteins alarmed

O'Connell's professed sympathies for the principles of Chartism made him a more difficult opponent to deal with than someone who was openly opposed to them as it implied his opposition was merely the product of strategic and tactical differences. If only the Chartists had realised the errors of their ways, all would have been well in his view. This meant that it was necessary for Chartists to try and diminish O'Connell's stature, hence the repeated cataloguing of his failures, and none relished this more than Feargus O'Connor, who furnished the most comprehensive catalogue of his former chief's failures in his *Series of Letters*. Reminiscent in some ways of a literary tradition of exposé, the letters are Gothic in their determination to unmask, to reveal that O'Connell was not all that he seemed. For O'Connor no less than for Shelley, evil invariably cloaked itself in deception, dissimulation and cant, a reminder that O'Connor was also a member of 'the gallery of nineteenth-century romantic populists', who moved with ease in the currents of late Romanticism, deploying its tropes and idioms to considerable effect.[57] This was one of the first of many times in which O'Connell would be cast in the melodramatic role of villain, though the problem was that in combating O'Connell's affective excesses by such sentimental means risked cancelling out the challenge. In his letters O'Connor presented himself as the one who first realised O'Connell for what he was, describing himself as the 'Marplot'. He soon realised that O'Connell's sole objective had been to acquire power for his own aggrandisement, a realisation that owed a great deal to Cobbett's earlier tirades, and to Oastler's cultural stylistics.[58]

O'Connor's letters read as a cautionary tale of what happens when politicians turn their backs on the people. In one of the letters he asked O'Connell to remember the fate of Dr Frankenstein. In raising up the people, O'Connell had created an uncontrollable monster who would, sooner or later, demand vengeance: 'I reminded you of Frankenstein; your conduct upon that question [repeal] it was; which first determined me to unmask you.'[59] O'Connor was not alone in deploying the Gothic motif, including references to *Frankenstein*, as a device for ridiculing O'Connell, as a cartoon by the political satirist John Doyle attests (Figure 7.1). The image seems to trade on the politics of fear: O'Connell nervously shouts 'hur-hur! rah for Repeal' and the Jacobin monster, symbolising the Irish people, retorts 'I have been your slave long enough, and now you shall be mine'.

Whether consciously or not, in referring to Frankenstein, O'Connor was inverting the use of this metaphor as O'Connell had himself been likened to Frankenstein's monster, created by English politicians who were now helpless before his power. An earlier cartoon by Doyle had depicted O'Connell in exactly these terms, entitled 'Political Frankensteins alarmed at the progress of a giant of their own creation'.[60] O'Connor also cast O'Connell as Dr Frankenstein for the part he had played in drawing up the People's Charter. Finding his own power threatened, O'Connell 'now dread[ed] the monster of [his] own creation'.[61] As these examples testify, by the 1830s and 1840s the Frankenstein metaphor for the unwitting creation of a dangerous monster had firmly lodged itself in the cultural vocabulary of the day. And in politics it became a metonym for fear, especially of the awesome power of the masses, hardly surprising given the conflation of the monster with godless Jacobin terror in some minds (note the cap of liberty aloft the pole held by the monster in Figure 7.1).[62] On another occasion, O'Connor implied that O'Connell was a monstrous creation composed of three parts: a native Irishman, but to this had been 'superadded the keen, glancing, penetration of a lawyer, and the wily, oily, smoothness ... of a cold-blooded, calculating, and dissembling politician'. The result was a 'political limb of Satan'. O'Connell was so afraid to reveal his true character that he kept it hidden in the 'stolen garb of truth, and covered by the mask of liberty'. 'The robe of truth, however, fits ill the recreant limbs of an imposter', O'Connor continued, and 'the keen-eyed observations of the English people soon discovered divers rents through which the vile carcass was made manifest'.[63] O'Connell was also likened to a 'hideous monster' who 'feasts, without remorse, upon their [the Irish people's] vitals'.[64] Elsewhere – in the poetry columns of the *Northern Star* – he was described as 'a hoary political vampire' that sucks 'the blood of thy own native land'.[65]

O'Connor and the Chartists juxtaposed their own carefully controlled affective politics against O'Connell's Gothic excesses – attempting to avoid the cancelling out referred to above. And here the LWMA was able to draw on its ascetic radicalism contrasting their restraint with O'Connell's appeal 'to the passions rather than to the intellect of men'.[66] The Irish Universal Suffrage Association – the body which led Irish Chartism – also 'stressed the importance of appealing to the reason of the people' and criticised 'O'Connell who appealed to their 'passions and prejudices'.[67] Once again, the Chartists

Figure 7.1 A New Illustration of the Story of Frankenstein, by 'H.B.' [John Doyle] (1843).

construed their anger as indignation; O'Connell's as rage. As Stauffer has usefully observed, 'to claim indignation is to appropriate a three-fold bonus for one's anger: it is justified (because it has been caused by evident wrong-doing), it is righteous (because it is felt on behalf of others), and it is digni-fied (because it has resulted from an affront to dignity worth defending'.[68] Thus armed, the Chartists were able to mount a challenge to O'Connell's popularity with the Irish masses. In language that would have done little to endear O'Connor to the Irish masses, he accused O'Connell of deliber-ately keeping the 'Irish people in a state of miserable destitution, in order that their minds may be held in a state of still more servile prostitution'.[69] The Irish masses, O'Connor implied, were creatures of their base passions and prone to excitement. Slaves to privation, they were blinded to their true interests, the continuance of which furnished the basis of O'Connell's power, a conclusion reached by other Chartists, too.[70] This situation was aggravated by the absence of a genuinely free press in Ireland. The result was that the Irish masses were thus incapable of rationally seeing O'Connell for what he was: 'the intellect is paralyzed by the body's suffering'.[71] Here was a con-venient explanation for the weakness of Chartism in Ireland.[72]

It could be argued that Chartist anger and hatred towards O'Connell functioned as a useful safety vent for the pent-up anger, frustration and resentment that was such an integral part of the Chartist experience. But such an interpretation would be to confuse cause and effect since it would be crass, and in any case difficult to prove, that Chartist leaders simply wheeled out O'Connell as a hate figure for the sole purpose of keeping order of the unruly troops. O'Connell in this reading becomes little more than catharsis, the visible and audible manifestation of which were the frequent groans that Chartist audiences uttered at the mention of his name.[73] Feelings seldom function in such straightforward ways: they are not like surging liquids striving to be set free (what has been termed the 'hydraulics' model of emotions). While feelings can be unstable and not easily shunted into safe and redundant cul-de-sacs, they can, to some extent, be switched on or off in the sense that feelings, including anger, can be summoned in the right place and time – as Chartist anger towards O'Connell suggests.[74]

What emerges in Chartist denunciation of O'Connell is a tension between, on the one hand, intense feelings of hatred, disgust and revulsion and, on the other, an effort to restrain these feelings and express them in ways that were perceived to be legitimate – the dilemma posed and resolved in part by ascetic radicalism. On the other hand, it is a measure, in part, of how acutely Chartists felt the charge of unrestrained passion that many trumpeted temperance, self-improvement and respectability. But feelings were key here as well: as we saw in the previous chapter, familial love, domestic bliss, kindness and pity, for example, were all part of this projection (a reminder that it was not only negative feelings that were part of the Chartist experience). So, too, was exercising restraint. Elite conventions of politics increasingly accented sober and ordered behaviour, especially with the decline of sentimentalism and the rise of the 'man of character', even if politicians did not always practise what they preached.[75] The world of popular politics, at least as perceived by the elite, lagged behind, affectively speaking, in the hands of demagogues like O'Connell and O'Connor.

The mode of expression and the spatial context was crucial for the legitimation of affective politics. It is revealing that most Chartist expressions of anger towards O'Connell occurred not as spontaneous outbursts of anger but in carefully staged and controlled contexts. Unfocused, vituperative invective was deemed inappropriate and self-defeating. To return to the opening vignette: the private exchange of letters between H.G. and Peter Brophy appears, at first glance, to be such an outburst. But on closer inspection, H.G.'s 'outburst' can be read as a carefully chosen device for deepening the bonds of friendship between two Chartists. To take another example, the Leicester Chartists expressed their contempt for O'Connell through a series of resolutions passed at a public meeting condemning his actions;

a widely used forum and procedure in elite circles, including parliament itself. Although O'Connor used his *Series of Letters* to unleash his invective against O'Connell, the use of public letters was a shrewd move on his part; again, publishing open letters was an accepted vehicle for public debate, including censure, while the epistolary format was closely identified with Romanticism. Part of the Chartist strategy was to retain the moral, rational high-ground by accusing O'Connell of false feeling to further his ends: J.P. Cobbett, speaking in the Chartist Convention of 1839, accused O'Connell of using 'crocodile tears' to get what he wanted (a charge repeated by Chartists on several occasions).[76] But this accusation of emotional fraudulence is not only grounded itself in a form of affective appeal – Chartists were denying O'Connell's feelings in this case – but such impassioned rhetorical performances could function as emotives, in Reddy's sense of the term: 'Emotives are influenced directly by and alter what they "refer" to ... Emotives are themselves instruments for directly changing, building, hiding, intensifying emotions.'[77] In other words, there can be no such thing as straightforward emotional fraudulence, especially where an audience is involved, and accusations of this – which were and are such an important part of political culture – are themselves forms of emotional work.

What is remarkable about O'Connor's *Series of Letters*, and indeed Chartist denunciations of him more generally, is that they are, on the whole, quite measured. One may conjecture that this was a deliberate tactic on O'Connor's part and, but for the occasional controlled outbursts, the letters read more like a barrister's prosecution brief. In a tantalising piece of 'pop-psychology', O'Connor alleged that O'Connell had amassed such a store of political information 'that your mind is the index of your words rather than of your feelings'. This is an interesting observation that confirms that feelings are not just bodily occurrences but also the product of the mind.[78] '[Y]our passions are only strong,' O'Connor continued, 'when accused personally for personalities, and then you defend yourself by being scurrilous in order to prove that you act under excitement. From these practices you have acquired so complete a command of countenance, that the novice would suppose your feelings wounded.'[79] In levelling these charges, O'Connor knew his man. O'Connell was well versed in the arts of rhetoric and oratory, having read widely as a young man the great works in these fields.[80] Doubtless he would have been familiar with the arguments of Seneca, Aristotle, Cicero and Horace, each of whom had praised the orator who pretends to be angry, whereas the 'genuinely angry person expressing his or her emotion will never do, ultimately because such expression amounts to self-absorbed verbal violence, rather than rhetorical manipulation of others'.[81]

But O'Connor wanted to ridicule O'Connell at every turn. On the one hand, he seems to imply that in following the precepts of classical oratory,

O'Connell was guilty of dissimulation. On the other hand, if O'Connell was genuinely enraged, he was guilty of transgressing the accepted conventions of public speaking. By accusing him of resorting to unrestrained passion – whether genuine or feigned – O'Connor turned the tables on O'Connell and thereby aligned him with the very forces he claimed to reject: the unrestrained passions of the mob. O'Connor forges such a link by referring to O'Connell's speeches as 'foam', with its connotations of vehement rage (in the sense of frothing at the mouth), and also by accusing him of having 'completely lost your temper'.[82] O'Connor then juxtaposes his own authentic feelings: 'How my indignation swells, when, in vain, I endeavour to arrange the catalogue of your treasons against Ireland.' The basis of O'Connell's oratorical power, O'Connor maintained, was his ability 'to feel the pulse of your audience' and to then suit the speech according to the affective wavelength of the audience: 'You have a happy knack of finding out the soft part of your audience, and then you laugh or cry as the case requires.'[83] Thus, although O'Connor presents his anger as just indignation ('manly indignation' as he put it on another occasion), he brands O'Connell's as irrational rage),[84] a distinction that is reinforced by his leading question 'you know you hate me – know I despise you'.[85] While hate is imputed to O'Connell, by using the word 'despise' to describe his own feelings, O'Connor carves out a detached and more measured affective position. O'Connor was to deploy this distinction on many subsequent occasions. Speaking to the Chartists of Barnsley in April 1839, he remarked that:

> This Daniel is a most extraordinary animal. When he is speaking of finance, he foams out of the mouth like a mad dog in the dog days. (Cheers and laughter.) – When he speaks of oppression, he sobs like the love-sick girl. When he speaks of religion, he affects sanctity, and turns up the whites of his eyes like a duck in thunder. (Roars of laughter). But when he jingles the coppers from the poor man's labour in his pocket, he grins like a Cheshire cat for cheese. (Renewed laughter.) ... This beast calls me violent, while the lava from his crater has long since singed every hair on his head. He is like a shaved pig. (Loud cheers, and roars of laughter.)[86]

To accuse O'Connell of conniving in the politics of unrestrained passion was to strike at the very chord of his political philosophy. As a number of his biographers have observed, he had read, as a young student in London, William Godwin's *Political Justice*, and it had made a deep and lasting impression on him.[87] He was particularly struck by Godwin's argument concerning the futility of violence and revolution, and, in conjunction with O'Connell's nerve-racking experience of having witnessed virtually first-hand the horrors of French revolutionary violence in the 1790s, this moulded him into a lifelong advocate of moral force and made him distrustful of unrestrained passion in politics. However, O'Connell's rhetoric, much like O'Connor's, could sail close to the boundaries of physical force: during his trial for sedition Joseph Rayner Stephens as part of his defence wanted to subpoena O'Connell 'for his numerous violent speeches'.[88]

Coming from O'Connor, who was perhaps only slightly less well versed in classical oratory and who certainly did not refrain from appealing to the passions, these charges appear disingenuous and hypocritical. In short, O'Connor was never going to be an effective critic of O'Connell's sentimental radicalism because of the many identical or similar traits in his own affective politics. The Chartist Thomas Wheeler described O'Connor's speaking style as one that varied 'from the deepest pathos to the loudest indignation'.[89] As O'Connor's enemies within Chartism multiplied, due to what was perceived as his dictatorial leadership, his affective politics were frequently highlighted as defective. The Bradford radical John Jackson remarked that 'O'Connor, to his own shame – were he susceptible of that emotion – has made it his chief aim to play upon the very worst passions of the human heart'.[90] Indeed, it has been argued that O'Connor learnt his 'mob-oratory' from none other than O'Connell, transplanting 'the techniques used with the Irish peasantry to the English industrial classes'.[91] Just how much O'Connor modelled himself on O'Connell – an accusation often levelled at him by his detractors – is something of a moot point, but it is highly probable that he was only too aware of the similarities between himself and O'Connell. In their seminal article on the gentleman-radical model of leadership, Belchem and Epstein did not include O'Connell, no doubt because he was such an unpopular figure with English audiences by the late 1830s.[92] And yet, if we widen our stubbornly Anglo-centric lens to include Ireland, it soon becomes evident that O'Connell was the gentleman radical *par excellence*, and in this respect was remarkably similar to O'Connor. Although both men were upper class they were outsiders as far as the English parliamentary classes were concerned; each claimed to have made many social and economic sacrifices by campaigning for civil liberties – even renouncing their elite social status and abandoning promising legal careers as barristers; they were both cast in the mould of the Romantic hero even to the detail of being incarcerated for their beliefs; both were consummate platform orators, equally passionate, noisy and loved by their many followers, though O'Connell was, perhaps, more eloquent; and they were equally dependent on financial contributions from the masses and while it seems beyond doubt that neither profited unduly from their respective movements they were both financially imprudent.[93]

While O'Connor and O'Connell brought a sense of fun, excitement, and theatricality to the radical platform,[94] compared with earlier gentlemen radicals, notably John Wilkes, they were more dangerous because of their seriousness and commitment. There was little about either O'Connor or O'Connell that would fit John Brewer's apt description of Wilkes: 'a court jester and a lord of misrule'.[95] The parallels between O'Connell and O'Connor do not end here. Both men were committed to sweeping parliamentary reform. In addition, there were strategic and tactical similarities between Chartism and repeal.[96] Although often interpreted as personifying the strategic rift in radicalism between physical force and moral force,[97] both men, in fact, confound this dichotomy in strikingly similar ways. While they repeatedly spoke out against physical force (they were equally vociferous in the denunciation of underground, violent protest), both resorted to threatening rhetoric. Hence, O'Connell found himself tarred with the brush of Jacobinism, just as O'Connor frequently did.[98]

O'Connor, possibly aware of the similarities between himself and O'Connell, was quick to retort that he had sunk his own personal fortunes in Chartism and, unlike O'Connell, he had suffered as a consequence. Having complained about the poor deal that the Irish masses were getting for their pence (a veiled reference to the 'rent', the pennies of the poor which were collected to finance O'Connell's career), O'Connor declared to his friend the radical stockbroker Thomas Allsop: 'The greatest indeed only consolation that I have in the midst of trials and persecutions is that I purchased only suffering for myself and at my own expense.'[99] Thus, in the end the qualification for O'Connor's virtue was suffering, the inference being that O'Connell had not; on the contrary, he was living a comfortable life of significance at the expense of his people. Unlike O'Connor, O'Connell had not been imprisoned for his beliefs (O'Connor was imprisoned in York Castle for eighteen months in 1840–41), though that was about to change as a result of the monster repeal meetings held in 1843 which led to his indictment for conspiracy. His stay would be even shorter than O'Connor's as he was released after only three months in conditions much more comfortable than they had been for O'Connor, much less Carlile or Lovett.[100] Thus, in staking his own claim to the leadership of the English radicals, O'Connor may have been concerned to put as much distance as possible between himself and O'Connell. The juxtaposition of two different affective politics was one of the means by which he accomplished this act of distancing. The fact that O'Connor felt the need to do this on numerous subsequent occasions, even when Chartism was at its height, is evidence that he continued to view O'Connell as a potential threat to his own leadership.[101] This was surely one of the reasons why O'Connor was often willing to devote so many column inches to ridiculing O'Connell in his newspaper the *Northern Star*. Festering wounded pride for the way O'Connell had ruined O'Connor's career as an Irish radical MP may also have played its part.

Gaelic Gothic?

Remarkably, Chartist anger towards O'Connell seldom manifested itself as either anti-Catholic prejudice or anti-Irishness, remarkable in that anti-Catholicism and anti-Irishness were such marked features of mid-nineteenth-century British society.[102] The absence of this is, again, further evidence of how restrained and controlled the Chartists were in their affective politics. What makes this absence doubly interesting is that there was a well-developed belief among Protestants that, while their own faith implied self-restraint, Catholicism – and above all, Irish Catholicism – was associated with passionate and violent extremes.[103] Although it is possible to read a Gothicised subtext to Chartist depictions of the Irish masses as irrational – recall O'Connor's claim that this underpinned O'Connell's power – this would be a wilful misreading of the evidence. As Luke Gibbons has shown, this particular vision of 'Gaelic Gothic', which pathologised the Irish as a disease, was associated with Chartism's enemies, notably Thomas Carlyle who linked the 'virulent effects of cholera' with the 'contagious influence of Irishness itself on the mobilisation and organisation of the working class under Chartism'. This spurious linkage – through 'disease, invisibility, and infiltration', Gibbon argues, had the effect of brutalising the English working class through their association with the Irish in the urban centres where Chartism drew its main support.[104] On the one hand, it would have been tactically astute of the Chartists to advance the citizenship claims of the English working class by defining themselves against the brutalised savage Celt who was thought to be affectively inferior. On the other hand, given the propensity of Chartism's enemies to demonise the English working class because of its associations with the Irish, it made little sense to draw attention to the putative affective inferiority of the Irish. This may explain why Chartists on the whole did not ground their own claims to citizenship by defining themselves against the 'savage Celt' in the way that some supporters of English working-class enfranchisement did in the post-Chartist years, or as some of the American Irish did against blacks.[105] In the 1830s and 1840s, this othering was the preserve of popular toryism, with the Irish as 'the internal "other" against whom the English worker defined (and elevated) himself'.[106]

Had Chartists wanted to, it would have been easy to deploy anti-Catholic prejudice. But the fact remains that most did not, and to have done so would have betrayed the dictates of ascetic radicalism by displaying inappropriate feeling. Indeed, some Chartists actively campaigned against 'No Popery' prejudices, by packing anti-Catholic meetings and defeating the resolutions, and in this respect they were heirs to Cobbett who had done so much to persuade the English working class to reject the 'No Popery' prejudices of their forebears.[107] *Pace* the claims of Linda Colley, who dumps much of the vestigial anti-Catholicism of the early nineteenth century on to the English working class,[108] the *Northern Star* took the view that it was the English aristocracy and middle class who continued to harbour these prejudices.[109] While such rhetoric must have struck a chord with some workers, there was no space for this sort of prejudiced feeling in Chartism. It was the English working class who had 'silenced the reproachful tongue of national inequality' and have treated the Irish 'not as aliens, but as brethren'.[110] Speaking at Liverpool, and no doubt tailoring his speech to suit his audience, O'Connor exclaimed, following Cobbett's line, 'had it not been for the inconsistency, cruelty, lust, and villainy of the bloody Harry ... all who then heard him would now be Catholics. (Immense cheering.)'[111] The crux of Cobbett's argument was that anti-Catholicism was nothing more than a triumph of passion over reason, a deliberate subterfuge employed by the beneficiaries of the Reformation to prevent people from pursuing a 'fair and honest enquiry' into the Reformation and its lasting effects.[112]

True, there is a sense in which anti-Catholicism and anti-Irishness were two outlets closed off to Chartists: they believed in civil and religious freedom and were thus above sectarian conflicts. The absence of anti-Irishness may have been an obvious concession to the fact that the foremost Chartist leader was himself Irish; and this may explain why the occasional outbursts of anti-Irishness were vented in places other than O'Connor's *Northern Star*. The short-lived London newspaper the *Chartist* occasionally resorted to anti-Irishness, referring on one occasion to O'Connell and his supporters as 'a crew of ragged bogtrotters'. The same article continued: 'Low-born beggar, we are at least Englishmen. Oppressed, tyrannically oppressed as we are, we are not come of a race half-savages, half-slaves.' But even this outburst was tempered by the acknowledgement that the English working class had no quarrels with the Irish themselves.[113] These occasional outbursts are consistent with what we know about anti-Irishness during this period: that it was not grounded in any (pseudo) scientific notion of race, but 'an awkward mix of climate, physiology, culture, mysticism, and the will of God', a mix that was 'much more about culture than about race'.[114]

Arguably of greater significance in explaining the relative absence of anti-Irishness and anti-Catholicism is the Chartist belief that O'Connell regularly appealed to the inverse of these baser prejudices: 'Orange, Protestant, English Chartists' was how he branded them in 1841.[115] As a further taster of the kind of invective O'Connell hurled, he dismissed Sharman Crawford – an Irish Protestant by birth – as 'an Englican [sic.] Saxon rat'.[116] O'Connor regularly accused O'Connell of trying to foster enmity between the Irish and the English, and was quick to juxtapose this with his own inclusive patriotic feelings. O'Connor looked to a 'union of sentiment' between the Irish and English working classes based on kindly feeling'.[117] Speaking in the Chartist Convention of 1839, Mr. Wood 'felt confident that the greatest incubus on the liberty of Ireland was the power of O'Connell, who made every question a religious one'.[118] A number of Chartist communications to O'Connell and the Irish were indignant in their refutation of his charge that the English radicals cared little about Irish grievances. The LWMA was outraged at O'Connell's bigotry and countered this with the assurance that 'as the blood of both countries commingles in our veins ... so, assuredly, under the benign influence of free and equal institutions would our liberties and interests be blended and identified as one united and happy people'.[119] Bronterre O'Brien similarly lambasted O'Connell for the blanket way he denounced all Englishmen as 'Saxons', emphasising in particular the affective consequences of such labelling: 'It makes an Englishman's blood boil to hear the term Saxon, uttered reproachfully.'[120] This indignation was also instrumental in that the Chartists were seeking to enlist the Irish masses in their campaign for democratic rights, and thus it is hardly surprising that these prejudices were not aired in these communications. The co-operation between English and Irish workers was evidence that for many, 'class consciousness appears to have eclipsed ethnic consciousness', sanctified by a veritable union of hearts in place of the hated Act of Union. [121]

Conclusion

This chapter has presented a problem by way of two questions: why were the Chartists *so* angry at O'Connell, and what, in this context, is meant by anger? In trying to answer these questions, the purpose has been to suggest just how important fine-grained portraits of feelings are in sketching out affective life. The why of anger also speaks to the how of anger – to the Chartist practice of anger – that in turn makes this anger specific to time and space. While anger may have been the starting point for our historical analysis, we have also seen how feelings are seldom, if ever, comprised of a single feeling, and what looks like anger on the surface is, in fact, something else – above all, indignation. Further, although their opponents often painted them as creatures of base passions, what strikes the historian is just how restrained and controlled the Chartists were in venting their feelings, thus highlighting some of the key tensions between and within ascetic radicalism and sentimental radicalism. The negative feelings that Chartists associated with O'Connell were not spontaneous, irrational outbursts but carefully controlled and selected. Indignation, like resentment, appealed to a higher sensibility that transcended mere anger and rage and thereby demonstrated the fitness of working men for the franchise. Expressing feelings of indignation suggested that Chartists were capable of moral reasoning, of the kind that was seen as necessary for citizenship.[122] There was much more to this cluster of negative feelings than loyalty to O'Connor or a 'turf-war' between Chartism and Repealers. O'Connell was seldom far from the mind of Chartism, especially in its early phase when references to him were ubiquitous. He posed a serious threat to Chartism, and through his attacks he raised questions that went to the very heart of the movement. As we have seen, O'Connell was an important, inspirational but also dangerous figure from the radical tradition, not just because he was still alive but because he personified a rival and potentially attractive model of radical leadership and strategy which, in the eyes of many Chartists, threatened the independence and working-class character of their movement. It is surely no coincidence that the Chartists began to pay less attention to him precisely at the moment when his power began to wane. Increasingly preoccupied with Irish popular politics, and subsequently the Famine, O'Connell ceased to play any significant part in British popular politics after 1841–42, hence he was no longer perceived as a significant threat to Chartism. It was a measure of how far O'Connell and the Chartists had drifted apart by 1844 that when news reached Britain of O'Connell's incarceration there were sympathetic voices in the Chartist movement. As the Leicester-based *Chartist Pilot* confessed, 'Towards *all* men suffering for alleged conspiracy, we feel the most ardent sympathy'. 'We cannot shut our eyes to the fact,' the *Pilot* continued, 'that notwithstanding all O'Connell's insults to Chartists, and abuse of Chartism, he nevertheless, has claims upon us now, of a diversified character.' The *Pilot* then proceeded to list all of O'Connell's betrayals, before concluding that 'his present humiliated position demands from every Chartist in the empire a strong, clear and unequivocal condemnation of the tyranny which has consigned him to prison ... This we owe to O'Connell.'[123] The fact that some Chartists felt they owed anything at all to O'Connell by 1844 is a tantalising insight into the complexity of their relationship. Even in its darkest and most fractious moments, it was never one of contemptuous, peremptory dismissal. Like most fraught relationships, there was more going on here than meets the eye: hatred, loathing, disgust, or the other negative feelings that Chartists felt towards O'Connell were codes denoting much deeper and more complex attitudes, assumptions and positions.

As this chapter has suggested, to fully understand the ways in which Chartists and O'Connell defined themselves and one another, we need to introduce a third dynamic in their affective politics: their respective relationships with the state and the British political elite. The British political elite accused O'Connell and the Chartists with inciting the masses to violence through appeals to the base passions, and to accuse each of being indistinguishable from the other. At the same time, we have also seen how, once again, political reason itself was an affective construct, and that the elite had no monopoly of it. The elite, too, also resorted to deploying the baser prejudiced feelings of anti-Catholicism and especially anti-Irishness. As far as the elite were concerned, there was a profound dissonance between the affective politics of Chartism and the broader hegemonic emotional regime that they policed.[124] Chartism and Repeal, and the trenchant opposition to which they gave rise, were crucial parallel episodes in the fashioning of a restrictive, elitist, British citizenship which demonised any dissent which could be construed as base passion – a lesson that was not lost on the leaders of the revived radical movement for parliamentary reform in the 1860s.[125]

Notes

1 National Archives of Ireland, Chief Secretary's Office Registered Papers/ Outrage Papers, 1841: 8/60904 (Dublin), 'H.G' to Peter Brophy, 30 August 1841, fol. 359.

2 Matthew Roberts, 'Daniel O'Connell, repeal and Chartism in the age of Atlantic revolutions', *Journal of Modern History*, 90 (2018), 1–39. In this article, I also summarise the long-standard debate on the relationship between Chartism, Ireland and the Irish.

3 Thomas Dixon, 'What is the history of anger a history of?', *EHCS*, 4 (2020), 1–34.

4 Dixon, 'What is the history of anger', p. 31.

5 *London Evening Standard*, 5 November 1839.

6 Feargus O'Connor, *A Series of Letters from Feargus O'Connor, Esq., Barrister at Law, to Daniel O'Connell, Esq., M.P. containing a review of Mr. O'Connell's conduct during the agitation of the question of Catholic emancipation, together with an analysis of his motives and actions, since he became a member of Parliament* (London, 1836).

7 TNA, HO 64/11, secret service report, 13 November 1830, fol. 121.

8 *London Dispatch*, 9 December 1838.

9 *Discussion in the Lyceum Rooms, Glasgow, on the Public Character of Daniel O'Connell* (Glasgow, 1840), p. 8.

10 William Lovett, *The Life and Struggles of William Lovett* (London: Macgibbon & Kee, 1967 [1876]), pp. 240–4.

11 *NS*, 12 January 1839; Henry Miller, *Politics Personified: Portraiture, Caricature and Visual Culture in Britain, c.1830–80* (Manchester: Manchester University Press 2015), p. 11.

12 Patrick Joyce, *Democratic Subjects: The Self and the Social in Nineteenth-Century England* (Cambridge: Cambridge University Press, 1994), p. 177.

13 R.G. Gammage, *History of the Chartist Movement, 1837–1854* (London: Merlin, 1969 [1854]), 14; Patrick M. Geoghegan, *Liberator: The*

Life and Death of Daniel O'Connell, 1830–1847 (Dublin: Gill & Macmillan, 2010), p. 46.

14 *Hansard*, House of Commons, vol. 60, 14 February 1842, col. 428 (O'Connell quoted by W.B. Ferrand).

15 Patrick M. Geoghegan, *King Dan: The Rise of Daniel O'Connell, 1775–1829* (Dublin: Gill & Macmillan, 2008), p. 262.

16 *NS*, 23 May 1840.

17 Lovett, *Life and Struggles*, p. 159. On the affective aspects of O'Connell's court-room performances, see Katie Barclay, *Men on Trial: Performing Emotion, Embodiment and Identity in Ireland, 1800–45* (Manchester: Manchester University Press 2018), *passim*.

18 *Yorkshire Gazette*, 17 August 1839.

19 *Hereford Journal*, 24 April 1839.

20 TNA, HO 40/51, Albert Smith, 'V. R. Illegal Meetings', 13 August 1839, fol. 430.

21 TNA, HO 40/37, John Howard to Home Office, 25 April 1839, fols 193–5; Lancaster Trials, 1843, in *State Trials* (new series), iv, col. 1183, quoted and cited in Patricia Hollis (ed.), *Class and Conflict in Nineteenth-Century England, 1815–1850* (London: Routledge and Kegan Paul, 1973), p. 234.

22 *New Telegraph*, 12 July 1843.

23 *Saunders's News-Letter*, 29 November 1843.

24 Carol Zisowitz Stearns and Peter N. Stearns, *Anger: The Struggle for Emotional Control in America's History* (Chicago: University of Chicago Press, 1986), p. 233.

25 *London Democrat*, 8 June 1839.

26 *NS*, 7 December 1839.

27 *Advocate and Merthyr Free Press*, December 1840. For other similar references to the working class as 'animated machines, without hearts', see *NS*, 8 December 1838 (Rotherham WMA), 6 August 1842 (demonstration at Stepney Green).

28 *London Democrat*, 20 April 1839; *NS*, 18 April 1840.

29 As recent work has made clear, Chartism registered the Romantic preoccupation with authenticity of feeling: Matthew Roberts, 'Romantic memory? Forgetting, remembering and feeling in the Chartist pantheon of heroes', in Matthew Roberts (ed.), *Memory and Modern British Politics, 1789 to the Present* (London: Bloomsbury, forthcoming).

30 Mike Sanders, 'The platform and the stage: the primary aesthetics of Chartism', in Peter Yeandle, Katherine Newey and Jeffrey Richards (eds), *Politics, Performance and Popular Culture: Theatre and Society in Nineteenth-Century Britain* (Manchester: Manchester University Press 2016), p. 55.

31 *NS*, 15 December 1838. For Brewster, see Malcolm Chase, *Chartism: A New History* (Manchester: Manchester University Press, 2007), pp. 49–56.

32 Thomas Dixon, 'History in British tears: some reflections on the anatomies of modern emotions', A lecture delivered at the annual conference of the Netherlands Historical Association, Koninklijke Bibliotheek Den Haag, 4 November 2011, http://emotionsblog.history.qmul.ac.uk/wp-content/uploads/2012/03/History-in-British-Tears.pdf [accessed 24 April 2020].

33 Stearns and Stearns, *Anger*, p. 16.

34 Ute Frevert, *Emotions in History: Lost and Found* (Budapest: Central European University Press, 2011), p. 1.

35 *NS*, 12 January 1839.

36 Joanna Bourke, 'Fear and anxiety: writing about emotion in modern history', *History Workshop Journal*, 55 (2003), 115.

37 *Western Vindicator*, 30 November 1839.

38 *Charter*, 29 December 1839; *True Scotsman*, 15 December 1838; O'Connor, *Series of Letters*, p. 57.

39 William Cobbett, *Cobbett's Address to the People of Ireland* (Dublin, 1825), p. 16, copy in National Library of Ireland. See also William Cobbett, *Big O and Sir Glory: or; 'Leisure to Laugh': A Comedy in Three Acts* (London, 1825).

40 *NS*, 23 May 1840.

41 *NS*, 24 February 1838.

42 *Discussion in the Lyceum Rooms*; *NS*, 21 March 1840.

43 *NS*, 13 June 1840.

44 *NS*, 21 August 1841, 6 November 1841.

45 *NS*, 4 and 13 April 1839; Thomas Milton Kemnitz, 'The Chartist Convention of 1839', *Albion*, 10 (1978), 161–4, 169. On the links between O'Connell and the League see Paul A. Pickering and Alex Tyrrell, *The People's Bread: A History of the Anti-Corn Law League* (London: Continuum, 2000), chapter 4.

46 *Charter*, 2 February 1840; *Chartist Pilot*, 22 June 1844; *Hansard*, House of Commons, vol. 58, 25 May 1841, cols 754, 764–5.

47 E.P. Thompson, *The Making of the English Working Class* (New York: Vintage, 1966), pp. 622–3; John Belchem and James Epstein, 'The nineteenth-century gentleman leader revisited', *Social History*, 22 (1997), 173–92.

48 Lovett, *Life and Struggles*, p. 156; *London Dispatch*, 18 December 1836.

49 William Farish, *The Autobiography of William Farish: The Struggles of a Handloom Weaver* (London: Caliban, 1996 [1889]), p. 77. See also the famous description of O'Connor by the Barnsley linen weaver John Vallance, quoted in James Epstein, *The Lion of Freedom: Feargus O'Connor and the Chartist Movement* (London: Croom Helm, 1982), p. 34.

50 Jonathan Shay, *Achilles in Vietnam: Combat Trauma and the Undoing of Character* (New York: Scribner, 1994). Although Shay is clearly concerned with war, and while my purpose is in no way meant to devalue the trauma that accompanies warfare, political conflict and mass movements which pose risks to those involved in them can be seen as similar, albeit less dangerous and emotionally taxing, for their participants especially when confronted by a state willing to use force. After all, the psychological states that Shay identifies with war – terror, shock, horror, grief at the death of friends and – his main focus – moral injury resulting from betrayal by leaders of 'what is right' – are not exclusive to warfare.

51 Lovett, *Life and Struggles*, p. 165; *Charter*, 1 September 1839 (R.J. Richardson's letter); *True Scotsman*, 30 May 1840. For this incommensurability see M.A.G. Ó Tuathaigh, 'The Irish in nineteenth century Britain: problems of integration', *Transactions of the Royal Historical Society*, 31 (1981), 171.

52 Ryan David Dye, 'Church or country? The Irish migrant experience in Liverpool, 1829–1886' (PhD dissertation, Northwestern University, 2000), p. 123.

53 'To the People of Ireland, Daniel O'Connell', 31 October 1843, broadside in Boston Public Library (MA, USA), CAB.24.24.1 v.2; O'Connell to P.V. FitzPatrick, 17 July 1841, in Maurice R. O'Connell (ed.), *The Correspondence of Daniel O'Connell*, vol. 7 (Tallaght: Irish Academic Press, 1978), p. 106.

54 Memorandum, State Prosecution – Ireland, copy in BL, Additional MS 40540, Sir Robert Peel Papers, n.d. [February 1844], f. 258.

55 Roberts, 'Daniel O'Connell', pp. 23–33.

56 Public Record Office of Northern Ireland, William Sharman Crawford Papers, D856/D/44–70, WSC to John Sharman Crawford, 31 December 1836.

57 Miles Taylor, *Ernest Jones, Chartism, and the Romance of Politics, 1819–1869* (Oxford: Oxford University Press, 2003), p. vi; Epstein, *Lion of Freedom*, p. 10; Paul A. Pickering, *Feargus O'Connor: A Political Life* (Monmouth: Merlin, 2008), pp. 26–7. For this interpretation of Shelley see Andrew M. Stauffer, *Anger, Revolution, and Romanticism* (Cambridge: Cambridge University Press, 2005), chapter 5.

58 O'Connor, *A Series of Letters*, p. 15. For the formative impact of Oastler on O'Connor, see Matthew Roberts, *Chartism, Commemoration and the Cult of the Radical Hero* (Abingdon: Routledge, 2020), pp. 165–6.

59 O'Connor, *A Series of Letters*, p. 24. For O'Connor's other references to Frankenstein see pp. 29, 33, 43 of his *Series of Letters*; NS, 17 July 1841.

60 For a description of this cartoon, see Anon., *An Illustrative Key to the Political Sketches of H.B.* (London, 1841), p. 64; James N. McCord, 'The image in England: the cartoons of HB', in Maurice R. O'Connell (ed.), *Daniel O'Connell: Political Pioneer* (Dublin: Institute of Public Administration, 1991), p. 60.

61 NS, 28 December 1839.

62 Michael Scrivener, '*Frankenstein*'s ghost story: the last Jacobin novel', *Genre*, 19 (1986), 299–318; Marilyn Butler, 'The *Quarterly Review* and radical science, 1819', in her edition of Mary Shelley, *Frankenstein, 1818 Text* (Oxford: Oxford University Press, 1994), pp. 229–51.

63 NS, 2 May 1840.

64 NS, 23 January 1841.

65 NS, 12 June 1841.

66 Lovett, *Life and Struggles*, p. 159.

67 Takashi Koseki, 'Patrick O'Higgins and Irish Chartism', *Hosei Ireland-Japan Papers*, No. 2 (1990), 9.

68 Stauffer, *Anger*, p. 42.

69 O'Connor, *A Series of Letters*, p. 13.

70 E.g., *Northern Liberator*, 27 April 1839 ('Rich and Intense Irish Gratitude'); NS, 8 July 1843 (letter by W.H. Clifton).

71 O'Connor, *A Series of Letters*, p. 46.

72 E.g., Patrick O'Higgins' letter in NS, 29 February 1840.

73 E.g., NS, 27 January 1838 (meeting of London Radical Association).

74 For a summary and critique of the hydraulics model see Barbara Rosenwein, 'Worrying about emotions in history', *American Historical Review*, 107 (2002), 834–7.

75 Matthew McCormack and Matthew Roberts, 'Chronologies in the history of British political masculinities, c.1700–2000', in Matthew McCormack (ed.), *Public Men: Masculinity and Politics in Modern Britain* (Basingstoke: Palgrave, 2007), pp. 187–202; Rachel Ablow, 'Victorian emotions', *Victorian Studies*, 50 (2008), 375.

76 *Chartist*, 9 February 1839; *Charter*, 5 January 1840; *NS*, 23 January 1841. For a discussion of O'Connell in Chartist poetry see Mike Sanders, *The Poetry of Chartism: Aesthetics, Politics, History* (Cambridge: Cambridge University Press, 2009), pp. 132–4.

77 William M. Reddy, 'Against constructionism: the historical ethnography of emotions', *Current Anthropology*, 38 (1997), 331.

78 On these theoretical issues in relation to history see William M. Reddy, 'Historical research on the self and emotions', *Emotion Review*, 1 (2009), 302–15; Susan J. Matt, 'Current emotion research in history; or, doing history from the inside out', *Emotion Review*, 3 (2011), 117–24.

79 O'Connor, *A Series of Letters*, p. 13.

80 Oliver MacDonagh, *O'Connell: The Life of Daniel O'Connell, 1775–1847* (London: Weidenfeld & Nicolson, 1991), p. 23.

81 Stauffer, *Anger*, p. 20.

82 O'Connor, *A Series of Letters*, p. 27.

83 *Ibid*, pp. 13–14, 64.

84 E.g., writing in the *NS*, O'Connor opened one of his letters thus: 'As I proceed with my narrative my wrath increases, my blood boils, and my heart swells with manly indignation, at the very thought of the "base, bloody, and brutal" manner in which my loved country has been swindled out of her rights.' *NS*, 1 May 1841.

85 O'Connor, *A Series of Letters*, p. 26.

86 *NS*, 13 April 1839.

87 O'Connell had also read Godwin's novel *Caleb Williams*, which was a cautionary tale of the consequences of uncontrollable rage. MacDonagh, *O'Connell*, pp. 35, 39.

88 TNA, HO 73/55, Charles Mott to Poor Law Commissioners, 22 March 1839, fol. 192.

89 Pickering, *O'Connor*, pp. 149–151.

90 John Jackson, *The Demagogue Done Up: An Exposure of the Extreme Inconsistencies of Mr Feargus O'Connor* (Bradford, 1844), p. 64.

91 A.R. Schoyen, *The Chartist Challenge: A Portrait of George Julian Harney* (London: Heinemann, 1958), p. 16.

92 Belchem and Epstein, 'Gentleman leader'.

93 Geoghegan, *King Dan*, pp. 50–1; Geoghegan, *Liberator*, pp. 39, 79. In his biography of O'Connor, Epstein remarks that 'O'Connor was a romantic in an age steeped in popular romanticism'. Epstein, *Lion*, p. 10.

94 Belchem and Epstein, 'Gentleman leader', pp. 179–80.

95 John Brewer, *Party Ideology and Popular Politics at the Accession of George III* (Cambridge: Cambridge University Press, 1976), p. 163. For O'Connor's theatricality, see Pickering, *O'Connor*, 85–6, 119–20, 150–1.

96 Roberts, 'Daniel O'Connell'.

97 Donald M. MacRaild, *The Irish Diaspora in Britain, 1750–1939* (Basingstoke: Palgrave, 2011), p. 118.

98 Pickering, *O'Connor*, chapter 2.

99 LSE, Thomas Allsop Papers, COLL 0525/2/2, Feargus O'Connor to Thomas Allsop, 1 July 1843.

100 For O'Connor's treatment in prison, see Pickering, *O'Connor*, pp. 91–2; for O'Connell's, MacDonagh, *O'Connell*, p. 529.

101 E.g., O'Connor's response to O'Connell's overture to the Birmingham Chartists: *NS*, 8 June 1839.

102 John Wolffe, *The Protestant Crusade in Great Britain, 1829–1860* (Oxford: Oxford University Press, 1991); Donald M. MacRaild, '"No Irish need apply": the origins and persistence of a prejudice', *LHR*, 78 (2013), 269–99.

103 This was certainly one theme in the Gothic literature of the period. See Fred Botting, *Gothic* (London: Routledge, 1996), p. 64.

104 Luke Gibbons, *Gaelic Gothic: Race, Colonization, and Irish Culture* (Galway: Arlen House, 2004), pp. 46, 49–50. See also Roger Swift, 'Thomas Carlyle, "Chartism", and the Irish in early Victorian England', *Victorian Literature and Culture*, 29 (2001), 67–83.

105 Margot Finn, *After Chartism: Class and Nation in English Radical Politics, 1848–1874* (Cambridge: Cambridge University Press, 1993), p. 186; Catherine Hall, Keith McClelland, and Jane Rendall, *Defining the Victorian Nation: Class, Race, Gender and the Reform Act of 1867* (Cambridge: Cambridge University Press, 2000), chapter 4; Noel Ignatiev, *How the Irish Became White* (London: Routledge, 1995).

106 John Belchem, *Merseypride: Essays in Liverpool Exceptionalism* (Liverpool: Liverpool University Press, 2006), p. 160.

107 *NS*, 19 December 1840 ('No Popery' meeting in London); Matthew Roberts, 'Catholicism and constitutionalism in William Cobbett's English and Irish medievalism', in David Matthews and Mike Sanders (eds), *Medievalism from Below: Subaltern Medievalisms in the Nineteenth Century* (Cambridge: D.S. Brewer, 2021), pp. 19–38.

108 Linda Colley, *Britons: Forging the Nation, 1707–1837* (New Haven: Yale University Press, 1992), pp. 330–4.

109 The 1826 general election, fought largely around the issue of Catholic emancipation, illustrated this very powerfully, as did Dr. James Kay-Shuttleworth's study of working-class life in Manchester which scapegoated the Irish just as the local authorities did. E.g., the 1826 Yorkshire Election posters: 'Milton and Marshall with Popery, Low Wages, and Power Looms', WYAS, KC174/34. 'No Popery' was the rallying cry of the Tory candidates. For Kay-Shuttleworth see Mervyn Busteed, *The Irish in Manchester, c.1750–1921* (Manchester: Manchester University Press 2016), pp. 23–30, 33.

110 *NS*, 12 June 1841.

111 *NS*, 19 May 1838.

112 William Cobbett, *History of the Protestant Reformation in England and Ireland*, vol. 1 (London, 1824), paras 4, 6, 25.

113 *Chartist*, 23 March 1839. For a similar outburst see 9 June 1839. The Edinburgh-based *True Scotsman* referred to O'Connell on one occasion as 'the great Irish Jesuit', quoted in W. Hamish Fraser, *Chartism in Scotland* (Pontypool: Merlin, 2010), p. 95.

114 D.G. Paz, 'Anti-Catholicism, anti-Irish stereotyping, and anti-Celtic racism in mid-Victorian working-class periodicals', *Albion*, 18 (1986), 615.

115 *NS*, 21 August 1841.

116 *Wexford Independent*, 23 October 1841.

117 *NS*, 28 May 1842.

118 *NS*, 23 February 1839, 8 May 1841.

119 Lovett, *Life and Struggles*, p. 151. For other similar examples, see *McDouall's Chartist and Republican Journal*, 26 June 1841.

120 *Poor Man's Guardian, and Repealer's Friend*, No.1. For other examples see *NS*, 14 September 1839 (Lowery's letter), 21 November 1840 ('A Welshman'). For O'Brien's Irishness, see Michael J. Turner, 'Ireland and Irishness in the political thought of Bronterre O'Brien', *Irish Historical Studies*, 153 (2014), 40–57.

121 Frederick James Kaijage, 'Labouring Barnsley, 1815–1856' (PhD dissertation, University of Warwick, 1975), p. 516; Paul A. Pickering, *Chartism and the Chartists in Manchester and Salford* (Basingstoke: Macmillan, 1995), pp. 95–6; Roberts, 'Daniel O'Connell', 15–17.

122 Resentment also functioned in a similar way. See Kathryn Temple, ' "Mixed emotions": love, resentment and the Declaration of Independence', *EHCS*, 2 (2018), 47, 51.

123 *Chartist Pilot*, 22 June 1844.

124 William M. Reddy, *The Navigation of Feeling: A Framework for the History of Emotions* (Cambridge: Cambridge University Press, 2001), p. 124.

125 Hall, McClelland and Rendall, *Defining the Victorian Nation*.

Conclusion

The study has challenged the assumption – just as alive today as it was in the nineteenth century – that the political sphere was an arena of reason in which feelings had no part to play. One of the fictions of modern British politics, and no doubt elsewhere, is that politics is, or ought to be, rational. According to this Habermasian view, politicians try to monopolise the high-ground of cool (often assumed to be male) rationality while denigrating their opponents as irrational creatures of feeling or, somewhat paradoxically, unfeeling. In other words, the exclusion of working-class men from citizenship was further legitimated on the assumption that they were either too effeminate (as creatures of feeling) or else they were seen as animals, a gendered and bestial rebuff that underlines the significance of feeling in the political culture of the period. But as this apparent paradox reveals, claims to political rationality are themselves forms of affective politics as we have seen with ascetic radicalism. While hate and anger might be beyond the affective pale, righteous indignation was not only acceptable but called for in certain situations. Even Carlile's 'reason's republic' required men to have certain kinds of feeling, just as Robert Owen's utopian communities did.

Democratic passions has shown how claims to political rationality were not only paved with affective tensions, but that reason itself was an affective construct, much like Lorraine Daston has shown with claims to scientific objectivity. Apprenticeship into scientific knowledge not only inducts the neophyte into ways of seeing, manipulating and understanding but also ways of feeling. There is a clear parallel here with the way in which political authority operates and is perpetuated.[1] Although the advocates of ascetic radicalism deployed a dichotomy of reason versus passion, just as the enemies of radicalism did, as historians we need to be on our guard when historical actors and contemporary politicians juxtapose their self-proclaimed rationality against emotion. As with much else in political language, this was and is rhetoric crafted for a specific purpose, one of which is to delegitimise the politics of dissent, invariably in ways that exclude on the basis of class, gender, race, religion and other forms of identity. The affective basis of political reason, of the conceit of the political elite that theirs was a rational politics merits further research for earlier and later periods. So, too, do the strategies and tactics deployed by politicians and their supporters to insulate themselves from the charges of unfeeling. Recognising this, and laying bare the affective basis of politics, is vital to the health of democratic politics.

A crass reading of this study might lead one to assume that popular radicalism in its working-class incarnation failed because its leaders were too emotional. By this stage of the book, the profound misconceptions of that assumption should be self-evident (though clearly it was a view held by the enemies of radicalism). It would be more accurate to conclude that popular radicalism often failed because it did not succeed in getting the right balance between the ascetic and the sentimental; or, in other words, displaying the right sorts of feeling in the correct context. *Democratic passions* has demonstrated that feelings were a central, albeit contested, aspect of the political culture of the period. Radical leaders were accused of inflaming the passions; the state and its propertied supporters were charged with callousness and cruelty; and radicals grounded their claims to citizenship in the universalist assumption that workers had the same potential capacity for feeling as their social betters. While sentimental radicals like Oastler were accused of feeling too much, ascetic radicals such as Owen were rebuked for feeling nothing. In short, feelings were (and are) not incidental but central to political culture. As we have seen over the course of this study, discussions about the nature, place and significance of the passions had implications for the language and practice of politics. Feelings were invoked as a way of transforming abstract political issues into heartfelt, embodied responses. Where radicals seated the passions in the body, for example, was intimately related to their project of demonstrating that working-class men were feeling subjects and worthy of citizenship. At the same time, we have also seen how some radicals politicised feelings in ways that advanced the citizenship claims of white working-class men by, implicitly or explicitly, denigrating a variety of 'others', notably blacks, enslaved and women. In this respect, as in so many others, the body was political, with senses and feelings used in ways that made 'othering' and various forms of difference legible on and in the body.

The very act of naming feelings – the labels that were used – also had political significance and flowed from a particular affective politics. The word 'feeling' was much more neutral than the passions, with the latter's connotations of negative feeling. The word emotion, though occasionally used, had a very different meaning from what it does today, or even by the end of the nineteenth century. Judging by the affective vocabulary used by popular radicals, there seems to be little evidence that the 1790s had witnessed a decisive shift away from passion to emotion, as argued by Rachel Hewitt.[2] In claiming that people had capacity to alter how they felt, ascetic radicals would have been resistant to the modern psychological category of the emotions because of its 'involuntary view of emotions as forces outside our control'.[3] Emotions were outward expressions of inward feeling; in other words, they were outputs not inputs. Thus, it is important to pay careful attention to the affective language used by those in the past in ways that are sensitive to time and place, rather than subsume the affective realm under the catch-all psychological category emotion that is still too often assumed to be trans-historical.

We also need to be mindful of the ways in which feelings were politicised; it remains to be seen if other political movements and actors developed a similar affective politics in the first half of the nineteenth century and beyond. The most cursory search suggests that it is not difficult to find other historical parallels in which popular movements have been beset by a similar tension between expressing intense feelings and restraining them.[4] But as the tensions between the two forms of concurrent affective politics – the ascetic and the sentimental – in the first half of the nineteenth century implies, it would be both teleological and simplistic to suggest that the modern era has seen the rise of emotional restraint at the expense of sentimental outpourings. To argue this runs the risk of returning to the widely discredited arguments of Norbert Elias about the civilising process. It could be argued that the enfranchisement of many working-class men in 1867 was a reward, in part, for the restraint and patience under suffering, with further similar rewards for good affective behaviour handed out in 1884, 1918 and 1928. Indeed, this was the very reason Gladstone gave for his conversion to further franchise extension in the 1860s.[5] On one level, this is undoubtedly true: Gladstone's remarks about the respectable artisan being 'our own flesh and blood' would have been unthinkable to the vast majority of the political elite in the 1830s and 1840s. Part of what made this unthinkable was the assumption that the working classes were either creatures of passion or unfeeling brutes. Thus, it was the growing realisation that at least *some* working men had the capacity for refined feeling which facilitated the rapprochement between working-class radicalism and liberal parliamentary politics, which has given rise to an extensive historiographical debate on the mechanics of mid-century political and social stability.[6] Some of this clearly had roots in the 1830s and 1840s – in the ascetic radicalism of William Lovett, in the phrenology movement, and more generally in a radical critique of a parasitical aristocracy, based, in part, on a bodily politics which equated Old Corruption with bloating, debauchery, greed and selfishness. The Anti-Corn Law League, for example, could easily rival, and even occasionally surpass, Chartism in its attack on a fat aristocracy, which pointed to shared affective ground and would culminate in the moral populism of John Bright and Gladstone. This rapprochement was facilitated by more egalitarian and universalised readings of character, the body and the mind.[7]

Yet there are several problems with this argument. First, its cross-class potential was undercut by an assumption that the working classes did *not* have the same capacity for refined feeling in the 1830s and 1840s. Second, although that view was declining by the mid-Victorian decades – hence Gladstone's declaration – it had by no means disappeared. The 'Adullamite' opposition within the Liberal party to their own government's Reform Bill in 1866 spoke out against the 'passions of the multitude'.[8] And a significant part of the anxieties over democratisation in later Victorian Britain revolved around the potential dangers of unleashing base passions – another topic worthy of revisiting from a history of emotions perspective.[9] Third, there is a sense in which Gladstone's claim about working men showing restraint was legitimating rhetoric for a decision already made by the Liberal Party to enfranchise respectable artisans (largely for partisan reasons). In any case, the Reform League – the organisation which spearheaded the popular radical movement for parliamentary reform in the 1860s – and even more so the Suffragettes who were described as 'helots of passion' in the words of one of their many enemies – demonstrated the same tensions between the ascetic and the sentimental as did popular radicals before 1848.[10] And Gladstone's brand of moral populism in the later Victorian era took outrage, indignation and loathing to new heights, complete with 'emotional or histrionic behaviour'.[11] Tellingly, Lord Cranborne, the future Marquess of Salisbury, dismissed Gladstone's plea that working men were our own flesh and blood as 'sentimental rant'.[12] The claim that a present generation is more rational and less emotional than their forebears is a fiction that each generation tells itself.

By breaking away from such teleological assumptions and substituting them for a focus on the affective language used by those in the past, we begin to appreciate the explanatory power of feeling as a dynamic in political culture. Focusing on that dynamic, as this book has suggested, casts new light on issues of ideology, strategy and tactics, leadership as well as the relationship between political leaders and their supporters. For example, feelings constituted the means by which the distinctions between categories like physical and moral force were made. Further, we have also seen how important feelings were in the relationship between radicalism and the government and its propertied supporters, thus suggesting the rich potential of the history of emotions to shed new light on the relationship between social movements and the state. At the time of writing, as the Police, Crime, Sentencing and Courts Bill makes its way through the English parliament, feelings once again are prominent: anxiety, alarm and intimidation are each cited as justification for new sweeping police powers to clampdown on protest.[13] This also suggests the need to reinterpret legislation and the law from the perspective of the history of emotions. Today's protesters find themselves excluded from an emotional regime that is just as sensitive to what it views as inappropriate displays of emotion as the late Georgian and early Victorian political elite did in setting their faces against base passion. Times have changed, language evolves and feelings change, but the fundamental issue endures: feelings are political, and politics is, at root, about feeling.

Notes

1 Lorraine Daston, 'The moral economy of science', *Osiris*, 10 (1995), 2–24.

2 Rachel Hewitt, *A Revolution of Feeling: The Decade that Forged the Modern Mind* (London: Granta, 2017), pp. 7, 13, 142, 293–4.

3 Thomas Dixon, *From Passions to Emotions: The Creation of a Secular Psychological Character* (Cambridge: Cambridge University Press, 2003), p. 134.

4 Stephen Brooke, 'Space, emotions and the everyday: the affective ecology of 1980s London', *Twentieth-Century British History*, 28 (2017), 122.

5 Matthew Roberts, *Political Movements in Urban England, 1832–1914* (Basingstoke: Palgrave, 2009), p. 13.

6 The debate is reviewed in *ibid.*, chapters 4–5.

7 Norman McCord, *The Anti-Corn Law League, 1838–1846* (London: Allen and Unwin, 1968), pp. 26, 59; Paul A. Pickering, *The People's Bread: A History of the Anti-Corn Law League* (London: Continuum, 2000), pp. 1–2, 194; Patrick Joyce, *Democratic Subjects: The Self and the Social in Nineteenth-Century England* (Cambridge: Cambridge University Press, 1994); Miles Taylor, *The Decline of British Radicalism, 1847–1860* (Oxford: Oxford University Press, 1995); Alison Winter, *Mesmerized: Powers of Mind in Victorian Britain* (Chicago: University of Chicago Press, 1998). In future work, I plan to explore the affective politics of the Anti-Corn Law League and the affective aspects of mid-century stability.

8 *Hansard*, House of Commons, vol. 182, 12 March 1866, col. 114.

9 For democratisation, and the fears surrounding it, see Robert Saunders, *Democracy and the Vote in British Politics, 1848–1867* (Farnham: Ashgate, 2011), chapter 5; Joanna Innes and Mark Philp (eds), *Re-Imagining Democracy in the Age of Revolutions: America, France, Britain, Ireland, 1750–1850* (Oxford: Oxford University Press, 2013); Angus Hawkins, *Victorian Political Culture: Habits of Hearts and Minds* (Oxford: Oxford University Press, 2015), chapters 6–7.

10 For the Reform League and the passions, see *London Daily News*, 27 July 1866 ('The government and the Reform League'); *Ashton Weekly Reporter*, 9 February 1867 (Reform League tea party); *Burnley Advertiser*, 2 February 1867 (Burnley Reform League). For similar rhetoric in the 1880s in relation to franchise

extension, see *Leeds Mercury*, 8 September 1884 ('The Lords and the Franchise'); *Glasgow Herald*, 5 August 1884 ('Franchise Bill agitation'); *Morning Post*, 21 October 1884 ('Franchise agitation'). For the Suffragettes, *Shetland Times*, 30 September 1911 ('Helots of passion'); *Suffragette*, 31 January 1913 ('Lord Hugh Cecil'), 5 September 1913 ('Chastity and the health of men').

11 Joseph S. Meisel, 'The importance of being serious: the unexplored connection between Gladstone and humour', *History*, 84 (1999), p. 281.

12 *Hansard*, House of Commons, vol. 182, 23 March 1866, col. 875; D.A. Hamer, *Liberal Politics in the Age of Gladstone* (Oxford: Oxford University Press, 1972), chapter 1; John Belchem and James Epstein, 'The nineteenth-century gentleman leader revisited', *Social History*, 22 (1997), 173–92.

13 *Police Powers: Protests* (House of Commons Briefing Paper, Number CBP5013, 15 February 2021), pp. 7–10, 19.

Select bibliography

For secondary literature, see the references in the main text.

Archival sources

Library of Birmingham, Wolfson Centre for Archival Research

MS 753 (LF.76.13), William Lovett collection, 1836–42

Boston Public Library, Massachusetts

CAB.24.24.1 v.2, broadsides

British Library, London

Add(itional) MS 27791, Francis Place papers, narrative of political events, 1830–35
Add MS 27820–35, Francis Place papers, collections relating to working men's associations, 1832–9
Add MS 35145, Francis Place Papers, Autobiography, vol. iv, 1809–36
Add MS 34245 A-B, Correspondence and papers of the General Convention, 1839
Add MS 37773–4, Working Men's Association minutes, 1836–42
Add MS 35151, Francis place paper, correspondence, 1837–50
Add MS 40540, Sir Robert Peel Papers, Correspondence, 1844
Add MS 41748, Correspondence between Richard Oastler and Thomas Thornhill, 1834–40
Add MS 46344, John Burns papers
Add MS 78161, William Lovett papers, 1828–76
Francis Place Collection, set 55, case of William Lovett and John Collins, 1839–41

Cheetham's Library, Manchester

B.9.41.52(1), Scrapbooks of W.R. Hay

Columbia University, New York, Rare Books and Manuscript Library

Seligman Collection, Richard Oastler pamphlets and broadsides

Historical Society of Pennsylvania, Philadelphia

2129, William Cobbett Papers, 1792–1835 (transcripts of letters from other archival collections)
250, Simon Gratz Autograph Collection

Huntington Library, San Marino, California

RC, Richard Carlile papers, 1817–1843

John Rylands Library, University of Manchester

FDN4, John Fielden papers, correspondence with Richard Oastler, 1836–39

London School of Economic, Archives

COL0525, Thomas Allsop papers, correspondence with Richard Oastler, Bronterre O'Brien and Feargus O'Connor, 1830s–1850s

The National Archives, Kew

HO 20/10, Home Office Prison correspondence papers, interview of Chartist prisoners, 1840
HO 40/3–59, disturbance correspondence, 1816–40
HO 42/157–203, domestic correspondence, 1816–20
HO 44/38, reports on Owenism, 1840
HO 44/52, secret service reports, 1839
HO 52/1–2, 8–21, 35–47, counties correspondence, 1820–40
HO 64/11–19, secret service reports, spies and informers, 1827–34
HO 73/52–5, Poor Law Commission correspondence, 1837–39
TS 11/1030, Treasury Solicitor's papers, Crown v Joseph Rayner Stephens, 1839

National Archives of Ireland, Dublin

Chief Secretary's Office, registered papers/outrage papers

National Co-operative Archive, Manchester

ROCC, papers and correspondence of Robert Owen

Nuffield College, Oxford

MSS Cobbett, William Cobbett papers, 1797–1860

People's History Museum, Manchester

LP/VIN1, Henry Vincent papers, 1837–42

Public Record Office of Northern Ireland, Belfast

D856, William Sharman Crawford papers

Senate House Library, London

Goldsmiths'-Kress Library of Economic Literature, Oastler and the factory movement collection, broadsides

Sheffield Archives

RP, Samuel Roberts papers

West Yorkshire Archives Service (WYAS), Bradford

DB 27, Political reform movements

WYAS, Kirklees

DD/T/C, Thornhill estate correspondence, 1841
KC174, G.W. Tomlinson collection

WYAS, Leeds

WYL22, Richard Oastler papers, 1832, 1843
WYL 623, Humphrey Boyle papers

Yale University Library, Manuscripts and Archives

MS 782/7/1/15, Cecil Herbert Driver papers, letters of Richard Oastler to Thomas Daniels

Images

BM Satires 10614, 'Posting to the election', by James Gillray (1806)
BM Satires 11047, 'The loyal address', by James Gillray (1808)

BM Satires 11338, 'True Reform of Parliament', by James Gillray (1809)

BM Satires 11372, 11378, 11384, 'Life of William Cobbett', by James Gillray (1809)

BM Satires 12867A, 'A patriot luminary extinguishing noxious gas!!!', by George Cruikshank (1817)

BM Satires 13283, 'The political champion turned resurrection man', by I.R. Cruikshank (1819)

BM Satires 13895, 'The Radical Ladder', by George Cruikshank (1820)

BM Satires 14194, 'Revolutionary Association', by I.R. Cruikshank (1821)

Huntington Library, Rare Books, 240387, *Political Sketches &c*, by 'H.B.' [John Doyle], vols 1 (1829), 8 (1843)

Printed primary sources

A Letter to William Cobbett, by A Briton (Birmingham, 1819)

A Report of the Proceedings and Speeches of a Public Meeting held in the Primitive Methodist Chapel, Oldham, 14 March 1835 (Oldham, 1835)

The Book of Wonders (London, 1821)

The Christian House, Built by Truth on a Rock; or an Antidote to Infidelity (London, 1820)

Debate on the Evidences of Christianity between Robert Owen and Alexander Campbell (London, 1839)

Discussion in the Lyceum Rooms, Glasgow, on the Public Character of Daniel O'Connell (Glasgow, 1840)

The Factory Lad, or the Life of Simon Smike Exemplifying the Horrors of White Slavery (London, 1839)

Illustrative Key to the Political Sketches of H.B. (London, 1841)

Life of William Cobbett (London, 1835)

The Loyal Man in the Moon (London, 1820)

Parliamentary Debates, Vol. XLI (London, 1820)

Prospectus and Rules of the Working Men's Association (London, 1836)

The Queen and Magna Charta, or the Thing that John Signed (London, 1820)

The Rotten House of Commons (London, 1836)

Rules and Regulations of the General Convention (Lambeth, 1839)

Sketch of the Life and Opinions of Richard Oastler (Leeds, 1838)

Third Letter from John Nott to his Fellow Townsmen (Birmingham, 1819)

Trial of Thomas Hardy for High Treason (London, 1794)

Trial of Edward Marcus Despard for High Treason (London, 1803)

Trial of Robert Emmet for High Treason (London, 1803)

Trial of W. Lovett, Journeyman Cabinet-Maker for Sedition (London, 1839)

Adams, M., *A Parody on the Political House that Jack Built* (London, 1820)

Brown, Paul, *Twelve Months in New Harmony* (Cincinnati, OH, 1827)

Carlile, Richard, *The Order for the Administration of the Loaves and the Fishes* (London, 1817)

—— *A Letter to the Society for the Suppression of Vice* (London, 1819)

—— *To the Reformers of Great Britain* (London, 1821)

—— *The Gospel according to Richard Carlile* (London, 1827)

Carlile Campbell, Theophilia, *The Battle of the Press: The Life of Richard Carlile* (London, 1899)

Cobbett, William, *A Year's Residence in the United States of America* (London, 1818)

—— *Cottage Economy* (London, 1821)

—— *History of the Protestant Reformation in England and Ireland*, 2 vols (London, 1824)

—— *Cobbett's Address to the People of Ireland* (Dublin, 1825)

—— *Big O and Sir Glory: or; 'Leisure to Laugh': A Comedy in Three Acts* (London, 1825)

—— *Advice to Young Men and (Incidentally) to Young Women in the Middle and Higher Ranks of Life* (London, 1829)

Croft, W.R., *The History of the Factory Movement, or Oastler and His Times* (Huddersfield, 1888)

Easby, John, *J.R. Stephens Unveiled* (Manchester, November 1837)

Flower, George, *History of the English Settlement in Edwards County, Illinois* (Chicago, 1882)

Gregory, Benjamin, *Side Lights on the Conflicts of Methodism* (London, 1898)

Hazlitt, William, *The Character of W. Cobbett* (London, 1835)

Holyoake, G.J., *Life of Joseph Rayner Stephens: Preacher and Political Orator* (London, 1881)

Hone, William and Cruikshank, George, *Life of Billy Cobb and the Death of Tommy Pain* (1819)

Jackson, John, *The Demagogue Done Up: An Exposure of the Extreme Inconsistencies of Mr Feargus O'Connor* (Bradford, 1844)

Kydd, Samuel, *The History of the Factory Movement from 1802 to the Enactment of the Ten Hours Bill in 1847*, 2 vols (London, 1857)

Lovett, William, *Social and Political Morality* (London, 1853)

—— *Elementary Anatomy and Physiology* (London, 1853)

Lovett, William and Collins, John, *Chartism: A New Organisation of the People* (London, 1840)

O'Connor, Feargus, *A Series of Letters from Feargus O'Connor, Esq., Barrister at Law, to Daniel O'Connell, Esq., M.P. containing a review of Mr. O'Connell's conduct during the agitation of the question of Catholic emancipation, together with an analysis of his motives and actions, since he became a member of Parliament* (London, 1836)

Oastler, Richard, *Infant Slavery* (Preston, 1833)

—— *Speech Delivered at a Public Meeting held in Huddersfield Market Place, 18 June 1833* (Leeds, 1833)

—— *A Letter to the Shareholders of the Bradford Observer* (Bradford, 1834)

—— *A Well Seasoned Christmas-Pie* (Bradford, 1834)

—— *A Letter to those Sleek, Pious, Holy and Devout Dissenters* (Bradford, 1834)

—— *The Huddersfield Dissenters in a Fury* (Leeds, 1835)

—— *A Letter to a Run-A-Way M.P.* (Leeds, 1836)

—— *A Letter to the Arch-Bishop of York* (Huddersfield, 1836)

———— *Mr Oastler's Three Letters to Mr Hetherington* (London, 1836)

———— *A Letter to those Mill-Owners who continue to Oppose the Ten Hours Bill* (Manchester, 1836)

———— *Damnation! Eternal Damnation to the Fiend-Begotten, 'Coarser Food' New Poor Law* (London, 1837)

———— Eight Letters to the Duke of Wellington (1838)

———— *The Right of the Poor to Liberty and Life* (London, 1838)

Owen, Robert, *Lectures on the New State of Society* (London, 1835)

———— *An Outline of the Rational System of Society* (Leeds, 1840)

———— *Catechism of the New Moral World* (London, 1840)

———— *Lectures on the Marriage of the Priesthood of the Old Immoral World* (Leeds, 1840)

———— The Book of the New Moral World (1840)

———— *A Supplementary Index to the Life of Robert Owen: Volume 1A* (London, 1858)

Palmer, Elihu, *Principles of Nature* (London, 1819)

Paulding, James Kirke, *The Merry Tales of the Three Wise Men of Gotham* (New York, 1826)

Stephens, J.R., *The Political Pulpit* (London, 1839)

———— *The Political Preacher* (London, 1839)

Whitley, T.W., *The Parliamentary Representation of the City of Coventry from the Earliest Times to the Present* (Coventry, 1894)

Autobiographies and edited papers

Bamford, Samuel, *Passages in the Life of a Radical*, 2 vols (Manchester, 1844)

Brougham, Henry, *The Life and Times of Henry, Lord Brougham*, 3 vols (New York, 1871)

Cobbett, Anne, *Account of the Family* (London: William Cobbett Society, 1999)

Cobbett, William, *The Autobiography of William Cobbett*, ed. William Reitzel (London: Faber, 1947)

Colchester (ed.), *Diary and Correspondence of Charles Abbot, Lord Colchester*, 3 vols (London, 1861)

Croker, J.W., *The Croker Papers*, ed. Louis J. Jennings, 3 vols (London, 1884)

Gammage, R.G., *History of the Chartist Movement, 1837–1854* (London: Merlin, 1969 [1894])

Hodder, Edwin, *The Life and Work of the Seventh Earl of Shaftesbury*, 3 vols (London, 1886)

Farish, William, *The Autobiography of William Farish: The Struggles of a Handloom Weaver* (London, 1996 [1889])

Hazlitt, William, *The Complete Works of William Hazlitt*, ed. P.P. Howe, 21 vols (London: J.M. Dent, 1930–34)

Lovett, William, *Life and Struggles of William Lovett* (London: Routledge & Kegan Paul, 1967 [1876])

Lowery, Robert, *Robert Lowery: Radical and Chartist*, ed. Brian Harrison and Patricia Hollis (London: Europa, 1979)

Trollope, Thomas Adolphus, *What I Remember*, 2 vols (London, 1887)

Wakefield, C.M., *Life of Thomas Attwood* (London, 1885)

Editions of primary sources

Bush, M.L. (ed.), *What Is Love? Richard Carlile's Philosophy of Sex* (London: Verso, 1998 [1826])

Claeys, Gregory (ed.), *Selected Works of Robert Owen*, 4 vols (London: Pickering and Chatto, 1993)

Cobbett, William, *Rural Rides*, ed. Asa Briggs, 2 vols (London: Dent, 1957)

Davis, Michael T. Davis, McCalman, Iain and Parolin, Christina (eds), *Newgate in Revolution: An Anthology of Radical Prison Literature in the Age of Revolution* (London: Bloomsbury, 2005)

Grande, James, Stevenson, John and Thomas, Richard (eds), *The Opinions of William Cobbett* (Farnham: Ashgate, 2013)

Hollis, Patricia (ed.), *Class and Conflict in Nineteenth-Century England, 1815–1850* (London: Routledge & Kegan Paul, 1973)

Howe, Anthony (ed.), *The Letters of Richard Cobden: Volume 1 1815–1847* (Oxford: Oxford University Press, 2007)

Morpurgo, J.E. (ed.), *Cobbett's America: A Selection of the Writings of William Cobbett* (London: Folio, 1985)

O'Connell, Maurice R. (ed.), *The Correspondence of Daniel O'Connell*, 8 vols (Tallaght: Irish University Press, 1972–80)

Royle, Edward (ed.), *The Infidel Tradition: From Paine to Bradlaugh* (London: Macmillan, 1976)

Smith, E.A. (ed.), *A Queen on Trial: The Affair of Queen Caroline* (Stroud: Alan Sutton, 1993)

Ward, W.R. (ed.), *Early Victorian Methodism: The Correspondence of Jabez Bunting, 1830–1850* (Oxford: Oxford University Press, 1976)

Parliamentary Papers (PP)

PP. 1831–2 [706], *Select Committee on Bill for Regulation of Factories*

Newspapers and periodicals

Titles with an * have been consulted in hard-copy or on microfilm; the remainder in digital.

Advocate and Merthyr Free Press

Ashton Chronicle

Ashton Weekly Reporter
Ballot
Bell's Life in London
Black Dwarf
Blackwood's Edinburgh Magazine
Bolton Chronicle
Boston Investigator (Boston, MA)
Bradford Observer
Brighton Co-operator
*British Labourer's Protector
British Statesman
Burnley Advertiser
Charter
Chartist
*Chartist Pilot
Christian Observer
Cleave's (Satirist &) Gazette of Variety
Cobbett's Evening Register
Cobbett's Weekly Political Register
Correspondent (New York)
*Cosmopolite
Coventry Herald
Crisis
*Deist
Economist (1821)
Edinburgh Monthly Review
*Extinguisher (Stokesley)
*Fleet Papers
Free Enquirer (New York)
Glasgow Herald
Hampshire Telegraph
Hereford Journal
Hereford Times
Isis
Kentish Mercury
Leeds Intelligencer
Leeds Mercury
Leeds Patriot
Leeds Times
*Lion
London Daily News
*London Democrat
London Dispatch
London Evening Standard
Manchester Times

*Manchester and Salford Advertiser
Moralist
Morning Chronicle
Morning Post
*National Association Gazette
New Harmony Gazette
New Moral World
New Telegraph
New Times
Northern Liberator
Northern Star
Operative
Pioneer
Poor Man's Guardian
*Prompter
Public Ledger
Radical Reformer
Republican
Saunders's News-Letter
Sheffield Iris
*Sherwin's Political Register
Shetland Times
Sligo Journal
Staffordshire Gazette
*Stephens' Monthly Magazine
*Stockport Advertiser
Suffragette
The Times
*True Scotsman
True Sun
*Twopenny Dispatch
*Western Vindicator
Wexford Independent
White Dwarf
Wooler's British Gazette
York Herald
Yorkshire Gazette*

Digitised sources

American Philosophical Society, Col. Richard Gimbel collection of Thomas Paine papers, http://diglib.amphilsoc.org/
British Library Nineteenth Century Newspapers, http://gale.cengage.co.uk

British Museum, Collection online, BM Satires www.britishmuseum.org/research/ collection_online/search.aspx
British Newspaper Archives, www.britishnewspaperarchive.co.uk/
Hansard's Parliamentary Debates, http://hansard.millbanksystems.com
History of Parliament Online, www.historyofparliamentonline.org
International Institute of Social History, Amsterdam, Owenite societies archives, https://search.iisg.amsterdam/Record/ARCH01167
National Portrait Gallery, collections, www.npg.org.uk/collections
Newspaper Archive, https://newspaperarchive.com/uk/
Nineteenth Century Collections Online, http://gale.cengage.co.uk

Index

Page numbers for illustrations are in *italics*, and for notes in the format 89n142.

EU authorised representative for GPSR:
Easy Access System Europe, Mustamäe tee 50,
10621 Tallinn, Estonia
gpsr.requests@easproject.com